MIRROR . . .

The Importance of Looks in Everyday Life

STATE UNIVERSITY OF NEW YORK PRESS

Soc
HQ
801
H354
1986

SUNY Series in Sexual Behavior
Donn Byrne and Kathryn Kelley, Editors

Published by
State University of New York Press, Albany

For information, address State University of New York
Press, State University Plaza, Albany, N.Y., 12246

Library of Congress Cataloging in Publication Data

Hatfield, Elaine.
  Mirror, mirror.

  (SUNY series in sexual behavior)
  Bibliography: p. 377
  Includes index.
  1. Courtship. 2. Interpersonal attraction.
3. Beauty, Personal. 4. Sex (Psychology)
5. Mate selection. I. Sprecher, Susan, 1955–
II. Title. III. Series.
HQ801.H354 1986   646.7′2   86-5776
ISBN 0-88706-123-0
ISBN 0-88706-124-9 (pbk.)

10 9 8 7 6 5 4 3 2 1

Dedicated to
Charles Hatfield and Eileen Hatfield
and
Charles William Fisher and Abigail Sprecher Fisher

CONTENTS

LIST OF TABLES

ACKNOWL-
EDGMENTS

We would first like to thank our families for their ideas and support of this book. Elaine would like to thank Richard and Kim Rapson; Charles, Eileen, and Mary Hatfield; and Patricia, James, Jeremy, Joshua, Jordan, and Shayna Rich. Susan would like to thank Charles Fisher; Milton, Shirley, Terry, Dawn, Larry, Jan, and Cynthia Sprecher; and Bill, Sharon, Rebecca, and David Ring.

We would also like to thank our colleagues and friends who read drafts of the book: Geraldine Alfano, Leslie Donavan, Diane Felmlee, Gerald Marwell, Kathleen McKinney, Nancy Neuman, Gerelyn O'Brien-Charles, Terri Orbuch, Patt Schwab, and Robert Smith. Thanks to Amy Grever and Carol Yoshinaga for typing this manuscript and to Chris Peters from the University of Wisconsin for providing assistance on Illustrations. Charles Fisher helped secure permission to use the various tables, graphs, and quotations.

To all the men and women interviewed for the book we express our gratitude.

CREDITS

Figure 1.3 Reprinted with permission from *Body and Clothes,* by R. Broby-Johansen (Copenhagen: Gyldendalske Boghandel, 1966).

Figure 1.5 Reproduced with permission of Pinacateca di Brera, Milan.

Figure 1.6 Reprinted with permission from *The Gibson Girl* by S. Warshaw (Berkeley, Calif.: Diablo Press, 1968).

Figure 1.7 Illustration first appeared in Wiggins, Wiggins, and Conger, "Correlates of heterosexual somatic preference," *J. of Personality and Social Psychology* © 1968 by the American Psychological Association. Reprinted by permission of the author.

Figure 1.8 Reprinted with permission of Paul J. Lavrakas, "Female Preferences For Male Physiques," *J. of Research in Personality* 9:324–334.

Figure 1.9 Reprinted with permission of Janet C. Vidal, 1984.

Figure 9.4 © 1982 Nancy Burson in collaboration with Richard Carling and David Kramlich.

Figure 9.9 Courtesy Soloflex, Inc.

Figure 11.2 © 1981, Universal Press Syndicate. Reprinted with permission. All rights reserved.

Figure 12.1 Courtesy Baker-Van Dyke collection.

FOREWORD

It is a pleasure to be asked to say a few prefatory words to this volume, which brings together under one cover for the first time what behavioral scientists have learned about the effects of physical attractiveness. Writing this introduction is a special pleasure because the book's senior author, Elaine Hatfield, has played a major and seminal role in the development of this knowledge.

Because the general public has shown a great deal of interest in information about the effects of beauty, in the recent past many journalists, freelance writers, and others have requested reprints of studies for writing their own books about the impact of physical appearance in our lives. However admirable these efforts may be, it is safe to say that none can have the authority and perspective of the pages that follow.

For one thing, researchers in an investigative area know where the bodies are buried—the "reasonable" hypotheses that turned out not to be so reasonable after all and whose disconfirming data now languishes in dark file drawers, never to see the light of publication and dissemination. For another, researchers know how to evaluate and weigh the quality of data and know where the subtle interpretive traps lie. Most importantly, researchers who have worked on a problem for a long time remember when what seems so obvious and readily accepted today was not only not obvious in the past but even failed to meet rudimentary standards of common sense. In the case of the effects of physical attractiveness, they remember when there was a scientific taboo against recognizing and systematically studying this variable at all.

This taboo against the investigation of appeariential variables upon human behavior reigned not in psychology's dim and distant past, but was alive and well until relatively recently. Just twenty years ago, Gardner Lindzey, president of the Division of Personality and Social Psychology of the American Psychological Association, took the field to task for ignoring the influence of morphological variables, "even aesthetic attractiveness," upon behavior. His remarks, many of which were scathing, detailed many reasons for the then prevalent belief in the scientific community that the study of appeariential variables was an "unsanitary practice," one that relegated those who persisted in exploring them to the tawdry side of the street in the social and behavioral sciences.

A few years after Lindzey's comments, Elliot Aronson (1969) an eminent researcher in the area of interpersonal attraction, commented upon the curious absence of systematic examination of the effect of one morphological variable, physical attractiveness, upon behavior. He also offered one possible reason for its neglect. "It may be," he said, "that, at some level, we [researchers] would hate to find evidence indicating that beautiful women are better liked than homely women—somehow this seems undemocratic." Presumably, it would have been equally uncomfortable for researchers, most of whom at that time were male, to find that handsome men were better liked than homely men. His comment, however, reflected the belief of the day (still covertly held by some researchers in contrary to established fact) that if physical attractiveness *did* by any chance have some impact, that impact was probably confined to women—and to women of dating and mating age at that.

These professional injunctions to those attempting to understand the dynamics of human social behavior had little noticeable effect. Then, in 1966, Elaine Hatfield and her colleagues published a study whose findings could not be ignored. The occasion for the study was Hatfield's employment by the University of Minnesota Student Activities Bureau, requiring her to help construct the university's program for "Freshman Welcome Week". That this new Ph.D., a top-rated graduate of the Stanford doctoral program in psychology, found employment only in an auxiliary service agency while her fellow male students secured prestigious professorships in psychology departments reflected the times and a different kind of societal taboo. Trained as a researcher and given a benevolent head of the bureau (who later recalled to a group of Minnesota faculty some of the unusual requisitions for research materials he signed while Hatfield was in his employ, including one, he remembered, for "chocolate-covered grasshoppers"), Hatfield saw her assignment to "do something" for Welcome Week as a research opportunity.

So, interested in the dynamics of interpersonal attraction, Hatfield decided to put together a "computer dance" for the incoming freshmen, a dance where purchase of a ticket would guarantee the student a date. The research question she asked was simple: Which dates, randomly paired, would like each other? Her hypothesis also was simple: People of relatively equal "social desirability" would hit it off better than people mismatched in social assets. But what determines a person's social desirability? "Personality" surely would be important, she reasoned. Fortunately, all incoming freshmen had completed various kinds of personality assessment devices, so information on this score was available. "Social skills," too, could be expected to play a role, and information on this dimension was also available. "Intelligence," especially in the college setting, undoubtedly would be an important asset, and, of course, all freshmen had submitted grade averages and completed aptitude tests to gain admittance to the university. These attributes headed the lists of all previous studies asking people what they looked for and valued in a date or mate. Thus, personality, social skills, and intelligence were to be combined into a "Social Desirability" score for each person buying a ticket to the dance.

At the last minute, however, Hatfield had an afterthought. She asked the students selling tickets to the dance to jot down their impressions of the physical attractiveness of the purchaser. Needless to say, these impressions provided only rough assessments. In the general confusion surrounding the ticket sale and in the few seconds it took to take money, make change, and issue a ticket, the ticket-taker's impression could not have much reliability and validity and thus could not be expected to predict much of anything. Nevertheless, the data were collected and analyzed.

I was a graduate student in the Laboratory for Research in Social Relations at the time and remember well when Hatfield was asked how the computer dance study had "turned out". "It was a flop," she said. Her "matching hypothosis" had not been confirmed. People of equal social desirabilities did *not* like each other better than mismatches. In fact, she went on, there was only *one* predictor of whether a person would like his or her date and, in the case of men, whether he would actually make an effort to contact the date again. That predictor was those rough physical attractiveness assessments. The more physically attractive a person was, the more they were liked by their date. This predictor held true whether the person was a woman *or* a man.

This news was greeted by total silence. Finally, someone said, "That was *it*?" "That's it," she replied. "Intelligence, social skills, personality— they didn't predict." Needless to say, these results cast a pall over the lab. The finding was embarrassing. Among other things, it gave the lie to our collective professions that what we really valued in potential dates and mates was a good personality—honesty, kindness, and all the other sterling virtues. The finding also mocked the advice, then routinely given to those who found themselves lonely and rejected, to wit: "Improve your personality and your character!"

It was not, of course, that we didn't suspect appearance played *some* role in how a person was regarded by others. But this was the early sixties—when appearance was almost universally regarded as a frivolous and superficial attribute. At this time people requesting plastic surgery to modify some aspect of their appearance were routinely subjected to tests to ascertain that they were free of psychopathology— a certification difficult for the candidate to achieve since a request for plastic surgery was itself considered a symptom of neuroticism. During this era the only reasonable justification for orthodontal surgery and treatment, or indeed routine dental treatment, was considered, by insurance companies, dentists, and clients alike, to be improvment of "function"—not aesthetic appearance.

All that, and more, has changed. For example, judges, juries, and lawyers representing clients whose appearance has been adversely altered through the negligence of others now take into consideration *more* than just impaired physical function. The probability that a disfigurement also leaves the victim with impaired self-esteem and impaired social and economic opportunities is also considered. The dental profession now worries about *more* than whether their treatment will leave the patient with the perfect "bite". Finally, therapists and counselors do not automatically conclude that social rejection is always the result of unattractive interior qualities.

Many of these changes can be traced back to that first uncomfortable and embarrassing finding, and to the fact that Elaine Hatfield was not content to bury her data. Against the advice of some senior colleagues, who believed the finding was "theoretically uninteresting" and therefore unworthy of consideration by professional journals, she wrote up her "serendipitous finding," as she called it then, and so the effort to trace the dimensions of this variable upon people's lives began in earnest.

All good researchers must be willing to observe not only that the emperor's new clothes are *not* magnificent but, when necessary, to call attention to the fact that he seems to be parading around in his underwear. Fortunately, researchers are not often called upon to make such assertions. When they are, however, and when they persist in their contention that we seem to be kidding ourselves, our understanding of our world changes; thus, our ability to make reasonable and considered choices for ourselves and for our own lives expands.

Since providing better information for making life choices is the bottom line of all research, I was particularly pleased to see that the relative importance of physical attractiveness is not ducked in the final chapters of this book. Just as it was wrong and misleading to underestimate the impact of physical attractiveness in peoples' lives, it is surely equally wrong to overestimate it—to forget that decisions on expending time, money, and energy to improve or maintain attractiveness have to be made in the context of many other considerations, and that while making gains on the attractiveness dimension, other things, often of greater value, may be lost.

I cannot resist concluding these comments with the most recent example of the effects of a single-minded determination to place beauty above all other considerations. The example comes not from the United States, with its multibillion dollar cosmetic industry and infinite numbers of diet centers, fat farms, and physical fitness and rejuvenation spas. It comes from Communist China. Concerned with the growing number of unwed men and women in their country, the Chinese government recently sponsored a nationwide campaign to "pair them off". To that end, "night dancing parties," marriage introduction services, and organized singles outings were introduced. The government's campaign, however, was a failure. Why? Apparently there are not enough "beautiful people" to go around. The *People's Daily* (as reported by the Associated Press in *The Minneapolis Star and Tribune*, August 31, 1984) complains: "Men's and women's criteria for selecting mates are not practical. The situation is unsettling. When matchmaking workers ask a man what kind of mate he desires, he says, 'I want a beautiful woman.' The result is they do not find anyone suitable." Apparently the joys of marriage and parenthood combined with governmental sanction and enticement do not outweigh, at least in contemporary Chinese eyes, the discomfort of being paired with someone who does not meet their high standards of beauty.

Is this subject "theoretically uninteresting"? That apples fall down, rather than up, must have seemed just as theoretically uninteresting at one time. But no one interested in predicting the trajectory of an apple loosed from its bough could afford to ignore that mundane fact, and no effort to understand human behavior in general, and social interaction in particular, can afford to overlook the factor of appearance.

Ellen Berscheid

Minneapolis, Minnesota
September, 1984

PREFACE

We all face a fundamental paradox. We have to admit that appearances matter. We know that small details of our appearance can be critical determinants of how well we will do in love, at work, and in life. And yet . . . and yet. Each of us knows we do not really "measure up," and we feel slightly ashamed that we expect other people to do so. How can we deal with this dilemma? This book will attempt to address that issue.

In chapter 1 we ask, "What is good looks?" and review what anthropologists, sociologists, and psychologists know about that question. We examine whether there is any agreement both between and within cultures as to what is considered beautiful or handsome.

In chapters 2 and 3, we review the evidence that, in the main, people believe "what is beautiful is good and what is ugly is bad." We will discover that people *believe* good-looking people possess almost all the virtues known to humankind, and that, as a consequence, they *treat* the good-looking/ugly very differently.

In chapters 4, 5, and 6, we discuss how well attractive versus unattractive persons fare in the dating, mating, and sexual marketplaces. We review several studies indicating that although most people desire attractive partners most often, because of the dynamics of supply and demand, they end up pairing with someone of about their own level of attractiveness.

We turn to more specific physical characteristics in chapter 7. We discuss the stereotypes held about people with specific physical characteristics. We explore the impact of height, weight, and such incidentals as hair color, eyes, and beardedness on our social encounters.

In time, most people come to see themselves as others see them— to act as others expect them to act. Eventually, good-looking and unattractive people become different types of folk in their self-images, personalities, and interactional styles. In chapter 8, we examine this *reality* of physical attractiveness.

In chapter 9, we trace the impact of beauty through the life cycle. We examine what happens to our bodies as we age and how this change affects other areas of our lives. We discover that beauty begins to matter in the nursery and continues to matter through old age.

Throughout the majority of the book we discuss the pleasant aspects of being attractive. Yet every silver lining has its cloud. The ugly truth about good looks, the disadvantages, are discussed in chapter 10.

This discussion leads us to the question of what to do if we are unattractive. Is it worth it to try every means to make ourselves more appealing? Cosmeticians, beauticians, orthodontists, and plastic surgeons would lead us to believe that we can (and should) do all we can to improve our looks. But such enterprises have serious costs even in the short run. They are expensive, exhausting, and require us to focus almost every waking moment on being something we are not. Worse yet, people banking everything on looks may find they have won the battle but lost the war. In the end, and in spite of evidence we have cited heretofore, factors other than beauty turn out to be important in producing life-long happiness. In chapters 11 and 12, we present what social psychologists and therapists have to say about the advantages and disadvantages of trying to improve our appearance. We learn that most of us do our best if we engage in fulfilling activities—concentrating on sharpening our skills in intimacy, pursuing friendship, investing energies in our careers. Apparently, what is important is to accept ourselves as we are and to set out on a search for what life has to offer.

Chapter 1

GOOD LOOKS— WHAT IS IT?

When we were deciding how to write this book, our first step was to gather a great sampling of people. We sought people very different from one another—men and women of various races, ages (3 to 97), and occupations; people strikingly good-looking to downright homely; people who had very different life experiences. These are the people who make up THE GROUP. We began by asking THE GROUP: "If you came upon a 2,000 A.D. computer capable of answering your deepest, most hidden questions about beauty and handsomeness, what would you ask?"

THE GROUP's reply was quick: "What is it?" They mentioned people *they* thought were strikingly beautiful or handsome . . . or painfully ugly—"What makes these people so distinctive?" Then, THE GROUP began, shyly, to ask more personal questions: "Do you think *I'm* good-looking?" "What's my best feature?" "My worst?" "What would I have to do to be *really* good-looking?" "What's it like to be extraordinarily good-looking?"

Figure 1.1. A tribesman admires his ceremonial appearance. Photograph by Jack Fields, 1969.

In this book, we will try to provide social psychologists' answers to all these questions and more. But first, we will have to begin at the beginning and discuss, "What is this thing called good looks?"

- How would *you* define good looks? Could you explain what a "beautiful woman" and "handsome man" are to a blind person?

- Who are the most attractive men and women you ever saw? What makes them so appealing?

- Who is the homeliest person you ever saw? What made him or her so unappealing?

GOOD LOOKS—WHAT IS IT?

Webster's New World Dictionary defines good looks as:

BEAU·TI·FUL (byōōt′e fel) *adj.* having beauty; very pleasing to the eye, ear, mind, etc. —**interj.** an exclamation of approval or pleasure —**the beautiful 1.** that which has beauty; the quality of beauty **2.** those who are beautiful — **beau′ti·ful·ly** (-e flē, -e fel ē) *adv.* *SYN.*—**beautiful** is applied to that which gives the highest degree of pleasure to the senses or to the mind and suggests that the object of delight approximates one's conception of an ideal; **lovely** refers to that which delights by inspiring affection or warm admiration; **handsome** implies attractiveness by reason of pleasing proportions, symmetry, elegance, etc. and carries connotations of masculinity, dignity, or impressiveness; **pretty** implies a dainty, delicate, or graceful quality in that which pleases and carries connotations of femininity or diminutiveness; **comely** applies to persons only and suggests a wholesome attractiveness of form and features rather than a high degree of beauty; **fair** suggests beauty that is fresh, bright, or flawless and, when applied to persons, is used esp. of complexion and features; **good-looking** is closely equivalent to **handsome** or **pretty,** suggesting a pleasing appearance but not expressing the fine distinctions of either word; **beauteous,** equivalent to **beautiful** in poetry and lofty prose, is now often used in humorously disparaging references to beauty—*ANT.* **ugly**

HAND·SOME (han′sem) *adj.* [orig., easily handled, convenient < ME. *handsom:* see HAND & -SOME[1]] **1.** *a)* [Now Rare] moderately large *b)* large; impressive; considerable [a *handsome* sum] **2.** generous; magnanimous; gracious [a *handsome* gesture] **3.** good-looking; of pleasing appearance: said esp. of attractiveness that is manly, dignified, or impressive rather than delicate and graceful [a *handsome* lad, a *handsome* chair] —*SYN.* see BEAUTIFUL —**hand′some·ly** *adv.* — **hand′some·ness** *n.*

(From D. B. Guralnik, *Webster's New World Dictionary: Edition 2* [New York: Simon and Schuster, 1982], 124, 634.)

By *physical attractiveness* we mean *that which best represents one's conception of the ideal in appearance and gives the greatest pleasure to the senses.*

At first glance, it seems easy to say what is appealing, what is not. For example, early I.Q. testers assumed that any intelligent person could easily tell which is which. *The Stanford-Binet Intelligence Scale* (1937 edition) asked children to look at two line drawings and to indicate which woman was pretty and which was ugly. The "pretty" face had fine, delicate features and a neat hairdo, while the "ugly" face had a large nose, a large mouth, and unkempt hair. Obviously, the test constructors assumed they *knew* what beauty was and that any "bright" child would agree with them. Unfortunately, however, things are not so simple. The search for a standard of beauty has been a long one.

The Search for a Universal Beauty

Thoughtful people have spent an enormous amount of effort trying to discover what is universal about beauty. Greek philosophers were convinced that the Golden Mean was the basic standard of beauty (see Hambidge 1920; or Plato 1925). The Golden Mean represented a perfect balance. To be extreme was to be imperfect. (So much for the rare and exotic.) The Greeks' theory was elegantly, brilliantly simple. Unfortunately, it was wrong. The Romans were more interested in the rarities of particular faces and persons. Conceptions of ideal beauty resurfaced in the Christian era (see Figure 1.2).

In more recent times, Charles Darwin's efforts to define beauty are worth noting. Charles Darwin realized it was critically important for anthropologists to know what various peoples considered sexually appealing. Only then could they predict the course of sexual selection and, ultimately, human evolution. Darwin tried but failed. After surveying the standards of various tribes throughout the world, Darwin concluded: "It is certainly not true that there is in the mind of many any universal standard of beauty with respect to the human body" (1952, 577).

Henry T. Finck (1887) was the first early psychologist to pose a theory of beauty. Finck is a delight to read. It makes one feel smugly superior to encounter someone so self-righteous, so opinionated . . . and so wrong. Finck's singular thesis was that primitive people were nature's "experiments." Humankind started out, he thought, exceedingly ugly. But humankind continued to evolve, becoming more perfect, better-looking, all the time. Finally, evolution and good looks reached a pinnacle in the upperclass English gentleman. (Luckily, Henry Finck happened to be in just this category.)

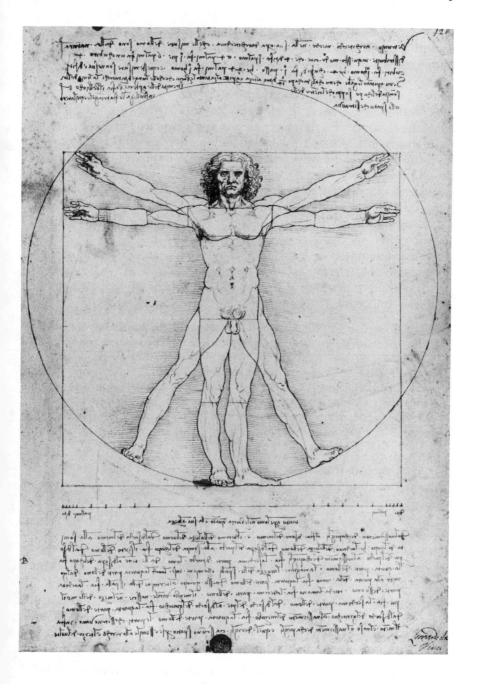

Figure 1.2. Leonardo da Vinci, *Illustration of Proportions of the Human Figure*, c. 1485–1490, pen and ink, 13½ × 9¾.

This tendency—to assume our own group contains the best of everything—is common. One example: Dental surgeons face the extraordinarily difficult task of developing a universal standard of beauty. (The only way to know whether orthodontics has helped or hurt is to have a standard of perfection against which to compare your work.) Most orthodontic indices, beginning with E. H. Angles' classification in 1908, have used an arbitrary classification standard. In each case, the test constructors selected their own face as the ideal! This unconscious chauvinism has had an ironic result. Since the dentists involved in scale development have been Europeans, when dentists in Hawaii tried to use the scales with Asian or black populations they soon discovered almost *all* their clients needed their teeth straightened. Finckism strikes again! (See Giddon [1980] or Uesato [1968] for a further discussion of this point.)

Finck attempted to provide a feature by feature analysis of what is good-looking. He began his dissertation with "The Evolution of the Big Toe" and moved slowly upward. The flavor of Finck's appalling Victorian smugness is recaptured in his opening passage:

> . . . Concerning savages, there is a prevalent notion that, owing to their free and easy life in the forests, they are healthier on the average than civilized mankind. As a matter of fact, however, they are as inferior to us in Health as in Beauty. Their constant exposure and irregular feeding habits, their neglect and ignorance of every hygienic law, in conjunction with their vicious lives, their arbitrary mutilations of various parts, and their selection of inferior forms, prevent their bodies from assuming the regular and delicate proportions which we regard as essential to beauty. (1887, 76)

Finck then itemized each trait—the feet, limbs, waist, chest, etc.—and explained why the Victorian gentleman surpassed all others in beauty appeal. (In a short 467 pages, he managed to insult every existing ethnic group.) The Hungarians are "of a repulsive ugliness in the eyes of all their neighbors." "The typical Jew is certainly not a thing of beauty. The disadvantages of genuine separation are shown not only in the long, thick crooked nose, the bloated lips, almost suggesting a negro, and the heavy lower eyelid, but in the fact that the Jews have proportionately more insane, deaf mutes, blind, and colour-blind" than other Europeans (p. 89). "The women of France are amongst the ugliest in the world" (p. 390).

What about the Americans? Finck quotes Lady Amberley:

> They all looked sick. Circumstances have repeatedly carried me to Europe, where I am always surprised by the red blood that fills and colours the faces of ladies and peasant girls, reminding one of the canvas of Rubens and Murillo; and I am always equally surprised on my return

by crowds of pale, bloodless female faces, that suggest consumption, scrofula, anaemia, and neuralgia. (p. 445)

Such was the tenor of Finck's scientific discussion. The problem with Finck's careful enumeration of ideal traits is that *nowhere* can we take him seriously.

The dream of anthropologists of discovering what constituted "universal beauty" was finally laid to rest in a landmark survey. Clelland Ford and Frank Beach (1951) studied more than two hundred primitive societies. They were unable to find *any* universal standards of sexual allure. Different cultures could not even agree completely as to what parts of the body were important. For some peoples, the shape and color of the eyes was what really mattered. For others, it was height and weight. Still others went right to the center of things—what mattered was the size and shape of the sexual organs.

To complicate things still further, even if two societies agreed on what was *important*, they rarely agreed about what constituted good looks in that area. For example, in some societies (like our own), a slim woman is the ideal. The opposite, however, is true in most other societies—the fatter the better. Table 1.1 lists traits people in various societies have considered hallmarks of beauty.

TABLE 1.1   **Societies' Preferences in Appearance**

	NUMBER OF SOCIETIES THAT ADMIRE THIS TRAIT
Slim body build	5
Medium body build	5
Plump body build	13
Narrow pelvis and slim hips	1
Broad pelvis and wide hips	6
Small ankles	3
Shapley calves	5
Upright, hemispherical breasts	2
Long and pendulous breasts	2
Large breasts	9
Large clitoris	1
Elongated labia majora	8

Note: Although Ford and Beach discuss the impact of "man's" appearance on sexuality, in this case "man" means "woman." Although the authors do not itemize the traits constituing handsomeness, other information makes it clear that in various societies there is equal disagreement as to what handsomeness is.

THE FACE

In many societies, the face—delicate boned or broad and sensual—is all that really counts.

Anthropologist Bronislaw Malinowski (1929) observed that, for the Trobriand Islanders: ". . . It is a notable fact that their main erotic interest is focused on the human head and face. In the formulae of beauty magic, in the vocabulary of human attractions, as well as in the arsenal of ornament and decoration, the human face—eyes, mouth, teeth, nose and hair—takes precedence" (pp. 295–296).

Those societies that are experts on the face do not agree as to what kind of face is best. Most peoples consider light skin to be most appealing. But many, like the Pima, prefer dark skin; some, like the Dobuans, consider albinos to be particularly repulsive. For the Wogeo, things are even more complicated: tawny-colored Wogeoians prefer light-skinned mates; the cocoa colored prefer dark-skinned mates.

Figure 1.3. In some African tribes, the women insert pieces of wood as large as plates behind their lips. Ubangi women.

THE BODY

In many societies, good looks equals a good body. But again, even the societies that worship fine bodies do not agree on what constitutes a good body. In most societies, robust women are seen as possessing the most sex appeal. Clelland Ford and Frank Beach observe:

> [Holmberg writes of the Siriono:] Besides being young, a desirable sex partner—especially a woman—should also be fat. She should have big hips, good sized but firm breasts, and a deposit of fat on her sexual organs. Fat women are referred to by the men with obvious pride as *EréN ekida* (fat vulva) and are thought to be much more satisfying sexually than thin women, who are summarily dismissed as being *ikáNgi* (bony). In fact, so desirable is corpulence as a sexual trait that I have frequently heard men make up songs about the merits of a fat vulva . . . . (1951, 88–89)

In many primitive societies, people are balanced on the fine edge of survival. A fat wife is a status symbol. She graphically illustrates her husband's ability to provide . . . to excess.

SEXUAL TRAITS: GETTING DOWN TO FUNDAMENTALS

It is easy for us to understand how critically important sexual characteristics are. The question "Are you a breast man, a leg, or an ass man?" attests to Americans' focus on sexual traits. American men have long been fascinated by big breasts (Morrison and Holden 1971). In 1968, Francine Gottfried of Brooklyn—a twenty-one-year old whose measurements were 43–25–37—generated a riot among staid, Wall Street businessmen simply by walking to work in the morning. At first, only a few bankers, brokers, and clerks waited on the street corner to watch her walk by. Then the crowds grew. The news media began to report on the phenomenon. The crowds swelled. On September 21, 1968, a cheering crowd of more than 10,000 jammed Broad Street (in front of the New York Stock Exchange) and nearby Wall Street. Newspapermen and cameramen from as far away as Australia waited for pictures. Ticker tape floated down from the buildings. Police stood by with bullhorns. In the pushing and shoving, some in the throng were nearly trampled. There was the distinctive thumping sound as the metal roofs of four automobiles buckled under the weight of excited spectators, who had climbed on top for a better view. Francine Gottfried of Brooklyn did not enjoy the spectacle as much as the bankers. She failed to put in an appearance (*New York Times*, 21 Sept. 1968).

Americans' obsession with breasts might tempt you to assume the fixation is a cultural universal. It is not. In different cultures, the "ideal" size and shape of a woman's breasts vary. Some peoples prefer small, upright breasts. (The Wogeo think breasts should be firm with the nipples facing outwards. A young girl with pendulous breasts, "like a grandmother," is pitied.) Other peoples like long and pendulous breasts.

For some peoples the external genitals, the labia majora and minora and the penis, are important. In many societies, elongated labia majora are considered erotically appealing. Young girls are advised to pull the clitoris and the vulvar lips to enhance their sex appeal. Before puberty, girls on Ponape undergo treatment designed to lengthen the labia minora and to enlarge their clitoris. Impotent old men pull, beat, and suck the labia to lengthen them. The girls put black ants in their vulva so that their stinging will cause the labia and clitoris to swell. In America, most men are not particularly focused on this area. Pornographic magazines featuring "beaver shots" appeal to a minority. (Another society's obsessions always seem strange to us.)

In many societies, men's sexual organs are equally important. In the New Hebrides, men choose to emphasize their sexual appeal (see Figure 1.4). Anthropologist B. T. Sommerville (1984) observed:

> The natives wrap the penis around with many yards of calico, and other materials, winding and folding them until a preposterous bundle of eighteen inches, or two feet long, and two inches or more in diameter is formed, which is then supported upward by means of a belt, in the extremity decorated with flowering grasses, etc. The testicles are left naked. (p. 368)

In the 1600s European men often wore codpieces in a similar effort to emphasize their assets. Originally, a codpiece was a metal case to protect men's genitals in battle. Eventually it became a gaudy silk case of colors contrasting with the rest of the costume. Sometimes it was enlarged with stuffing and decorated with ribbons and precious stones (see Figure 1.5).

Lest other society's obsessions with men's genitals seem exotic, note that *Rolling Stone* once devoted an entire issue to describing how magazines such as *Playgirl* and *Viva* test, cajol, and massage the centerfold's penis to just the right stage of arousal (McCormack 1975). Elvis Presley often used a toilet paper tube under tight pants while performing on stage to augment his penis size (Wallace 1981).

As we have seen again and again, however, only a few societies focus on the external genitals, and those that do fail to agree on what constitutes beauty. The New Hebrides model and the Marlboro man *are* miles apart.

Figure 1.4. In the New Hebrides, men wrap their penes in cloth to form an impressive bundle, held in place with a leather belt. Courtesy, Musée de l'Homme, Paris.

Figure 1.5. Portrait of Antonio Navagero by Giovanni Battista Moroni, 1565.

IN SUMMARY

Today, scholars have admitted defeat in their search for a universal beauty. After a painstaking search, after numerous false leads, all their hopes of uncovering such ideals have been shattered. Anthropologists have ended where they began—able to do no more than point to the dazzling array of characteristics that various people in various places, at various times, have idealized.

(Reading this research, one feels a sense of irony. Most of us spend so much time worrying about our bodies, trying to emphasize our "good points" and minimize our "bad" ones. It is disconcerting to realize that with a slight change of time or place all these standards would be turned topsy-turvy.)

Although anthropologists have also been unable to unearth any universal standards for good looks (or for bad looks) *within* any society, there *is*, however, considerable agreement on what is appealing and what is not.

The Search for a Local Beauty

In Western society, the media promotes a standard of beauty. Gerald Adams and a colleague (Adams and Crossman 1978) describe television's image of beauty:

Masculinity is judged by overall appearance and impression. The commercials on television will suggest the main attributes a man needs to be considered attractive and desirable. "The dry look" is important. "Reaching for the gusto" is absolutely essential. Using Right Guard and smelling of Brut, English Leather, Old Spice, Musk or one of a half dozen other men's colognes are also necessary. And depending upon the "type", he will drive a certain make and model of car, smoke a certain brand of tobacco, and above all, read "Playboy" magazine. He doesn't have to have a face like Paul Newman or Robert Redford, or a physique like Adonis, though it won't hurt if he does. Primarily, he must be trim, rugged but not too rugged, manly, and have a nice smile. Femininity, on the other hand, is characterized by perfection in every detail. Unlike masculinity, femininity cannot be acquired merely by using the right deodorant and applying a number of external props. A woman must have hair with body and fullness that is marvelously highlighted. Each feature must be an equal contributor to her pretty face. She must have eternally young and blemish-free skin. Her figure must not only be trim, but meet certain "idealized" standards to be considered beautiful. Her hands must be silky soft and not too large. Her nails must be long and perfectly trimmed. Her legs must be shapely, firm, and preferably long. To attain all this, she must "enter the garden of earthly delights" and use "Herbal Essence Shampoo"—hair conditioners scented with lemon, strawberry or apricot, which give marvelous body . . . and rinse or dye, which will make her the "girl with the hair". Her skin must be nurtured with moisturizers and emollients so she can look eternally young. Her figure should surpass that of a Greek goddess by being amply bosomed and slim waisted, but rounded in the hips. As for her legs, "gentlemen prefer Hanes." For finishing touches, she should use "sex appeal toothpaste" and put her "money where her mouth is". She should know that "Blondes have more fun" and Lady Clairol blondes have the most fun of all. For a foundation, she should wear the "cross your heart bra" and never be without her "18-hour girdle". Finally, above all else, her beauty must look natural. (pp. 21–22; reprinted by permission of Libra Publishing)

Americans and Europeans agree with the media on what is appealing and what is not. In a typical study (this one conducted in Great Britain), Iliffe (1960) asked readers of one of the large newspapers how "pretty" they thought twelve women's faces were. The photos where chosen to represent as many types as possible—they varied in slope of eye, coloring, shape of face, etc. Thousands of readers replied, the critics ranging in age from eight to eighty. They came from markedly different social classes and regions, yet they had similar ideas about what is beautiful. (Additional evidence that, within a society, there *is* consensus on what is beautiful comes from the work of Cross and Cross [1971] and Kopera, Maier, and Johnson [1971].)

We asked THE GROUP what traits they thought made men and women appealing. Here are some of their answers.

A physically attractive woman is someone with beautiful hair, expressive eyes, high cheekbones, perfect breasts, great ass and legs.

Beautiful people have distinctive features.

Figure 1.6. Charles Dana Gibson, *The Jury Disagrees*

A beautiful woman is someone with big eyes, a pretty smile, a thin tapered nose, oval-shaped face, perfect teeth. Usually women have to be perfect to be beautiful. Men don't have to be perfect.

Distortions are ugly. Someone who has a very large nose or big forehead, a lot of freckles, or something like that, is unappealing.

I'm thinking of a man I know who is gorgeous. He has blond hair, light blue eyes, high cheekbones, a long face, and a perfect nose.

I don't like the 5'11" All-American blond with voluptuous curves. It's boring, I like the unusual—a German look . . . a beautiful Scandanavian look.

When I think of beauty, I think of *Vogue* and high fashion. Since I don't like that, I don't know what beauty is.

No fat chicks here.

I think men whose bodies have gone to seed are a little disgusting.

Beauty is perfection. That perfection can manifest itself in a variety of ways—first and foremost would be in physical aspects.

Though there are differences among these statements, the similarities and agreements are more common.

Several studies have examined how people react to different body configurations. Nancy Hirshberg and her colleagues (Wiggins et al. 1968) conducted the most careful study of what men think is beautiful in women. They prepared 105 nude silhouettes like those in Figure 1.7.

The first silhouette had a Golden Mean sort of body—she had average-sized breasts, buttocks, and legs. (If the Greeks were right, men should have preferred *her*—they didn't.) The remaining silhouettes' assets were systematically varied. For example, the silhouettes were given unusually large breasts (+2), moderate-sized breasts (+1), standard breasts (0), moderately small breasts (−1), or unusually small (−2) breasts. The silhouettes' legs and buttocks were varied in the same way. Young men were asked to pick the figures they liked best.

The Golden Mean theory turned out to have *some* validity. Most men thought the women with medium-sized breasts, buttocks, and legs were more attractive than those with unusually small or large features. The men's ideal, however, was a woman with oversized breasts (+1), medium to slightly small buttocks, and medium-sized legs. (Similar results were secured by Beck et al. [1976] and Horvath [1979].)

What about women? What do they find appealing in *men*? Paul Lavrakas (1975) followed the procedure we have just described in order to find out. He constructed nineteen different types of men's bodies on

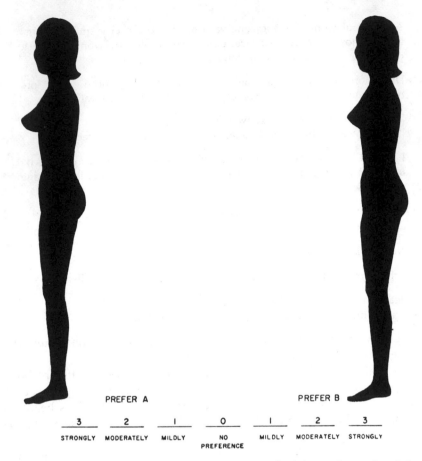

PREFER A   PREFER B

3	2	I	0	I	2	3
STRONGLY	MODERATELY	MILDLY	NO PREFERENCE	MILDLY	MODERATELY	STRONGLY

Figure 1.7.   An illustrative stimulus pair. A standard figure is on the right; the one on the left has +2 breasts, and standard buttocks and legs.

graph paper—combining the same-size head with bigger or smaller arms, torsos, and legs—as shown in Figure 1.8.

He interviewed women aged eighteen to thirty as to which men's bodies they liked best. He found women preferred men with a Robert Redford tapered "V-look." They liked men with medium-sized shoulders, a medium-thick waist and hips, and thin legs. The build they most disliked was the "Alfred Hitchcock pear-shaped look" (men with small shoulders and wide hips). (Similar results were secured by Beck et al. [1976] and Horvath [1979].)

CAN MEN AND WOMEN EVER AGREE ON ANYTHING?

According to the folklore, men and women supposedly have markedly different standards of beauty. Presumably, women prefer delicate, lady-

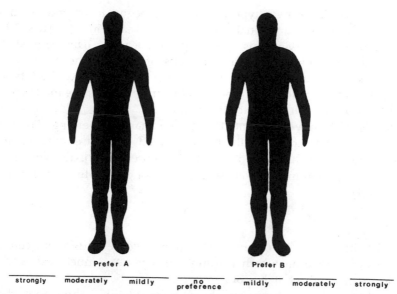

Fɪɢ. 1. An illustrative stimulus pair.

Figure 1.8. An illustrative stimulus pair.

like women; men prefer earthy, sexy ones. Women are supposed to find pretty men irresistible; men value rugged good looks.

To our surprise, we found this stereotype *untrue*. Men and women show surprising agreement on what is good-looking and what is not (see Kopera et al. 1971; Rokeach 1943).

CHANGING STANDARDS OF BEAUTY

Standards of beauty are never static. They are forever changing—especially for women. At the turn of the century, the Gibson Girl was the ideal. She was tall and full-breasted. In the 1920s, the "Flapper" sped into view. Women cut their hair, removed the scarves and other stuffing from their bodices, and began to bind their breasts. (The brassiere was originally invented to hide breasts.) From the 1920s on, ideals of beauty flickered from movie screens. In the 1950s, the leading Hollywood queen was Marilyn Monroe. She was the sex symbol of the era; once again beauty equaled voluptuousness. In the 1960s, Twiggy brought in the beanpole look, which did not last long. In the 1970s, with Raquel Welch, the shapely, sensuous look with legs returned. What about the 1980s? Today we admire a variety of beauty models. There are the Brooke Shieldses (all-American look), and the Dolly Partons—(with abundance.)

Very recently, a new type of ideal has begun to emerge—a more muscular, healthy, functional beauty. *Time* magazine (Corliss 1982) devoted a cover story to this "New Ideal of Beauty." *Time* argued that women are reshaping Americans' notions of beauty. The new woman is natural—graceful, slim, and far stronger than before. Their bodies are streamlined for motion, for purposeful strides across the mall, around the backcourt, and into the board room.

Ideals of beauty for women and men may be merging. For men, attractiveness has traditionally been equated with strength, stamina, fitness—all of which allowed men to be more functional. Women are finally joining men in the exercise gym and in corporate chambers (See Figure 1.9).

Summary

Scientists have found no universal beauties. People in different cultures do not even agree on which features are *important*, much less what is good-looking and what is not.

Within a culture, however, there *is* considerable agreement about looks. Luckily for the vast majority of us, there is not complete agreement. For example, Cross and Cross (1971), after reporting that Americans and Europeans agree, to some extent, on what kinds of faces are most appealing, report: "The most popular face in the sample was chosen as best of its group by 6 of 207 judges but there was no face that was never chosen, and even the least popular face was picked as *best* of its group (of six portraits similar in age, sex, and race) by four subjects" (p. 438).

The optimistic hope that someone, somewhere, sometime will think we are irresistible seems a realistic one.

WHAT DO YOU THINK OF YOURSELF?

Now that we have discovered what Americans and Europeans think is good-looking, we can turn to the most personal questions THE GROUP faced:

- How good-looking do you think you are?

- If you could enter one part of yourself in a beauty contest, what would that be?

- Are there certain parts of your body that are especially ugly?

- What do other people think of your looks?

Figure 1.9. Ms. University of Hawaii, Janet C. Vidad, at a beauty and physical fitness contest, 1984.

- Do they ever tell you you're physically appealing? Make cruel comments about your looks? How do you react to such comments?

- How self-conscious are you about your looks?

Scientists have developed a variety of techniques for assessing "Body Image."

We all know about "The Perfect 10". At the University of Wisconsin (Madison) sits The Pub, overlooking State Street. The front wall is solid glass. Men sit on stools, drinking beer, "watching all the girls go by." Each time a woman passes, men shout out "5" or "8" to indicate how good-looking they think she is. Madison women, a bit fiercer than most, occasionally retaliate. One Friday afternoon, a student named Leslie Donovan went down to The Pub with her Alpha Chi Omega sorority sisters, each armed with a stack of flash cards numbered 1–10. When a man shouted his rating, *they* held up a card indicating *his* score. (Ms. Donovan once held up a flash card with a "10" on it plus a note attached which said, "My name is Leslie. You can reach me at 222-0101.")

Generally, researchers use a straightforward technique for finding out how people rate themselves. They simply ask them. For example, we (Hatfield [Walster] et al., 1966) asked teenagers: "All in all, how good-looking do you think you are?"

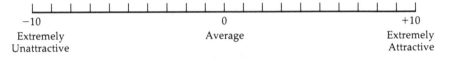

−10	0	+10
Extremely Unattractive	Average	Extremely Attractive

In this study, most teens thought they were less than a perfect 6.

Surprisingly, even though this method sounds simplistic, it is an effective way to find out what people think of themselves. This straight-forwardness is as good as some of the more elaborate scaling techniques that have been devised. Sometimes, simple is best. Usually, such rough and ready estimates have been enough. On occasion, researchers want to know more about the details of beauty. In such cases, they have proceeded to ask men and women how they felt about almost every feature of themselves—their face, height, weight, and other details.

For example, we asked readers of *Psychology Today* (a popular magazine) how they felt about their bodies (Berscheid, Hatfield [Walster], and Bohrnstedt 1973). More then sixty-two thousand readers replied. Take a moment to answer our Body Image questionnaire.

Body Image

How satisfied are you with the way your body looks?

1. Height:
   - ○ A Extremely satisfied.
   - ○ B Quite satisfied.
   - ○ C Somewhat satisfied.
   - ○ D Somewhat dissatisfied.
   - ○ E Quite dissatisfied.
   - ○ F Extremely dissatisfied.

2. Weight:

  ○ A Extremely satisfied.
  ○ B Quite satisfied.
  ○ C Somewhat satisfied.
  ○ D Somewhat dissatisfied.
  ○ E Quite dissatisfied.
  ○ F Extremely dissatisfied.

3. Hair:

  ○ A Extremely satisfied.
  ○ B Quite satisfied.
  ○ C Somewhat satisfied.
  ○ D Somewhat dissatisfied.
  ○ E Quite dissatisfied.
  ○ F Extremely dissatisfied.

4. Eyes:

  ○ A Extremely satisfied.
  ○ B Quite satisfied.
  ○ C Somewhat satisfied.
  ○ D Somewhat dissatisfied.
  ○ E Quite dissatisfied.
  ○ F Extremely dissatisfied.

5. Ears:

  ○ A Extremely satisfied.
  ○ B Quite satisfied.
  ○ C Somewhat satisfied.
  ○ D Somewhat dissatisfied.
  ○ E Quite dissatisfied.
  ○ F Extremely dissatisfied.

6. Nose:

  ○ A Extremely satisfied.
  ○ B Quite satisfied.
  ○ C Somewhat satisfied.
  ○ D Somewhat dissatisfied.
  ○ E Quite dissatisfied.
  ○ F Extremely dissatisfied.

7. Mouth:

  ○ A Extremely satisfied.
  ○ B Quite satisfied.
  ○ C Somewhat satisfied.
  ○ D Somewhat dissatisfied.
  ○ E Quite dissatisfied.
  ○ F Extremely dissatisfied.

8. Teeth:

- ○ A Extremely satisfied.
- ○ B Quite satisfied.
- ○ C Somewhat satisfied.
- ○ D Somewhat dissatisfied.
- ○ E Quite dissatisfied.
- ○ F Extremely dissatisfied.

9. Voice:

- ○ A Extremely satisfied.
- ○ B Quite satisfied.
- ○ C Somewhat satisfied.
- ○ D Somewhat dissatisfied.
- ○ E Quite dissatisfied.
- ○ F Extremely dissatisfied.

10. Chin:

- ○ A Extremely satisfied.
- ○ B Quite satisfied.
- ○ C Somewhat satisfied.
- ○ D Somewhat dissatisfied.
- ○ E Quite dissatisfied.
- ○ F Extremely dissatisfied.

11. Complexion:

- ○ A Extremely satisfied.
- ○ B Quite satisfied.
- ○ C Somewhat satisfied.
- ○ D Somewhat dissatisfied.
- ○ E Quite dissatisfied.
- ○ F Extremely dissatisfied.

12. Overall facial attractiveness:

- ○ A Extremely satisfied.
- ○ B Quite satisfied.
- ○ C Somewhat satisfied.
- ○ D Somewhat dissatisfied.
- ○ E Quite dissatisfied.
- ○ F Extremely dissatisfied.

13. Shoulders:

- ○ A Extremely satisfied.
- ○ B Quite satisfied.
- ○ C Somewhat satisfied.
- ○ D Somewhat dissatisfied.
- ○ E Quite dissatisfied.
- ○ F Extremely dissatisfied.

14. Chest (males), Breasts (females):
    O A Extremely satisfied.
    O B Quite satisfied.
    O C Somewhat satisfied.
    O D Somewhat dissatisfied.
    O E Quite dissatisfied.
    O F Extremely dissatisfied.

15. Arms:
    O A Extremely satisfied.
    O B Quite satisfied.
    O C Somewhat satisfied.
    O D Somewhat dissatisfied.
    O E Quite dissatisfied.
    O F Extremely dissatisfied.

16. Hands:
    O A Extremely satisfied.
    O B Quite satisfied.
    O C Somewhat satisfied.
    O D Somewhat dissatisfied.
    O E Quite dissatisfied.
    O F Extremely dissatisfied.

17. Size of abdomen:
    O A Extremely satisfied.
    O B Quite satisfied.
    O C Somewhat satisfied.
    O D Somewhat dissatisfied.
    O E Quite dissatisfied.
    O F Extremely dissatisfied.

18. Buttocks (seat):
    O A Extremely satisfied.
    O B Quite satisfied.
    O C Somewhat satisfied.
    O D Somewhat dissatisfied.
    O E Quite dissatisfied.
    O F Extremely dissatisfied.

19. Size of sex organs:
    O A Extremely satisfied.
    O B Quite satisfied.
    O C Somewhat satisfied.
    O D Somewhat dissatisfied.
    O E Quite dissatisfied.
    O F Extremely dissatisfied.

20. Appearance of sex organs:
   - O A Extremely satisfied.
   - O B Quite satisfied.
   - O C Somewhat satisfied.
   - O D Somewhat dissatisfied.
   - O E Quite dissatisfied.
   - O F Extremely dissatisfied.

21. Hips (upper thighs):
   - O A Extremely satisfied.
   - O B Quite satisfied.
   - O C Somewhat satisfied.
   - O D Somewhat dissatisfied.
   - O E Quite dissatisfied.
   - O F Extremely dissatisfied.

22. Legs and ankles:
   - O A Extremely satisfied.
   - O B Quite satisfied.
   - O C Somewhat satisfied.
   - O D Somewhat dissatisfied.
   - O E Quite dissatisfied.
   - O F Extremely dissatisfied.

23. Feet:
   - O A Extremely satisfied.
   - O B Quite satisfied.
   - O C Somewhat satisfied.
   - O D Somewhat dissatisfied.
   - O E Quite dissatisfied.
   - O F Extremely dissatisfied.

24. General muscle tone or development:
   - O A Extremely satisfied.
   - O B Quite satisfied.
   - O C Somewhat satisfied.
   - O D Somewhat dissatisfied.
   - O E Quite dissatisfied.
   - O F Extremely dissatisfied.

25. Overall body appearance:
   - O A Extremely satisfied.
   - O B Quite satisfied.
   - O C Somewhat satisfied.
   - O D Somewhat dissatisfied.
   - O E Quite dissatisfied.
   - O F Extremely dissatisfied.

(Berscheid, Hatfield [Walster] and Bohrnstedt 1972; Reprinted from *Psychology Today* July, 1972, pp. 58–59.)

Now you know how satisfied you are with your appearance. Do you have more self-confidence than most? . . . or less? Let's find out.

Lest We Forget: A Note

You might have felt—as you struggled through the Body Image questionnaire—that we asked too much. Not so for most people. Many people who responded complained we had neglected to ask about the very traits they thought were most important: "I thought your quiz very odd," wrote one New York man. "Nothing about chest hair, pubic hair, or beards." "How one sees oneself in motion—awkward, graceful, rigidly erect, slumping. . . ." "Why didn't you ask about physical deformities?" asked one unhappy man. "My rib cage is deformed as a result of rickets (not to mention a curvature of the spine and a short leg)." "How about blindness?" . . . "bowlegs?" . . . "deafness?" . . . "mastectomies?" One man was annoyed that we did not ask how people felt about their colon, what with constipation and such! Granted we did not ask everything, but we can see how people feel about the things we *did* ask about.

To find out how people in general felt about themselves, we selected a sample of two thousand questionnaires for closer scrutiny. We selected a sample that came as close to the national statistics as possible. It consisted of 50 percent men and 50 percent women. Forty-five percent were 24 years old or younger, 25 percent were between 25 and 44, and the rest were 45 or older.

Table 1.2 shows how satisfied most people are with themselves.

Appearance

American society places so much emphasis on looks. How do most people feel they measure up *overall*? Only about half the people are extremely or quite satisfied with their looks. Slightly more men than women (55 percent versus 45 percent) are this satisfied. One California man, who was extremely satisfied with his looks, observed: "I have to admit that I consider myself to be a gorgeous person. Your questionnaire made me aware of my body, not just a finely crafted machine, but as a being that is beautiful in an artistic way."

A trivial 4 percent of men and 7 percent of the women are quite or extremely *dissatisfied* with their overall appearance. The following replies are typical of people in that category:

> What we ugly people need is a special book of etiquette that advises us how to behave under the following circumstances: How to respond to remarks like "you sure are ugly." When you see all the easy jobs go to

TABLE 1.2   **Satisfaction with Body Parts**

	QUITE OR EXTREMELY DISSATISFIED		SOMEWHAT DISSATISFIED		SOMEWHAT SATISFIED		QUITE OR EXTREMELY SATISFIED	
	WOMEN	MEN	WOMEN	MEN	WOMEN	MEN	WOMEN	MEN
Overall Appearance	7%	4%	16%	11%	32%	30%	45%	55%
face								
overall facial attractiveness	3	2	8	6	28	31	61	61
hair	6	6	13	12	29	22	53	59
eyes	1	1	5	6	14	12	80	81
ears	2	1	5	4	10	13	83	82
nose	5	2	18	14	22	20	55	64
mouth	2	1	5	5	20	19	73	75
teeth	11	10	19	18	20	26	50	46
voice	3	3	15	12	27	27	55	58
chin	4	3	9	8	20	20	67	69
complexion	8	7	20	15	24	20	48	58
extremities								
shoulders	2	3	11	8	19	22	68	67
arms	5	2	11	11	22	25	62	62
hands	5	1	14	7	21	17	60	75
feet	6	3	14	8	23	19	57	70
mid torso								
size of abdomen	19	11	31	25	21	22	29	42
buttocks (seat)	17	6	26	14	20	24	37	56
hips (upper thighs)	22	3	27	9	19	24	32	64
legs and ankles	8	4	17	7	23	20	52	69
height, weight and tone								
height	3	3	10	10	15	20	72	67
weight	21	10	27	25	21	22	31	43
general muscle tone or development	9	7	21	18	32	30	38	45
sex organs								
chest/breast	9	4	18	14	23	24	50	58
size of sex organs	1	6	2	9	18	19	79	66
appearance of sex organs	2	3	5	6	18	19	75	72

the pretty girls, when they are no more capable than you [sic]. What are you supposed to do when people stare at you? When little children run when they see you! When, as a child, you have to listen to people say that your parents must have committed some grave sin. When you realize that hardened criminals are better off than you because they can at least go to a big city and get lost in the crowd. When people mistreat you and accuse you of being evil. And finally, how are you equipped to behave, when you cannot see any evidence that God loves you?

> At the age of twelve, I realized that I was a homosexual. To relieve my tension, I ate and ate until, at the height of five-seven, I weighed 180 pounds and became known as "Fats." At the age of 14, while taking a shower, I realized that no one, absolutely no one would ever love me— I was a fat slob. The next month I lost 30 pounds. It worked. I am now 23 and am 6 foot and weigh 155. I have a lover for the first time in my life who is more than a one-night stand. I am glad that I had that experience. I somehow appreciate inner beauty more than the plastic, store-bought, television ad beauty that drives so many in this world. (P.S. My lover is beautiful. I refuse to answer if I was attracted to his inner or outer beauty first.)

In general, then, men do have better body images than do women. This finding is especially disturbing in light of the fact that women are those most likely to believe that "physical attractiveness is very important in day-to-day social interaction."

For most women, the longing to be beautiful runs deep.

> Throughout my childhood I was praised as the intellectual, quiet, thoughtful, conscientious, humorous child of the family—but I desperately wanted to be pretty. I am nearly thirty years old, a "success" in a field few women enter, a "good" speaker, conversationalist, and clown, in a mild sort of way. I am happily married and feel "valued" by my family, but I'd chuck it all if some Mephistophelian character offered me the option of the kind of long-legged, aquiline, tawny beauty praised in myth and toothpaste ads.

A few women noted they were *trying* to overcome their obsession with beauty:

> At a consciousness-raising session, several friends and I decided to go around in a circle and name our most hated features. Hearing each other, we realized how minutely our "ugly" features were noticed. It was definitely a good thing to do.

One's Face Is One's Fortune

Almost everyone was happy with his or her face; only 11 percent of the women and 8 percent of the men expressed any dissatisfaction.

People were not uniformly delighted with every aspect of their faces, however. Both men and women were unhappiest with their teeth—almost one-third were dissatisfied—one-fourth of the respondents complained about their complexions, and one in five did not like their noses.

Sexual Characteristics: How Do You Stack Up?

Given Americans' preoccupation with sex and sexual performance, we thought it possible that most men would be worried about the size of their penises and most women would complain about the size of their breasts. Sex researchers have often observed that couples are unduly worried about just that (Masters and Johnson 1970; Zilbergeld 1978). In fact, Masters and Johnson (1970) were so apprehensive that if word leaked out as to what constituted the "average" breast or penis size, those who fell short would have great difficulty dealing with the facts. Thus, these advocates of academic freedom refused to publish this information.

Ann Landers (1979) receives many, many letters from women worried that their breasts are too large or too small. In 1979 she ran a letter from a woman in Cincinnati who was painfully self-conscious about her small breasts. (A boyfriend had just taken a look at her breasts and told her to "put some calamine lotion on them and they would be gone by morning." She was humiliated and hurt.)

Her letter stimulated a flurry of letters from women suffering from *too much* of a good thing. One woman reminded her that both psychological and medical problems came with big breasts. Men were only interested in one ("or should I say two") things. She had to dress carefully, avoiding low necklines, clingy fabrics, and knits. Her brassiere required special padding on the strap, and the straps still cut into her shoulders. Ann suggested surgery for breast reduction.

We received many such letters, but they are the exception. Only 9 percent of women are very dissatisfied with their breasts. One woman in four is dissatisfied.

What about men's concern about their sexual endowments? We discovered that only 15 percent of men are *at all* dissatisfied with the size of their penises; barely 6 percent are "extremely" or "quite dissatisfied". Evidently, only a few men worry about such things. However, we got letters from men concerned about other aspects of their masculinity:

> You ask men how they feel about the size of their sex organs. But this is not the crux of the problem. No doubt millions of men, and I among them, have fretted endlessly over the size of their penises, but after all,

except among nudists, this isn't a very crucial matter in day-to-day interaction. It is a secret that can be fairly well kept. There is one secret that can't be kept—how masculine your secondary sex characteristics are—the amount and distribution of your hair, the broadness of your shoulders, narrowness of hips, etc. When I was an adolescent, I had the misfortune to see a sex manual which showed male and female-pubic hair distribution. Horrors—my own pubic hair was the perfect model of the feminine pattern—and still is!

I am going through severe depression, for the following reason: I am *extremely* unattractive. By 22, a man should look very different from the opposite sex. I don't. My beard growth is nil. The texture of my skin on my face is, if anything, softer and smoother, more "feminine" than most women's. Indeed, on first glance, I am often mistaken for a girl by store clerks and others. This has had a devastating effect on my life. I am a musician, and until I was about 18, when I still looked like a kid, I was able to play with musicians older and more experienced than I, because of my talent. It was assumed that I would "grow out of it." Now, I cannot manage to get into a band, even when the musicians are inferior to me. Needless to say, my social life is just as depressing. In fact, I have none to talk about. My dermatologist sent me to an endocrinologist, as he suspected there might be a hormonal imbalance, but the tests were all negative. I am truly desperate!

There is, however, one group of men exceptionally concerned with their looks and with penis size: gay men. Ten percent of the men and 5 percent of the women who answered our *Psychology Today* questionnaires had some experience with homosexual activity. Those men who had never experimented with homosexual activity were likely to have a higher body image score than were gay men (33 percent versus 25 percent). Fully 45 percent of the gay men had below average images of their penises on a two-item measure ("satisfaction with size" and "appearance of genitals"), compared to only 25 percent of the other men.

Apparently, gay men, because of men's emphasis on looks in sexual encounters (see Hagen 1979; Symons 1979), become unusually concerned about their bodies. Unlike other men, gay men may have discovered how important beauty is in attracting men; thus, they become as concerned as women have always been about "measuring up." Consistent with that argument is the finding that only gay men are so concerned with appearances. Lesbians are as likely to have a positive body image as other women.

Are women concerned about their genitals? Only 3 percent of the women were dissatisfied with the size of their sex organs. Only 7 percent were dissatisfied with the appearance of their sex organs. A few women worried about having a vagina too small or too large for their mate's penis. One woman complained that, while having a pelvic examination, her gynecologist observed: "Your husband must complain about sex with you. You are *very* large, you know."

Weight

To say that most people are generally satisfied with their bodies overall is not to say they are happy with every aspect of their looks. Society places an enormous emphasis on a trim figure. One man volunteered: "As for me, FAT people make me sick. I've never had a fat friend or bedded a fat woman." Almost half of the women and about one-third of the men said they were unhappy with their weight. Twice as many women as men were *very* dissatisfied (21 percent versus 10 percent).

Perhaps because excess weight tends to settle in the mid-torso area—abdomen, buttocks, hips, and thighs—people worried about their weight were also unhappy about these particular body parts. Some 36 percent of the men fret over that spare tire problem. Women worry about the size of their hips—49 percent were dissatisfied. (We will discuss this issue in greater detail in chapter 6.)

Women are sensitive to the issue of weight. Wardell Pomeroy, who collaborated with Alfred Kinsey in their early interviews (Kinsey et al. 1948, 1953) on sex, discovered that the *most* embarrassing question he could ask women was: "How much do you weigh?" (This question was more embarrassing than "How often do you masturbate?" "Have you ever had an extramarital affair?" "A homosexual affair?")

When women try to ignore their weight problem, the "bare" facts can suddenly strike them, as Ellen Goodman (1980) describes:

> In my life as a clothing consumer I have been subjected to a series of sudden visions known as Dressing Room Revelations. . . . Most of them were unpleasant . . . brought to me by that demon of technology, the three-way mirror. . . . It was in a dressing room, for example, that I discovered what I look like from the back. This is something I really didn't have to know. I could have led a decent, understanding life blissfully ignorant of this information. (p. 11)

Height

There is a great deal of evidence that, in our society, height—especially for men—is extremely important. (We will discuss this issue, too, in chapter 7). We had expected to find widespread dissatisfaction with height—we thought men would want to be taller and women would be afraid of being too tall. Not so. Only 13 percent of both sexes expressed any discontent with their height, and actual height was not related to body satisfaction.

ARE YOU AS GOOD-LOOKING AS YOU THINK YOU ARE?

When you filled out the Body Image questionnaire, you had a chance to say how good-looking *you* think you are. Would most people agree with you? To find out how objective men and women are about themselves, researchers' first step was to develop an "objective" measure of looks. This test turned out to be surprisingly difficult. After several false starts, scientists finally settled on a well-worn method—the method of consensus (see Berscheid and Hatfield [Walster] 1974). Researchers simply ask a number of judges to rate men and women's looks. Judges have their own biases, of course. One judge may like tall, Nordic types, another, short, athletic types, but if you get enough judges, these biases tend to cancel out one another. The method of consensus may be a form of shared ignorance . . . but it is a form of "ignorance" that works (Hatfield [Walster], Aronson, Abrahams, Rottmann 1966).

Scientists have asked, "Do people see themselves as others see them?" The answer appears to be, "through a glass, darkly." There is *some* correspondence between people's ideas on how good-looking they are and the opinions of more objective judges, but the relationship is far from perfect (see Berscheid et al. 1971; Huston 1972; or Stroebe et al. 1971). Two contradictory processes—the Modesty effect and the Henry Finck syndrome—combine to reduce our ability to see ourselves as others see us.

The Modesty Effect

Cavior (1970) asked fifth-grade girls and boys how they rated compared to other boys and girls in their classes. He found that 75 percent of the girls thought they were the least attractive girl in their class! The girls were not just being modest. They were simply focusing on defects in their appearance that the more objective judges thought were trivial. The girls had adopted an absolute standard of attractiveness—they compared themselves to a "perfect 10" and concluded they did not measure up. The judges, less ego involved, had adopted a relative standard. They asked themselves: "How good looking is this girl *compared to other fifth grade girls?*"

Cavior also found that fifth- and sixth-grade boys' and girls' guesses as to how their classmates would rank them were almost always wrong. These eleven to twelve year olds had little idea how they rated with their friends. They had a slightly better idea about how relative strangers would feel about them.

The Henry Finck Syndrome

Sometimes false modesty is not the problem—sometimes it's just the opposite. Like Henry Finck, we take it for granted that our country, our race, our family look as people *ought* to look. For example, Malff (reported in Huntley 1940) found that young adults rated their own thinly disguised profiles, hands, faces, etc. more favorably than others rated them, *even though they were unaware it was their own features they were rating*. These two opposite processes—false modesty and unconscious arrogance—both contribute to people's inabilities to see themselves as others see them.

As we get older, we do get a little wiser. With age people get to be somewhat better at guessing how others see them. Somewhat better . . . but far from perfect. For example, Berscheid et al. (1971) found that adults' self assessments on the *Secord and Jourard Body Cathexis Scale* (a type of body image scale) had no relationship to outside observers' judgments about their appearance! Other researchers have found only a minimal relationship (see Huston 1972; Murstein 1972; Stroebe et al. 1971).

So, if you want to know what other people like or dislike about you, you better ask them.

A Note: If you arrange things properly, you can guarantee you will rate a "perfect 10".

1. Ask people with high esteem what they think of your looks. Scientists have found that people who rate themselves highly are equally generous in rating others (Morse, Reis, Gruzen, and Wolff 1974).

2. Avoid beautiful people. They have been found to be harsher in their judgments. They consider themselves to be the Golden Mean and, in contrast, you lose (Hatfield [Walster] et al. 1966; Tennis and Dabbs 1975).

3. Avoid critics who spend a lot of time thumbing through movie magazines, watching "Charlie's Angels" on television, etc. When they compare the stars to you, you lose out in luster. The contrast effect again (Kenrick and Gutierres 1980; Melamed and Moss 1975). This observation may be reason enough to cancel your date's *Playboy* or *Playgirl* subscription.

4. Ask men or women who are sexually aroused what they think of you. While aroused, men and women have been found to be unusually appreciative of the opposite sex's looks . . . and unusually harsh in their judgments of the same sex, who are potential rivals. This fact may be reason enough to present your date with a subscription to *Playboy* or *Playgirl*.

5. Ask someone of the opposite sex who has been drinking in a singles bar, just before closing time. Scientists have found that people

do get better-looking just before closing time, probably because men and women are eager for company and can afford to be generous (Pennebaker et al. 1979).

6. Ask someone who owes you money.

7. Ask people who look like you. If they have the same color hair, the same body frame, and a mole in the same place, they are going to think you are gorgeous (D. Byrne 1971).

8. Ask people who know you. They are going to be more lenient in judging you (Cavior 1970; Cavior, Miller and Cohen 1975).

9. Be sure to ask your mother! It's her obligation to think you are good-looking.

Chapter **2**

WHAT IS BEAUTIFUL IS GOOD: THE MYTH

Most of us feel a little uneasy about our feelings toward attractive versus ugly people. On one hand, we know that beauty *should* not be important. (We are a little ashamed when we remember how we teased a fat "mama's" boy in grade school or stood by while others did so. We blush when we recall what fools we made of ourselves over a good-looking athlete in high school, and how we persevered in spite of our shame because he was so good-looking.) On the other hand, in our hearts, we know beauty is important to us . . . sometimes *very* important.

You may get some sense of how complicated your feelings are about beauty and ugliness by sorting through your reactions to two cases illustrating the strong effect physical appearance may have. How do you react to the following cases?

EXAMPLE 1:

Recently (Van Buren 1976), a mother wrote that, although she knew that she should be grateful to have a thirteen-year-old daughter who was healthy and bright, she found it impossible to love her daughter because the girl was so ugly. The mother felt guilty because she could not help but be cruel to the girl. The mother and father were attractive. They had done everything they could to help the daughter look better— she had a good hair cut, her teeth were straightened, she had been treated for acne, she had nice clothes, but still, she was searingly homely. The mother asked "What can I do?" Abby's answer was swift and sharp. "You are the ugly one, only your ugliness doesn't show." Is Abby right? Or is this mother simply more honest about her feelings than most of us are? Or, consider this case:

EXAMPLE 2:

Candace (Candy) Weatherby Johnson was a dazzling blonde model when she married multimillionaire Jacques Mossler. Soon thereafter, Candy and her nephew, Lane Powers, stood accused of murdering Mossler. The press labeled the murder trial "the trial of the century." It's no wonder. The prosecution dwelt on Candy's incestuous relationship with her nephew, her shady associations with the underworld, and her involvement in murky Texan politics. Percy Foreman, the flamboyant lawyer for the defense, dwelt on Mossler's "Jekyll and Hyde" personality, his "insatiable sexual appetite—his transvestitism, voyeurism, masochism, and sadism; his adulterous and homosexual encounters—his ruthless business dealings;" all of which, Foreman contended, gave hundreds of people a motive to kill him.

The jury deliberated for three days. Finally, they found Candy "not guilty." The press continued to question the verdict. Did the all-male jury let Candy off because they could not believe so beautiful a woman could commit so violent a crime? Had Candy's beauty worked against her? Would she never have been brought to trial if she were not so beautiful, so rich, and politically well connected (see Dorman 1969)?

Do you think beauty affects judgments of character and innocence? In general, how much of an advantage is beauty? Is it ever a disadvantage? In the next few chapters, we will review the evidence scientists have collected to help us answer such questions.

AN OVERVIEW

Scientists find that most people, most of the time, are favorably biased in their reactions to good-looking people. This discovery is certainly not new. The Greek philosopher Sappho (1965) stated, "What is beautiful is good." Schiller (1982) added, "Physical beauty is a sign of interior beauty, a spiritual and moral beauty. . . ." Today's scientists, however, have come to a little better understanding of just how, where, when, and why physical appearance is important.

There seem to be four steps in the stereotyping process that ensures that beauty equals goodness.

1. Most people feel that discriminating against the ugly is not fair, but yet. . . .

2. Privately, most of us simply take it for granted that attractive and unattractive people are different. Most often we perceive that attractive people have the more desirable traits.

3. As a consequence, we *treat* good-looking versus ugly people quite differently; the good-looking get the better treatment.

4. How does such prejudice affect the victims of our discrimination? Over time, a sort of "self-fulfilling prophecy" occurs. The way we treat attractive versus unattractive people shapes the way they think about themselves and, as a consequence, the kind of people they become.

In the next few chapters, we will present an encyclopedic review of the evidence that, in general, good looks are an enormous advantage.

SIDENOTE: THE EXPERIMENTAL METHOD

Scientists have discovered most of what they know about society's biases in favor of the attractive by conducting experiments. Most people, however, do not have a very clear idea about what actually happens in a psychology experiment. What about you? What images come to your mind?

Basically, the raison d'être of an experiment is to answer a question. For example, in the early 1970s, scientists were interested in the question, "Do most of us perceive attractive versus unattractive people differently?"

First, scientists shaped the question into a *hypothesis*—a specific prediction. Early scientists predicted that "attractive men and women will be perceived as more appealing in every way than the unattractive."

The next step in an experiment is to arrange things so that one can determine whether or not the hypothesis is true. An experiment can be conducted almost anywhere. The experiments we describe in this book have been conducted in a variety of settings—in universities, laboratories, supermarkets, classrooms, bars, and telephone booths.

In experiments, three key concepts are *independent variables, dependent variables,* and *randomization.* The experimenter manipulates the *independent variable.* In the *experimental group,* the experimenter manipulates the variable he is interested in. For example, an experiment might ask people to look at a picture of Brooke Shields and to speculate about what she is like personally. Other people, those in the *control* (or comparison) *group,* might be asked to look at a picture of a Plain Jane and to guess about her personality and character. Here, the experimenter is manipulating the independent variable—beauty.

The experimenter suspects that people's guesses about the girls' personalities and characters will depend on which picture they have seen—the gorgeous girl or the plain one. For this reason, men and women's reactions in an experiment are called *dependent variables.* By comparing people's ideas on what a beautiful Brooks versus a Plain Jane is like, scientists can get some hunches about the stereotypes about beauty.

Another characteristic of a good experiment is that subjects are *randomly assigned* to different conditions. In the above experiment, the experimenter might toss a coin and decide which picture the judges receive. There is a 50-50 chance any judge will end up judging Brooke Shields. Of course, there is also a 50-50 chance it will be Plain Jane. Such randomization is critically important. It insures that the experimenter cannot, consciously or unconsciously, bias the results. For example, the experimenters could assign generous-spirited people to judge

CONTROL GROUP   OUT OF CONTROL GROUP.

Figure 2.1. Cartoonist Peter Mueller's wry depiction of experimental versus control groups. Copyright 1984, P. S. Mueller.

Brooke and crotchety ones to judge Plain Jane to insure they get the results they expect.

We have talked about experiments in abstract terms, but what would it be like to actually participate in an experiment? Let's find out: Walking past the library one day, you see a sign:

> VOLUNTEERS WANTED FOR A
> FIRST IMPRESSION STUDY
> Please sign up below

Just for the fun of it, you decide to sign up for the experiment. A few days later you find yourself in the psychology building at the University of Hawaii. When you report, you find that two other volunteers have been scheduled for the same time. The laboratory is cozily furnished—it contains portraits of King Kalakaua and Queen Liliuokalani, a table, three chairs, and a thick, beige carpet.

The experimenter, a graduate student, tells the three of you a little more about what you are about to do.

> We are interested in how accurate people can be when required to form first impressions of others on the sketchiest of information. We'd like to show you some photographs of students—Hawaiians, Japanese, Chinese, and Haoles [a Hawaiian expression for "Caucasian"]—enrolled at the University of Hawaii. Since they've lived in Hawaii all their lives, we know a great deal about them. Better yet, we plan to keep in touch with them, so eventually we'll be able to find out how things worked out for them in the long run. We'll be able to compare your first impressions with the factual information we have about them. Do you have any questions?

No one can think of anything to ask, so the exercise begins. The experimenter hands each of you a packet. Your packet contains two photographs—one of a strikingly good-looking man and one of an equally good-looking woman. It also contains two rating forms on which you can indicate your impressions. For a split second, you wonder if there is more to this task than meets the eye. You try to catch a glimpse of the contents of the packets given to the other two subjects, but they are too far away . . . and already busy at work. Your suspicions evaporate as you become engrossed in trying to accurately guess what these strikingly good-looking people are like.

To make it *really* seem like you are participating in this study, we have included some photographs (Figures 2.2 and 2.3) and one of the two rating forms below. What impressions does each person give you? Choose one of the pictures and fill out the checklist of adjectives.

Figure 2.2. Kim Rapson, 1976.   **Figure 2.3.** Joshua Rich, 1979.

What sort of impression did he or she make on you?

Altruistic	1	2	3	4	5	6	7	Selfish
Exciting	1	2	3	4	5	6	7	Boring
Genuine	1	2	3	4	5	6	7	Phoney
Sexually permissive	1	2	3	4	5	6	7	Sexually conservative
Sincere	1	2	3	4	5	6	7	Insincere
Warm	1	2	3	4	5	6	7	Cold
Modest	1	2	3	4	5	6	7	Conceited
Happy	1	2	3	4	5	6	7	Sad
Submissive	1	2	3	4	5	6	7	Assertive
Self-confident	1	2	3	4	5	6	7	Self-doubting
Weak	1	2	3	4	5	6	7	Strong

Finally, the hour is up. The experimenter gathers up the packets. As she delivers them to an adjacent room, you steal a chance to talk to the other two students. You discover that one had been asked to give her first impressions of what she describes as an "average-looking" couple. The third volunteer, on the other hand, reveals that his couple had been extraordinarily unappealing.

The experimenter returns, and so do your suspicions. You are convinced there is more to this experiment than you have been told. You are about to interrogate the experimenter, but she is one step ahead of you. She coughs, smiles mischievously, and begins a revealing discourse. You discover your hunch—that there was more to the experiment—was right. No one was interested in comparing your first impressions with factual information about the people in the photographs. Even if someone had been interested, no information existed on the individuals! That introduction was a "cover story" to prevent you from guessing the true purpose of the experiment.

What, then, was the true purpose? To discover whether or not people are biased in favor of the good-looking. The photographs of the three couples were different in attractiveness. One couple was extraordinarily good-looking (you got that one), one average, and one ugly in *appearance* (This was the independent variable). The experimenter was interested in people's first impressions of these couples (the dependent variable). The experimenter can get a hint about the stereotypes the three of you (and others, as well) hold about beautiful people by comparing your reactions. By the way, you have just been *debriefed*— you have been told the true purpose of the experiment.

A Look Behind the Scenes

Before an experiment begins, a great deal of preparatory work must be done. In the above experiment, the investigator began by assembling a set of photographs of men and women varying in appearance. Where do such photographs come from? In many studies, researchers have selected photos of good-looking, average, and ugly men and women from college or high school yearbooks. In other studies, researchers have searched for appropriate models and taken photographs of them. For example, when Elaine Hatfield began beauty research back in the 1960s, she would stop people on the street she thought were good-looking (or homely) and ask if they would allow her to take their picture for use in her research.

She quickly learned an unexpected lesson. Occasionally, when she stopped someone she thought was unusually handsome or beautiful and lured him or her back to the laboratory, she found that not everyone agreed with her evaluation. The first time this happened she was stunned. She hauled in a man she thought was breathtakingly handsome, and her colleague, Dr. Ellen Berscheid, bluntly asked which group he was intended for—good-looking, average, or ugly. Dr. Hatfield was dumbfounded! Surely Dr. Berscheid was kidding. She wasn't. Eventually they discovered they had opposite, but predictable, biases. Dr. Hatfield tended to think that dark, muscular, athletic men and women were good-looking; Dr. Berscheid liked tall, thin, ethereal blonds.

After researchers have assembled photographs they think are appropriate, therefore, their next step is to make sure other people agree with their impressions. Researchers use the "truth by consensus" method to settle disputes about how good-looking people are. If virtually all "judges" rate certain photographs as "attractive," then they can confidently be defined as attractive. Similarly, if almost everyone rates the photographs as "unattractive," they can be labeled that way. Luckily, as we observed in chapter 1, people generally agree about who is attractive and who is not.

While most studies have used photographs or slides of only the face, in a few studies experimenters have studied people's reactions to the entire body. For example, one investigator had his graduate students bring in photographs of their parents in bathing suits. Occasionally, videotapes are used. One investigator, for example, prepared a videotape of a beautiful versus a homely young woman stealing a book from the bookstore. Given the chapter 1 definition of beauty, videotapes have an obvious advantage. Videotapes allow us to respond to several aspects of good looks—vivaciousness, posture, style of movement, and so on—rather than limiting response to structural beauty.

Live models have been used in a few experiments. For example, in the study you just participated in, you could have received a note in your packet like this:

> The other volunteers think you are rating photographs in your packet, as they are. However, as you have noticed, you don't have any photographs. We want you to rate the other two volunteers. Inconspicuously, study them. What are your first impressions of them?

You might have noticed a lot about the other volunteers. Certainly you would have noticed how good-looking they are. But you would also notice how they are sitting, whether they look bored or interested in what they are doing, and perhaps most importantly, how they respond to you (did they smile or ignore you?).

To insure that it is looks (and not boredom or friendliness) that matters, researchers generally use the same person as the appealing and unappealing model. Sometimes, the model is made as unappealing as possible. She looks like the "before" picture in the magazine ads. She has an unflattering makeup, mismatched clothes, and is wearing a stringy, dirty-haired wig. At other times, she is made extremely good-looking. For example, in the "after" condition, the model should be beautifully made up, fashionably dressed, and have neatly styled hair. If you're curious about how the same person can look either attractive or ugly, see Figure 2.4.

Getting the photographs, slides, videotapes, or actual models for the experiment is the biggest job. There are many other tasks involved in conducting an experiment however. For example:

1) The investigator must get permission from a University Ethics Committee to conduct the experiment. Such committees are formed to protect participants from any physical or psychological harm. The investigator has to convince the committee that participants will not be harmed in any way, and that, if deception is involved, participants will be thoroughly debriefed. The experiments reported in this book were all screened to insure that none of the participants were embarrassed or hurt in any way.

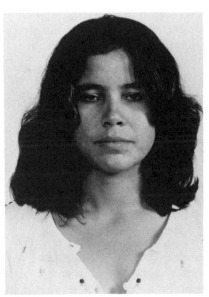 

Figure 2.4. Before and after photos, courtesy Frances Loo (stylist). Makeup, Lyle Nelson; photography, Gerald Bishop (Tiare Lee, model).

2) The investigator must decide what questions to ask the subjects—exactly what kinds of "first impressions" he's interested in. Two compulsive researchers (Allport and Odbert 1936) once compiled a list of all possible adjective pairs that could be used to describe people. Their list contained 18,000 items! Good luck to researchers who think people will respond to such lists! All seasoned researchers know there is a limit to how much can be asked of people. Quality not quantity of data is the goal.

3) If an experiment is to be realistic, the "setting" has to be carefully prepared. In one study we will discuss later, dimes were placed in pay telephones. In another experiment, a car with a flat tire was left "stranded" on the highway.

4) Participants have to be found. Sometimes, investigators solicit volunteers from classes. Sometimes, signs (similar to the one illustrated earlier) are used. At other times, participants are whoever happens to be around, e.g., whoever enters the phone booth or drives by the car with a flat tire.

In conclusion, an enormous amount of work went into preparing each of the experiments in this book. Space does not permit detailing each experiment, but now you can fill in those details yourself.

BEAUTY = THE BEST OF EVERYTHING

How biased are *you* in favor of the good-looking?

Do you generally react differently to good-looking people than to ugly ones? How? For example: Do you have a better impression of good-looking people than ugly ones? Did you ever dislike someone just because of his or her looks?

Do you generally treat good-looking people differently than ugly ones? How?

Can you think of any time when good looks are a *disadvantage?*

Most people believe you should not "judge a book by its cover"; but, most of us do. Why? Perhaps because often we have no real alternative. When we have to make a quick decision about who to sit next to at lunch, who to hire to run errands, who to share a cab with in the train, or who to ask out, sometimes appearance is all we have to go on.

Appearance is the sole characteristic apparent in every social interaction. Other information may be more meaningful but far harder to ferret out. People do not have their IQ's tattooed on their foreheads, nor do they display their diplomas prominently about their persons. Their financial status is a private matter between themselves, their bankers, and the Internal Revenue Service. And scientists would not know how to interpret the structure of someone's genes, even if they could be presented for inspection. Thus, it is not surprising that, like it or not, beauty counts.

Classic Beauty Studies

Two early experiments were the first to verify that most people do assume, "What is beautiful is good, what is ugly is bad."

In one experiment, Elaine Hatfield, Karen Dion, and Ellen Berscheid asked college men and women to look at pictures of good-looking, average, or homely men and women. They discovered that most people assumed good-looking men and women possessed nearly all the good traits known to humanity. The good-looking were supposedly more sexually responsive, warmer, more sensitive, kind, interesting, strong, poised, modest, sociable, and outgoing, were more "exciting dates" and more "nurturant," and had a "better character" than less appealing persons.

Not only were beautiful people expected to have better personalities, they were also expected to have more fulfilling lives! The researchers asked respondents to guess what lay ahead for the individuals they saw pictured. Without fail, people predicted the beautiful and handsome would have happier marriages, would secure better jobs, and would have happier and more fulfilling lives. On only one dimension were people suspicious of beauty—they did not expect attractive people to make especially good parents. This classic study convinced social psychologists that people do have stereotypes about the beautiful/ugly (Dion, Berscheid, Hatfield [Walster] 1972).

Other researchers have confirmed that people generally believe in the "goodness of beauty." Miller (1970a) documented that good-looking people are assumed to be more appealing on the following dimensions: curious, complex, perceptive, confident, assertive, happy, active, amiable, candid, serious, pleasure seeking, outspoken, flexible.

The attractive are also perceived as creators of their own destinies. Attractive men and women are seen as "masters of their own fate, as individuals who behave with a sense of purpose and out of their own volition." Unattractive men and women are seen as "coerced and generally influenced by others or by environmental conditions" (Miller 1970b).

The Ugly Truth About Beauty

Most people give the beautiful rave reviews, but not everyone. Tolstoy once observed cynically: "What a strange delusion it is to fancy beauty is goodness!" Most of the time, we are caught up in beauty's lure, but in a few instances, we cannot help but recognize that the beautiful's shining armor has a few chinks.

For example, in a study titled, "When Beauty May Fall," Dermer and Thiel (1975) asked women to rate the beautiful on a few more traits than researchers had studied in the classic studies described above. As before, this study showed that attractive women were judged more favorably on most dimensions. They were expected to be "more sociable, sexually alluring, successful professionally, and personally happy." However, attractive women were also expected to be more vain, egotistical, materialistic, snobbish, likely to get a divorce, and likely to have extramarital affairs. The researchers predicted that unattractive women would be particularly jealous of attractive women and especially harsh in their judgments. They found some evidence for this prediction.

One attractive twenty-four-year-old woman from THE GROUP described how such jealousy led her friends to mistreat a beautiful woman:

> There's a woman I work with now, who's extraordinarily beautiful—Italian, very dark, and her features are well-proportioned. But I think she has a disadvantage. When you are an especially beautiful woman, other women tend to treat you badly. Unattractive women can be very catty toward a beautiful woman. This woman doesn't have very many women friends. Even her sister is jealous of her! But she *is* extremely pretty. I noticed that right away. Even I reacted that way to her. I remember thinking, "Oh, she's really pretty, but she's probably not the kind of girl I like."

We will focus on the special problems attractive men and women confront in chapters 10 and 12.

BEAUTY = THE MOST LIKELY TO SUCCEED

Do you know anyone who was given special advantages at school or work because he or she was good-looking?

Do you know of anyone discriminated against because he or she was "funny-looking"?

Do you think there is ever a disadvantage (at school or work) in being too good-looking?

Contrary to the popular belief that "beauty and brains don't mix," there is considerable evidence that parents, teachers, and employers equate "looks" with creativity and intelligence.

Figure 2.5. Elaine Hatfield and Patricia Hatfield Rich, 1947.

Figure 2.6. Douglas H. Haller and Gary Marchand, 1960.

Discrimination in Educational Settings: The Book Is Judged by Its Cover

GRADE SCHOOL

Teachers take it for granted that beauty and brains go together, and they grade accordingly. Are good-looking people, in fact, smarter than others? (Some of the early eugenicists certainly thought so.) Or is grading simply prejudiced? The evidence suggests the latter.

Dr. Margaret Clifford, an educational psychologist, and Elaine Hatfield found such a bias in their research (Clifford and Hatfield [Walster] 1973). They asked four hundred fifth-grade teachers to take a look at children's academic files. Inconspicuously pasted in the corner of one of the report cards was the child's photograph. As you might expect, the class photograph was a bogus one. Some teachers saw a picture of a quite attractive boy or girl. Others saw an exceedingly plain child. Except for the picture, teachers received identical information about the children, and there was a great deal of it. The academic record revealed the student's grades in reading, language, arithmetic, social studies, science, art, music, and physical education. It reported on their attitudes and work habits. It even contained a tally of their absences during the school year.

The "insignificant" class photo had a great impact on the teachers' attitudes, in spite of the abundance of information about the child. Teachers assumed that cute boys and girls were more intelligent, that their parents were more interested in their educations, and that these children were more likely to get advanced degrees than the homely boys and girls. Teachers expected cute students to be popular and to get along unusually well with their classmates, as well as being brainy. All this, when according to the facts, the children's records were identical! (Similar results were secured by Adams [1978]; Adams and Cohen [1976]; and Clifford [1975]. However, studies by Adams and LaVoie [1974] and LaVoie and Adams [1974] failed to replicate these results.) It has also been found that physical education teachers expect attractive children to perform better in physical activities (as well as to be better teammates) (Martinek 1981).

In the above studies, the children were average to good students. What about children with special disabilities? In one study, elementary teachers were shown the record of an attractive or unattractive eight-year-old boy or girl. Once again, except for the photograph, the children's academic records were identical. This time, however, the student had a low IQ (78), below average academic functioning, and seemed immature: Would the teachers recommend the child be placed in a class for the mentally retarded? Teachers were more likely to recommend the child be placed in a class for the mentally retarded if he/she was unattractive. They also believed unattractive children would have poorer psychological functioning and would experience more academic and social difficulties (Ross and Salvia 1975).

Teachers are not the only ones expecting more from cute children. Parents do too. In one study, 106 mothers and 91 fathers of elementary schoolchildren were shown a hypothetical student progress report, accompanied, of course, by a photo of either a cute or a rather homely child. Parents assumed the cute children had better personalities, were more popular, and were more likely to be elected to class offices. However, the parents did not expect attractive children to be better academically than unattractive children (Adams & LaVoie 1975).

Teachers *expect* good-looking children to be brighter than homely ones, but do they grade accordingly? The evidence suggests they might. Recently, several investigators have set out to examine what actually goes on in the classroom. Apparently, better-looking students do get better report cards. Researchers found this is true in Michigan (Felson 1980; Lerner and Lerner 1977), in central Pennsylvania (Salvia, Algozzine, and Sheare 1977), in fact, almost everywhere except, for some reason, in Muscatine, Iowa (Clifford 1975).

Faced with this real world evidence, we are motivated to return to our original question and ask why beauty and brains go together. Are good-looking people smarter? Or are teachers prejudiced? Again, the evidence suggests the latter. Researchers find a link between beauty and brains only when teachers have a chance to influence grades—i.e., when grades are based on the teacher's general impressions or on essay exams. When performance is measured by IQ scores or scores on standardized objective tests (Clifford 1975), the homely student suddenly "blossoms," and they do just as well as anyone else. Thus, clearly prejudice, not performance, links beauty and brains (Clifford 1975).

THE PYGMALION EFFECT

There is some evidence that sometimes teachers' expectations affect even IQ scores. How do parents and teachers' biases affect children? G. B. Shaw had an answer. He argued that people become what they are expected to become.

> You see, really and truly, apart from the things anyone can pick up (the dressing and the proper way of speaking, and so on), the difference between a lady and a flower girl is not how she behaves, but how she's treated. I shall always be a flower girl, and always will; but I know I can be a lady to you, because you always treat me as a lady; and always will. (Quoted in Rosenthal and Jacobson 1968, 183)

A classic experiment (Rosenthal & Jacobson 1968) dramatically demonstrated the operation of just such a "self-fulfilling prophecy." The experimenters were convinced that teachers' expectations about what students will become have a dramatic impact on what they *do* become. They arranged an ingenious experiment to demonstrate this occurrence.

Oak School is in the midst of a working class community. Many of the children are from broken homes. Fathers, when around, are mostly unskilled or semiskilled workers. Mothers and children often subsist on welfare funds. The Harvard professors contacted Oak School and offered to give first- to fifth-grade children the "Harvard Test of Inflected Acquisition". The professors *claimed* the test could identify students who would show unusual academic progress during the coming year.

The scientists administered an IQ test to the Oak School students. They then simply chose 20 percent of the children *at random* (pulling names out of a hat) and announced to the teachers that the IQ test had identified *these* children as special students. They were the "late bloomers," destined to show marked intellectual improvement within the year.

George Bernard Shaw would have smiled at the results. When the psychologists returned to Oak School a year later, and again two years

Figure 2.7. The Pygmalion effect. ©1959. United Feature Syndicate Inc.

later, and gave the same IQ test to all the same children, they discovered that the "late bloomers" had done just what they had been expected to do. Their IQ's had risen dramatically. These gains seemed especially pronounced for first and second graders (perhaps their self-concepts were still in the formative stage), but considerable effects were detected even among the fifth graders.

How could this phenomenon have happened? Perhaps Oak School teachers were more pleasant, friendly, and enthusiastic toward the children they expected great things from. Perhaps they paid more attention to them.

If "attention" is an advantage (and surely it must be), attractive children again have the advantage. Attractive children are unusually likely to be referred for special supplemental services—such as psychological, speech, reading, or testing services (Barocas and Black 1974). Attractive children are also more likely to receive encouragement from their teachers. Investigators observed teacher-student interactions in kindergarten, fourth, and seventh grades. Teachers' biases could not be detected with younger children, but by the seventh grade, their biases began to show. By the seventh grade, teachers were simply more receptive to and supportive of the attractive children (Adams and Cohen 1974).

The above research evidence is reflected in a comment made by a thirty-two-year-old male elementary teacher from THE GROUP:

I've taught first, fourth, and sixth graders. I hate to admit it, but the attractiveness of the children is probably important in how I react to them. For first grade, however, I don't think it was that important. Probably because they were all so cute and energetic. But when you're dealing with fourth and sixth grades, there starts to be variation in how they look and develop. And I have found that I may call on the attractive kids more often than the unattractive ones. But it's hard to separate attractiveness from personality. If the child is outgoing—and often cute kids are outgoing—then I'm going to interact with them more.

If students have the abilities, they are going to make it regardless of what they look like. But if they are average or below in abilities, it may help to be attractive. I found myself working very hard to draw out a sixth-grade girl who was shy and withdrawn. But I probably worked this hard because she was so pretty. I might not have worked as hard with an ugly child.

Perhaps teachers are more demanding, perhaps teachers try harder themselves with attractive children. In any case, research in this area provides compelling evidence that teachers' expectations (whether generated by physical appearance or "special tests," as in the Oak School study, can spark a self-fulfilling prophecy. More discussion of how the self-fulfilling prophecy operates awaits in chapter 8.

Figure 2.8. Jeremy Rich, 1977.

Figure 2.9. Carol Yoshinaga, 1984.

HIGH SCHOOL AND COLLEGE

In a revealing biography of rock star Janis Joplin, Myra Freidman (1974) describes how Joplin's unattractiveness affected her school life. Before adolescence Janis had been chubby. At adolescence, her chubbiness bloated to heft. She developed a disfiguring case of acne, severe enough to require sanding.

Janis became hated. She recalled that other teens threw things at her and called her names ("pig" was the favorite). Parents warned their children to avoid Janis' bad influence. Her teachers? In spite of the fact that she was smart and got good grades, they too disliked her personality. Her appearance was contemptible. She had repulsive body mannerisms. Friedman observes that Janis, to protect herself from disintegrating under the pressures, handled her conflicts, terrifying as they were, by acting them out.

Are teachers prejudiced in high school and college? Unfortunately, little empirical research has been done to examine this question. But we can speculate about what happens . . .

By high school, teacher-student interactions probably become a little more complicated than ever before. For example, women teachers may be biased in favor of handsome, athletic boys; but, for the first time, men teachers may be a little jealous of all that youthful virility.

Similarly, the reverse would be true—women teachers may be envious of good-looking girls, while men teachers favor them. There is no evidence, however, that such a jealousy effect operates.

The stereotypes about various kinds of beauty may get more differentiated in high school. For example, the beautiful blonde cheerleader may be stereotpyed for the first time as a dumb blonde, having little dedication to scholarly endeavors. A brawny, six-foot football player may be victimized by similar stereotypes.

What about college? In college, classes are often large. There may be four hundred to five hundred students in a single, large lecture hall. On first thought, you would think that in a large, impersonal class, where grades are given mechanically on an objective basis, all bias would disappear. Finally, the good-looking and the homely would have an equal chance. Ironically, the impersonality of large classes may make good looks essential. There is some evidence that in college, where most professors are men, the better-looking the college woman, the better grades she gets (Singer 1964). One reason for this result may simply be that pretty women are easier to remember. Singer (1964) describes what may happen:

Attractive girls get the benefit of doubts in grades. This would require two assumptions. First, faculty give the benefit of the doubt when grading to those whose names and faces they associate and remember. Second, there are none so likely to have their names and faces remembered as attractive girls in the class. Although we have no evidence directly relating to this point, many of our colleagues acknowledged that they can recall the names of pretty girls in their classes. (p. 144)

WHAT IS BRAINY MAY BE BEAUTIFUL AS WELL

The preceding evidence indicates that good looks are an important determinant of teachers' attitudes toward students. Can anything be done to help teachers behave more fairly—to lessen beauty's impact? Just reminding people of their biases probably helps to some extent. There *is* evidence that as teachers become better acquainted with their students, they are better able to view them as people rather as stereotypes. For example, when teachers learn not just what their students look like but a little about them—their sex, academic standing, race, and IQ—physical attractiveness becomes far less important (Kehle, Bramble, and Mason 1974). In one study (Solomon and Saxe 1977), people knew both how good-looking and how bright a college woman was (her grade point average and *Graduate Record Examination* scores were said to be either high or quite low). Looks were important, but not as important as IQ and performance. The bright woman was judged as having a more appealing personality and was expected to have greater occupational success and happiness.

Clifford (1975), an educational psychologist, has commented:

Although attractiveness may be a reliable determinant of an individual's initial impression formation, it is not necessarily a predictor of long-term academic effects. It may well be that as educational discriminators (e.g., verbal classroom behavior, conduct patterns, assignment scores) become available, teachers' initial expectations based on attractiveness are altered. (p. 208)

In other research, scientists made a fascinating discovery that we will discuss at greater length later. Apparently, students' intelligence and personality characteristics influence their attractiveness! Judgements of beauty (theoretically only "skin deep") are profoundly affected by inner beauty! For example, children thought to have academic or athletic assets are perceived as more attractive, at least by other children (Felson and Bohrnstedt 1979). In other words, although the beautiful are perceived as being talented, it is also true that the talented are perceived as being beautiful.

In summary, the "superstar," not the "superbeauty," gets to the head of the class. However, the path to the top may be somewhat rocky. The superbeauty is more easily noticed than the superstar. Children's IQ scores are not brazen in bold letters on their T-shirts; they do not wear good conduct medals. So it is easy for teachers to forget the objective evidence when coming face-to-face with the child's appearance everyday. Superstars may have to prove themselves over and over again.

AN APPLE FOR THE TEACHER

Teachers are not the only ones prejudiced . . . their little charges are too (Chaikin et al. 1978). In one study, nine-to thirteen-year-old boys and girls watched a videotape of a teacher presenting a lecture on basic concepts in psychology. The teacher was made to look either attractive or homely (her hair was pulled back tightly, dark circles were smudged under her eyes, her face was pale, shadows on her face were used to make her look "hard"). After the lecture, the students were asked to evaluate the teacher. The teacher's attractiveness had a dramatic impact on the ratings. They rated the attractive teacher as a "better teacher," "more enjoyable to have as a teacher," "more interesting." They also thought that, with an attractive teacher, it was easier to concentrate on the lesson, that the lesson was more enjoyable and more interesting to listen to, and that the teacher had tried harder (even though the teacher had behaved identically in the different videotapes). The students were also given a quiz testing their comprehension and retention of the lecture. In this case, teachers' looks did not matter. The students performed equally well—or poorly—regardless of how their teacher looked.

In another study (Goebel and Cashen 1979), it was found that students from second grade through college thought attractive teachers did their job better than did unattractive teachers. Attractive teachers were seen as more friendly, better organized, more likely to encourage students to interact—in short, as being better teachers overall. Worst yet, students suspected that the homely teachers would be most likely to load them up with too much work.

Possibly, a self-fulfilling prophecy occurs with teachers as well as with students. Children expect more from attractive teachers—and get more! Interactions between attractive students and attractive teachers must be especially rosy.

On-the-Job Discrimination

Title VII of the Civil Rights Act of 1964 forbids job discrimination on the basis of race, creed, color, sex, or national origin. It says nothing, however, about attractiveness. Perhaps it is not surprising that Title VII fails to prohibit such discrimination—the Federal government itself has long been a blatant offender.

The biases of J. Edgar Hoover, former director of the FBI, were legendary:

> Hoover was a petty man. . . . G-men were neat, serious, disciplined, all white, all male, and any deviation from the norm could cost an agent his job, from being overweight to bald.
>
> One day, for example, according to the tapes, Hoover was on an elevator at the FBI building in Washington when he spotted a young man with acne wearing a red vest. Hoover ordered the man fired, and he said that whomever hired him was to be punished. "We're not going to have anybody working for us who wears a red vest and has a pimply face," he said. (Thomas 1982, 6)

Today, in government circles, little has changed. Nancy Reagan originally opposed the appointment of Presidential Press Secretary James Brady ("The Bear") (later seriously wounded by an assassin) because he was not good-looking enough to fit the Reagan image. After Brady was hired anyway, his press colleagues surrounded him with, "She's grown accustomed to my face" (*Time*, 13 April 1981, p. 48).

Figure 2.10. Mary Hatfield, 1971.   **Figure 2.11.** Richard L. Rapson, 1980

DISCRIMINATION IN HIRING

Most of us would be willing to concede that, in some occupations, it *is* legitimate for employers to make good looks a prerequisite for employment. For example, it seems reasonable that the Charles Stern Agency of Los Angeles would insist (as they do) that the men they hire for television commercials be over six feet, athletic-looking, and weigh 150–170 pounds, that *Vogue* would insist their models be stunningly beautiful. We do not mind if coaches insist on tall basketball players, if circus owners prefer midgets, or if dentists hire dental assistants with straight teeth.

For most occupations, however, it seems unfair for employers to discriminate. Generally, there is not an obvious link between good looks and competence. Elegant secretaries can not type faster than plainer ones. Tall executives can not think faster than short ones. Yet, employers often do use looks as a hiring standard, even in these situations.

Several years ago, *Time* magazine carried a little blurb about "Equality for Uglies" (21 February 1972). It presented an observation by *Washington Post* Columnist William Rasberry:

> According to Rasberry, discrimination against ugly women ("there's no nice way to say it") is the most persistent and pervasive form of employment discrimination. Men, he argues, face no bias, except in the movies and in politics. Rasberry's sympathies lie not with the "mere Plain Janes, who can help themselves with a bit of pain and padding," but with the losers, the "real dogs," who supposedly would be working full-time if their features were more regular. Such discrimination, he insists, is all the more insidious because no one will admit that it exists. No personnel officer in his right mind will tell a woman, "Sorry, lady, but you need a nose job, and your lips don't match." And a woman so insulted would not be likely to publicize it. (p. 8)

Most often, employers' biases in favor of good-looking candidates are probably unconscious. Sometimes, however, personnel managers' biases are fully conscious. Hiring on the basis of looks may be especially pervasive when a job requires employees to deal with the public. The employer may know there is no real difference in competence between an attractive and an unattractive employee, but there *may* be a difference in how they are received by the public or by clients that could mean a difference in profit.

A twenty-one-year-old waitress from THE GROUP described the hiring procedures in the large restaurant where she works:

At my restaurant, I can see that the better looking waitresses get the job. Hostesses especially are known for being "cute" and having great bodies—that's the reason they are hired. A couple of hostesses were fired right off the bat—even though they were doing an O.K. job. But you could tell they weren't drawing men. The managers were keeping records. And they found that when certain "cute" hostesses were working, more customers came in and kept coming back. These hostesses were promoted and the others were let go.

I know a lot of people who have applied at our restaurant—stacks and stacks of applications. And a lot of people are turned away who are competent. The ones who are hired have to be attractive.

SUCCESS: WHAT THEY SEE IS WHAT YOU GET

Personnel managers are consistent in their biases; they are willing to admit they discriminate against *everyone* on the basis of looks—male and female. In one study, 60 percent of personnel managers stated that when deciding to hire a manager, they tried to determine whether or not the prospective manager *looked* like a manager (Quinn, Tabor, and Gordon 1968). Most personnel managers consider a "good appearance" even more important than a college education or being innovative, loyal to the firm, or sensitive to others (Bowman 1962, 1964).

There is also good evidence that this bias is not just "talk." Managers do not just *say* they prefer good-looking applicants; they put their biases into practice. In the typical experiment, personnel interviewers are asked to work through a pile of job applications. The set is "rigged"—the applicants' sex, competence, and physical attractiveness have been systematically varied. Which applicants are hired? The compent were preferred to the incompent, men were preferred to women, the good-looking to the less attractive.

In one study (Dipboye, Fromkin, and Wiback 1975), thirty male industrial management students and thirty professional personnel interviewers from a wide range of companies evaluated a batch of resumes for the position of head of a furniture department. Each of the men received twelve resumes. A photograph (of either a good-looking or an unattractive applicant) was attached to each resume. Some of the applicants were women; some were men. The applicant's scholastic standing varied. Some of the applicants had good grades in their high school and college marketing classes; others did not. Some applicants were just average scholastically.

Who was hired? Even today, it is still a man's world—men were far more likely to get the position than were women. (additional evidence for this contention comes from Cash, Gillen, and Burns 1977; and Schuler and Berger 1979). Competence was the most important factor in determining who was hired. Applicants with good scholastic qualifications were preferred over those with low standings. Finally, for both men and women, it was an enormous advantage to be good-looking. Even professional interviewers, who had training and experience, discriminated on the basis of sex and physical attractiveness.

We interviewed one male recruiter for a large firm. He admitted that discrimination on the basis of physical attractiveness does occur:

> I don't do it overtly, perhaps I inadvertently do it—weigh looks. But I know a lot of guys really do it. They'll say, "Boy, she's good looking." They'll even put it down right on the recruiting papers—"nice looking."
>
> Good looks has become an attribute. In other words, it doesn't hurt. If you have two women walk into your office to be recruited, and both have the same grades, the nice looking one will get hired and that's a simple fact. Probably because the nice looking one can do more things than the not nice looking one—i.e., use her sex appeal, etc. to smooth over some clients.

"I'VE BEEN THERE"—AND IT DOES NOT HELP

Most personnel directors are biased, then. But certainly personnel interviewers of mediocre appearance themselves, who have personally suffered from injustice, can identify with "flawed" applicants. Surely, they would not discriminate in hiring. They must prefer someone of about their own level of attractiveness.

In "Know How to Interview for a Job," Milton Rockman (*Wisconsin State Journal*, 18 July 1982) argues that interviewers look for others similar to themselves in appearance:

> It is unfortunate, but true, says Donald H. Sweet, vice-president of Costello-Erdlem & Company, a Wellesley, Mass. consulting firm and former personnel director of the Celanese Company, that interviewer biases affect their hiring practices. Despite frequent disclaimers, many tend to hire on the basis of superficial first impressions involving appearance, clothes, height, or personal chemistry. They look for individuals much like themselves with whom they can feel comfortable. Sweet calls it "clonal hiring." (p. 22)

The evidence indicates that first impressions do count . . . but that everyone prefers the attractive applicant. So much for the kinship of suffering.

In one study, "personnel interviewers" (college students) were asked to evaluate a series of applicants for a managerial job. At the time they began their research, scientists expected the "interviewers" to be most biased in favor of those looking like themselves—no better and certainly no worse. Attractive interviewers were expected to prefer attractive applicants, and unattractive interviewers to prefer unattractive applicants.

This optimistic prediction, however, was soon disconfirmed. Everyone preferred the good-looking applicants. Both attractive and homely interviewers were more likely to recommend hiring the attractive applicant . . . and at a higher starting salary (both men and women were biased in favor of male applicants also) (Dipboye, Arvey, and Terpstra 1977). Job discrimination seems to occur regardless of who is sitting behind the desk.

DISCRIMINATION AGAINST THE ELDERLY—IS THE SIN BEING OLD OR UNATTRACTIVE?

Older workers confront overpowering discrimination. A Department of Labor survey found many jobs only open to people fifty-five-years of age and younger. Sometimes even people in the forty-five to fifty-five age range are discriminated against. At times it is not clear why older people are discriminated against. Sociologist Inge Powell Bell (1979) argues that physical attractiveness could be important:

> The problem of discrimination against older men and women is complicated by the fact that a study would have to take into account whether discrimination was practiced because of expected lack of physical strength, long training or internship programs, or physical attractiveness. The former two considerations figure much more frequently in the case of men and certainly have more legitimacy as grounds for discriminating than the factor of physical attractiveness, which usually arises solely because the woman is seen as a sex object before she is seen as a productive worker. As long as this is the employer's orientation, it will probably do little good to cite him the studies proving that middle aged women office workers are superior to young women in work attendance, performance and ability to get along agreeably with others. (p. 241)

WHEN BEAUTY="DON'T CALL US, WE'LL CALL YOU"

Of course, there are some instances when great beauty can be a handicap in getting a job. Marilyn Monroe, for example, was turned down for the part of Grushenka in Dostoyevsky's (1958) *The Brothers Karamazov* because she was too beautiful to be credible. Actress Morgan Fairchild has said, "I've lost a lot of parts because they said I was too beautiful, too classic, too glamorous. One producer told me, 'No one will identify with you' " (Kramer, *Parade*, 4 July 1982).

TOO MUCH OF A GOOD THING

Psychologists (Heilman and Saruwatari 1979) have speculated that in traditional business circles, although dazzling women may have an advantage in securing traditional, low-paying, "feminine" jobs, they may have a distinct disadvantage in competing for traditional "men's jobs." To determine if this assumption is true, the researchers asked men and women to evaluate a collection of applications for a white-collar job. In some cases, the job was clerical; it was described as a Level 8 job with a salary of $6,000–$8,000. In other cases, the job was a managerial position—a Level 6 job, with a salary of $14,000–$16,000. Attached to the employment form was the applicant's photograph. The man or woman's photo, a bogus one, was either attractive or homely.

If the applicant was a man, good looks were an advantage in getting hired, regardless of whether the job was clerical or managerial. If the applicant was a woman, however, beauty only helped when the job was clerical. When the job was a high-status managerial one, "beauty was beastly." Interviewers assumed homely women were more qualified for the managerial job; they were more eager to hire them and at a higher starting salary.

Why would traditional employers discriminate against beautiful women for "fast track" positions? Apparently, a woman's attractiveness enhances the perception of feminity, and for these traditional men, feminity is supposedly incongruent with the skill and talent required in high-status managerial jobs. Beautiful women may seem ill suited for men's work. Homely women, on the other hand, are apparently seen as "one of the guys." The researchers concluded, "This finding sadly implies that women should strive to appear as unattractive and as masculine as possible if they are to succeed in advancing their careers by moving into powerful organizational positions" (p. 371).

In another study (Cash, Gillen, and Burns 1977), unattractive women were more likely to be considered for the traditional men's jobs of automobile salesperson and wholesale hardware shipping and receiving clerk than attractive women. On the other hand, attractive women were more likely to be considered for the "feminine" jobs of telephone operator and office receptionist.

Obviously, in traditional circles there seems to be a stereotype that high-status and "masculine-type" jobs may not be appropriate for women—particularly for attractive women (viewed as the epitome of all that is feminine). A note: We suspect the preceding studies might exaggerate the problems beautiful career women face. Our own exploratory work has begun to reveal two factors executive women must consider in dressing for success—good looks and appropriateness. (This last factor may be of overriding importance.) We suspect that women can look as beautiful as they want, as long as their hair is arranged in a businesslike style and they are dressed appropriately for the job.

In some of the preceding research (which seemed to depict beauty as a disadvantage) there was some confusion between beauty and appropriateness. The stimulus pictures showed that apparently a few of the beautiful women did not appear as businesslike as the plainer women. (Their hair was too long and sultry; they wore the wrong kind of eye makeup.) They were beautiful, but subtly wrong for an executive position. We suspect that beautiful women may actually be more marketable than plainer women, if everyone is dressed appropriately.

In any case, even if subsequent research shows we are wrong and that, currently, beauty and success do not mix, there is some suggestion that this situation may be changing. Recently, some educators became concerned that traditional sterotyping (i.e., that beauty and professionalism do not mix) might be preventing young women from pursuing careers in professional fields. They found, however, that among young people no such stereotyping exists. For example, in one study (Lanier and Bryne 1981), a group of high school students was shown twenty slides of beautiful to ugly women. They were told that some of these women were engineers, lawyers, doctors, oceanographers, architects, and executives. Could they guess which women were the professionals? A second group was shown slides of the same women and was told that half the women had taken some of the following courses in high school: mechanical drawing, physics, calculus, chemistry, and political science. Which women had taken these courses? Both high school boys and girls took it for granted that beauty and brains do mix. The new generation simply assumed the attractive women had the professional careers and had taken the traditionally masculine high school courses.

CONFLICTING MESSAGES TO WOMEN: HOW TO LOOK MASCULINELY FEMININE AND NOT COMPROMISE YOUR VALUES

For the moment, however, career women seem caught in a damned-if-you-do and damned-if-you-don't world. On the one hand, sometimes they are encouraged to look very feminine—if it helps get the job done. On the other hand, they can not be too attractive or they may not be taken seriously by those in power (as the previous studies indicate). Furthermore, if they are to be prepared for the world of tomorrow, they should always try to look their best. Career magazines—such as *Savvy* and *Working Woman*—reflect this confusion. Their ads suggest women should be softly feminine, muskily sexy, and relentlessly dominant, all at the same time (a hard bit of advice to follow).

Given this confusion, how *should* a woman dress for a job interview? Just what "look" is right will depend on the occupation, of course. The good looks that land a man a job as a United States senator or as a cowboy in a movie (i.e., tough, decisive, and virile) is different from the look that will land him a job in a male fashion magazine (pretty and elegant). The good looks that help get a woman a job on the floor of the stock exchange are different from the look that will get her a job as a bar girl in a Hotel Street dive.

Investigators have examined what people should wear when job hunting. (Rucker, Taber, and Harrison 1981) In a study sponsored by the Research Committee of the Western College Placement Association (Anton and Russell 1974), college recruiting officers and managers assessed applicants' job potential. Male applicants were most appealing when wearing suits, ties, sport coats, slacks, and dress suits in contrast to T-shirts, shorts, jeans, and sandals (as you might guess, the latter were taboo). Recruiters preferred women who wore blouses, heels, and nylon stockings when applying for a job. (They reacted negatively to sandals, shorts, jeans, and the "bra-less look.")

Kelley et al. (1976) found much the same thing. They concluded that dressing for the office should be a "conservative but fashionable look with an emphasis on being neat and well-groomed." Molloy in his books, *Dress for Success* (1975) and *The Woman's Dress for Success Book* (1977), has said, "Dressing to succeed in business and dressing to be sexually attractive are almost mutually exclusive." He suggests long sleeves and high necklines for women.

What a woman wears for a job interview and what she wears when secure in her job, however, are two different things. We conducted an interview with Brian Shapiro, a top accounting executive from a "Big 8" accounting firm in Los Angeles. He describes what happens in his profession:

> In the Big 8, there has always been a myth that you have to dress like "an accountant" to succeed. Of course, the question is, What do accountants look like? . . . and then, Why should they dress like *that?* There has always been a kind of "militarism" in the Big 8. You have to wear a suit. That was fine for years, but about the mid-70s, the women's movement finally began to infiltrate the previously untouched accounting community. There started to become a number of women accounting majors—and, of course, the large firms started hiring them. Now the problem became—We know that the men should dress in dark, conservative suits, but how should the women dress? We didn't know. On the one hand, we thought women should look professional. But on the other hand, shouldn't they look feminine too? Why can't accountants be feminine?
>
> Over the last six years, I have seen the predominantly male partner group adopt a double standard in what is demanded of women. On one hand, they want women to look old and conservative. On the other

hand, suddenly, they would like women accountants to look "sexy," because they think that's what the clients want to see. If you are going to hire women, why not use their sex appeal for professional gain—to obtain rapport with the clients? I hate to admit it, but I have seen it used. I have seen partners suggest that one woman, who is extremely well-endowed, wear certain outfits to certain jobs, when they know that, for instance, professionally teasing an "old letch" would help the firm. And it works . . . I have seen it done. If women auditors can learn to use their femininity, it seems to loosen up the clients. Like it or not, it works.

DISCRIMINATION IN SALARY AND PROMOTION

Not only are good-looking applicants more likely to be hired, but they are more likely to be hired at a higher starting salary. In one study, interviewers were told an applicant had been hired; they were asked merely to recommend a starting salary. Who were given higher salaries? Once again, the physically attractive, the highly qualified, and, of course, the men (Dipboye, Arvey, and Terpstra 1977). Another researcher (Waters 1980) discovered a "Cinderella syndrome." She found that personnel managers and employment counselors from Los Angeles to Chicago to New York gave a higher starting salary to a woman when she was made up attractively than when the same woman appeared to be plain. It was most important to be beautiful in secretarial positions, least important in managerial ones.

BEAUTY PAYS

Given all these considerations, the discovery that the good-looking are likely to end up with jobs higher in pay and prestige than their less appealing competitors probably comes as no surprise. In 1971–1973, Robert P. Quinn (1978) examined data from three national surveys conducted at the University of Michigan's Survey Research Center. All in all, more than 800 men and 470 women ranging in age from sixteen up and employed full-time were interviewed. Interviewers rated the person's physical appearance (were they "strikingly handsome or beautiful," "good-looking," "average-looking," "quite plain," or "homely?"). Interviewers recorded what participants' jobs were, and how much they got paid for doing them. They found that, for both men and women, physical attractiveness was tightly linked with income and occupational prestige (see Table 2.1).

The income of "handsome/good-looking" men was $1,869 higher than that of "plain/homely" men. The income of "beautiful/good-

TABLE 2.1   **The Relationship Between Looks and Career Success**

ATTRACTIVENESS	YEARLY INCOME	RATINGS OF OCCUPATIONAL PRESTIGE
Men		
"Strikingly handsome" or "good-looking"	$10,093	49.6
"Average"	$ 9,216	42.4
"Quite plain" or "Homely"	$ 8,224	31.4
Women		
"Strikingly beautiful" or "good-looking"	$ 5,874	50.8
"Average"	$ 5,043	42.0
"Quite plain" or "Homely"	$ 4,647	33.6

SOURCE: Table based on data available in Quinn (1972)

looking women was $1,227 higher than that of their "plain/homely" counterparts.

The researchers measured occupational prestige by Duncan's Socioeconomic Status Scale (Reiss, Duncan, Hatt, and North 1961). This scale lists almost every conceivable job (on a scale of 1 to 100) according to how much prestige people, in general, attach to the occupation. They found that good-looking men and women tended to have jobs rated around 49–50 in prestige. (The jobs in that range include clergymen, music teachers, floor managers, bookkeepers, photographers, student nurses, and managers of food stores.) Homely men and women held jobs of lower prestige, in the 31–34 range (including housekeepers, building superintendents and managers, boilermakers, machinists, and gasoline service sation managers). Obviously, good looks pay—in money and in prestige.

DISCRIMINATION IN EVALUATIONS OF ON-THE-JOB PERFORMANCE

If you are not much to look at, getting a job is difficult in the first place. If you do get a job, you may have to work extra hard to get a good evaluation. Considerable evidence exists documenting that teachers and employers treat plain women's (and perhaps men's) efforts with less respect than they deserve—especially when judgments have to be subjective.

WHEN PERFORMANCE IS IN THE EYE OF THE BEHOLDER

In one study (Landy and Sigall 1974), college men were asked to judge how "compelling," "logical," and "convincing" an essay was (the essay was on the role of television in society). Attached to most of the essays was a photograph of either a beautiful woman or of an ugly one. Other essays had no attached photograph. One of the essays was well written; a second was shoddily composed (there were errors in grammar, the logic was appalling, the ideas were bland and unexciting, and it was cliche ridden.) The men were most impressed by a given essay if they believed it was written by a beautiful woman. They were less impressed when they did not know what the authoress looked like and totally unimpressed when they believed she was ugly. The authoresses' looks were important even when the essay was first-rate, but they were critically important when the essay was not. Good looks seemed to make the grammar and logic less appalling, and the ideas a little less bland.

Judges display the same bias when assessing artists' work. In one study, both men and women judged paintings to be more appealing when they thought the artist was a pretty woman. They liked the work least when they thought she was plain (Murphy and Hellkamp 1976). (Similar results were secured by Holahan and Stephan 1981.)

Researchers also find we are "unbiased" in our biases. People are prejudiced in favor of the beautiful and against the ugly, regardless of the employee's, writer's, or artist's race, creed, or color (Maruyama and Miller 1980).

So far, we have discussed employer's biases against *women*. What about men? Does a *handsome* writer or artist have an advantage over an ugly one? If so, are men and women equally biased against men? Does a jealousy factor operate when employers are judging the work of striking people of the same sex? Kaplan (1978) argues that employers should be most biased in favor of attractive members of the opposite sex; they should be far less favorably disposed toward good-looking members of their own sex. In fact, employees might even be prejudiced against the latter. After all, these are their competitors! Experiments have been conducted to determine if jealousy shapes our evaluation of others.

In a pair of experiments, Kaplan (1978) investigated all the questions just raised. Men and women were asked to judge an essay, supposedly written by either a man or a woman who was either attractive or unattractive. The essay was on patriotism and was designed to emulate the style of an untalented college freshman. As before, men were markedly swayed by the woman author's beauty in assessing her competence. Women were not—in fact, the women judges actually judged the beautiful woman's work slightly more critically than the ugly woman's. What about the men's essays? Neither men nor women showed any bias in favor of the good-looking men! The conclusion? Apparently, *men* are most likely to confuse beauty with competence, and they are most likely to confuse the two only when judging women. (Unfortunately, since most employers are men, this bias may be fairly pervasive.) There is no evidence that people take men's looks into account when judging their performance (of course, given all the other data scattered throughout this book, subsequent research may show that handsome men are seen to perform handsomely too, but, as yet, such documentation does not exist).

One recent study found that "beauty does *not* equal talent." Holahan and Stephan [1981] found that, as in the studies above, when an essay was poor, a beautiful writer was judged to be more talented than the homely one. However, these authors found that when the essay was good, attractive writers were actually discriminated against. This is the first time anyone has secured such results. These conclusions, if they hold up, may suggest that men believe beautiful women are smarter, but [enough is enough] they cannot be *too* smart!)

Does egalitarianism affect men's responses to good-looking/ugly women? Psychologists have speculated that traditional men might be even more inclined than liberal men to forgive an attractive woman for her flaws. To test this notion, psychologists (Holahan and Stephan 1981) asked men and women about their sex role attitudes via the Attitudes Toward Women Scale (Spence and Helmreich 1972). On this scale, men and women with traditional attitudes are expected to agree with statements such as:

1. Women should worry less about their rights and more about becoming good wives and mothers.

2. The intellectual leadership of a community should be largely in the hands of men.

3. There are many jobs in which men should be given preference over women in being hired or promoted.

4. Femininism and women's liberation threaten to destroy the family institution and women's natural place in the world.

5. For the sake of their children, women should be willing to stay at home and not seek outside employment.

Men and women with liberal attitudes would be expected to disagree with the above statements.

As the authors suspected, only traditional men equated women's beauty with competence. In fact, liberal men evidently leaned over backwards to be fair—they actually showed a *slight* bias in favor of the homely women's essays. Women were fairly evenhanded in their judgements of beautiful versus ugly women, regardless of their traditionality.

The preceding study clearly shows that not everyone is strongly biased in favor of the good-looking. Different people have different experiences, and thus they develop different implicit personality theories—i.e., different conceptions of what traits go together. For most people, the belief that beauty equals competence is deeply ingrained. A few of us, however, are not so sure.

"DELIVERING THE GOODS"

Possibly, beauty is not always an advantage. It is extraordinarily difficult to judge the quality of an essay or a painting. In such circumstances, good looks can give the artist an edge. However, some performances are not so ambiguous—the lawyer either wins or loses the case, the salesman either makes or does not make the sale, the mathematician either solves the equation or waves his hands. When an employee does not complete the job, looks will probably not help bail him or her out, at least, not for long.

A California executive describes how looks can backfire.

> If someone is very good-looking, she is noticeable. It's impossible for an extremely good-looking woman to have a low profile. When she walks into a room, everyone looks. She can't blend into a crowd.
>
> Her high profile means that more people will be examining her strengths and weaknesses. Someone who is average-looking, can have lousy skills, but it won't be noticed until late in her career. No one is looking.
>
> In any technical profession, looks will get you in the door, but believe me, performance is what gets you promoted. Looks can backfire.

A middle-aged professional woman from THE GROUP argued there is extra pressure on an attractive woman to perform well.

> I think, initially, attractiveness is a plus. It's been true for me. I've gotten jobs because I'm reasonably attractive and present myself well. But while it's a big plus initially, somewhere along the line, someone inevitably says: "Wait a minute. Can she deliver the goods?" They may even be irritated *because* you are attractive, and so you had *better* deliver the goods! There is sort of a boomerang effect. They may even discount you—at least initially—because of your good looks. You have to prove your competence.
>
> Here's something that happened to me recently: I was elected to be on an important state committee—a 30-member committee, all men. But I was nominated in a devastating way. An important committee member stood up and announced in front of everyone, "We have to have Audry

on the committee—she's the prettiest thing here." I was stunned! Shocked! I couldn't say anything. I wasn't prepared for such a statement. This was supposed to be a professional group. We were all there because we had professional credentials. Such a statement seemed *so* unprofessional. After getting over my initial astonishment, my reaction was to get very, very angry. The thought crossed my mind that I would show them by refusing the honor. But then I calmed down, and remembered that I was there because I was representing people who weren't represented. I could serve a useful function on the committee. My reaction, as I was driving home from the meeting, went something like this: "Ok, now you know what the score is. Your looks put you on a committee, but now you're going to show them what a pretty face can do—you're going to show them that you can deliver the goods. And you're going to deliver the goods first-class!" And that's just what I did.

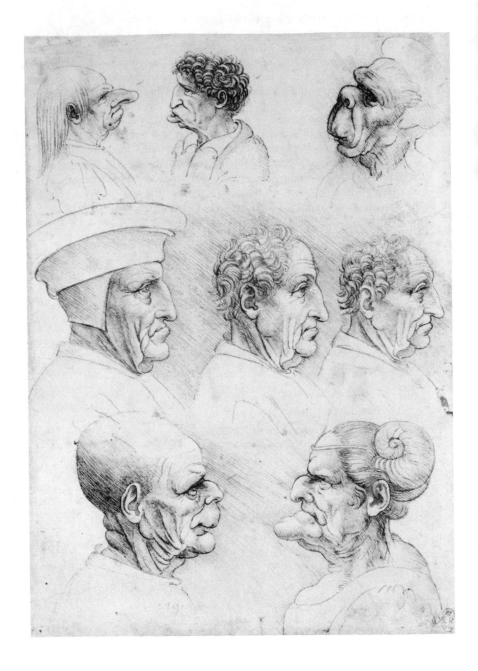

Figure 3.1. Leonardo da Vinci, *Study of Grotesque Heads*, c. 1490, pen and ink over red chalk. Courtesy, The Royal Library, Windsor Castle.

Chapter 3

The Ugly: Mad or Bad?

If you do not like someone's looks, it is easy to conclude there must be something "wrong" with them. Therapists point out there are three ways we discount people: we accuse them of being "stupid" (discussed in chapter 2), "mad," or "bad."

In this chapter, we are going to focus on the assumption that "what is ugly is mad and bad." First, we will examine people's perceptions of attractive versus unattractive people's mental health. Next, we will examine how attractiveness affects judgments about aspects of character, shaping even judgments of guilt and innocence in the justice system. Finally, we will go beyond examining stereotypes and will consider how attractive versus unattractive people in distress are actually *treated*.

BEAUTY = SANITY

Mental health professionals are not immune to the glow cast by beauty. There is compelling evidence that social workers, psychologists, psychiatrists, and the rest of us respond very differently to good-looking

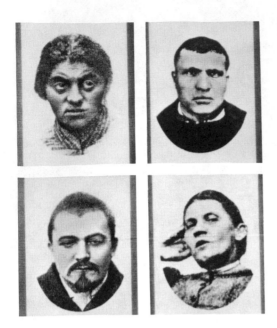

Figure 3.2. Lipot Szondi (Szondi, Moser, and Webb 1959) argued that psychologists could discover a person's genetic predisposition toward mental illness or criminality by observing the extent to which they were attracted by *or* repelled by the mentally ill or criminal. (The principle seems to be "birds of a feather flock together" *and* "opposites attract." The Sjondi Test required individuals to look at a variety of people, all outstandingly homely, and to say which they liked most or least. Those people chosen as the most and the least liked, he concluded, were most similar to that individual. Here, at least, ugliness was linked to madness and badness.

versus ugly people. In general, people tend to attribute greater psychological disturbance to homely people than to attractive ones.

Much of the evidence that beauty equals sanity comes from studies done with college students who were asked to imagine they are psychotherapists. Typically, the men and women listened to recorded interviews or watched videotapes in which clients recounted their problems. Then the "therapists" were asked to evaluate the clients and make suggestions for treatment. It seems very difficult for people to believe that good-looking clients are really disturbed and need professional help. They have no trouble at all imagining that homely men and women are in trouble (Cash, Kehr, Polyson, and Freeman 1977; Cash and Salzbach 1978; Hobfall and Penner 1978; Jones, Hansson, and Phillips 1978).

It is interesting to know that the man-on-the-street (or the student-on-campus) confuses comeliness with sanity; but, it is fascinating to discover that mental health professionals share their biases—and they do. In one study (Barocas and Vance 1974), it was found that counselors at the University of Rochester Counseling Center were influenced by the physical attractiveness of the troubled students they saw. They assumed their striking clients had better personal adjustment and better prognosis than did their unattractive clients.

Perhaps the most revealing information about therapists' biases comes from in-depth interviews. Family therapist Morton Perlmutter (Perlmutter 1978; also reported in Hatfield and Perlmutter 1983) questioned Wisconsin psychiatrists, psychotherapists, psychologists, and psychiatric social workers about the ways in which a client's looks affected the therapy process. Perlmutter's interviews were revealing. Client's appeal evidently has a profound impact on therapists' first impressions, their diagnoses, and even on the eventual outcome of therapy. Here are some of the things Perlmutter and others have learned.

THERAPISTS' SENSITIVITY TO ISSUES OF BEAUTY

Psychotherapists were well aware that the clients' beauty or ugliness is a critical issue for them. They readily admitted they prefer YAVIS (young, attractive, verbal, interesting, and successful) clients and avoid OUIBF (old, ugly, inarticulate, boring, failures) (Schofield 1964).

They were also aware that, in spite of their liking for beautiful clients, it is difficult to deal with them. (Since almost all the psychotherapists Perlmutter interviewed were men, when he speaks of therapists' problems in dealing with good-looking "clients," he is really referring to the problems men have dealing with beautiful women.) Therapists admitted they have mixed motives when dealing with good-looking clients. On the one hand, they are sensitive to professional ethical standards and want to be objective. On the other hand, they know objectivity is impossible. Therapists are attracted to strikingly beautiful women, and they can not help hoping the women return their interest.

THERAPISTS' SELF PERCEPTIONS

When dealing with pretty patients, therapists found themselves acting out stereotyped roles. The men acted in a more machismo way, the women in a softer, more feminine way. (Other data show that people do try to look their best when confronting beautiful people, and "their best" generally means conforming to traditional sex roles [see Shaw and Wagner 1975].)

In general, therapists tried to be charming, alluring, and desirable with their attractive clients. One therapist served coffee to beautiful women, while expecting his other clients to help themselves. A few therapists admitted they had a hidden desire to become more intimate with their good-looking patients and thought of seducing them. (Sometimes, therapists' desires are not so hidden—12 percent of men therapists and 3 percent of women therapists admit they do engage in sexual intimacies with their clients) [McCartney 1966; Pope, Levenson, and Schover 1979].)

THE DIAGNOSES

Perlmutter found that, most of the time, therapists and clients had a fairly easy time settling on clear-cut and limited goals. When dealing with beautiful women, however, therapists tended to get confused about just what their goals were. They might start out with clear-cut objectives, but they found themselves continually revising things. Frequently, their diagnoses were complex and mixed.

In the end, the therapists tended to settle upon *intrapsychic* interpretations of beautiful women's problems. They generally decided the beautiful woman herself was the key, making it unnecessary to bring in her husband or family. In support of Perlmutter's findings, Schofield (1964) discovered that attractive men and women are more likely to obtain individual psychotherapy than are homely clients.

The therapists Perlmutter interviewed assumed that beautiful clients were mentally healthier than run-of-the-mill clients. (Probably therapists' biases are reinforced by the fact that, when people are acutely distressed, it is extraordinary difficult for them to look their best.) A number of other researchers have found that laymen and psychologists are swayed by appearance when attempting to decide how mentally healthy another person is.

Other evidence indicates that being influenced by a client's looks may depend on the therapist's particular style of therapy. For example, Muirhead (1979) interviewed two types of therapists—Freudian therapists and more eclectic ones. (Eclectic therapists try to take the best of everything from existing schools of thought.) The therapists were shown a photograph of a client. Some of the clients were handsome or ugly men, others were beautiful or ugly women. The therapists then reviewed the client's background information. The client was presented as a bright college student from a normal, middle-class family, with no known history of mental illness.

Finally, the therapist listened to a psychiatric interview. During the session, the clients complained they were tense for no apparent reason. They felt listless. They wasted a lot of time just sitting around watching television. Recently, they had started to have some problems with their parents. They knew their parents had good intentions, but they expected too much. There was too much pressure. They were angry at their folks. They felt guilty, too. The therapists had to decide: was the client crazy, or just like the rest of us?

Unexpectedly, this study found that the philosophical orientations of the therapists had a substantial impact on their evaluations. For some reason, Freudian therapists (and only the Freudians) had difficulty remaining objective when their client was a beautiful woman. They thought the beautiful woman was unusually well adjusted. In fact, they rated her more positively than an unattractive woman on a number of dimensions. She was judged to be brighter, better able to express herself, less in need of support, better adjusted sexually, and more self-revealing and less defensive. Conversely, therapists of every theoretical orientation looked at men objectively: they evaluated handsome and homely men in an evenhanded way. (Similar results have been secured by Barocas & Vance, [1974]; Cash, Kehr, Polyson, and Freeman, [1977]; Cash and Salzbach [1978]; Hobfall and Penner [1978]; Jones, Hansson, and Phillips [1978].)

THE THERAPISTS' GOALS

Perlmutter found that therapists are influenced by their clients' "market value" when deciding what their patients can reasonably expect out of life. There is some evidence that therapists, like the rest of us, may value appearance so much that it affects the goals they set for therapy. Therapists may encourage (even demand) that attractive people insist on getting everything they want—from their intimates, their bosses and coworkers, and from life in general. They may be less adamant in setting the same goals for homely clients.

There is even evidence that people's judgments as to whether or not women have something to live for may depend on their beauty! Psychologists (Pavlos and Newcomb 1974) asked men to read a case history about a woman who had attempted suicide by taking an overdose of medicine. The woman was said to have either treatable cancer with a prognosis for complete recovery *or* terminal cancer with no hope. Attached to the case material was a photograph of an attractive woman, a photograph of an unattractive woman, or no photograph at all. The men were asked to indicate how "justified" the woman was in attempting suicide. When the cancer was treatable, a beautiful woman was seen as less justified in attempting suicide than a homely one. Apparently, it was assumed the beautiful woman had everything to live for. On the other hand, when the cancer was terminal, the beautiful woman was seen as more justified in attempting suicide. Perhaps it was assumed that when there was no hope, the attractive woman had more right to feel despair at how the cards had been dealt.

THE TREATMENT: THE FIFTY-MINUTE HOUR—AT LEAST

The therapists Perlmutter (1978) interviewed reported that they spent more time with their beautiful patients. Usually, before settling down to business, therapists and clients engage in small talk. When their patients were beautiful, therapists reported spending an unusual amount of time "warming up." They also spend more time in chit-chat at the end of the hour. Perhaps they were reluctant to terminate the session. All in all, therapists ended up spending far more time with lovely clients than with any others.

Other researchers (Barocas and Black 1974; Katz and Zimbardo 1977) have confirmed that attractive men and women do get more of their psychiatrist's time than do other patients.

WHERE DOES IT ALL END? THE OUTCOMES OF THERAPY

In sum, therapist/client relationships are very different when clients are attractive. Are attractive clients also more likely to get well? As always, it depends.

In general, Perlmutter concluded that therapist's biases work to the good-looking client's advantage. Therapists try harder, and their efforts work. Most good-looking patients solve their problems with unusual swiftness (Farina et al. 1977 report similar results). Perlmutter provides one example:

> The client was a startlingly beautiful housewife. She was so tradi-
> tional, she was unable to deal with her children, however. The oldest
> boy, who was 14, thought that he was the man of the family. He
> bossed her around, and if she "talked back," he hit her. She was a
> smoldering volcano; unable to express anger directly. (When upset, she
> became incapable of speaking; she signaled her distress by waving her
> arms wildly). The therapist took a personal interest in her case. He saw
> her three to four times a week. When her insurance ran out, he contin-
> ued to see her, for free. He helped her a great deal. The family rela-
> tions improved enormously. This time, the therapist's exceptional atten-
> tion had exceptional results.

Barocas and Black (1974) and Katz and Zimbardo (1977) insist such cases are typical. They find that, in general, good-looking patients receive more, and better, treatment than do their so-so counterparts.

The results are not always so positive, however. When therapists are unusually concerned about achieving success, sometimes they begin to try harder, in fact, too hard, possibly resulting in poor therapy. Perlmutter cites an example:

Two therapists reported difficulties with the same woman. She was a handsome woman, who had poliomyelitis in adolescence and, as a result, had lost the musculature in her calves. Therapist #1 saw her for a few sessions, but soon realized it was impossible to continue seeing her. His physical attraction to her, and his pity for her, rendered him ineffective. He found himself observing: "How can anyone so beautiful be so maimed?" and having fantasies about how he might rescue her . . . instead of working on her problems.

Therapist #1 referred her to Therapist #2. He suggested to Therapist #2 that she needed quick symptom relief. (She was phobic; she worried that she'd fall over in her wheelchair and be hurt. She was worried that people would invade her house and injure her. She was suicidal.) Once *these* symptoms were ameliorated, Therapist #1 thought long-term psychotherapy could begin.

Therapist #2, too, had problems. *He* decided to persevere in therapy, however. In retrospect, he realized that had been a mistake. He admitted that he, too, had become so personally involved with her, that he had failed as a therapist. He never attempted quick symptom relief. In fact, he persisted in denying that she had any real problems—he would insist "You're as capable of getting around as the rest of us." Obviously she was not. What he really needed to do was to acknowledge her limitations—to consult with an expert in such handicaps, who could teach her to deal with her handicaps. After three years of therapy, she showed no improvement. If anything, she was worse.

Good looks is usually an advantage, but not always.

The Patient Strikes Back

It is not just therapists who are biased—clients are too. The experimental evidence makes clear that patients have more confidence in good-looking therapists than in less attractive ones.

In one study (Cash, Begley, McCown, and Weise 1975), students watched a young, professional, male counselor in action (via a videotape). The man's appearance was altered cosmetically—sometimes he was unusually appealing, sometimes not. The attractive counselor was judged to be more intelligent, friendly, assertive, trustworthy, competent, warm, and likeable. He was also expected to be a better counselor. Other research indicates these biases also occur with female counselors (see Cash and Kehr 1978; Lewis and Walsh 1978).

What happens, however, when you see a counselor for session after session? Does the effect of physical attractiveness wear off? To examine this question, researchers (Vargas and Borkowski 1982) had men observe a woman counselor dealing with a client over several sessions. For some observers, the counselor was very good-looking. Sometimes, she was made quite homely. The first session was an intake interview.

During the next two sessions, the client discussed his problems—he had difficulty knowing what to say to women and had trouble getting dates.

The researchers were interested in just how much a therapist's beauty can affect her perceived effectiveness, so they made up two sets of tapes. In the first set of tapes, the counselor—good-looking or not—was very good. She used Rogers' (1951) client-centered approach, and was empathetic, genuine, and encouraging. On other tapes, she did a terrible job of counseling. She even insulted the client by making comments such as, "If you've been here for two years and have only had a couple dates, that's pretty bad." After the third session, the men were asked to evaluate the counselor.

It was found that, regardless of whether the counselor was skilled or unskilled, physical attractiveness gave her an extra boost in how effective she was perceived to be—even after three sessions. In judging the counselor's future success in treating problems, however, the men were influenced by the physical attractiveness of the counselor only if she was skilled. If the counselor was incompetent, apparently enough was enough. Even if she was pretty to look at, men were not willing to say they would go back for more. Apparently, for both therapists and their clients, it is a real advantage to be YAVIS.

BEAUTY = CHARACTER

In the last chapter, we discussed parent's and teacher's biases in judging students' academic work. What about the other side of the report card—the citizenship side? You may remember the praise (or critical remarks) teachers jotted down on your report card: "Gets along well with classmates," "A disturbing element," 'Picks on smaller children . . . and the teacher." Seemingly, ugly children are more likely to get a poor citizenship report, even when they behave exactly like attractive children. Ugly adults also face the same negative judgments.

Ugly As Sin: Juvenile Style

In a now classic study, psychologist Karen Dion (1972) suspected that adults would react very differently to cute versus homely children when they misbehaved, even if they had done exactly the same thing. She asked college women to read through a teacher's "notes," describing a child's activities during the day. Attached to the notes was a photograph of either a cute or a homely seven-year-old boy or girl. The teacher's notes were rigged. They described an incident in which the child hurt either a dog or another child and in either a trivial or in a

Figure 3.3. Jordan Rich, 1980.   **Figure 3.4.** Shayna Rich, 1982.

fairly serious way. For example, Note #1 described an aggressive act so minor it could hardly be called aggression. The child merely stepped on a sleeping dog's tail and caused it to yelp. Note #2, however, described an act against a dog which was far more serious. This time the note read:

> At the one corner of the playground a dog was sleeping. Peter stood a short distance from the dog, picked up some sharp stones from the ground, and threw them at the animal. Two of the stones struck the dog and cut its leg. The animal jumped up yelping and limped away. Peter continued to throw rocks at it as it tried to move away from him.

Notes #3 and #4 described an incident in which the cruelty was directed toward another child. Note #3 described a mild incident in which the child threw a snowball that hit another child's leg, causing the leg to sting. In the more serious incident, Note #4 reported the child had packed a snowball with ice and aimed it at another child's head; the child suffered a deep and bleeding cut.

Were women swayed by the children's looks when making judgments about their characters? As long as the children's misbehavior was mild, women were reasonably objective. They found both attractive and unattractive children "not guilty." As the children's cruelty became more serious, however, women's emotions began to get in the way of their objectivity. An unattractive child was more likely to be seen as guilty than an attractive child.

The women also explained the misbehavior of attractive and unattractive children in different ways. Women tended to attribute a homely child's misbehavior to a "rotten" personality and character. On the one hand, the attractive child's actions were attributed to temporary mood states and situational forces. For example, when an attractive child had hurt the dog or child, women typically made comments such as:

> She appears to be a perfectly charming little girl; well-mannered, basically unselfish. It seems that she can adapt well among children her age and makes a good impression . . . she plays well with everyone, but like anyone else, a bad day can occur. Her cruelty need not be taken too seriously. (reported in Berscheid and Hatfield [Walster] 1974, 193)

However, when the same act was committed by a plain child, women typically said such things as:

> I think the child would be quite bratty and would be a problem to teachers . . . she would probably try to pick a fight with other children her own age . . . she would be a brat at home . . . all in all, she would be a real problem. (p. 193)

"Would the child do it again?" the women were asked. Probably—if the child is ugly. Women thought the ugly child was most likely to be a "repeat offender."

A Note: Not every study has found that teachers are more lenient toward good-looking children. One study found that, occasionally, teachers are harsher in their treatment of attractive boys and girls. They expect adorable children to behave well, and thus they are unusually disappointed when they don't. Perhaps it is also a threat to self-esteem when teachers or parents find they can not even control a seemingly "perfect" child. In one study, Marwit, Marwit, and Walker (1978) asked student teachers and practicing teachers from the St. Louis public schools to look at a cute versus a homely ten-year-old boy's classroom behavior (he either threw a tantrum in class or stole lunch money from his teacher's desk) and to say how serious they thought the misbehavior was. Student teacher's judgments were not affected by the boy's looks. Actual teachers, however, were biased, but in this case, they were the least tolerant of the attractive child's misbehavior. Apparently, although teachers are generally tolerant of cute children, there are limits to their tolerance.

Disciplining Attractive Versus Unattractive Children

Given the diverse perceptions of the women in the above study by Dion (1974) as to why appealing versus homely children behaved as they did, we might expect women' opinions to differ about how the troublemaker should be treated. Surprisingly, the women did *not* recommend different punishments for the attractive and unattractive children. All the women agreed the teacher should discuss things with the child, regardless of how attractive or homely the child. Women were opposed to withdrawal of love, physical punishment, and other alternative forms of punishment for all the children. Nevertheless, one wonders whether an unattractive child perceived to be a chronic troublemaker would not be "reasoned with" more swiftly than would a good-looking child, and whether the discussion would not proceed along somewhat different lines.

Although the women in the Dion study did not believe in physical punishment, obviously children do get physically punished. In fact, two million children are abused each year, and at least two thousand of them die from their injuries. A duet of experiments explored the chilling notion that parents direct their hostility toward the most unattractive child in the family (Berkowitz and Frodi 1979). Researchers involved women in an investigation of the dynamics of parent-child relationships in two complicated experiments. The researchers arranged for a couple to have either a delightful or a stressful encounter with each another. The question was: How would the couple's encounter affect the way the mother treated the child? Would it matter what the child looked like?

Women were asked to act along with a man (actually an experimental confederate) as parents to a ten-year-old child. First, the researchers arranged for the "couple" to have either a delightful or a stressful encounter. In these experiments, the child's looks were systematically varied. Sometimes the boy or girl was very good-looking (the child's natural appearance). Sometimes, however, the same child was made up to be singularly unappealing. He or she had dark circles under the eyes and stringy hair.

The researchers found that even in the best of times (when the "couple" had had a pleasant encounter), women were less gentle with the unappealing child than with the cute one. They were more likely to punish a homely child than an attractive child for errors made in homework. When the woman was angry at the man, however, things got worse, and even more unfair. In more trying circumstances, women were reasonably restrained with cute children, but they really "took things out" on homely ones. Evidently, beauty protects children from others' anger; ugliness makes them a moving target.

A recent Associated Press story provides a telling example of this finding. The headline read:

> KIDNAPPER SAYS TOT IS TOO PRETTY TO KILL
>
> METAIRIE, La. (AP)—A 17-month old girl, snatched from her home by a gunman who stuffed her into a gift-wrapped box, was found unhurt after a man telephoned her anxious parents and said she was too pretty to kill, authorities say.
> "He called and told us . . . she was such a beautiful baby, otherwise he would have wasted her," the toddler's father, Ron Hocum, said later Tuesday. (Associated Press, 4 February 1981)

A critic might object that these studies were limited to examining only how strangers treat children. The studies do not tell us how real parents reach to their own children. This criticism loses some of its punch, however, when we recall that, in real life, people in authority (social workers, policemen) often know little about the children with whom they must interact except how attractive they are. These strangers, however, certainly have power over the children.

There is some evidence, however, that, in real life, physically unappealing children are more likely to be battered. Why is this? Does the neglected, battered child become ugly? Or is the child battered because he or she is ugly? Probably both processes operate. Berkowitz and Frodi (1978) comment:

> These physical characteristics can obviously result from the treatment their parents give them but once formed they can also heighten the chances that the children will be mistreated again. The foundation is laid when the youngster's appearance is unpleasant to their mothers and fathers. As a result, the parents may develop even more negative feelings about their children, and consequently they are more inclined to beat them. If the adults then happen to be angry for some reason, their offsprings' looks might be the extra spark to a violent outburst, especially when the children are misbehaving. (p. 20)

Taken at face value, the preceding studies suggest that, in general, parents and teachers do tend to direct their anger toward unattractive children and that the latter get punished most harshly.

Ugly or Sexy = Sinful in Adulthood

Adults may not get citizenship reports, but their characters are judged by others and these judgments can be influenced by how they look.

Figure 3.5. Hieronymus Bosch, *Ascent to Calvary*, c. 1505. Bosch painted in an era that believed a man's face reflected his inner nature. Christ's killers, as hideous as caricatures, are living images of bestiality.

One fascinating study went a step further than the usual studies by finding that beauty is good in some contexts but a distinct disadvantage in others.

Most people have been in situations where another's comments seem difficult to interpret. "I wonder what they meant by that?" you ask. On the one hand, the remark might be very innocent. But then again. . . . An experiment was conducted to examine just this situation (Hochberg and Galper 1974). Men and women were asked to look over some "case histories." One history sketched a conversation between a secretary and her boss. The other case was an encounter between a social worker and her client. Each conversation ended with an ambiguous statement. "What," men and women were asked, "does the secretary or social worker 'really mean' by that [the ambiguous statement]?" The participants were also shown a snapshot of the secretary's or social worker's face. Sometimes she had a "highly sexual" (or attractive) face and, at other times, a "socially undesirable" (or unattractive) one.

The encounter between the secretary and her boss was reported as follows: The secretary had just been assigned to the company's vice-president—a young, fast-rising, married man. He thanked her for taking dictation, and she asked, "Is there anything else you would like?" The men and women in the experiment were asked what she really meant by this question: (1) that she was available for a more intimate relationship, (2) that she was flirting but had no intention of following through (3) that she was skilled in *all* aspects of scretarial services— arranging schedules, devising filing systems, etc., or (4) that she was simply being polite and courteous (Holchberg and Galper 1974, 40).

The men and women's attributions depended on what the secretary looked like. They were less likely to assume her intentions were honorable if she had a sexy face. This result demonstrates that attractiveness is not always equated with innocence.

The encounter between the social worker and her client was described in equally ambiguous terms. The social worker was sent to interview a woman on welfare. The client was suspected of holding a job while receiving welfare payments. The interview makes it clear that the client is guilty of fraud; in fact, she has even acquired a modest set of investments. After outlining the penalties for such fraud, the social worker says to the client (who is in tears): "It doesn't have to be as bad as that. You seem to be an intelligent woman, and I like you. Let's talk about it some more." The experimenters asked, what does she really mean by this comment? (1) That if the client paid back the money she had stolen she may get off with only a reprimand; (2) that there must be some way out of the mess; (3) the social worker was just being kind and reassuring, to stop the client from crying; (4) that the social worker would cover up the fraud if given a sufficient bribe.

The looks of the social worker also had an influence on the attributions made about her. It was a more likely assumption that an ugly social worker would accept a bribe rather than an attractive social worker.

Other studies have also found that character judgments of adults are influenced by what the individuals look like and that, in general, "what is ugly is deviant." We have already discussed how more symptoms of psychopathology are attributed to unattractive people than to attractive people. It has also been found that physically unattractive people are more likely than the attractive to be seen as having epilepsy (Hannson and Duffield 1976), as being politically radical, and as being homosexual (Unger, Hilderbrand, and Mader 1982b).

What about in disciplining adults—do looks matter in this area? Next, we will consider how attractiveness is important in the justice system.

BEAUTY = A FRIEND IN COURT

Does appearance influence justice? Clearly, judges and lawyers think so. Albert L. Twesme, chief justice of the Seventh Judicial District of the State of Wisconsin, observes:

Figure 3.6. Charles Hatfield, 1943.

I have spent 34 years as a trial judge in Wisconsin. It has always been my observation that anyone connected with a thief, including the attorneys, almost always does better if he appears in proper clothing and with proper grooming. Attorneys are well aware of this.

In my many years on the trial bench, I have seen many men and women brought into court, charged with an alleged crime. The first time they appear in Court, they have usually just been arrested. Their "Initial Appearance" is very brief. They are merely informed of the charges pending against them and their Constitutional rights. Inasmuch as they have just recently been picked off the street, brought to jail and then to Court, they have had no opportunity to alter their appearance. Many are dirty, disheveled and unkempt.

The next time I see them is at the trial before a jury. When they appear at the trial it is sometimes difficult to recognize them as the same persons! At the trial they are clean, well-groomed and dressed in proper attire. What caused the difference? I would say that the attorneys as well as the clients are fully aware of the importance of appearance, and feel that their appearance is vitally important to the decision makers, whether the decision maker be the jury or judge. I'm sure that if the clients are not aware of this important factor, the attorney is, and will do everything possible to present a favorable appearance for his client as well as for himself.

I recall an extreme case in which the attorney was caught in a situation where his appearance was not exemplary and he lost the case. His mishap impressed upon me very vividly the importance of appearance in the courtroom.

This lawyer had a physique common to many people. He had a very large pot belly. To hold his pants up he wore only a belt which, because of his shape, served its purpose well since it was anchored above the pot belly. In his final argument to the jury he became very emotional and used a great number of gestures. One of his gestures included stretching his arms up straight towards the ceiling directly above him. This caused a disaster! In that fatal move his pot belly disappeared and his pants fell to his ankles. He turned away from the jury, bent over and tried to retrieve his pants. In doing so, the back fly of his long winter underwear spread open and his posterior was exposed to the jury. But since his pot belly had returned to its normal position, he was unable to unbuckle his belt nor could he pull up his trousers. He then continued to bend over with his hands to his ankles as he waddled out of the courtroom. He did return to the courtroom to finish his argument, but needless to say, all persons present were looking at the floor with their hands over their mouths trying to conceal their amusement. He lost the case. The next day the local daily paper published an article about the case on the front page with the headline, "Lawyer loses pants in lawsuit."

At the time this happened there was a very popular TV series on the air entitled, "I've Got a Secret." Although I talked to the lawyer several times, I was never able to convince him to appear on the show!

In the trial of any civil or criminal jury case the judge is required to instruct the jury on the law as it applies to that particular case. Included in those instructions are matters that are to be taken into consideration by the jury. In those sets of instructions there is one instruction that is given in each case. It is called the "Credibility of the Witnesses." The judge very clearly calls the jury's attention to one of several things they can take into consideration in determining "Credibility." It says in part, "In determining the weight and credit you should give to the testimony of each witness, you should consider . . . his appearance on the witness stand. . . ."

It seems apparent that, since this exact instruction is given in each case, our judicial system has long recognized the importance of "appearance" in the courtroom. (personal communication)

Lawyers agree that people should dress appropriately for their court appearance, but they disagree about just how to go about it. Each lawyer may give a different piece of advice. Attorney David Schutter says he tries to get his clients to look as if they have tried their best to dress for the courtroom but just do not know how. "I once told a client to borrow a shirt from his brother, who was bigger than him; a jacket from his father who was smaller than him; and to go out and buy a tie that was out of style" (Harada-Stone 1983, B–1).

District Judge Marie Milks advises her clients to dress respectfully and to cover tatoos and other markings that might bring negative associations to jurors' minds. Attorney F. Lee Bailey (who represented newspaper heiress Patricia Hearst) says he advises all his clients to dress "conservatively, not flashily." (During Patti Hearst's 1976 trial, there was much comment on her transformation from a revolutionary in khaki shirt and baggy pants at the time of her arrest into a woman who wore nail polish and dresses and pantsuits when she appeared in court.)

San Francisco's Melvin Belli, the self-described "King of Torts," represented Erin Felming in the Groucho Marx estate case. He compares going to court with going to church—"you dress up for it." Belli does not allow anyone on his side to wear "wild ties or suits" in court. "If your main witness comes in with jewels and a fancy hairdo, that can swing the balance." Belli tells clients and witnesses not to chew gum and not to wear dark glasses, white shoes, or message T-shirts and sweat shirts (Abrams 1983, B-1)

Although legal professionals vary on the specifics of what to wear and how to wear it, they agree it is important to present a good appearance. They *know* that appearance does matter in the courtroom. The evidence we will review next clearly shows that judges and jurors are people, like everyone else. When faced with momentous and difficult decisions, they use everything they have. Their decisions are influenced by the appearance of lawyers, of the plaintiffs and defendants, and of the witnesses.

The Defendant Puts in an Appearance

People believe physical attractiveness should not be important in the courtroom (Efran 1974). They argue that only the defendant's previous history and character should influence the jury's decision. Yet, there is

Figure 3.7. Wanted by the FBI.

clear evidence that most people are unable to put their prejudices aside and to act on their convictions.

WENDING YOUR WAY THROUGH THE JUSTICE SYSTEM

Actually, there are several steps in the justice process from the commission of a crime until a case is tried. At each of these points, authorities have to make choices. The choices they make have an enormous impact on the adversaries' lives. Most cases start simply enough. Imagine, for example, a police car cruising along a dimly lit street at 3:00 A.M. Out of the corner of her eye, the patrolwoman spots a fight. She is a little nervous, a little excited. It has been a long night. She and her patrol partner jump out of the scout car and run over to break up the fight. The choices they make, from this point on, will determine what happens to the brawlers. The first decisions the police will have to make are:

Who started things? Who should be taken into the station? What are they guilty of? Was this just a "friendly scuffle" or assault and battery?

Once charges are filed against the brawlers, more choices remain. The prosecuting attorney and defense attorney will try to negotiate an out-of-court settlement. The lawyers' predictions about how well they can do in court will affect the sort of plea-bargaining in which they are willing to engage. If the case does go to court, more choices remain. The jurors have to decide whether or not the defendant is guilty and, if so, what his or her sentence should be. It is easy to see how the defendant's looks might be important at every step of such a justice process.

Criminologists have collected evidence showing that if defendants are good-looking people:

1. they are less likely to get caught at illicit activities;

2. if caught, they are less likely to be reported;

3. even if the case does come to court, judges and jurors are more likely to be lenient with them.

Let's review all this evidence:

WHO GETS CAUGHT? WHO GETS REPORTED?

In one daring study (Mace 1972), psychologists persuaded 440 young men and women to shoplift items from ten large stores in a major city. Clerks were less likely to spot shoplifters who were well-groomed and neatly dressed than to catch those with long, stringy hair and sloppily groomed. Presumably, clerks are less likely to suspect good-looking customers of shoplifting and are thus less likely to be watching their every move.

Clerks are not the only ones that notice shoplifters. Customers also notice strange behavior in those around them. It has been found that customers are more likely to report bogus shoplifters if the lawbreakers have an unappealing appearance rather than an appealing one (Steffensmeier and Terry 1973). In two different chain grocery stores and in a discount department store, an accomplice blatantly shoplifted in the presence of customers. The man or woman shoplifter dressed either in a "straight" style or in a "hippie" style. The straight shoplifter looked like a typical professional out on a shopping break. A "hippie" shoplifter was described in the following way: "He wore soiled patched blue jeans, blue workman's shirt, and blue denim jacket; well-worn, scuffed shoes with no socks. He had long and unruly hair with a ribbon tied around his forehead. He was unshaven and had a small beard" (p. 442).

Hippie shoplifters were not only more likely to be reported, but they were reported with more enthusiasm. For example, one customer said, "That son-of-a-bitch hippie over there stuffed a banana down his coat." (Incidentally, men and women were equally likely to be reported for shoplifting.) Apparently, if you are going to be a thief, you would do well to be neatly dressed.

PRETTY IS AS PRETTY CAN GET AWAY WITH

Why are people eager to report to authorities the illicit behavior of homely people and so reluctant to turn in attractive people? One study, which explored how people felt about the plight of attractive versus unattractive shoplifters, helps us understand why.

In this experiment (Deseran and Chung 1979), men and women were asked to act as store detectives. The researchers claimed to be investigating the process by which the detectives, who monitor the television cameras in department stores, make their decisions on whether various "suspicious actions" of shoppers are "reportable."

The men and women were asked to view a scene on videotape and to pay close attention because questions would be asked later. The "detectives" observed a woman browsing in a bookstore. After thumbing through a few books, she stuck one of the books into her handbag, sauntered past the cashier, and went out the door. In one version, the woman looked like a "hippie"—her hair was frizzy, she was not wearing makeup, and she wore a sweater with no bra, a long denim skirt, and sandals. In another version, the same woman was "straight" in appearance—her hair was neatly styled, she wore makeup, and she had on a conservative blouse, skirt, and shoes.

The "detectives" were asked how upset the woman would probably be if she were caught, tried, and convicted of shoplifting. Observers took it for granted the "straight" woman would suffer most if she were convicted of shoplifting. For example, they assumed she would be more emotionally upset and more concerned about what her family and friends would think of her than would be the "hippie" woman. Observers, then, may be more hesitant to turn in conventional-appearing people (who look "just like them") than people who are unattractive and seem very different from themselves.

This bevy of experiments suggests that bias in favor of the attractive occurs long before a case ever gets to the courtroom. Overall, the evidence indicates:

> Attractive people, especially if they are neatly dressed in the conventional manner, are less likely to be *caught* committing a crime. (Since they are less likely to be suspected, their actions are not as carefully

scrutinized, and their crimes go relatively undetected.) Even if they are caught, attractive people are less likely to be *reported*. (In part, this may be because people who observe them like them. In part, it is because people care more about what happens to them; they emphasize how personally devastating it would be for them to be convicted of a crime.)

WHO GETS PUNISHED?

"Gentlemen of the jury," said the Defense Attorney, now beginning to warm to his summation, "the real question here before you is, shall this beautiful, young woman be forced to languish away her loveliest years in a dark prison cell? Or shall she be set free to return to her cozy little apartment at 4134 Seaside Street—there to spend her lonely, loveless hours in her boudoir, lying beside her little Princess phone, 312–6642?" (*Playboy's Complete Book of Party Jokes* 1972, 148)

For ethical reasons, legal scholars are prohibited from observing, much less conducting, experiments with real jurors who are deliberating real cases. They can, however, do the next best thing. They can study the reactions of jurors and lay people to transcripts or videotapes of court cases. Such simulated jury studies clarify that the defendants' looks are critically important in determining whether or not they are found guilty and, if so, how severe a sentence they receive.

In one early study (Efran 1974), students were asked to make judgments about other students who were accused of cheating. If cheaters were good-looking, they were less likely to be found guilty and were given less severe punishments. Good looks have also been found to be important in other studies, at least under certain conditions (Leventhal and Krate 1977; Sigall and Ostrove 1975; Solomon and Schopler 1978; Steward 1980; Storck and Sigall 1979).

Most of the studies that examine the importance of looks in the courtroom have studied the impact on sentencing of extraordinarily good looks versus ugliness. What if defendants are "average" in appearance? Will they get lenient sentences like good-looking defendants, severe sentences like homely ones, or somewhere in between? Most researchers have assumed a so-so defendant would fall somewhere in between. They are probably right, but one pioneering study suggests "it ain't necessarily so."

Solomon and Schopler (1978) were curious about the fate of people with average looks. The researchers speculated that average-looking defendants may actually receive harsher sentences than either strikingly good-looking or ugly defendants. When jury members are asked to make a decision, they use everything they have to come to the right decision. Any information deviant from the normal may be given greater weight. Unusually attractive defendants might be judged most leniently on the assumption that "what is beautiful is good." Homely defendants, on the other hand, may also be judged somewhat leniently out of pity. An average-looking defendant, however, does not get the benefit of the doubt for either reason; thus, he or she may get the harshest sentence.

In a study designed to test this idea (Solomon and Schopler 1978), men at the University of North Carolina evaluated a case of a young woman accused of embezzling $10,000. The woman was either attractive, average-looking, or unattractive. As might be expected, the attractive woman received the most lenient sentence. On the average, the men suggested a sentence of about 12 months. They were much harsher with unattractive women—they gave her an average prison sentence of 18½ months. The average-looking woman, however, received the harshest sentence of all. The men wanted to lock her up for 19½ months!

WHEN THE FRIEND IN COURT FAILS

While clear that, generally, an attractive defendant has a real advantage, there are, naturally, some exceptions. Sometimes, appearance does not seem to matter one way or the other. In rare instances, good looks seem actually to act *against* a defendant as shown in the following three cases.

1. Whether the appearance of defendants works for or against them seems to depend on the type of crime they have committed. When the crime (say burglary) could be committed by anyone (as is usually the case), good-looking or not good-looking, attractive defendants get the usual advantages. They are unlikely to be found guilty, but even if they are, they get less severe sentences than others. If it seems the defendants used their good looks to prey on others, however (i.e., "con artists" who use their charisma to swindle others), evidently that is the last straw. Bogus jurors hold the swindlers' good looks against them; this time it is the attractive defendant who receives harsher treatment.

For example, in one study (Sigall and Ostrove 1975), if the defendant committed a regular burglary—breaking into a neighbor's apartment and stealing $2,200—an attractive woman was judged more leniently than an unattractive woman. However, when the defendant "ingratiated herself to a middle-aged bachelor and induced him to invest $2,200 in a nonexistent corporation," the beautiful woman was assigned an unusually long prison sentence. The homely swindler did better.

2. Another study found other limits to our "love affair" with good-looking people. People will give the attractive the benefit of the doubt under normal conditions. But if the crime gets too serious, the good-looking lose their advantage (Piehl 1977). Mock jurors were asked to

review a case involving a traffic accident and to sentence the offender to a term of imprisonment fitting the seriousness of the crime. "Jurors" read one of three different versions of the case, each describing different consequences. When the consequence was trivial, a good-looking woman offender was given a lighter sentence. However, when the offense was serious (she killed an innocent motorist), the attractive woman "had the book thrown at her." (For other research indicating that jurors sometimes lean over backwards to avoid being biased—ending up being biased in favor of homely defendants, see Friend and Vinson [1974].)

3. Finally, other studies suggest that individual biases may be tempered somewhat by the jury process. In one study (Izzet and Leginski 1974), men and women were asked their first impressions of a defendant in a negligent automobile homicide case. At first, men and women expressed the usual biases in favor of attractive defendants. They felt attractive defendants deserved a less severe sentence than others. Then, however, jurors were asked to state their recommended sentence, to list their reasons for deciding on that sentence, and then to deliberate with other members of the "jury." All this talk had its effect. In the end, the attractiveness effect disappeared! Regardless of how attractive the defendant was, in the end it was the facts of the matter that counted: all the defendants got the same sentence. Another study (Baumeister and Darley 1982) demonstrated that when more factual information is added to the case, biases in favor of attractive defendants also decline. This research suggests that, as simulated jury studies come closer to replicating *actual* courtroom settings, we find that jurors are less swayed by defendants' looks than has been assumed.

SUMMING UP FOR THE DEFENSE

We have found that good-looking defendants have several advantages.

1. They are less likely to be caught.

2. If caught, they are less likely to be reported.

3. If their case comes to court, judges and jurors are more likely to be lenient.

The research, then, suggests that people ought to appear at their best in court. Probably, dressing appropriately is all one can do. Some books suggest people can do more—that one can *Dress for Courtroom Success*. They explain how the underworld Mafia figure can, with the right tailor, turn into a Walter Mitty; how the arrogant showgirl can appear to be a simple housewife. Such transformations are probably not possible. We communicate our personalities in a thousand different ways.

Even when we try to fool others via dress and demeanor, our person-alities tend to shine right through (Mossis 1981).

Paul Mullin Ganley, a prominent Honolulu trial lawyer, describes one such case of "show and tell."

> A while back I had my arm twisted by a judge and reluctantly under-took the representation of a young cocktail waitress fighting to regain custody of her child from the State. As it turned out, she was a warm, loving mother—but she certainly didn't look the part. I coached her on how she should try to appear in court, but she kept missing the point. Each outfit she wore to my office for my perusal appeared to be sleazier than the last. I was greatly relieved when I met her at court on the day she was to take the witness stand; she had gotten the idea—she really looked nice and sweet. She had on a cardigan sweater, tailored slacks, appropriate heels and not too much makeup. As she sat in the witness chair awaiting the judge to enter to reconvene the trial, I noticed she had buttoned her sweater only part way up. Thinking it looked a little bit untidy, I advised her to "button it all the way up . . . or take it off." I then walked to the back of the courtroom and stepped into the hall to encourage waiting witnesses to be patient. When I returned to the courtroom, I was stunned. She had removed her sweater to expose her long-sleeved T-shirt, which was fine except that the front of the T-shirt had colored pictures of two large fried eggs at strategic feminine points. To make things far worse, the yolks were transparent. I literally ran toward the witness stand, repeating in my stage whisper that she should "put on the sweater!" But just then the judge came out of his chambers, everyone rose, he took one look and with a disapproving judicial eye said, "Too late, Mr. Ganley, too late."

Too often, our real personalities shine through.

The Victim

Thus far, we have focused on the role the defendant's appearance plays in the courtroom. What about the plaintiff's appearance? Presumably, victims are not on trial. But researchers have found the victim's at-tractiveness can play a critical role in decisions reached in the courtroom.

Criminologists have been intrigued with finding out the role of both the defendant's and the victim's attractiveness in rape trials. In such cases, it is easy to see how the jurors, in their attempt to piece together what happened and why, might be influenced by *both* the defendant's and the victim's appearance. Most criminologists are convinced rape is a crime of violence (Amir 1971). Many feminist writers agree (Brown-miller 1975). In approximately 70 percent of all rape reports, the offender threatens force against the victim. Occasionally, physical force is used.

This statement by a rape victim from a police report illustrates such a case:

> He hit me in the face and knocked me on the floor. He pulled off my robe and nightgown and I screamed and he threatened to kill me. He stuffed the nightgown in my mouth and tied the rest around my throat and the gown strangled me. He tied my hands behind my back and he pressed my neck so hard I passed out. Then he asked me if I needed air and I nodded and he let it loose a bit but still kept it in my mouth. He tied my legs up to the tie on my hands . . . then he got my butcher knife from the kitchen and ran the point all over my body. (Chappell and James 1978, 59)

The public, however, still tends to assume rape is a crime of passion. In judging such "crimes of passion," the parties' appearance may affect the attributions jurors make about the crime.

IF THE RAPIST IS TRIED AND CLAIMS INNOCENCE

Most rapists have a clear idea of the kind of woman they look for. Schram observes that when offenders were asked to describe their victim preferences in detail, the picture that emerged was of the "all American woman"—a nice, friendly, young, pretty, white housewife or college student. These same offenders were asked to indicate what would be an undesirable victim. Leading the list were children and women who were crippled, dirty, sick, pregnant, retarded, fat, middle-aged, or prostitutes (see Chappel and James 1978, 8–9).

Thus, in a trial, the credibility of the rapists' claim of innocence may depend on the looks of his victim. If she is stunningly beautiful, the jury may wonder "How could he resist?" and they may doubt his denials. If the victim is ugly, however, they may doubt *her* claims. One social worker we interviewed complained bitterly about a rape case she had handled. A retarded woman was brutally beaten and raped. The woman was big and awkward. She mumbled; she drooled. Everyone who knew the rapist was convinced he was guilty. He was a violent man. He had beaten and raped women before. But the jury could not believe in the crime. "Why would he want to rape *her*?" one juror asked. Thus, we might suspect defendants are more likely to be assumed guilty if their victims are beautiful. In one study (Thornton 1977), researchers found that "jurors" believed both a stunning woman's and a homely woman's account of being raped, but they gave the assailant a longer prison sentence when he raped an attractive woman. (Perhaps they felt he had done greater harm, somehow!)

The credibility of the accused rapist's claim to innocence may also depend, of course, on what *he* looks like. In one study (Jacobson 1981), men and women read a case description like the following (Jacobsen's description was adopted from Jones and Aronsen, 1973).

It was ten o'clock at night and Judy W. was getting out of an evening class at a large Midwestern university. She walked across the campus toward her car, which was parked two blocks off campus. A man was walking across the campus in the same direction as Judy W. and began to follow her.

Less than a block from Judy W.'s car, the man accosted her. In the ensuing struggle, he stripped her and raped her. A passerby heard her screams and called the police. They arrived at the scene within minutes.

Judy W. told the police that she had never seen her attacker before that night. Based on her description, the police arrested Charles E., a student whom they found in the vicinity of the attack. Judy W. positively identified Charles E. as the man who raped her. Charles E. swears that he is innocent. He testified that he was just taking a break from studying by going out for a walk and that it was just a coincidence that he was in the vicinity and that it was a coincidence that he matched Judy W.'s description of her attacker. (p. 251)

The defendant's appearance turned out to be tremendously important in determining whether or not judges "let him off the hook." If Charles E. was handsome, men and women were likely to think he was just out for a walk and that his resemblance to the rapist was coincidental. Not so, if Charles E. was homely. Then he was likely to be seen as guilty. Judges were also asked how long a prison sentence they would recommend for Charles E. if he were found guilty. If these judges had their druthers, the handsome defendant would have to spend about ten years in prison, while the homely defendant would be locked up for almost fourteen years.

Judy W.'s attractiveness also had some effect. In accordance with previous research, judges were more likely to assume Charles E. was guilty when Judy W. was ravishing. They were also less sympathetic to a rapist of an attractive woman than to a rapist of an unattractive woman. (Deitz and Byrnes [1981] also found that an unattractive rapist is more likely to be considered guilty than an attractive rapist).

IF THE RAPIST HAS NOT BEEN APPREHENDED

Unfortunately, sometimes we never learn much about the rapist. It has been estimated that as few as 3 percent of rapists are actually convicted for the crime (Gage and Schurr 1976). Often rapists are not convicted because they are not caught in the first place, or, if caught, they never make it to the courtroom.

Even though the rape case may never make it to trial, people hearing about the case still form opinions about it. In these cases, however, things work a little differently. Here *only* the physical at-tractiveness of the victim can have an influence. The rapist remains faceless. Some evidence does indicate that the physical attractiveness of the victim matters. For example, in one study (Seligman, Brickman, and Koulack 1977), researchers told men and women they were inter-ested in people's reactions to local crimes. They asked the individuals to look at a wire service photo and a news story about an incident that happened to a twenty-seven-year-old nurse. The newspaper articled described the following incident: As the nurse was returning home from the hospital about 12:30 A.M., she was followed by a man who pulled her into an alley and—depending on the version of the story the subject received—either (1) hit and kicked her, (2) took her purse, or (3) raped her. Her attacker fled by climbing a fence and had not yet been appre-hended. The photograph in the newspaper article pictured either an attractive or a homely nurse.

Did mock "jurors" see any relationship between the nurse's at-tractiveness and the crimes that occurred? If the woman was attractive, both men and women thought she was unusually likely to be a rape victim. Jurors were asked if the nurse "might somehow have provoked the man into treating her as he did." It is obvious to people why the rapist might attack the beautiful woman—her mere existence is enough to explain the rape. It is not so obvious why he would want to rape the ugly nurse. In the rape case, jurors tended to assume the unattractive nurse must have behaved provocatively, that she must have "asked for it." For the mugging and the robbery, on the other hand, attractive and unattractive women were perceived as equally likely to be victims and also equally likely to provoke (or not to provoke) the incident. (A study by Tieger [1981] secured much the same results.)

Rape is not the only crime in which the victim's attractiveness matters. One study found that defendants were most likely to be convicted when their victims were portrayed by the attorney as both "beautiful and blameless." In this study, the crime was automobile theft (Kerr 1978).

Summing Up for the Defense

These studies indicate that, in general, the handsome and the beautiful have a friend in court. Good-looking defendants are less likely to be found guilty, and, even if convicted, they are more likely to receive lenient sentences. Good-looking victims are better able to make their cases stick. In the last section of this chapter, we will see how looks affect our willingness or reluctance to help others.

BEAUTY=A "FRIEND IN NEED"

Who is more likely to receive assistance—a good-looking person or an ugly one? From reading this book, you would probably respond, "The attractive person, of course." And you would be right—most Good Samaritans have an eye out for good-looking Pharisees.

What about when you need "to get by with a little help from a friend?" To whom are you most likely to turn? If, out of habit, you

Figure 3.8.   Courtesy, Eileen Kalahar Hatfield, Boblo Island, Michigan, 1929.

answer, "A good-looking friend," think again. This time you may well be wrong. For most people, the friend to turn to when in need is a homely friend. Here is the evidence to support these contentions.

Who Gets Help?

In fairy tales, the damsel in distress is inevitably beautiful. It's lucky that she is. A number of experiments document that a beautiful damsel is more likely to get help than an ugly crone; and, if by chance he should ever be in need of aid, the ruggedly handsome knight will more likely receive help than his homelier peers.

Imagine yourself in the following situation: You walk into a phone booth and find a dime lying on the shelf below the phone. It is not much, but you are secretly pleased about your find. It saves you from having to dig out your own dime. As you are leaving the booth, either a lovely woman or plain one approaches you and says, "Excuse me, I think I might have left a dime in this booth, did you find it?" What would you say? Would it matter if the woman was homely versus attractive? Most individuals are more likely to return the money if the woman is good-looking. In one study (Sroufe, Chaikin, Cook, and Freeman 1977) that staged this situation, 87 percent of men and women returned the dime to an attractive woman, while only 64 percent returned the dime to the same woman dressed up to be homely.

Similarly, men are more willing to go to the trouble of doing trivial favors, such as mailing letters or giving directions, for attractive women than for unattractive women (Wilson 1978), especially if she begins her request by introducing herself (Harrell 1978). A cynic might insinuate that men are willing to help beautiful damsels in distress because, if she were to utter, "How can I possibly repay you?" they could easily come up with an answer. Perhaps, but that is not the whole story. Researchers find that people are simply more likely to help beautiful women (and men), even if the aided persons will never know who helped them.

In one experiment, when men and women walked into a telephone booth at the Detroit airport, they found an application form clipped to a stamped envelope. A note was attached to it: "Dear Dad. Have a nice trip. Please remember to mail this application before you leave Detroit on your flight to New York." It was signed either "Love, Linda" or "Love, Bob." Obviously, "Dad" had forgotten.

The envelope was addressed to the psychology department at a local university. The application contained the name of either Linda or Robert Smith and other standardized information: home address, educational background, professional references, grade point average, and

Graduate Record Examination scores. Attached to the application was the ubiquitous picture of a good-looking or of a homely man or woman.

Did the harried callers take the time to mail the application? They probably realized that, if they did not, the applicant would lose his/her chance to go to graduate school, but what a bother. They had to seal it all up and find a mailbox—and they were busy. It was found that men and women were more likely to take the time to mail the application if the applicant was good-looking than if he or she was ugly (Benson, Karabenick, and Lerner 1976). (Knowing what we do about the importance of beauty, it is perhaps fortunate the "Good Samaritans" didn't steal the ugly applicants' application fees). The favors were done even though "Linda" or "Bob" or "Dad" would never be around to ask, "How can I repay you?"

Perhaps it's understandable that when we're just talking about returning dimes, giving directions and mailing letters, favoritism will influence our willingness to proffer aid. But some researchers have speculated that, when the chips are really down, beauty does count for less. Emergencies require immediate and impulsive action. Often there is not much time to even notice what the damsel in distress looks like. Or is there? Well, even if the Good Samaritans *could* notice, some have speculated that, in an emergency, almost everybody who needs help *will* get it, regardless of their looks. But do they?

Researchers have conceived of some ingenious experiments to test these ideas. To everyone's surprise, researchers find that, even in an emergency when time is short and things are critical, beauty still counts. For example, when speeding down a highway, a driver catches a glimpse of a woman stranded beside a car with a flat tire. The driver has enough time to assess her looks before deciding whether or not to stop to help. Apparently, in this situation attractive women are more likely to get their tires changed than homely women (Athanasiou and Greene 1973).

Another example: If men are approached on the street by a woman with her arm swathed in a blood-soaked bandage and she asks for money to get a tetanus shot (she was bitten by a rat while conducting an experiment), they are more likely to donate money to her if she is beautiful (West and Brown 1975). In this study, it was also found that if the emergency did not seem to be so severe (there was no blood-soaked bandage), there were no differences in the donations to an attractive versus an unattractive woman. This study suggests that, when the chips are down, beauty might count for even more, not less.

(As these stories of "damsels in distress" get increasingly bizarre, you may wonder: "What's next?" We'll stop here.)

Why are people so extraordinarily willing to help good-looking people? Edmund Burke observed in the eighteenth century that "beauty in distress is much the most affecting beauty" (Burke 1909). Several explanations for these experimental results have been offered:

1) Possibly good-looking people are simply better liked at first sight than ugly ones. Scientists have found that most people are eager to help those they love, willing to help those they like, and reluctant to do anything for those they dislike. In fact, most people seem to take genuine pleasure in the *sufferings* of their enemies (Rubin 1973; Bramel et al. 1968). One reason people are so willing to help good-looking people, then, is that they like them.

2) A second reason people may run to aid the good-looking is that when the latter express their gratitude it can be unusually rewarding. (Especially if they add: "What can I ever do to repay you?")

3) In almost all the preceding experiments, the knight in shining armor was a man, and the damsel in distress was a woman. That scenario is consistent with traditional sex role stereotypes. If beautiful women are seen as more feminine (as they seem to be), they may also appear to be more helpless (Bar-Tal and Saxe 1976b). Thus, it may not be surprising that attractive women get more help. Consistent with this argument is the finding that men are more likely to help women in dresses than women wearing more masculine-looking clothes (Harris and Bays 1973).

Beautiful women, then, are seen as feminine and needy. Ugly women are perceived as able to take care of themselves. In fact, of course, the reverse is probably true. It is the ugly—the old, the sick, the poor—who are generally most in need of help, but least likely to get it. One woman from THE GROUP observed:

> I always thought that I wouldn't mind being a woman so much, if I could be a beautiful woman. When there's a debate about the ERA or something, my men friends talk about all the advantages women have. What they really mean is *beautiful* women. I wouldn't mind the fact that it's a man's world, if I had someone to open doors for me, carry my packages, and so forth, but I don't. I can remember when I was hiking around Lassen with some male chums. When we came to a difficult part in the trail, all the men stopped, cleaned out their pockets, and handed me all this junk, asking if I'd put it in my pack so they wouldn't be "unbalanced" during the climb. There I was, trying to scramble up the rocks with this big pack, swinging wildly from side to side. When you're an ugly woman, you don't get tender attention—you get all the dirty jobs, because you're inferior. You're expected to clip the hedges, shovel the sidewalk, take the car in for servicing. Your time doesn't count for anything.

In contrast, here is the self-disclosure made by a very attractive, professional woman: "I can manipulate people because of what I look like. I can get advantages—people pay a little more attention—they are just a little more willing when I ask for something. I'm aware of this and probably use it."

The evidence suggests the above women are right. Good Samaritans are most likely to help good-looking Pharisees and tend to leave ugly ones lying by the side of the road. But what about people who are paid and expected to provide help—doctors, nurses, policemen, social workers? Do they discriminate on the basis of the looks of their patients or clients? Maybe. Maybe not. We have already devoted a whole section to how therapists can be influenced by the attractiveness of their clients, but such biases may not occur in other helping professions—or, at least, not on the surface.

We would think, for example, that medical professionals are above being influenced by the physical attractiveness of their patients. In one study, 108 first- and second-year medical students in a southern United States medical school were presented with photographic identification cards and hypothetical reports of illness for eight students. The illnesses included mononucleosis, bronchitis, a migraine headache, a re-injury of a recurrent knee problem, lryngitis, acne, a cold sore, and a common cold. The medical students were asked to imagine they only had one hour on a busy Saturday morning at a college health center and that all eight students had been waiting anxiously since 10:00 A.M. Their task was to review the medical reports and rank the students in the order they would see them. (The researchers had arranged it so that the illnesses and the photographs were paired in different ways.) Attractive patients were not put at the head of the line. These future medical professionals were influenced only by the severity of the illness and not by the patients' attractiveness (Silvestro 1982).

So far, we have focused on only one side of the coin—how Good Samaritans respond to good-looking versus ugly Pharisees. What about the other side of the coin? Who do the *Pharisees*—in desperate need of help—ask to come to their aid?

Who Is Asked to Give Help?

"Them who's got" may get, but the evidence suggests that "them who's got" are not likely to be asked to *give*. A wide array of experiments document this contention. In the typical experiment, researchers bring people into a university setting and assign them to tasks far beyond their abilities. Workers may be missing certain parts or information they need to complete a project. Will they ask for assistance?

In such a situation, everyone has mixed feelings about asking for help. On the one hand, it becomes increasingly obvious that one is a fool not to ask for help. Time is running out, and there is no chance of getting anywhere without aid. On the other hand, no one likes to ask for help. It lowers our self-esteem and is acutely embarrassing (Homans 1974; Joffe 1953). It leaves us feeling vaguely in debt (Dillon 1968; Gross, Piliavin, Wallston, and Broll 1972; Hatfield, Walster, and Piliavin 1978).

It may be difficult, at best, for people to ask for help, but for most people, it is next to impossible to admit they need help from a strikingly good-looking person. They may be too much in awe of the attractive person's presumed intelligence and competence. They also want to be liked and they certainly do not want to inconvenience someone so good-looking. They care too much about what the person thinks of them to risk asking for help. So, in general, it is difficult for people to ask help of attractive people.

However, some things do reduce people's reluctance to seek help from others, attractive or otherwise. Anything that makes it *legitimate* to ask for help, helps. In fact, when it is legitimate to ask for help, we might even expect a bias in the opposite direction. When asking for help is legitimate, people might be especially prone to seek out the attractive.

For instance, it is "legitimate" to ask for help from someone *supposed* to provide us with help. Doctors, counselors, clergymen, teachers, and experimenters are there to help us out. Under such circumstances, the potential Good Samaritan's looks should have very little bearing on whether or not they are sought out for help. If we ask our dashing professor to help us with a paper, he might end up asking us out for coffee. If we ask the blonde stewardess if the flight is on time, she might stick around for a drink.

We can envision a second type of circumstance that makes it "legitimate" to ask for help. We may be so extraordinarily busy solving some difficult and important task (that only we can solve) that we do not mind asking for a little assistance—someone to make us a sandwich, sharpen our pencils, or turn down the nuclear reactor. In such situations, our self-esteem should not be affected by asking for help.

There is considerable evidence that the above logic is sound. For example, Stokes and Bickman (1974) found that it did not matter what a woman experimenter looked like if she was in a helping role. In those circumstances, women were quite comfortable asking the experimenter, beautiful or not, for assistance on an impossible task. However, if the same woman was introduced as just another student, hence, not an authority, women were less willing to approach a beautiful woman than a plain one.

In another experiment conducted at the Tel-Aviv University in Israel (Nadler 1980), it was found that women's willingness to approach an attractive woman for help was tempered by whether or not they expected to subsequently have a face-to-face meeting with her. The women were assigned the jobs of figuring out the meanings of certain rare Hebrew words. They were provided with the opportunity to consult with a partner on any words they did not know. Yet, the women were reluctant to do so. It was bad enough if the potential helper was an average-looking woman. It was more difficult if she was beautiful, and nearly impossible if she was beautiful and the women knew they would have to interact with her later. Apparently, the women were unwilling to expose their inadequacies to an attractive other if they expected to have to confront the person later.

Although people are concerned about exposing their weaknesses to those people they value (attractive people), there are sometimes special reasons to ask help of an attractive person of the opposite sex. Men in laundromats ask beautiful women their advice about detergents. Women attending football games ask questions of attractive men sitting next to them. In each case, the ploy is the same—to make the acquaintance of someone they want very much to see again.

In fact, a recent study demonstrates that at least women use just such ploys. In this study, Nadler, Shapira, and Ben-Itzhak (1982) observed potential Good Samaritans' responses to both men and women "Pharisees" (who were either unusually attractive or homely). Men and women listened to a detective story and then were asked to solve the mystery by answering sixteen questions about the story. The questions concerned the detail provided in the story and included inquiries such as, "What was the color of Helga's skirt when she met Heinrick at the bar?" It was arranged so that some of the questions were unanswerable, given the information provided in the story. Since the amateur detectives did not have enough information to answer the questions, they were allowed to ask help from their partners on as many questions as they wanted.

As in previous studies, men and women were extremely reluctant to ask good-looking members of the same sex for help. When the partner was the opposite sex, men were still more reluctant to ask help if she was attractive. The men seemed reluctant to admit to a beautiful woman that they needed any help. Women, on the other hand, were eager to ask handsome men to come to their aid. The women in the study asked for more help from an opposite sex partner if he was attractive than if he was unattractive. (And it is likely they had more in mind than just finding out the color of Helga's skirt.) As the authors suggested, women were probably just as concerned as men were with presenting a favorable self-image. However, displaying dependency on the opposite sex is a part of the feminine sex role, not a part of the masculine sex role.

Summary: Apparently, good-looking people are most likely to get a "little help from their friends" and least likely to be asked to give help.

Figure 4.1. Thomas and Mary Carey Kalahar, 1910.

Chapter 4

Romantic Beginnings

Recently, *Nutshell* magazine investigated the fantasies and realities of college romance. Following are two views—first from a man's perspective, then from a woman's:

> That's the way all of us are. Even the shy, sweet ones. Like everyone else, we college men are products of our environment. . . . We're warped by the media. We're conditioned by Charlie's Angels, by *Playboy* Advisor and *Penthouse* Forum and the *Sports Illustrated* bathing suit issue, by all those impossibly smooth airbrushes centerfolds, by rock 'n' roll lyrics and TV ads. We've got all that glamour coming at us, but we've also got a completely separate thing going with the Girl Next Door, who's healthy and wholesome and fun. We batter, bash, tug, and heave, but we can't quite seem to reconcile the two.
>
> . . . Mitchell, who's a little more cynical than most, says right away that the only thing college men want is to sleep with beautiful college women. . . . That is the way it is. Everybody has his own private rating system—not just 8's and 10's, but for some guys a real ob-

session. That's what college teaches us: how to gather and correlate data. Dan blames his attitude on a course he took during his sophomore year, "Game-Playing and Decision-Making"; now he assigns attractive women coefficients and plots out probabilities like a technician in the Pentagon war room. . . . An accounting student I once knew used a sliding scale based on 100. "I'd be happy," he would tell me, "with an 80." Sure— who wouldn't be? (Luke Whisnant, a graduate student at Washington University, Schwartzbaum & Whisnant, 1982, 44)

I thought college men would be tall and wear flannel shirts. I thought they'd play Frisbee and quote Hesse; I thought they'd be good kissers and drink wine. Some of them, I fancied, might smoke pipes. One of them, I dreamed, might win my heart.

But as I searched, they seemed to grow shorter, t-shirt season ended only when the ski parkas came out. Frisbee was played with their dogs; pipes were more often of the water variety, and kissing was passe. The vogue, they would have had me believe, was to go directly from vertical activities (such as first-time introductions) to horizontal activities (such as could easily be accomplished in our co-ed dorms).

. . . Why should I have thought college men would miraculously be older, cuter, and more sophisticated than the guys who had finished high school with me just two months before?

Why? Because hope springs eternal. Because I was on my own, away from home for the first time, with a new Indian-print bedspread, a high school graduation gift—stereo, my own checking account, and a stack of fat college-issue fashion magazines filled with hundreds of examples of what to wear on campus to attract tall, cute, flannel-shirted, pipe-smoking, wine-drinking, sophisticated, good-kissing men (Hesse quotations optional).

Getting those hopes dashed did not take long. A week of orientation, a few into-the-night blab sessions with my suitemates, a disastrous mixer or two, a few close encounters of the nerd kind, and the dazzling truth began to seep in: These guys were human. Just like us, but shorter. (Lisa Schwarzbaum a freelance writer In Schwartzbaum & Whisnant, 1982 p. 42)

Men want to date ravishing women. Women want their dates to be handsome as well as competent and TALL. But dreams are not the same as reality. The interplay between fantasy and reality will be the theme of this chapter.

Before we discuss how physical attractiveness operates in both the fantasy and reality of the dating marketplace, let's begin at the beginning. Just how many people are out their bargaining in the marketplace, and who are they?

THE "LONELY HEARTS" ARE NOW "SWINGING SINGLES"

Remember "Old Maid"? Whoever got stuck with the homely old crone was clearly the loser. This card game symbolizes the stigma once attached to being single, particularly if one was a woman. Single women, "old maids," or "spinsters," were assumed to have no choice in the matter—they were single because no one found them attractive enough to marry. Single men were "bachelors"; it was assumed they chose to remain single because they loved an exciting life.

Today, it is more acceptable to remain single—even for women. In fact, in 1978 about 48 million adult Americans (about one-third the adult population) were single. Here are some other facts:

- Most college students are single.

- More than one-half of Americans aged 18 to 39 are single.

- At any age, there are more single women than single men. This gap increases with age. For people in their forties, there are 233 unattached (never married, divorced, widowed) women for every 100 men. (Blumstein and Schwartz 1983; Francaeur 1982).

Today, many people are choosing to remain single for a longer period (or all) of their adulthood. There are several reasons why they are choosing not to marry. Many women find this choice gives them greater freedom to pursue a career. Other individuals have developed negative attitudes about marriage, perhaps from growing up in a broken home. Some develop such negative attitudes about attachment to one person that they choose to be "creatively single." Roger Libby (1977) defines a "creatively single" person as one who chooses not to be dependent on any one person—emotionally, financially, or sexually.

Other people, however, are reluctantly alone. Rather than choosing not to select, they are not selected. These people may have problems being selected because of unattractiveness or lack of social skills. The emptiness and despair of such singles is portrayed in the following comment by a young, single man:

> I have cried over my general inability to meet women—once even in my car in the parking lot of a disco in L.A. after having an extremely difficult time conversing with a number of girls who I was really attracted to (which is rare). I have been intrigued with the subject of suicide and realize that it is the most effective way to cure one's depression. . . . My depressions always center around my inability to meet women. Period. I really envy guys who have the "gift of gab" and who can just walk up to strange women and start a conversation. If I

had that ability, it would solve all my problems, I'm convinced of it. (Hite 1981, 255–256)

Although many single people are involved in romantic relationships, many are not. There are many adults truly unattached. Although they may not always stay home on Saturday night, there really is no special person in their lives. They are the *Availables*.

If you are one of these "Availables," this chapter is written particularly for you. Those already intimately involved with someone will find their concerns discussed in chapter 5—"More Intimate Affairs." Those more interested in sex than romance and love get their turn in chapter 6—"Let's Get Physical." However, we would recommend that, to get the big picture of love and romance, you read all three chapters.

THE DATING GAME

Imagine that a friend has given you a six-month membership to a video dating service. Such services have been springing up all around the country. They go by names such as "Great Expectations," "Couple Company," and "People Resources" (Kellogg 1982). During your orientation meeting, the service asks you to submit a small snapshot and a handwritten autobiography. The second step, which may seem a little more intimidating, is to make an appointment for an interview that will be videotaped. You will sit down face-to-face with the interviewer and answer a series of questions—ranging from your views on politics to your views on relationships. Your interview then becomes part of a film library, available for viewing by other members.

Your membership also allows you to browse through the pictures, autobiographies, and videotapes of the other members. Any time you have some free time, you can drop in to the video dating center, and leaf through a large catalogue, which contains the other members' photographs and biographical material. From all those faces and stories, you pick out the very few whose videotapes you want to view. From those few videotapes, you have to decide just who you might be interested in meeting and possibly dating. Momentous decisions to be made.

As the newest member, you probably have some questions swirling through your mind:

1. How should I look for my videotaping? How should I dress— casually or in my best?

2. How should I present myself? Should I reveal my strengths *and* weaknesses? Or should I lie and make myself seem *really* desirable?

3. Who should I go out with? (All those videotapes!) What factors are important in a date or mate anyway? Should I care what my date looks like? Should I ask out the date I *want* (no harm in trying) or one I think I can *get?*

The questions spill out, one after the other. Luckily, social scientists have something to say about these issues. In this chapter, we will present evidence on just how important attractiveness is in the getting-together stage of dating. We discuss how much difference other characteristics, such as intelligence and personality, make. We discuss both the *fantasy* of the dating marketplace, what men and women would like if a genie granted them three wishes, and the *reality* of the dating marketplace, what people are willing to settle for after they realize they can not get all they want. We will see which matches tend to be good ones, which not.

How Important Are Looks in Romantic Beginnings?

Looks are important in most areas of life, but at the beginning of romance there is probably nothing that counts more. The men and women who sign up for video dating services are well aware of this importance. Most attempt to look their best for the taping. Women apply their makeup more carefully than usual and wear their best clothes. Men get fresh haircuts, shave, and dress more carefully than usual.

What do really homely people do? There are always the jokes:

"I'm planning to put a paper bag over my head and come as the mystery videodate."

"I've hired Jeff to stand in for me."

"Now that you mention it, I guess I'll cash in my membership and invest my money in something more profitable—perhaps in a money-market account."

These are wry remarks, but the concern behind them is well placed. Beauty may be only skin deep, but in romantic beginnings apparently the surfaces are what count. There is dramatic evidence indicating how important looks are in the beginning stages of dating.

OH GREAT COMPUTER IN THE SKY, MATCH ME WITH SOMEONE ATTRACTIVE

In the 1960s, Elaine Hatfield and colleagues (Hatfield [Walster] et al. 1966) organized a dance for freshman at the University of Minnesota.

Figure 4.2. The first ten seconds.

The men and women were told that a computer would match them with a blind date who would be just right for them. In truth, we matched couples on a more mundane basis—we simple drew names out of a fishbowl.

In the backs of our minds, we were expecting people to like their dates best if they were matched by "social desirability." Tom Sellecks would like Bo Dereks, Plain Joes would like Plain Janes, and, if by chance a gorgeous person and a homely person were matched, both would feel uncomfortable.

When the men and women arrived to purchase their tickets for the dance, we set out to assess their general social desirability. We assumed social desirability was influenced by attributes such as physical attractiveness, intelligence, personality, and social skills. Meticulously, we measured each of these personal characteristics. Participants' attractiveness was secretly assessed by four ticket sellers. Intelligence was assessed by high school grades and by scores on the Minnesota Scholastic Aptitude Test. To measure personality, we gave men and women a battery of personality tests, including the prestigious Minnesota Multiphasic Personality Test and the California Personality Inventory. We also assessed their social skills.

At the dance a few days later, the four hundred couples who attended did what people always do at dances—they danced, talked, and got to know one another. Then, during the 10:30 P.M. intermission, we swept through the building, rounding up couples from the dance

floor, lavatories, fire escapes—even adjoining buildings. We asked them to tell us frankly (and in confidence) what they thought of their dates.

What do you think we found? Perhaps you will be in a better position to answer this question if you return to the video dating scenario we set up for you. Imagine you have just viewed several videotapes. You have seen the whole range—everyone from the stunning actor (or actress), who promises cruises on his (or her) yacht, to the balding, pudgy mortician, who admits his (or her) hobby is collecting dead baby jokes. If you were guaranteed a date of your choice, who would you select—the actor (actress), the mortician, or someone in between? How attractive, personable, socially skilled, or intelligent would you want your date to be?

Here are some of the things we found:

1. If you are like the freshman who attended our dance, ideally you would prefer (in fact, insist) on going out with the most appealing dates available. Virtually everyone, including the homeliest men and women, asked to be matched with good-looking blind dates.

2. Everyone, good-looking or not, insisted their dates be exceptionally charming, bright, and socially skilled! ("To dream the impossible dream.")

3. Those whom fate matched up with a beautiful or handsome date wanted to pursue the dream. They wanted to see their computer match again. When we contacted couples six months after the dance to find out the extent to which people had, in fact, pursued their dreams, we also found that daters—good-looking or homely—had continued to pursue the best. The prettier the woman, the more she was pursued by everyone, homely or not.

4. Every effort to find anything else that mattered failed! Men and women with exceptional IQs and social skills, for example, were *not* liked any better than those less well endowed.

5. Finally, both men and women cared equally about their dates' looks. (See also Curran and Lippold [1975].) They secured similar results.

The inordinate importance of good looks in blind date settings has been substantiated by other investigators (see Brislin and Lewis 1966; and Tesser and Brodie 1971).

Some time ago, we asked you to think about what you wanted in a video date. How did your reaction compare with the preceding results? Of course, in your case you merely said what you would *like*. How would you feel if you were really going to ask the person out and if they could turn down your invitation? Let's carry the exercise a little further.

POSSIBILITY FOR TURNDOWN = TURNOFF

In the video dating scenario we presented, we guaranteed you a date with the person of your choice. In the computer dating study we actually conducted, the students were also pretty much guaranteed a date for the evening. But rarely does true life contain guarantees. The *reality* of the dating marketplace is somewhat different.

In fact, a video dating service generally operates as follows: For your membership fee you are allowed to send an invitation to only five or six members each month. If they so desire, these individuals can screen *your* videotape in return, and, *if* they are interested, a mutual selection is made and names/phone numbers are given to both parties. Obviously, invitations are not always reciprocated. Particularly desirable candidates, flooded with invitations, will not have the time to respond to all of them. Particularly unappealing candidates may issue five to six invitations, but no one may return their interest. Rejection is a possibility in all interpersonal interactions but is particularly characteristic of the getting-together stage of dating.

Would the knowledge that there has to be "mutual selection" affect your decisions about to whom you would send invitations? If you are like most other people, it will. You may be tempted to aspire for the best, but rejection stings; you may well settle for someone you think you can get. As we predicted several years ago, one's romantic aspirations are influenced by "the desirability of the goal and the perceived probability of attaining it" (Hatfield [Walster] et al. 1966).

Age and experience probably help people get a good sense of what is out there for them. A very experienced gay friend of Elaine Hatfield's observed that:

> Gay men who do a great deal of "cruising," can tell in the flicker of an eyelash who'd be interested in them, who'd not. In a bar or on the street, looks is all that matters; everyone has an exquisitely fine-tuned sense of who's available, who's not. There's a real pecking order.

Experiments indicate that, when there is a possibility of rejection, people become a little more realistic in their dating choices. In one study (Huston 1973), men were shown color Polaroid pictures of six women and asked to select one as a date. The women varied markedly in physical attractiveness. Men were also told either that the women had already seen a picture of them and had said they would be willing to date them *or* were given no information as to whether or not she was likely to date them. What type of woman were men most likely to select? Men were more likely to select a good-looking date when confident she would accept them rather than when they were uncertain about whether or not she would be interested.

The men in this study given no information about the women's desires were asked to estimate whether or not each woman would want to date them. The men assumed the beautiful women would be "harder to get." Furthermore, handsome men perceived their chances of acceptance by the women to be greater than did unattractive men.

Other researchers (Shanteau and Nagy 1979) have also examined whether the probability of acceptance is important in choosing a date. Women were asked to examine the photographs of several pairs of men and, in each case, to choose the one they would prefer to date. The men varied markedly in attractiveness. Below each photograph was a phrase indicating how certain (or uncertain) the man was that he wanted to date *her*—a conclusion he had supposedly reached after seeing her photograph. Both the attractiveness of the men and the probability of acceptance were found to be important. A man who was both attractive and willing to accept the date was seen as very desirable. A man who was unattractive and unlikely to accept a date was seen as particularly undesirable. (Other experiments, however, have been

BLOOM COUNTY

Figure 4.3. Advertising for a date.

less conclusive in indicating the effects of the possibility of rejection. See, for example, Berscheid, Dion, Hatfield [Walster] and Walster [1971].)

This research indicates that, ideally, people would prefer to date very attractive others, but, because rejection is costly, they end up choosing someone of about their same level of attractiveness. Social psychologist Bernard Murstein (1971) describes how the risk of rejection moderates dating aspirations:

> A man who is physically unattractive (liability), for example, might desire a woman who has the asset of beauty. Assuming, however, that his nonphysical qualities are no more rewarding than hers, she gains less profit than he does from the relationship and thus his suit is likely to be rejected. Rejection is a cost to him because it may lower his self-esteem and increase his fear of failure in future encounters; hence, he may decide to avoid courting women who he perceives as much above him in attractiveness. (p. 113–114)

That people do seem affected by the chances of rejection was also demonstrated in a study conducted in the naturalistic setting of singles

by Berke Breathed

bars (Glenwick, Jason, and Elman 1978). If men in singles bars follow an "idealistic" strategy (following their dreams), attractive women should be approached more frequently than unattractive women. On the other hand, if men follow a more "realistic" strategy (and fear rejection), the attractive and unattractive women should be approached equally often. Using four singles bars in Rochester, New York, the researchers observed unattached women and recorded how attractive each woman was, how many men initiated contact with her, and how long the contacts lasted. The researchers found that men seemed to be choosing a strategy to minimize rejection: Attractive women were not approached more often—or for longer periods of time—than less attractive women.

In Sum

While the students who participated in our early computer dating study (Hatfield [Walster] et al. 1966) desired the most attractive date, they were guaranteed the date and did not have to face possible rejection.

Other studies indicate that the possibility of rejection lowers men and women's aspirations somewhat. If you actually had to send a limited number of invitations to other video date members and "mutual selection" was necessary before names were exchanged, you would also probably be willing to settle for others of about your own level of attractiveness (or risk ending up with no one to call). We are all affected by the possibility of rejection. The dynamics of the marketplace operate to bring people together who are matched in physical attractiveness. Yet, there is no question most of us would prefer the most attractive partner we can possibly get.

DO THINGS BESIDES PHYSICAL ATTRACTIVENESS MATTER?

Most video daters know how they want to look during their interview—as appealing as possible. But how do they act? What personality traits, attitudes, and interests should they display? And does it really matter how they act, given the importance of physical attractiveness? Here are the kinds of questions that preplex video daters:

> How should I present myself? Maybe I should fake it. After all, my friend invested $350 in this for me. I want to be sure *someone* asks me out. But how do I fake it? Should I demonstrate superior intelligence, or will that just scare possible dates away? (And my God, how would I even know how to act intelligently?) Should I act self-confident, or shy and modest? (Maybe I should be a natural leader, yet someone who can blend into a crowd? Brilliant, but not too "heady." Strong and vulnerable? Uhhuh.)
>
> On the other hand, maybe I don't want to try to be something I am not (even if I could figure out just what *that* was). What good does it do to fake it, to attract someone who loves what you *say* you are but can't stand *you.* To discover too late that your perfect match never even took a second look at you, because you were busy pretending to be someone you thought he/she would like better.
>
> What to do? Maybe I'll just shade the truth a little.

In this section, we will present the bits of evidence social scientists have collected on what men and women want in those they date.

INTELLIGENCE, PERSONALITY, AND FRIENDLINESS DO SEEM TO MATTER

Many women are afraid that if they sound too bright they might scare dates off. While we would not recommend claiming degrees, honors, or IQ points one does not have, it does not hurt, and probably helps to take opportunities to demonstrate brilliance and competence. Experiments indicate people are more attracted to men and women who seem intelligent and competent (Aronson, Willerman, and Floyd 1966; Helmreich, Aronson, and LeFan 1970; Solomon and Saxe 1977).

It also seems to pay to act friendly. Dale Carnegie, who wrote *How to Win Friends and Influence People* (1936) several decades ago, gives just such advice. In his book, he offers six ways to make others like you:

Rule 1: Become genuinely interested in other people.

Rule 2: Smile.

Rule 3: Remember that a man's name is to him the sweetest and most important sound in any language.

Rule 4: Be a good listener. Encourage others to talk about themselves.

Rule 5: Talk in terms of the other man's interest.

Rule 6: Make the other person feel important—and do it sincerely.

Millions of copies of Carnegie's book have been sold. This success is probably because such advice is generally effective. Men and women like all the conventionally appealing things your parents (and Dale Carnegie) said they would. They like to be around "nice" and "friendly" people and those who have generally pleasant and agreeable characteristics (Kaplan and Anderson 1973). People also like those who like them. If Abigail learns that Benjamin likes her, probably Abigail will like Benjamin in return (Mette and Aronson 1974). (See Hatfield and Walster [1978] for a review of this literature.)

On the other hand, according to folklore, we should never "throw ourselves" at the people we find appealing. Socrates, Ovid, the *Kama Sutra*, Bertrand Russell, and "Dear Abby" all agree: Passion is stimulated by excitement and challenge. To find authors in such rare accord is refreshing. Luckily, research clearly shows that, this time, the sages are wrong. Researchers have conducted a number of experiments designed to demonstrate that men and women value hard-to-get dates more than easy-to-get ones. Inevitably, these experiments failed. They all had the same results: If anything, hard-to-get dates are liked less than easy-to-get dates. In general, then, there is no point in pretending to be what you are not. Some poeple prefer secure, easy-to-get dates; others like the excitement of a hard-to-get partner. It all balances out (see Hatfield [Walster] et al. 1973). (Some people like impossible-to-get partners most of all, making for a somewhat distant relationship.)

BUT SUCH INNER QUALITIES DO NOT SEEM TO MATTER AS MUCH AS PHYSICAL ATTRACTIVENESS

In the computer dance study (Hatfield [Walster] et al. 1966), we found that everyone hoped for the best. They wanted a stunningly good-looking partner—who was also bright and sparkling, with a wonderful personality. But rarely is life so accommodating. When people have to make compromises (which is most of the time), what is really most important—"superficial" appearances or more meaningful things such as intelligence, warmth, considerateness, and personality? In romantic beginnings, seemingly superficial appearances are what matter. The discovery that someone has a "great personality" *seems* to matter very little. Let us consider the research that leads to this conclusion.

In the computer dating study we just described, for most of the young people physical attractiveness was everything; but, maybe that is not so surprising. In certain settings—noisy mixers, singles bars, loud new-wave discos, or computer dances—about all daters can perceive is what their dates look like. In the midst of the din, daters certainly do not have much chance to display their knowledge of world affairs or advanced calculus. In such settings, about all people can go on is looks.

But in other settings, people do get a chance to find out more about one another. A video dating service gives one a chance to do just that. So do church discussion groups, encounter groups, and small parties. What about these settings? What matters most in such settings—how you look or what you are like? Let's see.

What People Say They Want

When teenagers and young adults are asked what characteristics are important in a date, they *say* there are many factors more important than looks. In one of the earliest studies conducted on dating relation-ships (Perrin 1921), men and women were asked to list the characteristics they cared about in a date. Men were more willing than women to admit they cared about looks, but it was not a very important item for anyone. For example, men insisted that a woman's "sincerity," "indi-viduality," and "affectional disposition" were more important than her looks. (Similar results were secured in another early study by Hill [1945].)

Half a century has not changed these preferences to any great extent. In recent studies (conducted in 1956, 1967, and 1977), when men and women were asked to rate eighteen personal characteristics they desire in a date or mate, good looks ranged from being ninth to eighteenth in importance (Hudson and Henze 1969; Hudson and Hoyt 1981; McGinnis 1956). Men and women said what they really valued was "dependable character" and "emotional stability." This research will be discussed in greater detail in the next chapter. Other investigators have found similar results (Miller and Rivenbark 1970; Tesser and Brodie 1971).

 People generally *say* looks are not too important to them, but their actions belie their statements.

Actions Speak Louder Than Words: What People Do Value

A variety of experiments suggest that looks are more important than people are able or willing to admit. In such studies, men and women are shown photographs of potential dates, who range from fairly homely to breathtakingly appealing. They are also given a brief personality sketch of each date. The potential date is described as having either a desirable personality trait or its opposite. Researchers conducted these experiments to see if attractiveness still has a powerful effect, even when compared to other powerful factors.

These studies suggest that looks overshadow everything else. It seems to matter very little to men (all the subjects in these studies have been male) if they are told their potential date is independent versus dependent (Meredith 1972), trustworthy versus untrustworthy (Shepard 1973), relaxed versus anxious (Mathes 1975), or boastful versus modest (Stretch and Figley 1980). Attractive dates were overwhelmingly preferred to unattractive ones, while trustworthy or honest or independent dates were preferred only slightly more (or sometimes not any more) than untrustworthy or dishonest or dependent dates.

Other evidence also confirms that good looks are more important than good character or personality in the dating marketplace. Elaine Hatfield and colleagues (Hatfield [Walster] et al. 1966) asked more than seven hundred young men and women, "How popular are you with the opposite sex?" and "How many dates have you had in the last six months?" As you might expect, attractive men and women were more popular and dated more often. In this same study, intelligence, personality, and social skills seemed to have little impact on popularity (similar results were found by Berscheid et al. 1971).

What can we conclude from all these studies? In romantic beginnings, attractiveness is exceedingly important. We are aroused by others who are physically and personally appealing. Appearance, which we tend to think of as only a superficial trait, appears to be far more critical in the dating marketplace than traits we think of as of deeper importance—such as intelligence, personality, and social skills. Why?

WHY DO WE PREFER A "10" TO A "6"?

We have documented that men and women do prefer "10's" over "6's," but we have not addressed *why* this is so. There are at least three reasons:

1 *Aesthetic Appeal:*   Just as it is pleasant to live in a beautiful environment, possess appealing paintings, and collect beautiful objects, it is also pleasant to be around beautiful people. Infants as young as four months prefer good looks to ugliness. Investigators (Kagan et al. 1966) showed infants faces that were either normal or terribly distorted. The infants were content to gaze at the normal face, but they reacted with anxiety, fear, and crying when shown the distorted face. Aesthetic concerns probably increase as we become older.

2 *The Glow of Beauty:*   Good looks radiate. Appearance influences how we think about other's nonphysical characteristics. Most people presume the Bo Dereks and Tom Sellecks of the world are perfect in every way. Attractive people are assumed to be unusually sensitive, kind, interesting, strong, poised, modest, sociable, outgoing, more exciting dates, and sexually warm and responsive (Berscheid and Hatfield [Walster] 1974). In chapters 2 and 3, we provided evidence that attractive people are perceived more positively in a wide variety of settings—in schools, on the job, by the mental health system, in the courtroom, and so on. It is not surprising, then, that attractive people are preferred as dating partners, for they are expected to have a monopoly on all the good things life has to offer.

Also, of course, the stereotypes about good-looking people just may contain a "kernel of truth." Possibly good-looking people, who are treated so graciously by others, actually become the beautiful and the best—sort of a self-fulfilling prophecy. (Such a possibility will be discussed in chapter 8.)

This explanation for why a "10" is preferred over a "6," therefore, suggests it has nothing to do with good looks, per se. The preference exists because of the inner qualities that are assumed to develop (or actually do develop) as a result of having an appealing exterior.

3 *Beauty "Rubs Off":*   There is also a selfish reason for wanting to associate with attractive people. Attractive men and women may be preferred because our self-esteem and prestige are bolstered when irresistible people find us irresistible. Sociologist Willard Waller (1937) spoke about this process in his discussion of the "rating and dating" complex. In describing college campuses several decades ago, he said men and women rated potential dates (1 to 10) and tried to date the

best. Their success or failure at this game provided evidence to them-selves and to others about just how valuable they were.

The "rating and dating" complex is not just a quaint reminder of the past. Even today, people gain by merely being seen with someone good-looking. In one study, for example, men were asked their first impression of another man. Tucked in at the man's side was a girlfriend, either ravishingly beautiful or exceedingly homely. (Sometimes the man was alone.) When a man was accompanied by a beauty, he was evaluated most favorably. Indeed, a man was better off being seen alone than when associated with a homely woman (Sigall and Landy 1973).

Do women gain just as much by being seen with a handsome man? Not necessarily. In another study (Bar-Tal and Saxe 1976), men and women looked at a series of slides of married couples and judged the husband and wife on several dimensions. If an ugly man had an unusually beautiful wife, the judges assumed he must have *something* to offer. They assumed he must be unusually bright, rich, or profes-sionally successful. The same assumptions were not made for the women. If an ugly woman had an unusually handsome husband, she gained nothing in how she was judged. She was evaluated strictly on her own merit.

Physical attractiveness matters, then, and we have considered some of the reasons why. But is physical attractiveness equally important to everyone? Is it equally important in all settings?

THERE ARE SOME LIMITS TO THE PREFERENCE FOR THE MOST ATTRACTIVE

Probably everyone, then, cares about looks a little. But surely there is variation among people in just how important physical attractiveness is. The importance of physical attractiveness should also vary across situations. In this section, we will discuss how physical attractiveness may be more important: (1) to some people than to others; and (2) in certain settings. We will present what past research indicates and will also speculate a little on our own. This area is one in which much more research is clearly needed. Certainly, there are many homely men and women eager to find out the exceptions to the general preference for good looks.

For Some People, Looks Do Not Matter Quite So Much

Some people seem to care far more about looks than do others. We will consider four characteristics that may influence how important a good-looking dating partner is: (1) age; (2) self-esteem; (3) personality; and (4) gender.

YOUTH: WHEN HOPE SPRINGS ETERNAL

Young people are often especially concerned about looks. At least, our personal experiences would suggest this is so.

> Elaine Hatfield once gave a surprise birthday party for Michelle, a 12-year old who was staying at her house. Since Michelle is an unusually adult little girl, rather than inviting Michelle's friends, we invited a collection of older people—including some well-known authors, psychologists, artists, and craftspeople. As we sat talking after dinner, Michelle was asked how she liked junior high school. She said that, at first, as a newcomer, she had been considered "A Nothing" . . . but, she said blithely, "it is just a matter of time until I'm one of the most popular girls."
>
> Intrigued by her confidence, a physicist asked, "What does it take to be a 'super-star'?" Michelle answered matter-of-factly, "Girls have to have big breasts; boys have to be athletes." (She considered her own budding breasts to be big; we could barely see their lines under her dress.) The table suddenly became very quiet. The "adults" were reminded of their own painful high school experiences. "Surely," said the physicist (who was obviously not an athlete) with uneasy enthusiasm, "there are other ways for a boy to be popular. What if he has a great sense of humor?" Michelle pronounced with finality, "Well, he could be a *friend*, but no one would want him for a *boyfriend*." The laws of the dating jungle are relentless, and there is perhaps no worse time than junior high and high school for those who don't "stack up."

Looks may be especially important to young people because of their need to conform in order to be popular (or at least to be accepted) by their peers. While it may sound bizarre today, when Elaine Hatfield was an undergraduate at the University of Michigan in the late 1950s, one of the prestigious sororities fined sisters who dared to "damage the house reputation" by dating ugly men. While sororities today probably no longer have fines for "dating down," there is still a great deal of pressure to date men from the right fraternities (the fraternities that have good-looking men!). Young men have the same kinds of pressures to date beautiful women.

We suspect that by the time men and women reach middle age, they have learned that looks matter less, while wit, intelligence, personality, and character matter more. Although common sense suggests that looks matter more to younger people than to older individuals, little evidence exists to verify this notion. Unfortunately, no computer dating studies have been conducted with senior citizens. One study that did look at older people's general impressions of physically attractive *versus* physically unattractive people found that older people are not immune to the physical attractiveness stereotype. Age does not seem to diminish the belief that "what is beautiful is good' (Adams and Huston 1975). However, only further research will indicate whether older people are as likely as younger people to insist on the most attractive dating partner they can get.

SELF-ESTEEM

Fundamental to how we feel about others is how we feel about ourselves. Just how is self-esteem related to dating choice? There really is not a simple answer. Self-esteem could have two different effects.

First, people with low self-esteem are often afraid they will be rejected. They fear stepping out of line and being different. They seek social approval. Shy teenagers, unsure of themselves, find it very difficult to date a person friends find unappealing. High self-esteem individuals, on the other hand, are not so desperate for social approval. They can afford to date someone much less attractive than they are. They have enough prestige "credits" to be unconcerned about the "rating and dating" complex we described earlier. (Gergen [1974] discusses self-esteem and interpersonal attraction.)

But there is another possibility. When people have high self-esteem, they have the confidence to approach anyone they desire. Thus, they are more likely to take a chance and approach a good-looking man or woman (who is also intelligent, charming, and considerate). In a delightful experiment, Sara Kiesler and Roberta Baral (1970) demonstrated this hypothesis—the greater a person's self-esteem, the more likely he or she is to approach striking dates. The researchers recruited college men to participate in a study on intelligence testing. After the men completed the first portion of the IQ test, they were told how they were doing. The researchers tried to raise the self-esteem of some of the men by giving them fake IQ test results indicating they had done very well. The self-esteem of the other men was temporarily lowered by telling them they had done poorly. At intermission, the experimenter suggested they take a coffee break. They walked to a nearby canteen and sat down. Once they were seated, the experimenter's assistant walked over and joined them. On some days, the assistant was beautifully made up and dressed. On other days, she was made up to be downright ugly. (She wore heavy glasses and her hair was pulled back with a rubber band. Her blouse and skirt clashed and were sloppily arranged.) During the coffee break, the experimenter left, ostensibly to make a phone call. The man was left alone with the woman. The assistant carefully noted how much interest the man expressed in her.

Did he offer to buy her a coke? Did he ask for her phone number? Did he even go so far as to ask her out? When the man's self-esteem was unusually high, he was most romantic with the attractive woman. On the other hand, if his self-regard was at rock bottom, he was more comfortable approaching the homely woman.

What can we conclude about the possible effects of self-esteem on responsiveness to physical attractiveness? We would hypothesize that if individuals do not have to risk rejection (for example, women have traditionally been asked out rather than doing the asking), then a deficit of self-esteem will lead them to aspire to the most attractive partner possible. Because their esteem needs are unfulfilled, such persons are especially in need of any prestige that could "rub-off" on them. On the other hand, if people have to risk the chance of rejection (they have to do the asking and are not sure of the outcome), impoverished self-esteem might lead them to flee any chance of having their self-esteem assaulted even further.

THE MACHO PERSONALITY

Are there certain personality types especially captivated by looks? One study examined the relationship between having a "macho" personality and reacting to physically attractive *versus* unattractive persons of the opposite sex (Touhey 1979). Men and women were asked to complete the Macho Scale, which measures the extent to which people possess traditional sexist stereotypes, attitudes, and behaviors. What are macho men and women? In general, these individuals agree with statements such as:

1. It's alright that most women are more interested in getting married than in making something of themselves.

2. A wife shouldn't contradict her husband in public.

3. I would not want to be part of a couple where the male was considerably shorter than the female.

4. For the most part, it is better to be a man than to be a woman.

5. "Henpecked" is a good word for describing some husbands.

(from the Macho Scale by Villemez and Touhey 1977)

The researchers showed men and women a photograph of someone of the opposite sex who was either attractive ("neatly groomed, smiling, relaxed, and approachable") or unappealing ("disheveled and squinting . . . sported a less inviting demeanor"). They were also given biographical information. Finally, they were asked how much they liked this person of the opposite sex and if they wanted to date him or her.

First, it must be pointed out that most of the men and women cared at least a little about looks. In general, an attractive model was liked more than a homely one. However, it was the highly macho men and women who cared most desperately. They were unusually eager to date good-looking partners and unusually quick to reject homely ones. They seemed less influenced by the biographical information. In fact, they had a hard time even remembering what was in it. The non-machos were far less swayed by looks and did remember the contents of the biographical information.

Another recent study (Anderson and Bem 1981) produced similar results. Men and women who were sex-typed, adhering tightly to traditional male/female roles, (as measured by the Bem Sex-Role Inventory) were more likely than androgynous men and women to be more responsive to attractive than to unattractive strangers.

GENDER: DO MEN CARE MORE THAN WOMEN?

> The ideal beauties teach women that their looks are a commodity to be bartered in exchange for a man, not only for food, clothing, and shelter, but for love. Women learn early that if you are unlovely, you are unloved. The homely girl prepares to be an old maid, because beauty is what makes a man fall in love. . . . A man's love is beauty deep. Beauty is man's only and sufficient reason for lusting, loving, and marrying a woman. Doesn't a man always say you're beautiful before he says I love you? Don't we all think it strange when a man marries a girl who isn't pretty and not at all strange when he marries a dumb beauty? Is it therefore surprising that even the great beauty fears a man's love will not survive her looks, and the average woman is convinced that no man can really love her? (Stannard 1971, 124)

According to popular belief, in the dating and mating game men care more than women about having a good-looking romantic partner. This assumption is so built into our belief systems that if the words "man" and "woman" were switched in the above paragraph, it would seem very strange indeed. Try it:

> The ideal muscle men teach men that their looks are a commodity to be bartered in exchange for a woman, not only for food, clothing, and shelter, but for love. Men learn early that if you are unlovely, you are unloved. The homely boy prepares to be a bachelor, because looks are what makes a woman fall in love. . . .

Is physical attractiveness really more important to men than to women, or is this mere belief? Theorists have assumed that men are more obsessed than women with appearance. Sociobiologists contend that men and women are *genetically* programmed to desire different things from their intimate relations (see Hagen 1979; Symons 1979; and Wilson 1975). Symons (1979) argues that gender differences are probably the most powerful determinants of how people behave sexually. Symon's sociobiological argument proceeds as follows: According to evolutionary biology, animals inherit characteristics that ensure they will transmit a maximum number of their genes to the next generation. It is to men and women's advantage to produce as many surviving children as possible. But men and women differ in one critical respect—to produce a child, men need only invest a trivial amount of energy; a single man can conceivably father an almost unlimited number of children. On the other hand, a woman can conceive only a limited number of children. It is to a woman's advantage to ensure the survival of the children she does conceive. Symons observes, "The enormous sex differences in minimum parental investment and in reproductive opportunities and constraints explain why *Homo sapiens*, a species with only moderate sex differences in structure, exhibits profound sex differences in psyche" (p. 27).

What are the gender differences Symons insists are "wired in"? According to Symons,

1. Men desire a variety of sex partners; women do not.

2. Men are inclined to be polygamous (possessing many wives). Women are more malleable in this respect; they are equally satisfied in polygamous, monogamous, or polyandrous marriages (possessing many husbands).

3. Men are sexually jealous. Women are more malleable in this respect; they are concerned with security—not fidelity.

4. Men are sexually aroused by the sight of women and women's genitals; women are not aroused by men's appearance.

5. For men, "sexual attractiveness" equals "youth." For women, "sexual attractiveness" equals "political and economic power."

6. Men have every reason to pursue women actively. They are programmed to impregnate as many women as possible. Women have every reason to be "coy." It takes time to decide if a man is a good genetic risk—is likely to be nurturant and protective.

7. Men are intensely competitive with one another. Competition over women is the most frequent cause of violence. Women are far less competitive.

Figure 4.4. Sociobiologists believe men are wired up to care about beauty and youth. ©1959 United Feature Syndicate, Inc.

Presumably, men are genetically "wired up" to care about beauty and youth in their lovers. Women, on the other hand, are attracted by political and economic power instead. (Henry Kissinger once observed that "power is the best aphrodisiac.")

The sociobiologists' arguments sound good, but there is a more compelling, albeit a more prosaic, explanation for why beauty is so important to men. Traditionally, men have had more social and economic power than have women. Thus, men can afford to select a beautiful and sexy mate without worrying too much about her other assets. Women have to be more practical. As one shrewd observer (Waller 1938, 162) noted: "There is this difference between the man and the woman in the pattern of middle-class family life: a man, when he marries, chooses a companion and perhaps a helpmate, but a woman chooses a companion and at the same time a standard of living. It is necessary for a woman to be mercenary." Feminist Arlie Hochschild (1975) agrees.

Other theorists (Bar-Tal and Saxe 1976) have observed that, traditionally, women are expected to provide the husband with affection, to be sexually responsive, to be a good housekeeper, and to take care of the children. Thus, beauty provides an important external cue as to whether or not a woman can adequately fulfill her traditional role. In contrast, women look for men who will be good providers—they search for men of good education and occupation rather than men of good looks.

Theorists believe that men *are* more concerned about beauty than women—but *are* they? They are. When men and women are asked what they want in a date, men admit they are more concerned about appearances than are women. Several years ago, one thousand college men and college women were asked what qualities they desired in a dating partner (Coombs and Kendell 1966). Men were more insistent on having a good-looking partner. In answer to the question, "To what extent is it important that your date be good looking or attractive?" 22 percent of the men, but only 7 percent of the women said it was "very important." What did women want? They were more likely than men to expect all the following qualities in a date: he should be of the same race, the same religion, a good dancer, possess high campus status, high scholastic ability, wear stylish clothes, and belong to a fraternity. A variety of other studies indicate that men are more concerned than women with appearances in a variety of settings—first encounters, work, dating, and marriage (Coombs and Kendell 1966; Hewitt 1958; Miller and Rivenbark 1970; Stroebe, Insko, Thompson, and Layton 1971; Vail and Staudt 1950; Williamson 1966).

Men's concern with beauty is also reflected in their behavior. Two researchers (Harrison and Saeed 1977) examined over eight hundred lonely hearts advertisements that appeared in a national weekly tabloid. Such ads are placed in all types of newspapers and go something like the following:

> NON-GENERIC MALE, 36, wants to meet pretty, slim, working woman; 25–35 ish; must be well read, articulate, witty, with a finely tuned sense of the absurd. No Psychobabble, please. Write Chuck, Box 403 B

> GAY? I am dissatisfied with the gay bar scene; frustrated by the lack of constructive human contact. I wish to meet a like-minded gay man. If you're interested too, call Bill at 658–0965.

> WOMAN, tired of the obsession with superficial appearances, wants man who is concerned with deeper qualities—one who possesses spiritual concerns, a passion for life. . . . Send picture.

> PRETTY WOMAN, I WOULD LIKE TO MEET YOU. I know beauty is only skin deep. I did not used to care so much about beauty, but now I will not settle for less than the best. I also treasure an alert mind, w/serious interests (whether they be electrical engineering or scuba diving). Kindness and basic human decancy. In the past, I wanted a woman who was an outstanding success; now I care more about per-

CATHY

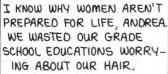

by Cathy Guisewite

Figure 4.5. Preparing for life. © 1981, Universal Press Syndicate. Reprinted with permission. All rights reserved.

sonal qualities. Filing clerk, unemployed artist, fallen woman, or fast track exec.—it's the person rather than the occupation I care about. Write Oscar, Box 921.

The researchers found that men and women are well aware of men's special concern with appearances. As expected, they found that women were more likely than men to offer attractiveness, while men were more likely to seek it. As far as financial security, women were more likely to seek it, while men were more likely to offer it. Finally, another major sex difference was that women were likely to seek someone older, while men were likely to seek someone younger.

Other evidence indicates that attractiveness is more tightly linked to dating popularity for women than for men (Berscheid et al. 1971; Krebs and Adinolfi 1975; Hatfield [Walster] et al. 1966). Beautiful women have more dates than homely women, while a man's attractiveness (or lack thereof) is not as important in determining how busy his social calendar is.

This greater obsession in men with looks is not limited to our society. Interestingly, Ford and Beach (1951), who studied men and women in 190 societies, also concluded: "One interesting generalization is that in most societies, the physical beauty of the female receives more explicit consideration than does the handsomeness of the male. The attractiveness of the man usually depends predominantly upon his skills of prowess rather than upon his physical appearance" (p. 86).

One observation: Traditionally, men have cared about beauty while women were concerned with finding a good provider. These gender differences, however, may be on their way out. As women begin to have successful careers and become financially independent, they may have the luxury of insisting that their men be handsome and athletic (consider the popular song by Diana Ross, "I Want Muscles"). Many men may decide to accept the changes women are demanding. They may be willing to sacrifice having a beautiful date in order to have someone who can share the expenses. In the future, we may start to see less traditional and more individually tailored matches.

In conclusion, then, if you want to capitalize on your looks, you should spend your time with young people who have "appropriate" levels of self-esteem and who hold traditional macho values (and it helps if you are a woman). On the other hand, if you do not want your dating success to be totally determined by your looks, seek out people with the opposite characteristics.

Thus far, we have considered what types of *people* care most about beauty. Now let us consider the settings in which beauty matters more (or less).

IN SOME SETTINGS, LOOKS MATTER MORE (LESS)

We opened this chapter by asking you to imagine you were seeking dates via a video dating service. While such services do exist, most people meet romantic partners in more typical ways—at work, school, parties, bars, and through friends. Does physical attractiveness matter more (or less) in some of these settings than in others?

Where and How People Meet and Begin Dating

In what settings do most people meet? Dr. Gerald Marwell, our colleague and friend at the University of Wisconsin, recently became interested in this question when he realized there is a striking lack of information on how couples actually "get together." Susan Sprecher joined him and others in a research project designed to find out the process by which young adults meet and begin dating (Marwell, Sprecher, Mc-Kinney, DeLamater, and Smith 1982).

We interviewed a random sample of over one hundred college sophomores from the University of Wisconsin-Madison. We asked them to think of their most recent relationship:

> We want you to think of the last person you met since coming to the university with whom you have had some experience in which the two of you were definitely a "couple." You might have met only that evening for the first time, or you might have met previously. But at least for an hour or so, the two of you were together in what was clearly a couples relationship.

We wanted to learn about a variety of encounters—from the short-term to the long-term encounter.

We then asked men and women a set of questions about these romantic beginnings, for example: Where did you first meet this person? Were you introduced to him/her? If you were not introduced, who initiated the meeting—you or him/her? The most common meeting location was at parties—in either dorms, apartments, or fraternities. Classes were the next most frequent meeting place, followed by bars and nonparty dorm locations. For a more exact breakdown on the settings in which college couples met, see Table 4.1.

A substantial portion of relationships got their start from introductions from a third party. Someone, usually a friend, introduced 33 percent of the men and 43 percent of the women to their date. For those couples not introduced by a third party, typically the man was the initiator. Half the women and one-third of the men reported that their partner was the initiator. Forty percent of the men, but only 15

Figure 4.6. How do people meet?

TABLE 4.1   **Where Do Most College Couples Meet?**

MEETING LOCATION	MEN	WOMEN
Party in apartment, dorm, or fraternity	28%	30%
Classes	25%	16%
Bar or restaurant	15%	21%
Dorm (but not a party)	23%	7%
Other public university location (cafeterias, library)	3%	13%
Other (sports, work)	7%	13%

percent of the women, said they were the initiator. The rest reported that both initiated the meeting, or that it was just happenstance.

Although men *and* women believe men are the initiators of romantic first meetings, as indicated in the above study careful observation of men and women getting together indicates this may not be so. Timothy Perper and Susan Fox (1980) observed single people of varying ages in New Jersey and New York City bars. These investigators overturned one of our most beloved cultural myths—that the man is usually the aggressor. They found the woman often makes the first move. But because her move is subtle—usually nothing more than standing close to him—understandably the man (and woman) might erroneously believe *he* started the interaction.

Both men and women seem to be equally effective in their pickup attempts. Perper and Fox (1980) found that neither gender dominates a successful flirtation. Indeed, it is hard to separate the influencing agent from the influencee. Each person takes a turn at signaling his/her interest. As the couple's relationship becomes more secure, flirtation strategies become more obvious:

[A woman] commonly touches the man before he touches her. Her touch is made, typically with the palm of the hand flat, and not with the fingertips, in a light, fleeting and pressing gesture. . . . She might brush against him with her hip or back, she may lean on him briefly, or she might brush against him while she turns to look at something. An alternative is for the woman to remove an otherwise nonexistent piece of lint from the man's jacket (men's jackets in bars collect such lint very readily). (p. 18)

Touching is safe. It can be interpreted as accidental if the other just is not interested. For this reason, women often use it as a way to initiate an encounter.

After a couple actually manages to meet, the rules for who asks whom out have traditionally been rather strict. The traditional woman could, at most, make herself attractive. She is not allowed to call the man or to start a new relationship. In contrast, the traditional man (shy or not) is responsible for initiating all relationships with women. Women, of course, are traditionally the ones who set limits. They have the power to say yes or no.

Traditional rules still seem to prevail. Men and women still state that men initiate new dating relationships (Allgeier 1981; Green and Sandos 1980). For example, in the study we conducted at the University of Wisconsin (Marwell et al. 1982), men were more likely to ask the women out than the reverse. Not everyone, however, is happy with this situation. Men, in fact, are more in favor of women initiating and paying for dates than women are! (see Allgeier 1981; McCormick and Jesser, 1982.) Times may be ripe for change.

In What Settings Are Good Looks Most Important?

The preceding statistics tell us *where* men and women usually meet and who initiates the encounter, but in which of these settings is beauty most important? Where least?

Social psychologist Bernard Murstein (1970) points out that settings can be characterized by how "closed" or "open" they are. In open fields, people have a great deal of choice about with whom they interact. The video dating setting is an example of an open field. There, you can look at the members and send out invitations, or you can just flip to the next page. Other examples of open fields include singles bars and large social gatherings.

In closed fields, people are forced to interact over prolonged periods of time. They often have little choice about interacting with each other. Work is an example of a closed field. Day after day the same people interact. They get to know one another well. The man or woman in the cubicle next to you may never hit the pages of *Gentlemen's Quarterly* or *Vogue*, but in time you learn that he or she has a great sense of humor, is kind and dependable, and, well, you've just grown accustomed to his or her face.

We speculate that beautiful people shine in open fields, while homely men and women do relatively better in closed fields. In open fields, looks are often all that can be known. In closed fields, both appealing and homely people profit from the chance to reveal their personalities to others.

We also predict that as long as men do most of the asking out, the physical attractiveness of women will continue to be an important determinant of their dating frequency. However, if women begin to initiate more interaction, physical attractiveness might come to be an equally important (or unimportant) influence on the dating popularity of men and women.

Advice To The Lovelorn

We have reviewed much of what social psychologists know about romantic relationships. (For a complete review, see Hatfield and Walster [1978].) Based on the material we have reviewed and some we have not yet considered, what advice can we give men and women interested in meeting others for romantic beginnings? Now that we know the reality of the dating marketplace, what can be done to make it more in tune with your fantasy?

• *If you are looking for a lover,* search for a friend. Recently, scientists have begun to study lonely people who hunger for romance and love (see Peplau and Perlman 1982). Russell, Peplau, and Cutrona (1980) have developed the most commonly used measure of loneliness—*the UCLA Loneliness Scale.* The scale contains items such as in Table 4.2.

Scientists find that most lonely people long for a romantic affair. But, paradoxically, single-minded men and women who set out looking for romance end up worse off than those who take time to make a few good friends along the way. In fact, the most effective strategy for finding a lover is apparently to concentrate, at first, on finding good friends. (The latter are generally easier to find.) Then, *they* can introduce you to romantic beginnings (Cutrona 1982).

TABLE 4.2   **The Revised UCLA Loneliness Scale**

Directions: Indicate how often you feel the way described in each of the following statements. Circle one number for each.

	NEVER	RARELY	SOMETIMES	OFTEN
1. I lack companionship.	1	2	3	4
2. There is no one I can turn to.	1	2	3	4
3. I am no longer close to anyone.	1	2	3	4
4. I feel left out.	1	2	3	4
5. My social relationships are superficial.	1	2	3	4
6. No one really knows me well.	1	2	3	4
7. I feel isolated from others.	1	2	3	4

Note: Reprinted by permission from D. Russell, L.A. Peplau, and C.E. Cutrona, "The Revised UCLA Loneliness Scale: Concurrent and Discriminant Validity Evidence," *Journal of Personality and Social Psychology* 39, no. 3 (1980): 475.

• *If you are good-looking* and want to capitalize on your looks, you might do well to see and be seen. Spend your time in open fields, such as single bars.

• *If you are average or less in looks,* you would do better to concentrate more on people you see in classes or work. Join small clubs and activities. These are closed fields. Let people get to know you in these settings.

• *If you are not shy* and you meet someone to whom you are attracted, ask him or her out—fine advice for men, but what about women? Traditionally, women have assumed that if they are "too forward," men will be scared off (McCormick and Jessor 1982). Researchers at the University of Wisconsin (no reference available), however, found that men are heartier than they are reputed to be. If a woman is reasonably attractive, with an acceptable personality, it makes little difference whether she asks the man out or waits patiently for him to get around to asking her out. Men simply like attractive women, whether they are passive or aggressive. What if a woman is not the kind of woman a man would normally want to date? Perhaps she is unattractive and acts obnoxiously. Again, whether she takes the initiative or waits futilely for him to matters little. Men dislike her (equally) either way. Thus, if taking the initiative—regardless of whether you are a man or a woman (attractive or unattractive)—you may lose a little pride, but you will not damage your chances for a good relationship. Furthermore, you will save a lot of time. (Similar results were secured by Muehlenhard and McFall [1982].)

What are your chances for success? Russell D. Clark and Elaine Hatfield (see Clark and Hatfield 1981) tried to find out via a simple experiment. We selected college men and women who varied from "slightly unattractive" to "moderately attractive" in appearance and asked them to help us run the experiment. We asked them to approach attractive men and women of the opposite sex and say: "I have been noticing you around campus and I find you to be very attractive." Then they were to ask them one of three questions: (1) "Would you go out with me tonight?" (2) "Would you come over to my apartment tonight?" or (3) "Would you go to bed with me tonight?"

To our surprise, we found it was surprisingly easy for men and women to get a date, if only they have enough courage to ask. More than half the men and women approached agreed to go out with a complete stranger!

Another surprise, in this day of equality, was the big difference in men versus women's willingness to have sex with a complete stranger. Men and women responded as tradition would predict. Men readily accepted sexual invitations, while women were extremely reluctant to do so. Women generally refused to go to a man's apartment or to have

TABLE 4.3   **Percentage of Compliance with Each Request**

SEX OF REQUESTOR	DATE	TYPE OF REQUEST APARTMENT	BED
Male	56%	6%	0%
Female	50%	69%	75%

sexual relations with him. Men, on the other hand, were fairly willing to go to strange women's apartments or to bed! Equally interesting were men and women's reactions to the requests. In general, men were intrigued by a sexual invitation. They made comments such as, "Why do we have to wait until tonight?" or "I can't tonight, but tomorrow would be fine." Often, the men that said "no" were apologetic—i.e., "I'm married," or "I'm going with someone." In contrast, the women's reactions to the intimate requests were, "You've got to be kidding," or "What is wrong with you, leave me alone."

• *If you are too shy to ask for a date,* rely on "social density" networks. Arrange it so you are always in the same place at the same time— surrounded by other people, of course. Then, one time, it will just seem appropriate to form a smaller group—just the two of you. Simply by happenstance (although a happenstance carefully planned) you may become a couple.

In the next chapter, we go beyond the first date, beyond romantic beginnings. Then, things get a little more complicated.

Figure 5.1. Rolland and Rosemary Chateauvert and Eileen Kalahar Hatfield, 1940.

Chapter 5

More Intimate Affairs

The first date I had with this man was just awful! He was so incredibly awkward on that date—spilling things, saying the wrong things, simply not knowing how to handle himself. However, when the evening came to an end, and he asked me out for a second date, I didn't hesitate for a second. Any man that gorgeous, I thought, should get a second chance. And I'm glad I gave him the benefit of the doubt. I ended up falling in love with him, and we've lived happily ever after. But if he hadn't been so handsome, I probably wouldn't have gone out with him for a second time. (Fifty-year-old woman from THE GROUP)

Getting the first date is only the first step on the road to forming long-term, intimate relationships. Looks may help you get the first date—possibly even a second—but then other characteristics become important. People begin to look beyond the outside wrappings to see what is on the inside. Slowly, they discover whether the person is everything they want him or her to be—or maybe even more (or less?). You will notice little things—her favorite television shows, whether she smokes, and how she behaves when she gets angry. You also search for major information: What are his dreams and goals? What is his history (any skeletons in the closet)? As you take in all this information, you are always asking: Is this what I want? Am I what he/she wants?

All these considerations begin to emerge as the first date turns into a second, a third, and a fourth. Perhaps looks do not become any less important, but other factors become more and more important.

PRINCES AND PRINCESSES STICK WITH EACH OTHER; FROGS AND FROGETTES GET STUCK WITH EACH OTHER

In chapter 4, we showed how the law of supply and demand operates in the dating marketplace to bring Gorgeous Georges and Georgettes and Plain Joes and Janes together for a first date. In this chapter, we will show that such "perfect matches" are probably the happiest and the most likely to last.

There is considerable evidence that couples matched in appearance do have a head start on happiness. In one study (Silverman 1971), couples were observed in several natural settings—in movie theater lines, in singles bars, and at assorted social events. A team of researchers rated the daters' looks. Not so surprisingly, it was found that most couples were remarkably similar in attractiveness. A handsome man was most likely to have a beautiful woman on his arm. A homely man was likely to be spotted buying a drink for a homely woman.

This study also found that "similarity breeds content." The more similar the couples in physical appeal, the more delighted they seemed to be with each another, as reflected in intimate touching. Sixty percent of the couples similar in attractiveness were engaged in some type of touching. On the other hand, only 22 percent of mismatched couples were touching.

Other evidence that dating couples tend to be matched in physical attractiveness was found by social psychologist Bernard Murstein (1972). He meticulously arranged to have judged for attractiveness photographs of several hundred couples going steady or engaged. Long-term dating couples were better matched in attractiveness than randomly paired couples.

Further evidence that "similarity breeds content" and may even lead to wedding plans was found in a study of 123 couples from the University of California, Los Angeles, who responded to campus advertisements for participants in a study on romantic relationships. Many of the couples were casually or seriously dating; a few were engaged or married. The partners came into the researchers' laboratory to have their pictures taken (their attractiveness was rated from these) and to complete a questionnaire on their relationship.

Couples well matched in attractiveness were most in love. They were most likely to score high on Rubin's (1970) Love Scale, which includes items such as:

1. I feel that I can confide in _____ about virtually everything.

2. If I could never be with _____, I would feel miserable.

3. I would forgive _____ for practically anything.

Nine months later, the couples were asked about their relationships once again. For the couples still together it was the "well matched" couples whose love was more likely to have swelled. Couples who were mismatched were more likely to have broken up.

In addition, the researchers found that although casual daters were fairly well matched and serious daters were even better matched, the engaged and married couples were the best matched of all. Seemingly, therefore, the relationships surviving the courtship stage and getting as far as the altar are those in which the couples are well matched (White 1980b).

We will now march you to the altar. (But don't worry. You can annul everything at the end of the section.) How important is attractiveness to *you* in choosing a mate with whom to spend a lifetime (or some fraction thereof)?

WHICH BRIDE/GROOM FOR YOU?

Queen Anne of Cleves was the first "picture bride." In 1540, Henry VIII of England wanted to make Germany an ally, so he began a search for a German bride. Anne of Cleves was a leading prospect. He sent court artist Hans Holbein the Younger to paint a "perfect likeness." Holbein painted a flattering portrait of Anne, and Henry fell in love. He traveled, laden with presents, to meet her boat. When he saw Anne, he was repulsed by her appearance. She was tall and gangly, and her face was pitted from smallpox. She was equally repulsed by the aging and portly Henry. Although they went through with the marriage, it was never consummated. Eventually they agreed on an annulment (see Illustration 5.2).

In spite of this difficult start, mail-order brides have long been a way for men and women to find mates. In frontier Alaska, in the Old West during gold rush days, and in Hawaii in the 1900s, men and women in search of partners exchanged pictures. If they liked what they saw, they married, sight unseen.

Figure 5.2. Hans Holbein, *Anne of Cleves,* 1539, oil on wood panel. Cour
tesy of Musée du Louvre, Paris.

The tradition continues. Today, *Japan International, Sherry West, Club Joy, Inter Pacific, The Waysider,* and *Candy Friend* are among the dozens of publications around the world that advertise mail-order brides. *Cherry Blossoms* is the best known; in Hawaii, over one thousand men subscribe to this catalog. As you can see from Illustration 5.3, men are assumed to be very concerned with the potential brides' vital statistics. No doubt the women are equally concerned.

• Sheila is a thirty-year-old Malaysian Indian housewife whose face would not launch a thousand ships. But what she gives you a glimpse of below the neck, in full color, even I have to admire. If she's only 35–26½–36 as she says, she must have a small rib cage. She likes parties, dances and films (the spicier the better!) and makes it clear that if she likes you, you will be welcome to visit her for fun and games.

• I am rarely at a loss for words, but this lady leaves me speechless (almost). She is English, an office worker, and she says she collects men. In the photo she shows off her legs from the ankles right up almost to the hip joint. So far so good. She's a little overweight, but that just makes more to hold onto. What I can't get over is the part above the neck. Somebody must have switched the heads. She looks much more like a stern old school marm than a modern swinger. Kind of makes me wonder what she does with the men after she "collects" them. Would you like to find out? $6

• This lady is good looking except for the disturbing wen on the end of her nose. It would be easy for a doctor to remove that blemish and two other less conspicuous ones on her face. Secretarial student, 18, name Josephine. $10.

• Ivy may not have the full figure of the preceding two ladies, but she has a full sense of humor. "Vital statistics? Forget it! Rather picture a bean pole and compare it to my body. You'll find no difference." "She's 29, Malaysian, works as a cartographer's assistant, has average looks (wears glasses) and I don't see that her figure is as bleak as she suggests.

—*Cherry Blossoms* (1982)

The *Cherry Blossoms* editors leave nothing to chance. For example, they give subscribers a pamphlet entitled, "How to Write to Oriental Ladies":

Use your judgment also about when to send your photo. If you are very good looking, your photo should help to bring an early reply. If you are not so attractive, it might be better to wait until you have established a correspondence. Use the extra time to have several pictures taken of yourself so you can pick out the best one (get some friend's opinions too). It's a good idea to be neatly dressed when the photo is taken. Most of our ladies are more concerned about your personality and values—and most importantly, your attitude about *them*—than they

Figure 5.3. Current day mail-order brides.

are about your appearance. But they do want to see what you look like, and it doesn't hurt to put your best image forward. (p. 12)

Pomeroy and Broussard, 1984

Cherry Blossoms editors recognize that looks will be critically important for getting initial attention through the mail, but as they told the interested men, "Most of our ladies are more concerned about your personality and values." Is this statement true, or were the editors only lending false optimism to the subscribers, perhaps to increase business? No, the editors were probably sincere, just as were all the young people who participated in the following studies on "campus values in mate selection," who claimed that physical attractiveness is not *that* important in a mate.

Early sociologists became intrigued with the question, "What are the factors important in mate selection?" What characteristics do people want in someone with whom they will live until death do they part? As far back as 1939, sociologist Rueben Hill (1945) had college students at the University of Wisconsin complete a questionnaire on "campus values in mate selection." When these students were asked how important and indispensable certain personal characteristics would be in a mate, appearance was fourteenth on the list for men and seventeenth on the list for women (out of eighteen traits). Most important in those days for both men and women were traits such as dependable character, emotional stability, pleasing disposition, and mutual attraction. Women were also particularly concerned that their mate be ambitious and industrious.

The "campus values in mate selection" study was repeated again and again—in 1956, 1967, and 1977 (Henze and Hudson 1969; Hoyt and Hudson 1981; McGinnis 1958). Slowly, over the years, looks have become more important to both men and women. By 1977, appearance was ninth on the list for men and fifteenth on the list for women. Dependable character, emotional stability, and a pleasing disposition were still indispensable in 1977, as in 1939. One interesting reversal is that men now care more about having a good-looking wife than about marrying someone who can cook or clean house; the opposite was true several years ago. (One alternative explanation can be presented for the above results: Instead of looks becoming more important over the years, perhaps people have just become more honest in admitting what really counts.)

What about you? What do *you* want in a mate? List all the traits you think essential in someone you would marry.

Could Not Live Without These Traits in a Mate:

1. _____

2. _____

3. _____

4. _____

5. _____

How do your requirements compare to other people's? Let's find out.

Elaine Hatfield and her colleagues at the University of Wisconsin interviewed several hundred couples—causally and steadily dating couples, newlyweds, and couples married up to sixty years (Hatfield et al. 1984; Traupmann and Hatfield 1981). They compiled a list of the characteristics everyone—from dating couples to long marrieds—think are critically important for a relationship. Obviously, although people do care what their partners look like, they care about a lot of other things too. Some examples:

Personal Concerns

1. Having a good-looking mate.

2. Having a mate who is friendly and relaxed in social settings.

3. Having a mate who is intelligent and informed.

Emotional Concerns

4. Being liked and loved.

5. Receiving affection—touching, hugging, kissing.

6. Experiencing a fulfilling sexual relationship.

7. Having a partner who is faithful.

8. Having a mate who supports your need to be a free and independent person.

9. Contributing time and effort to household work—grocery shopping, cleaning, yard work, etc.

10. Having a mate who is easy to live with.

11. Having a partner who takes a fair share of the responsibility for making decisions.

Opportunities Gained and Lost

12. Having the opportunity to partake of the many life experiences that depend on being married—for example, becoming a parent and even grandparent, the chance to be included in "married couple" social events; having someone to count on in old age.

13. Marriage requires people to give up certain opportunities in order to be in this relationship. The opportunities could have been other mates, a career, travel, etc. Having a mate who makes the sacrifice worth it.

Now that we have reviewed some of the things people *want* from love (and have found out they want good looks *and* everything else), we can proceed to a more unsettling question: What is realistic to *expect* from love?

LOVE IS A COMPROMISE

In *A New Look at Love*, Elaine Hatfield made what seemed to her an obvious statement: Marriage, like life, requires compromise. You can get many of the things you want, but not everything. Soon after the book appeared, she received dozens of letters from lovers furious that she suggested they might not get all they hoped from love. The lovers angrily argued that, not only did they want it all, but they refused to settle for anything less. In fact, a few lovers insisted they already had it all.

It is easy, of course, to see why people long to believe that "love conquers all." Our yearning for unconditional, totally fulfilling love is primitive. We would all like to believe that, even if we lost our looks, openly expressed our most unacceptable feelings, or refused to work, our lovers, family, and friends would continue to care for us. The accumulating evidence, however, forces us to be more realistic (see Hatfield et al. 1984; Hatfield and Walster 1978). Here is the reality:

- Although we can not get everything we want, we can get many of the things we long for.

- Marriage is to give and take—the more we are able and willing to give another, the more we expect to get, and do actually get, in return.

- Men and women who think they can give and give with no thought of return are deceiving themselves. Those who expect such selfless love from their partners most assuredly are deceiving themselves.

• Men and women are profoundly concerned with equity and fairness. Considerations of equity influence who we marry, how happy we are in our marriages, and how stable our marriages will be.

Let us review the evidence for the above statements:

Finding the Mate You "Deserve"

Marriage counselors often act as if everyone should hold out for the best in marriage. For example, Herter (1974) warns young men to use "logic and common sense" in choosing a wife. He advises them to make sure their wife possesses the following basic assets. She should:

1. Be beautiful.
2. Be younger than you.
3. Be shorter than you.
4. Be the same religion.
5. Be the same race.
6. Be willing to pretend to be equally intelligent or less intelligent than you.
7. Be a virgin at the time you meet.
8. Be willing to live with you for a year before marriage to see if things work out.
9. Be willing to let you participate in the sports you like.
10. Be tolerant of the work you do; be tolerant of your ambitions and abilities.
11. Be willing to have as many sons as you want.
12. Be sexually desirable.
13. Be free from diabetes.
14. Not be a regular drinker.
15. Have not used marijuana, LSD, or similar drugs.
16. Not have a family history of insanity.
17. Have large breasts.
18. Have consent of both parents.
19. Be a good cook.
20. Be a good sewer.
21. Not be a complainer or arguer.
22. Be clean and neat.
23. Not be overweight.
24. Not snore.

"Logic and common sense," says Herter. Ann Landers (1975) gives similar advice when counseling women about how to choose a husband.

Unfortunately, such "advice" is wildly impractical. Of course, Everyman and Everywoman desires perfection. Unfortunately, they are not very likely to get it. "When I was a young man," runs the old joke, "I vowed never to marry until I found the perfect woman. Well, I found her—but alas, *she* was waiting for the perfect man" (composer Robert Schumann, cited in Baron and Byrne 1983).

Many social psychologists have argued that equity considerations are important determinants of who marries whom. Peter Blau (1964), for example, argues that people end up with the mates they deserve. People must make potential lovers "offers they can't refuse." The most desirable suitors attract the most desirable mates; the rest must settle for the "leftovers." Market principles ensure that everyone ends up with the mates they deserve.

Erving Goffman (1952) puts the matter even more succinctly. He notes, "A proposal of marriage in our society tends to be a way in which a man sums up his social attributes and suggests to a woman that hers are not so much better as to preclude a merger . . . in these matters." (p. 456).

There is considerable evidence that people do generally end up with mates about as attractive as they are, and who have about as much to offer overall as they do.

Matching: Married Look-Alikes

Earlier in this chapter, we described how couples matched in attractiveness are more likely to find their way to the altar than are mismatched couples. Matched couples are also most likely to stay together long enough to celebrate their silver and golden anniversaries.

Studies in the United States, Canada, Germany, and Japan found that matched couples are more likely to get married *and* stay married than mismatched couples (Cavior and Boblett 1972; White 1980b). In one study, for example, several New England couples, ranging in age from twenty-eight to fifty-nine, agreed to participate in a study in exchange for a tour of a historical house (Murstein and Christy 1976). The authors assessed men and women's attractiveness in three ways: *self-ratings*, men and women rated their own looks; *spouse ratings*; and *objective ratings*, five judges rated photographs of the husbands and wives. The authors found that the more attractive the husband, the more attractive the wife—regardless of how looks were measured (similar results were secured by Price and Vandenberg 1979).

A similar study was conducted with elderly couples ranging in age from sixty-four to eighty-six in a small west coast town. A high degree

Figure 5.4. Married look-alikes. Reprinted with permission of Globe Photos, Inc.

of matching was found for the mates' looks when their appearance was rated by outside judges (Peterson and Miller 1980).

Matching in size also seems to be important. Two recent investigators, Maria Watkins and Arlen Price, surveyed 215 couples married in the San Francisco area in 1974 or 1975. Several tests were administered to the husbands and wives, including vocabulary and reasoning tests, and physical measurements. Then in 1982, the researchers were able to track down 167 of the original 215 couples. Of those couples, 52 had broken up and 111 couples were still together in 1982. What distinguished those who had broken up from those who remained together? Similarity on physical traits, no less. Those couples who remained together were more likely to be similar on height, weight, forearm length, and shoe size! It was found that similarity on physical attributes was even more important than similarity on education and vocabulary. (Reported in *Wisconsin State Journal*, Sunday, January 9, 1983, page 3/section 6.)

The tendency for look alikes to marry is so strong that as a parlor game, you can pick out who belongs to whom . . . and be pretty sure you'll be right. In one study (Terry & Macklin, 1977), men and women were given a series of photographs. Each set of photographs consisted of one man and four women. Which of the four women was the man's wife? Men and women turned out to be surprisingly good at spotting her. They were right about 60% of the time. (By chance, they should have hit the mark only 25% of the time.) How did they do it? Men claimed they assumed each man was married to the most beautiful of the four women! (Every man a winner!) Women tended to assume like marries like. They were, of course, right.

Matching: More Complex Cases

Of course, couples can be "well matched" in a variety of ways. For example, Jacqueline Kennedy chose Aristotle Onassis, who was not particularly good looking . . . but was unusually bright, charming . . . and rich. We probably all know of similar cases closer to home.

Murstein et al. (1974) provide a description of the way such complex matching operates:

> A handsome man is seen with a woman of mediocre attractiveness. "I wonder what he sees in her?" may be the quizzical question of a bystander. Quite possibly, she possesses compensating qualities such as greater intelligence, interpersonal competence, and wealth than he, of which the bystander knows nothing. . . .
>
> Another case of compensatory exchange might be indicated if an aged statesman proposed marriage to a young beautiful woman. He would probably be trading his prestige and power for her physical attractiveness and youth. (pp. 3–4)

The evidence supports the contention that people do engage in such complicated balancing and counterbalancing when selecting mates.

WHAT BEAUTY CAN BUY

$$

> "My face is my fortune," said the pretty maid in the nursery rhyme, by which she meant that her pretty face would enable her to get a husband—the prettier the face, the richer the husband. The prettiest faces in our society angle for the biggest fortunes. Why else is the office beauty the front office secretary? Why else are airline stewardesses, models and actresses chosen solely for their looks? Why, if not to put them in the most visible places in the market so that the richest men can see and buy them? Men have so structured our society that the most beautiful women, like all other valuable property, can go to the highest bidder. (Stannard 1971, 123)

Evidence does indicate that a woman's face is her fortune. For example, in the 1930s in Oakland, California, educators observed fifth-

and sixth-grade girls as they played on the school playgrounds. They rated each girl's facial beauty, coloring, figure, sex appeal, and grooming. Years later, sociologist Glen Elder (1969) tracked down these girls to find out what had become of them. He found that the more beautiful the preadolescent the better she had done. The beautiful girls apparently used their beauty to capture mates whose social promise and subsequent social power far exceeded their own. (Additional support for Elder's contention comes from Holmes and Hatch [1938]; Taylor and Glenn [1976]; and Udry [1977].)

Can a man also trade looks for a rich spouse? In a recent study (Udry and Eckland 1982), 1300 men and women were interviewed fifteen years after graduating from high school. The investigators were interested in whether the men's and women's attractiveness at the time they graduated from high school (as judged from their yearbook pictures) would be related to their future success. Once again, it was documented that attractiveness helps women find a high-status husband. The more attractive a woman was in high school, the more educated and rich her eventual husband was. Attractive men, on the other hand, did not seem to use their attractiveness to marry an educated, high-status woman. In fact, the more attractive the men, the less educated their wives! Why? The researchers write:

> Perhaps being good looking gives a man so many heterosexual opportu-
> nities that he loses sight of other objectives and marries at an earlier
> age, thereby probably marrying a younger woman than the less good
> looking man, and therefore a woman with less education. (pp. 7–8)

This study, unlike some others, found that good looks do not always help men. Attractive men were less educated and had lower-status jobs than did less attractive men.

The investigators also examined whether attractive versus unat-tractive men and women differ in their chances of getting married. For men, attractiveness did not seem to matter. Handsome men and ugly ones were equally likely to be married. Beauty was critically important for women, however. The most beautiful women were ten times more likely to have marched up to the altar than were homely ones.

A Loving Nature + Sacrifice + Money

Remember the *Psychology Today* interview we described in chapter 1 (Berscheid, Hatfield [Walster] and Bohrnstedt 1973)? In addition to asking the readers how they felt about their looks, we also asked how they felt about their most intimate affairs. Who, we asked, is the best-looking—you or your partner?

"Describe your partner's appearance":

- Much more attractive than I.
- Slightly more attractive than I.
- As attractive as I.
- Slightly less attractive than I.
- Much less attractive than I.

We predicted that if couples were mismatched in looks there would be a compensating mismatch in other areas. We were right. The men and women who were better-looking than their spouses admitted their partner's assets balanced things out. For example, they said their mates were unusually loving or self-sacrificing, or rich. Those who admitted they were not as good-looking as their partners insisted that they were, however, unusually loving or self-sacrificing, or rich.

Other evidence also suggests that men and women know attractiveness can be used to bargain for other "luxuries in life." One investigator (Dermer 1973) found that, the more attractive the woman, the longer the vacations she expected to take after she married and the fewer hours she expected to have to work to supplement her husband's income.

Recently, freelance writer Pat Monthei (1981) gave ordinary women advice on how to catch a good-looking man:

> I've never been a 10. As a matter of fact, I've been a 6 all my life. Despite my numerical disadvantage, every meaningful relationship (in my many years of using such words) has been spent with someone of a higher denomination. If there's an Adonis within my working sphere, I'll find him. Correct that, we'll find each other.
>
> . . . How does the average woman, like myself and a million other 6's, some 5's and a few 4's wind up with the perfect men. It's easy, if you follow a few basic rules. (p. 44)

The author then describes how you flatter him, feed him, and give him sex—basically, give him everything he wants. Such is the way an average-looking woman can get and keep a "10" man.

> *Dear Abby:* Our 19-year-old daughter Caroline has started going with a guy named Angelo. He never takes her anyplace. He just comes over every night to watch television and wear out our sofa . . . What should I do?
>
> Kitchen Sitter
>
> *Dear Sitter:* Send me a picture of Caroline and I'll tell you what to do.
>
> (Van Buren 1981, 181)

Ironically, sometimes the delicate balance of marriage means losing one's attractiveness. Money, status, a loving nature, and sacrifice can buy the opportunity to "let oneself go." The man who toils sixty hours a week for the family paycheck may feel he has the right to get a "beergut." Consider the opinion of one middle-aged woman from THE GROUP:

> I weigh over 200 pounds, but I don't care. I'm entitled to look the way I do. I'm the one who brings home the paycheck—and it's a damn good paycheck. My husband doesn't deserve a beautiful wife, *too!* It sort of evens it all up, if you know what I mean.

Apparently, then, we can use our assets either to attract partners with exactly the same assets or to attract partners possessing quite different assets. In general, in long-term relationships people attempt to work out a delicate compromise between what they give and what they get.

THE RELATIONSHIP BETWEEN THE PRINCESS AND THE FROG

What happens when people beat the odds? When, through some fluke, they end up with mates clearly superior (or inferior) to themselves? What happens when the princess marries the frog, kisses him, and discovers he really is only a frog after all? We will discuss three aspects of the relationship between the princess and the frog: (1) happiness; (2) sex; and (3) power.

The Princess and the Frog Do Not Live Happily Ever After

In mismatched relationships, participants generally become increasingly dissatisfied. It is obvious, of course, why the princess would be dissatisfied. She can never really forget she could have married a real prince. But, the "lucky" frog might have cause for unhappiness too. He is confronted with a wrenching dilemma. On the one hand, he is eager to keep the princess's love. After all, what are his chances of fooling a princess a second time? On the other hand, he is painfully aware that the princess has little reason to stay with him. He may feel a little guilty that he took the princess away from what she could have had.

Recently, we tested the notion that inequitable affairs are the unhappiest love affairs (Traupmann and Hatfield 1981). We interviewed more than six-hundred men and women—dating couples, couples living together, newlyweds, and older couples married for forty, fifty, or sixty years. Our first step was to find out if the couples' relationships were fair and equitable. We asked:

> Considering what you put into your relationship, compared to what you get out of it and what your partner puts in compared to what he (she) gets out of it, how does your relationship "stack up":
> −3 My partner is getting a much better deal.
> −2 My partner is getting a somewhat better deal.
> −1 My partner is getting a slightly better deal.
> 0 We are both getting an equal deal.
> +1 I am getting a slightly better deal.
> +2 I am getting a somewhat better deal.
> +3 I am getting a much better deal.

From these answers, we could easily calculate whether men and women felt they were getting more than they deserved, less than they deserved, or if things were "just right."

We found that couples in fair and equitable relationships were more content and happy than other couples. Men and women who admitted they were getting far more than they really deserved were uneasy. They were less content, less happy, and felt a lot more guilty than their peers. Apparently, an "embarrassment of riches" is just that—painfully embarrassing. Of course, those men and women who felt they were getting far less than they deserved were in even worse shape—they were a lot less content, a lot less happy, and a lot angrier than were their peers [see Berscheid et al. 1972; Hatfield, Walster, and Traupmann 1979; Matthews and Clark 1982; Schafer and Keith 1980; Sprecher 1980; Traupmann, Hatfield, and Sprecher 1981; Traupmann, Hatfield, and Wexler 1983; Traupmann, Peterson, Utne, and Hatfield 1981).

Perhaps the strongest proponents of the equity perspective have been family therapists. For example, Sager (1976) observes how important a contract is to marriage and notes the discontent that occurs when equity breaks down.

> In work with marital couples and families, the concept of individual marriage contracts has proven extremely useful. . . . The term *individual contract* refers to a person's expressed and unexpressed, conscious and beyond awareness, concepts of his obligations within the marital relationship, and to the benefits he expects to derive from marriage in general and from his spouse in particular. But what must be emphasized above all is the reciprocal aspect of the contract: what each partner expects to give and what he expects to receive from his spouse in exchange are crucial. Contracts deal with every conceivable aspect of family life: relationships with friends, achievements, power, sex, leisure time,

money, children, etc. . . . . It is most important to realize that, while each spouse may be aware of his own needs and wishes on some level of awareness, he does not usually realize that his attempts to fulfill the partner's needs are based on the covert assumption that his own wishes will thereby be fulfilled. When significant aspects of the contract cannot be fulfilled, as is inevitable, and especially when these lie beyond his own awareness, the disappointed partner may react with rage, injury, depression, or withdrawal, and provoke marital discord by acting as though a real agreement had been broken. (pp. 4–5)

Theorists from a variety of other areas agree that equity considerations are critically important in intimate relations (see, for example, Bernard 1964; Blau 1964; Lederer and Jackson 1968; McCall 1966; Patterson 1971; Scanzoni 1972 and Storer 1966).

Sex in Equitable Versus Inequitable Relationships

"I Have a Headache"
I have a headache.
We did it last month.
I just brushed my teeth.
I have to finish *War and Peace* first.
We're out of Kleenex.

After my nap.
I just had a shower and I don't want to get all sweaty.
My nail polish is still wet.
I can't light your fire without a blowtorch.
The cat feels left out.
I don't need to lose anymore weight.
The honeymoon is over.
I've got a sink full of dirty dishes.
Do you have an appointment?
Let's not and say we did!

—(from the poster, "101 Reasons Not to Have Sex Tonight," 1981 R-R Productions Ltd., New York, New York)

Theorists have observed that couples' dissatisfaction with mismatched relationships can be manifested in yet another way—by refusing to get intimate. This refusal makes sense. If couples feel fairly treated, if they love each other, and if they feel comfortable with one another, then sex should go well. On the other hand, if couples feel trapped in unjust relationships, hate one another, and feel uncomfortable in one another's presence, their deep-seated resentment or guilt may corrode their sexual encounters (see Barbach 1975; Berne 1964; Heiman, LoPiccolo, and LoPiccolo 1976; Hunt 1974; Kaplan 1974; Kinsey, Pomeroy, and Martin 1948; Kinsey, Pomeroy, Martin, and Gebhard 1953;

Figure 5.5. Theorists agree that equity considerations are critically important. © 1959 United Feature Syndicate, Inc.

Masters and Johnson 1966, 1970, 1976; Safilios-Rothschild 1977; Zilbergeld 1978).

In our research, we have found that couples usually have the best sex when they feel fairly treated [Hatfield et al. 1979, 1982]. Equitably treated men and women are generally most satisfied with their sexual relations. They also feel more loving and close (versus angry and distant) *after* sex than do other couples. Those who have a sneaky suspicion they may be getting *more* than they deserve from their marriages are generally slightly uncomfortable about sex; those who are certain they are getting *less* than they deserve feel quite uncomfortable (similar results were secured by Matthews and Clark 1982). (One member of THE GROUP observed he no longer was willing to have sexual relations with his wife. "It just wasn't fair," he observed. Over the years, he had kept his shape and had acquired prestige and wealth as well. What had she acquired?—an extra one hundred pounds.)

Some investigators have looked simply at how the partner's attractiveness affects the quality of sex. In a recent, large-scale study, sociologists Philip Blumstein and Pepper Schwartz collected information from thousands of couples from all over the country. The couples represented several different intimate lifestyles—married couples, cohabitors, gay couples, and lesbian couples. It was found that when men and women thought their partners were attractive, they had a better sex life. Having a physically attractive partner was particularly important for cohabitors. Lesbian couples, on the other hand, managed to be relatively unaffeted by conventional standards of beauty (Blumstein and Schwartz 1983).

The Power of What Might Have Been

Something else affects mismatched relationships. The princess starts to remember the attention she used to get from the prince (or two or three) she could have married. How could she ever have married a frog? The frog begins to wonder too.

Social psychologists Thibaut and Kelley (1965) have argued that every relationship is embedded in a network of other relationships—both actual and potential. Whether we are happy with our marriage and want to remain in it depends on the types of relationships we have experienced in the past *and* on the types of relationships we think are out there awaiting us. Thibaut & Kelley label the first our Comparison Level (CL) and the second our Comparison Level for Alternatives (CL Alt.). These "comparison levels" determine how satisfied we are with our present relationships.

1. THE CL

Zsa Zsa Gabor compares her eighth husband with her seventh, sixth, fifth, . . . on down to the first. John Derek compares Bo Derek with Ursula Andress and Linda Evans. If these individuals recall that things were better with their first spouse than they are now, they may become discontent. We know of an elderly woman who reentered the dating marketplace after her husband died. She was a gorgeous woman before her marriage. She had been the center of attention with men. She could pick and choose among the most handsome and finest men, and did— her husband. When she returned to the dating market again at seventy-two, she was bitterly disappointed. Once, she had the best. Now, handsome young men would not look at her. Even men her own age wanted younger women. The only men interested in her were "old and decrepit." She could not help comparing what had been with what was, and found that wanting. As a consequence, she had not yet found happiness in autumn love. So, if the princess's love affair with the frog is her first intimacy, she is more likely to be content than if she has come straight from the arms of a prince.

2. THE CL ALT.

Another comparison level that effects our present relationships is the "comparison level for alternatives." Here, we compare our present relationship to ones we perceive are obtainable *now*, if only. . . . This CL Alt. determines whether or not we stay in the present relationship. If our marriage seems less rewarding than the competition, we may pack our bags. To the arms of the more desirable partner we want to flee. Sometimes, people do leave and never return to their partners. Sometimes, they are fickle—divorce is costly, and what about the children? Back they come (from the driveway) and unpack their bags to try the relationship again.

If one partner has greater access to alternative relationships, this opportunity can affect the power dynamics in the relationship. The person with greater opportunities has more power. Usually, as we have demonstrated in earlier chapters, the more attractive person has greater opportunities—physical attractiveness equals power.

Evidence exists to support these assertions. In a study of 231 dating couples, Anne Peplau (1979) found that, if one partner was more attractive, he/she was also likely to have more say in the relationship. In other words, those with more dating alternatives tended to have greater power, and, as we might expect, attractive people were the ones with more alternatives. White (1980a&b) also found that, among casual and serious daters, the more attractive partners had more opposite sex friends.

Sociologist Willard Waller (1938) called the consequence of this imbalance the "principle of least interest." The person least interested in the relationship has greater control in the relationship. The good-looking partner often has the least interest, primarily because he/she has more opportunities to start over with someone else. One young woman we interviewed put it this way, "I wouldn't go out with someone too attractive because he would have too much power in the relationship. To keep his interest, I would have to do things his way, and who wants to sacrifice all that?"

This state of affairs can thus be very unsettling, particularly for the less desirable partner who is precariously balanced in a state of uncertainty and self-sacrifice.

PATCHING UP A MISMATCH

What happens when a couple is seriously mismatched? Do they simply "grin and bear it"? Rarely. Couples who discover their marriages are precariously balanced remedy the situation in a couple of different ways:

- Some couples face the facts and work to change things. They work out a more acceptable give and take. The partner who has been taking advantage of the other begins to bend a little. The "martyr" learns to speak up a little more and to demand more.

- Some couples stay stuck. They do not change their behavior— but they do change their own and others' *perceptions*. They try to reassure themselves, their mates, and their friends (plus the mirror) that the situation is really fairer than it seems.

Setting Things Right

In most love affairs, relationships start out right. Lovers end up with mates who, if not their ideal, at least seem to be the best they can hope for. But, over time, the marital balance inevitably shifts. The beautiful new bride, so delighted with her new husband, may later find this particular husband not at all what she had in mind. How did she know he would drop out of medical school? The grossly overweight man may suddenly lose 120 pounds through diet and jogging, only to discover he is now much less tolerant of his wife's shortcomings. What happens when the marital balance suddenly goes askew? For one thing, observers have noticed, participants usually move with surprising swiftness to "set things right."

Psychologist Gerald Patterson (1971) observed, "There is an odd kind of equity which holds when people interact with each other. In effect, we get what we give, both in amount and in kind. Each of us seems to have his own bookkeeping system for love, and for pain. Over time, the books are balanced." (p. 26).

There is considerable anecdotal evidence that, when couples become mismatched, they must do something to "fine tune" their relationships (Angell 1936; Cayan 1959; Komarovsky 1971). For example, it has been discovered that, often, when an individual's looks change drastically, trouble erupts at home. In an article in *Weight Watchers* magazine (Palmer 1974), Dr. Alfred Jones warned readers that:

> Marriage, like all relationships, is a balance. When one partner is overweight, that fact has been considered, perhaps unconsciously, in setting up the balance. Obviously, when you remove the obesity, you upset the balance. The relationship shifts and takes on a different complexion. (p. 50)

Further, Marjorie Palmer (1974) adds, once excess weight is gone,

> "Gone are . . . the attempts to buy love through acquiescence and the overweight's traditional don't-make-waves-they-throw-you-out policy. In their place comes new pride, an awareness of rights and a tendency to

speak up for those rights" (p. 23). The following case study illustrates her point:

Every year for 10 years, Bob and Maire Coleman [fictional names] went to the same place for vacation—a secluded cabin in the woods of northern Minnesota. Bob Coleman loved the cabin and the quiet, restful times he spent there. . . . In the early years of their marriage, it had occurred to him that the cabin didn't offer much change of pace for his wife. Marie weighed over 190 and all her days were spent in semi-seclusion. At home, she stayed in their apartment and cooked and cleaned, and at the cabin she did more or less the same thing. But she loved the North Woods as much as he.

Then one day Marie decided to do something about her weight. In six months she'd lost 65 pounds and looked pretty terrific, all curves and interesting angles where once there'd been only mounds of flesh. She felt better, too, more energetic and self-confident. For the first time in more years than she cared to remember, Marie was proud of her looks—and of herself.

Bob was proud of her, too. He'd forgotten how pretty she was under all that fat. He felt as if the bride of his youth had been returned to him and he sometimes smiled to himself because he, an old married man, was so excited by the wife he'd had for more than a decade. There was only one thing wrong: When it came time to plan their next vacation, Marie didn't want to go up to the cabin. She said she'd rather go to a resort this year. At long last, she pointed out to Bob that he might be on vacation while they were at the cabin, but for her it meant housework, running after kids and "business as usual." This year she wanted to relax and be waited on, too.

Bob was very disappointed, not only because he'd miss his cabin but also because of Marie's attitude. In the past, she'd gone along with his suggestions, but she was being downright stubborn about this vacation. He couldn't understand what had come over her.

What had come over Marie was a healthy and long-repressed interest in herself and her own happiness. She had never enjoyed her vacations at the cabin, but then, she never enjoyed much of anything when she was fat. One place was as good as the next, as long as she could hide her bulk. Now that she was thin, she felt capable of—and entitled to—a real vacation. Hiding in the cabin, cooking for Bob and the kids, wasn't good enough anymore. (Palmer 1974, 22–23)

Convincing Yourself What Isn't Is, and What Is Isn't

Of course, couples sometimes find it easier to change their minds than to change their behavior. Sometimes, couples threatened by the discovery that their relationship is precariously balanced prefer to close their eyes to the problem and to reassure themselves that, "Really, everything is fine, just fine." They might rely on several rationalizations: "An extra 25 pounds just makes me look voluptuous, doesn't it honey?"

In intimate relationships, it is fairly easy to believe what you want to believe. Love relationships are complex. Even in the best of circumstances, people often find it extremely difficult to decide what is fair. The variety of resources that can be exchanged in the intimate relationship is tremendous. Look back at the traits desired in companions listed earlier in this chapter. With so much being exchanged, it is easy to become confused about exactly what is fair. Should having high intellect be worth less, about the same, or more than physical appearance? We can argue endlessly with ourselves: Maybe he did let himself go, but he is faithful and maybe that should count for something. And so on. We realign just what is important until things seem a little fairer.

If couples complicate the question still further by trying to decide whether or not their marriages will work out *in the end*, equity calculations become virtually impossible. Thus, when confronted with the fact that the balance of their marriage has changed, some partners find it easiest to try to convince themselves that, eventually, the situation will somehow balance out again.

Calling It Quits

If a relationship becomes impossibly one-sided, the couples are generally tempted to sever the alliance. Most people, however, feel that marriage should last forever; "Till death do us part" is still the cultural ideal. In addition to the moral and religious issues, there are very practical costs to divorce. Divorce is costly in emotional and financial terms. When a married couple separates, parents and friends are stunned, close friends stop calling, one of the parents often loses custody of the children, and careers may fall apart (see Bohannan 1971; Hunt and Hunt 1977; or Napolitane and Pellegrino 1977). So, when married men and women, after trying to right their marriage, ruefully concede failure, they may first respond by withdrawing *psychologically* from the situation—by burying themselves in their work or by giving their all to the children, friends, or backgammon. Yet, if a marital relationship is unbalanced enough, for long enough, couples do sometimes opt for separation or divorce. Currently, over 40 percent of first marriages end in divorce (Mariman, Jamieson, and Floyd 1982).

There is evidence that equitable marriages are more solid and long-term than inequitable ones. Recently, we interviewed 118 newlyweds both immediately after their marriages and a year later (Utne, Hatfield, Traupmann, and Greenberger, 1984). We found that, even a few weeks after their marriages, couples who felt equitably treated in their relationships were more secure about their marriages. Men and women who felt they were getting far less than they deserved from their marriages (and who had every reason to wish something better might come along) were naturally quite pessimistic about the future of the relationship; but, so were those men and women who knew they were getting far more than they deserved from their marriages and thus had every reason to hope the relationship would last. They, too, had to admit their affairs were fairly shaky (see also, Hatfield et al., in press).

"She's Not Really Cheatin'; She's Just Gettin' Even."*

Equitable marriages may be stable marriages for yet another reason. In such marriages, couples are reluctant to risk having affairs. On the other hand, men and women who feel they are not being fairly treated in their marriage are especially likely to explore a fleeting, or more permanent, love affair (Hatfield, Traupmann and Walster, 1979).

Elaine Hatfield and Richard Rapson work as family therapists at King Kalakua Clinic in Honolulu. Most family therapists feel that one affair is generally the way one of the partners tries to desperately communicate with his or her mate that something is wrong in the marriage. Men, who can not win an argument with their spouse, "get even" by having an affair. Their partners have affairs to retaliate. To us, the affair always seems to have more to do with the marriage than with the fact that the new partner is irresistible.

To test the notion that equitable relationships would be "affair proof," we asked *Psychology Today* readers to express their feelings about dating, living together, or being married (Hatfield, Traupmann, and Walster, 1979). We asked readers two questions about their extramarital affairs: (1) How soon after they were married did they have their first affair? and (2) How many extramarital affairs had they had? We found that equitably treated and overbenefited men and women were very reluctant to experiment with extramarital sex. On the average, they were married twelve to fifteen years before they took a chance on getting involved with anyone else. On the other hand, men and women who felt cheated in their marriages began "cheating" outside their marriages far earlier—approximately six to eight years after marriage. Similarly, the overbenefited had the fewest extramaterial encounters (zero to one). Equitably treated men and women had a few more, and the deprived had the most extramarital liaisons of all (one to three).

Apparently, then, equitable relations are likely to be more stable than inequitable ones. In these cases *both* partners are motivated to be faithful.

* (Moe Bandy, Country and Western Song)

SUMMARY

Equity theory, then, does provide a convenient model for examining romantic and marital relationships. Its principles do seem to determine whom people marry and how the marriage goes—how the partners get along, day-to-day and thereafter, and how likely they are to stay together. (Of course, you can never get all scientists to agree on anything. A few psychologists have argued that equity principles should not be and are not always important in love relationships. For a review of critics' research, see Brunner [1945]; Chadwick-Jones [1976]; and Douvan [1974].)

Chapter 6

Let's Get Physical

In all areas of life, appearance matters. But there is one area in which the body, with all its splendors and flaws, becomes extremely important—sexual activities. Whether we are passionately kissing a new lover or an old husband, our bodies (and theirs) are the focus.

In this chapter, we will try to answer a series of questions about physical attractiveness and sexuality posed by THE GROUP.

- Do we *think* attractive people have different sexual desires and participate in different sexual behaviors than unattractive people?

- How does sexual arousal affect how attractive we perceive our lovers to be?

- What are good-looking men and women really like?

- Are beautiful women and handsome men more sexually active or just the opposite?

Figure 6.1. E. S. Master, *Lovers on a Grassy Bank*, Flemish engraving, c. 1430–1470. Courtesy, The Metropolitan Museum of Art, Harris Brisbone, Dick Fund, 1922 (22.83.14).

- Who arouses the most jealousy—the strikingly good-looking person who flirts with our date at a party, or an ugly rival? What if the rival replaces us?

FIRST IMPRESSIONS ABOUT PEOPLE'S SEXUALITY

"Does She (He) or Doesn't She (He)?"

We have spent a great deal of time reviewing the stereotypes for attractive people. There are biases in favor of beautiful people in the schools, in the justice system, in the helping professions, and in the dating and marriage markets. But what happens when we move the setting to the bedroom? What kinds of stereotyping can we expect to find there? Do most people assume attractive people are more (or less) "sexy"? Actually, perhaps this dearth of research is not so surprising, for sex has traditionally been a taboo topic. In fact, during the 1920s, a professor at the University of Minnesota was fired because he approved a questionnaire on sex. (Clear evidence of the researcher's depravity was provided by the fact that he had asked college students such personal questions as, "Have you ever blown into the ear of a person of the opposite sex in order to arouse their passion?")

In an early study, Elaine Hatfield and her colleagues (Dion, Berscheid, and Hatfield [Walster] 1972) asked men and women what they thought attractive versus unattractive people were like. What were their personalities like? What kinds of lives could they expect to have? Quietly sprinkled in among the sixty-five questions were two items on sexuality—how "sexually warm or cold" and how "sexually responsive or unresponsive" did these people seem to be? Most of those participating in this study assumed good-looking people would be unusually warm and responsive sexually.

In another recent study (Tanke 1982), men from two universities (the University of Minnesota and the University of Santa Clara in California) were given a biographical information sheet on a woman college student. Included in the information sheet was either an attractive photograph, an unattractive photograph, or no photograph. The men were asked to give their first impressions of the woman. A few items asked about sexuality. Interestingly, it was found that of all the trait ratings, the sexuality items were the most affected by appearances. Attractive women were perceived to be more sexually warm, exciting, and permissive than unattractive women. (Women with no photograph were intermediate between attractive and unattractive women on these dimensions.)

Recently, Susan Sprecher and her colleagues at the University of Wisconsin (Smith, Sprecher, and DeLamater 1983a) decided to delve into people's fantasies about good-looking versus plain-looking men and women's sex lives. They asked men and women to look at some photographs of striking versus plain men and women and to guess what they might be like sexually. Just for fun, you may want to rate yourself on the items used in the study (see Table 6.1).

The authors found that people were especially likely to see attractive men and women as sexually vigorous. For example, the attractive (in contrast to the unattractive) were expected to have a high sex drive, to be sexually active, to prefer variety in sex, to prefer experimental sex, to be sexually satisfied, to be sexually permissive, to enjoy sex, and to prefer several sexual relationships. Respondents also assumed attractive people would be more likely to play a dominant role in sex activities, to be sexually exciting, to be bold in sex, and to disclose

TABLE 6.1 **Sexual Traits**

High Sex Drive	1 2 3 4 5 6 7	Low Sex Drive
Sexually active	1 2 3 4 5 6 7	Sexually inactive
Prefers routine in sex	1 2 3 4 5 6 7	Prefers variety in sex
Plays submissive role in sex	1 2 3 4 5 6 7	Plays dominant role in sex
Prefers experimental sex	1 2 3 4 5 6 7	Prefers conventional sex
Sexually frustrated	1 2 3 4 5 6 7	Sexually satisfied
Gentle in sex	1 2 3 4 5 6 7	Rough in sex
Sexually exciting	1 2 3 4 5 6 7	Sexually unexciting
Bold in sex	1 2 3 4 5 6 7	Shy in sex
Unresponsive to needs of sexual partner	1 2 3 4 5 6 7	Responsive to needs of sexual partner
Sexually permissive	1 2 3 4 5 6 7	Sexually unpermissive
Enjoys sex	1 2 3 4 5 6 7	Doesn't enjoy sex
Prefers several sexual relationships	1 2 3 4 5 6 7	Prefers one lifetime sexual relationship
Discloses everything to others about own sexuality	1 2 3 4 5 6 7	Discloses nothing to others about own sexuality

SOURCE: Smith Speecher, and DeLamater, 1983a.

their sexuality to others. People perceived attractive *men* to be especially high on all these dimensions.

"Do They or Don't They?"

Of course, it takes two to tangle—two to engate in sexual relations. Throughout this book, we have seen that people form immediate impressions of individuals based upon physical characteristics. They are equally swift to form impressions about pairs, to speculate about romantically entwined couples. "I wonder how happy they are with each other?" "I wonder what they fight about?" "I wonder what kind of sex life they have?" "Are they into anything kinky?" If there are not many actual facts for answering such questions, the man and women's visible characteristics—their apparent ages and what they look like—may seem to be important clues. When considering the pair, however, there are two sets of characteristics involved—the man's and the woman's. Both individuals could be very attractive, both very unattractive, or they could be strikingly mismatched.

Imagine some of the couples you know—your parents, your best friends, your professor and his live-in girlfriend. Imagine what their sex lives must be like. Do the couples' looks shape your guesses? Do you assume that the cute young couple is shy about sex, or that they are having an intensely passionate affair? Is it somewhat easier to imagine an older couple having an active sex life if they are good-looking than if they are old and rickety? If the couple is mismatched in attractiveness, do you assume their sex life is also a little skewed?

PERCEPTIONS ABOUT OUR INTIMATES

Are perceptions of the sexuality of those to whom we are closest—our parents, mates, children—affected by their looks? Nobody knows for sure, but our best bet would be that they are not.

It is very hard for most people to imagine that those they love most of all (good-looking or not) are sexually active. No matter how attractive parents are, many people have difficulty believing they willingly engage in sex. In 1977, researchers asked 646 students at a large, midwestern university what kinds of sex lives they thought their parents had (Pocs, Godow, Tolone, and Walsh 1977). Although more than 90 percent said their parents were happily married and still in love, they did not think their parents had sex very often. Over one-half the students thought their parents had intercourse once a month or less; about one-fourth of the sons and daughters believed their parents never had intercourse or had it less than once a year. Only 4 percent thought their parents might have sexual intercourse three to four times a week, and no one said more than four times a week. Typical of the feelings of these daughters and sons is a statement made by one young woman: "When I was 16, my 40-year-old mother shocked me one day by announcing that she was pregnant. I knew the facts of life and all, but somehow I just didn't think of my mother as doing *that*" (reported in Pocs, Godow, Tolone, and Watsh 1977).

These perceptions can be compared to the available statistics on the sex lives of men and women of the same age group as the students' parents. Large-scale surveys on people's sex lives, such as those conducted by Alfred C. Kinsey (see Kinsey et al. 1948, 1953), report that married adults between the ages of forty and fifty have marital sexual intercourse about seven times a month, on the average.

Sons and daughters were also inaccurate about their parents' premarital and extramarital sex, oral-genital sex, and masturbation (see Table 6.2). In brief, they underestimated what their parents were probably doing. There was a slight tendency for daughters to be even more conservative in their estimates than sons.

Some of the students were even upset that they had been asked about their parents' sexuality. Nearly 20 percent ignored the questions about masturbation. A few students wrote comments in the margins of the questionnaire: "This questionnaire stinks." "Whoever thinks about their parents' sexual relations, except perverts?" "What stupid-ass person made up these questions?"

We would speculate that children probably view their parents as asexual regardless of their attractiveness. We have no more than anecdotal data on the linkage between parental attractiveness and offsprings' perceptions of their sexuality. We suspect sex is seen as more or less taboo, regardless of looks, however.

Parents may have equal trouble envisioning their children engaged in sexual activity. Again, we suspect that parents' estimates about their children's sexuality are not linked to the children's attractiveness. Again, however, we have no data to support such speculations.

Perceptions of Casual Acquaintances

There is, however, evidence that our impressions of less intimate couples' (especially strangers') sexuality may well be influenced by how they look. In another study Susan Sprecher conducted with her colleagues (Smith, Sprecher, and DeLamater 1983b), she examined how sexually active couples were perceived to be. Men and women viewed pictures of a man and woman who had been steadily dating for about six months. (In truth, the pictures were randomly matched.) Sometimes

TABLE 6.2   **The Beliefs *vs*. The Reality**

| ACTIVITY | KINSEY'S FINDINGS VS. DAUGHTERS' BELIEFS | | | |
	DAUGHTERS GUESSED THEIR MOTHER DID	ACCORDING TO KINSEY	DAUGHTERS THOUGHT THEIR FATHER DID	ACCORDING TO KINSEY
Masturbation	31%	62%	62%	93%
Premarital petting	63%	99%	80%	89%
Premarital sex	10%	50%	33%	92%
Extramarital sex	2%	26%	7%	50%
Oral-genital sex	25%	49%	29%	59%

| ACTIVITY | KINSEY'S FINDINGS VS. SONS' BELIEFS | | | |
	SONS GUESSED THEIR MOTHER DID	ACCORDING TO KINSEY	SONS THOUGHT THEIR FATHER DID	ACCORDING TO KINSEY
Masturbation	49%	62%	73%	93%
Premarital petting	69%	99%	81%	89%
Premarital sex	22%	50%	45%	92%
Extramarital sex	2%	26%	12%	50%
Oral-genital sex	30%	49%	34%	59%

SOURCE: Based on data supplied by Pocs, Godaw, Talone, and Walsh, 1977.

the man and woman were both stunning, sometimes they were both homely, and sometimes they seemed badly mismatched.

The researchers asked the participants to guess how often the couple engaged in various types of sexual activities—kissing, intercourse, oral sex. Of the matched couples, there was a tendency to perceive the attractive couples as more sexually involved than the unattractive couples. This tendency was especially evident for oral sex. Apparently, the men and women had difficulty fathoming two unattractive people having oral contact with each other's genitals.

Interestingly, although the participants in the study assumed the attractive couples were more intimate and more actively sexually, they were not at all sure such intense relationships would last; in fact, they actually assumed the attractive couples would be *less* likely to be together one year later and to marry someday than the homely couples. No doubt, they suspected the attractive people would receive more opportunities to break away from the current relationship, to be swept up in a new one.

When the researchers compared the impressions formed of matched versus mismatched couples, they found a slight tendency for matched couples to be perceived as more sexually involved than mismatched couples, but the relationship was not very strong. There was, however, a strong feeling that matched couples were more likely to be still together in one year and to be married someday.

The Double Standard

Susan Sprecher and her colleagues (Smith, Sprecher, and DeLamater 1983b) tested one especially interesting hypothesis. According to Equity Theory (discussed in the previous chapter), people who feel they have more to contribute to a relationship than their partners do should feel entitled to "call the shots" sexually. But what does that mean?

In the past, a double standard existed. Men were allowed—if not encouraged—to demand sex whenever and wherever they could. Women were to save themselves for marriage. Today, remnants of the double standard still exist (see Baker 1974; Ehrmann 1959; Kaats and Davis 1970; Reiss 1967; Schofield 1965; Sorenson 1973).

In light of this double standard, men or women, who feel they should have things their way sexually, may actually demand quite different things. Attractive *men* (with homely mates) might demand intimate sexual behavior. In contrast, attractive *women* (with homely mates) may expect their partners to wait until *they* are ready for sex— and that may be a long wait.

Evidently, college students still assume this is the way things are. When men and women were shown pictures of a couple mismatched in looks when the man was the more attractive partner, they assumed the couple was likely to be sexually involved. When the woman was more attractive, however, they assumed the couple was probably not as sexually involved.

In sum, the results of several studies indicate that, in the eye of the beholder, there is a link between people's appearance and their sexuality. Handsome men and beautiful women are seen as being more exciting and active sexual partners.

SEXUAL AROUSAL AND PHYSICAL ATTRACTIVENESS

"Meat Markets": Attractiveness—Prime Cut

In single bars, couples meet for a "one night stand" or a more enduring affair. In a crowded, noisy bar, appearance matters. (It is often all that *can* matter.) Many men and women complain they are constantly being inspected and rated in such places. Once, Susan Sprecher went to a singles bar in Honolulu with her girlfriend, Linda. Linda is very attractive and was soon asked to dance. As she stood up to walk to the dance floor, her new dance partner followed behind, rubbing his hands together and muttering, "Oh good, she's a tall one." Susan was reminded of a customer admiring a choice cut of meat the butcher has held up for inspection. And, of course, women play the same game. Linda declined a second dance offer with the man because he was not very good-looking. This meat market scenario is repeated millions of times each night, from the Hawaiian Islands to the eastern seaboard. People inspect what is being offered, and when only the outside packaging is visible, they choose the better-looking packaging.

"Don't The Girls All Get Prettier At Closing Time?"*

Interestingly, perceptions about others' attractiveness may change as the night proceeds and/or as our desires change. Several years ago, country and western singer Mickey Gilley (1975) wrote a hit song containing the lyrics:

> All the girls get prettier at closing time, they all get to look like movie stars . . . ain't it funny, ain't it strange, the way a man's opinions change when he starts to face that lonely night.

Recently, Pennebaker and his colleagues (Pennebaker, Dyer, Cualkins, Litowitz, Ackerman, Anderson, and McGraw, 1979) decided to test this hypothesis.

A team of researchers entered three bars near the University of Virginia campus in Charolottesville at three different times of the evening—9:00 P.M., 10:30 P.M., and 12:00 midnight (the bars closed at 12:30 A.M.). They approached the patrons, one at a time, and asked if they would mind answering a few questions for a psychology study. How would they rate the other patrons, male and female, on a scale of one to ten? They found that Mickey Gilley is right—"All the girls [and boys] get prettier at closing time" (in Charlottesville, Virginia, anyway). As the night went on, patrons judged potential pick-ups as more and more appealing.

Were the drinkers merely radiating a rosy glow? Would they have rated anyone's looks more generously, male *and* female? Of course not, for who wants to think the competition is getting more appealing? As the night wore on, men and women continued to rate their competition with unfailing accuracy.

* Mickey Gilley, Country and Western song

Figure 6.2. Clodion (Claude Michel) 1738–1814, *Bacchante and Faun* ("The intoxication of wine") (s). Terracotta, height 23¼ in., Rococo paganism. Courtesy, The Metropolitan Museum of Art, bequest of Benjamin Altman, 1913 (14.40.687).

Susan Sprecher and her colleagues conducted a similar study in bars near the campus of the University of Wisconsin (Sprecher, De-Lamater, Neuman, Neuman, Kahn, and Orbuch, in press). To their surprise, they *failed* to secure the results found in the Virginia study. They did not find that attractiveness ratings of the opposite sex increased as bar closing time approached. The preceeding authors argued that the inconsistent results of the two studies could perhaps be explained by the fact that the bars in Madison, Wisconsin, were quite different from the bars in the Virginia study. The largest "pick-up" bars near the Madison campus were chosen for that study. Hundreds of young men and women were drinking, dancing, and talking. The bars used in the study conducted in Virginia were probably much smaller, with smaller bar crowds. It may not be that "all the girls [and boys] get prettier at closing time," as Gilley assumed. What may really be going on is, "as I grow accustomed to your face, it becomes more beautiful." In a small bar where there is a limited number of potential pick-ups to watch, these other patrons can become very familiar by the time the night is over. We notice what they drink, how they dance, who they are with, and we may even have a chance to talk to them. When the bar is large, however, and there are many available partners to watch, it becomes impossible to notice as much about each person. Other research has found that people give higher physical attractiveness ratings to familiar people than to those who are unfamiliar (Cavior 1970). So what can we conclude? Girls (and boys) may get prettier at closing time, but it probably depends on the type of bar.

One thing that does happen in a bar as the night goes on is that people typically get more tipsy. Can alcohol possibly affect our perceptions of others' attractiveness? In the study Susan Sprecher and her colleagues conducted in Madison, they asked the patrons how much they had drunk since 6:30 that evening. They found no relationship between the amount of alcohol consumed and perceptions of attractiveness of the other patrons. They did not even find a relationship between amount of alcohol consumed and answers to the question, "How interested are you in meeting someone of the opposite sex here tonight?" So much for alcohol as an aphrodisiac. Next time your friends tell you how to score over candlelight and wine, tell them to save the money on the wine.

GOOD LOOKS = SEXUAL AROUSAL = BEAUTY IS IN THE EYE OF THE BEHOLDER

It has long been known that a good-looking sexual partner is one of the best aphrodisiacs. Recently, however, scientists have discovered that the link between good looks and sexual arousal is a two-way street. Not only do good looks generate sexual arousal, but sexual arousal leads us to exaggerate others' appeal as well. Possibly, in fact, as the night goes on in the singles bar, people become more and more sexually aroused and increasingly eager for contact.

With two colleagues, Elaine Hatfield (Stephan, Berscheid, and Hatfield [Walster] 1971) set out to test a simple hypothesis: When we are sexually aroused our minds wander, and soon our dazzling fantasies lend sparkle to drab reality. To test this notion, college men were contacted and told that the researchers were studying dating practices. If they agreed to participate, the men would be asked their first impressions of a potential date.

The participants were to drop by the researchers' office to pick up their dates' names. When the men appeared, the investigators said they were running a little late. It was suggested that while the men sat around waiting, they while away the time by reading articles lying around the office. This material had been carefully selected. Some men were given a fairly boring article to read, describing the sex life of herring gulls. Other men were given a *Playboy*-type article (a romantic seduction scene designed to be arousing).

The researchers returned, showed the men pictures of their date, a pretty blond co-ed, and told them a little about her. (She appeared reasonably intelligent, easy to get along with, active, and moderately liberal.) What did the men think of her? Well, that depended on what they had been reading.

The investigators had hypotehsized that an unaroused man would be fairly objective; his fantasy life was in "low gear" and it would be easy for him to see women clearly. A sexually excited man, however, should have a harder time of it; the luster of his daydreams would keep rubbing off on his date-to-be. When a man is feeling sexy, he should have a tendency to see women as sex objects, and he should exaggerate two of her traits: (1) her sexual desirability; and (2) her sexual receptivity.

As was predicted, the more aroused these men were, the more beautiful they thought their date was. In addition, the more aroused, the more likely the men were to assume their date would be sexually receptive. Unaroused men judged their date-to be as a fairly nice woman. Aroused men suspected she was probably fairly "amorous," "immoral," "promiscuous," "willing," "unwholesome," and "uninhibited." (This finding gives us a new insight into the rapists' claim that "she asked for it.")

But There Are Limits . . .

When sexually aroused, do we exaggerate the appeal of *every* potential sex partner? Apparently not. A recent study (Istvan, Griffitt, and Weidnen, 1983) clearly shows that we only shape things a bit if the potential dates are already fairly attractive. We do not bother if they are unappealing. (Our repulsion might even lead to a "boomerang effect"—when sexually aroused, we may find unattractive people unusually unappealing.) In this study, some men and women were excited sexually (they were shown a series of sexy slides); others were lured into a low-key mood (they looked at slides of geometric figures). They were then asked to look at a striking, average, or downright homely member of the opposite sex. What did they think of him or her—of his/her hair, face, eyes, breast/chest, waist, hips, and overall body? How sexually attractive was he/she? How desirable was he/she as a date or mate?

The aroused men and women did exaggerate the sexual attractiveness of good-looking and average-looking persons. Aroused men and women were especially generous in their evaluations of the person's sexual characteristics—breasts, chests, waist, and hips. Aroused men and women also saw the average and highly attractive persons as more desirable dates and mates. But even when aroused, men and women did not extend their generosity to the homely. In fact, they were even more critical than usual of the homely person's sexual attractiveness. They also were more critical of their value as dates. The men and women seemed to be rejecting the idea that unattractive people could be potential partners.

It Is All In The Label

> It's not true that only the external appearance of a woman matters. The underwear is also important.
>
> (Firestone 1970, 134)

Other evidence also indicates that only attractive people are seen as appropriate for passionate fantasies and desires. As stated by Berscheid and Hatfield [Walster] (1974),

> In our culture, people assume that passionate fantasies are inspiried only by attractive human beings. If one admitted that he is sexually attracted to a hunchback, an octogenarian, or a man with no nose, he is branded as sick or perverse. The evidence suggests that most individuals docilely accept the prescription that beauty and sexual and romantic passion are inexorably linked (p. 374)

Sex researchers (DeLamater 1982; Gagnon and Simon 1973) have used the term "sexual script" to refer to a set of social definitions that indicate who is appropriate as a sexual partner and what kinds of behaviors are appropriate. Cultural norms specify that the actor sharing the stage of our sexual scripts be as attractive as possible. This norm may be so strong that it can influence whether we label the physical arousal we may be experiencing as the emotion of passionate love. Let us see how this theory works.

THE TWO-COMPONENT THEORY OF PASSIONATE LOVE

(1) What Is Passionate Love?

For centuries, theorists have bitterly disagreed over what passionate love really is. Is it an intensely pleasurable experience or an intensely painful one (see Kendrick and Cialdini 1977; or Stoller 1975)? Hatfield and Walster (1978) in *A New Look at Love*, and Hatfield [Walster] and Berscheid (1974) argue that both pleasure and pain can fuel passion. They would endorse the old adage, "The opposite of love is not hate but indifference." Their argument proceeds as follows: Both our mind and body make a unique contribution to our emotional experiences, both must be in sync if we are to have a true, spontaneous emotional experience.

(a) It Is All in Your Mind—Or Partly Anyway

Our semiconscious assumptions about what we *should* be feeling in a given situation have a profound impact on what we *do* feel in that situation. By adolescence, our culture, our families, and our own experiences have instilled firm ideas as to what it is "appropriate" to feel at different times. We know we should feel ecstatic when something unexpectedly good happens and depressed when everything goes awry. We are entitled to feel angry when humiliated, and we ought to feel grateful when someone treats us more kindly than we deserve.

Society offers us many images of passionate love. As a consequence, we can potentially experience passion in a wide variety of ways. Recently, when University of Minnesota psychologists asked college students, "What is passionate love?" they got strikingly different answers. Most students assumed love is a very pleasurable state. They associated love with the joy of loving and being loved, with the pleasure of having someone *finally* understand you, with sexual fulfillment, with having fun, and so on. ("Oh, painful things could happen," they admitted, "but that is extremely rare.")

Some students' remarks, however, were not so glowing. Love may have its moments, they said, but, all in all, it is a fairly unsettling state. They associated love with anxiety (would they be loved in return?), with emotional and sexual longing, and with uncertainty, confusion,

Figure 6.3. Francois Auguste Rene Rodin, *The Kiss* (1886–1898). Marble, height 5′11¼″. Courtesy of Musée Rodin, Paris. Photograph by Bruno Jarret.

and pain. Dorothy Tennov interviewed more than five hundred passionate lovers. She discovered that *passionate* love is associated with both intensely positive and intensely negative experiences. According to Tennov, "limerence" (passionate love) has the following components:

(1) intrusive thinking about the limerent object (LO),

(2) acute longing for reciprocation,

(3) mood dependent on whether or not LO reciprocates

(4) inability to react limerently to more than one person at a time

(5) some fleeting and transient relief from unrequited limerent passion through vivid imagination of LO's reciprocation,

(6) fear of rejection and unsettling shyness in LO's presence

(7) intensification through adversity (at least, up to a point),

(8) acute sensitivity to any act, thought, or condition that can be interpreted favorably, and an extraordinary ability to devise or invent reasonable explanations for why the neutrality that the disinterested observer might see is, in fact, a sign of hidden passion on the LO's part,

(9) an aching of the "heart" when uncertainty is strong,

(10) a feeling of walking on air when reciprocation seems evident,

(11) an intensity of feeling that leaves other concerns in the background,

(12) a remarkable ability to emphasize what is truly admirable in LO and to avoid dwelling on the negative, or even to respond positively to the negative

So, while love means pleasure for some, others equate it with pain. These very different ideas of passion profoundly affect our emotions and, ultimately, the ties we make in the name of love. For nearly everyone, however, good looks are seen as the sine qua non of passion. Love may be triumph or tragedy, but, in our minds, the participants are all expected to be good-looking.

(b) The Body Counts Too

All emotions must have a second, indispensable, component: there must be physiological arousal. Joy, anger, passion, envy, and hate are all accompanied by telltale "symptoms"—a flushed face, a pounding heart, trembling hands, accelerated breathing.

There are physiological reasons why love might be linked to both pleasure and pain. Physiologically, love, delight, and pain have one thing in common—they are intensely arousing. Joy, passion, excitement, as well as anger, envy, and hate all produce a "sympathetic" response in the nervous system. This response is evidenced by the "symptoms" associated with all these emotions: a flushed face, sweaty palms, weakness, butterflies in the stomach, dizziness, a pounding heart, trembling hands, and accelerated breathing. For this reason, theorists point out that either delight *or* pain (or a combination of the two) has the potential of fueling a passionate experience.

An abundance of evidence supports the common sense contention that, under the right conditions, intensely positive experiences such as euphoria, sexual fantasizing (Stephan et al. 1971), an understanding partner, or general excitement (Zuckerman 1974) can fuel passion. But there is also some evidence for the more intriguing contention that, under the right conditions, anxiety and fear (Hoon et al. 1977), jealousy (Clanton and Smith 1977), loneliness (Peplau and Perlman 1982; Russell et al. 1978), anger (Barclay 1969), or even grief can fuel passion. For example, in one study, psychologists (Dutton and Aron 1974) discovered a close link between fear and sexual attraction. The investigators compared reactions of young men crossing two bridges in North Vancourver. The first bridge, the Capilano Canyon Suspension Bridge, is a 450-foot long, five-foot wide span that tilts, sways, and wobbles over a 230-foot drop to rocks and shallow rapids below. The other bridge, a bit farther upstream, is a solid, safe structure. As each young man crossed the bridge, a good-looking college woman approached him. She explained that she was doing a class project and asked if he would fill out a questionnaire for her. When the man had finished, the woman offered to explain her project in greater detail "when I have more time." She wrote her telephone number of a small piece of paper so that the man could call her if he wanted more information. Which men called? Men who met the coed under frightening conditions were more likely to call. (Nine of the thirty-three men on the suspension bridge called her; only two of the men on the solid bridge called.) This research suggests that people may sometimes passionately love others, not in spite of the difficulties others cause them, but because of them.

Recently, more laboratory research indicates that, under the right conditions, any state of intense arousal can be interpreted as the stirrings of desire—even if the result of an irrelevant experience such as listening to a comedy routine, jogging, or listening to a description of a mob mutilating and killing a missionary (White et al. 1981). Strange as it sounds, then, evidence suggests that adrenalin makes the heart grow fonder. Delight is surely the most common stimulant of passionate love, yet anxiety and fear can sometimes play a part.

In brief, scientists have accumulated considerable support for the two-component theory. Both mind and body are critically important in shaping our emotions. Our minds determine what specific emotions we feel; our bodies determine whether or not we feel any emotion at all. As suggested earlier, any kind of arousal (positive or negative) may more likely be labelled passionate love if the recipient happens to be attractive rather than unattractive.

Two experiments designed to directly test the two-component theory of passionate love (White, Fishbein, and Rutstein 1981) indicate how important the physical attractiveness of a potential date-to-be can be in determining whether arousal is labeled as passion or repulsion. In the first study, arousal was created in some men by having them run in place for two minutes. Other men, in a low arousal condition, ran in place for only fifteen seconds. Immediately after this exercise, the men viewed a videotape of either a stunning or a homely woman and then completed several attraction measures. They were asked, for example, how sexy the woman was, how much they would like to date her, how much they would like to kiss her, how much they would like to work with her, if she were the type of person they would like to get to know better, and how well they thought they could get along with her. It was found that aroused men liked the attractive woman more than did the unaroused men. The unattractive woman, however, was liked less by the aroused than by the unaroused men. In the second experiment by the same researchers, men either heard a positive arousal tape (comedian Steve Martin's album "A Wild and Crazy Guy"), a negative arousal tape (a description of the killing and mutilation of a person) or a neutral arousal tape (a description of the frog's circulatory system). Regardless of whether the initial arousal was positive or negative, arousal led to attraction if the woman was attractive but to repulsion if the woman was unattractive.

Is It Good or Bad to Be Perceived As Sexy?

In chapters 2 and 3, we found that most people are far more tolerant of good-looking people's deeds—for good or ill. Is this attitude true for sex as well? Is a beautiful/handsome person who is sexually active considered "sensual," while an active, ugly person is considered "sluttish" or a "Don Juan"? Apparently not. Regardless of what men and women look like, critics apparently give sexual activity mixed reviews.

In one study (Janda, O'Grady, and Barnhart 1981), researchers interviewed men and women about their attitudes toward beautiful versus ugly women portrayed as having liberal, neutral, or very conservative sexual attitudes. Here are two of the "autobiographical" sketches used in the study. You can easily identify which is the sexually liberal and which is the conservative sketch.

> The most pleasant thing about ODU [Old Dominion University] is the sexually liberated attitude that everyone seems to have. I slept with six different guys last year and there were no problems at all. Nobody seems to have any hang-ups about it. After all, if you're attracted to someone, why shouldn't you have sex with him? All my girlfriends

seem to feel pretty much the same way. I'm really looking forward to this next year. I've already met several guys I'm attracted to, and I'm anxious to develop relationships with them. (p. 192)

> I've had a very favorable reaction to ODU. I was somewhat worried about going to college because I've heard that college kids are pretty sexually permissive, but that hasn't been my experience. All the guys I've gone with have respected me, and all my girlfriends are also waiting for the right person to come along before having a sexual relationship. Most of the kids I have met have pretty high moral standards and I really appreciate that. (p. 192)

Try envisioning both a beautiful and an ugly woman expressing each of these sentiments, in turn. Can you detect any difference in the way you would feel about a beautiful versus an ugly conservative woman? A beautiful versus an ugly liberal woman? Most people do not.

Contrary to expectations, in this study no differences were found in how men and women felt about beautiful versus homely women who were sexually active. Regardless of what they looked like, sexually permissive women were seen as both appealing and unappealing. For example, permissive women were seen as bad, immoral, and irresponsible, as well as warm, friendly, and likeable.

We can confirm that people have mixed feelings about sexually active women. According to folklore, men find women who play hard to get the most appealing. Socrates, Ovid, Terence, the *Kama Sutra*, and "Dear Abby" all agree that the person whose affection is easily won is unlikely to inspire passion. Ovid (1963), for example, argued:

> Fool, if you feel no need to guard your girl for her own sake, see that you guard her for mine, so I may want her the more. Easy things nobody wants, but what is forbidden is tempting. . . . Anyone who can love the wife of an indolent cuckold, I should suppose, would steal buckets of sand from the shore. (pp. 65–66)

Bertrand Russell (in Kirch 1960) remarked:

> The belief in the immense value of the lady is a psychological effect of the difficulty of obtaining her, and I think it may be laid down that when a man has no difficulty in obtaining a woman, his feeling toward her does not take the form of romantic love. (pp. 10, 11)

In 1973, Elaine Hatfield and her colleagues (Hatfield [Walster], Walster, Piliavin, and Schmidt 1973) decided to find out why men preferred women who played hard-to-get. They were so swayed by the stereotype, it never occurred to them to ask if men *did*. Thus, they began by asking men why they prefer hard-to-get women. In informal interviews, the men explained that an easy woman spells trouble. She is probably desperate for a date. She is probably the kind of woman who would make too many demands on a man. She would want to get serious right away. She might have herpes. (As the joke goes, "What's the difference between love and herpes?" Answer: "Herpes lasts forever.")

The men assumed, on the other hand, the "hard-to-get" woman would be a valuable woman. A woman can only afford to be choosy if she is popular—and a woman is popular for some reason. When a woman is elusive, it is usually a tip-off that she is unusually pretty, has a good personality, is sexy, and so on. Men were also intrigued by the challenge the elusive woman offers; one can spend a great deal of time fantasizing what it would be like to date her. Other men thought their prestige would be boosted by attracting such a woman. In brief, nearly all men took it for granted (as we did) that men prefer hard-to-get women. They could supply abundant justification for this supposed prejudice.

A few isolated men disagreed adamantly. These dissenters stated that an elusive woman is not desirable. Sometimes she is not only hard-to-get, she is impossible to get because she is misanthropic and cold. Sometimes a woman is easy-to-get simply because she is a friendly, outgoing chum who boosts one's ego and ensures that dates are "no hassle." We ignored the testimony of these deviant types. We shouldn't have. Research by this team and others has demonstrated the error of the initial premise. Hard-to-get women are not especially desired. Neither are easy-to-get women. The preferred women are those who are "selectively hard-to-get." In other words, most men like the women interested in them but in no one else. Beauty gives no immunity. Regardless of their looks, easy/hard-to-get women get mixed reviews.

Good-looking men and women are *expected* to lead more interesting sex lives. They certainly have unusual *opportunities* to do so. But do they really? We will now turn to this issue.

DO GOOD-LOOKING MEN/WOMEN HAVE SEX SOONER?

There is never a one-to-one relationship between men and women's appearance and their sexuality. People engage in intimate relationships for a crazy multitude of reasons, thus there are always surprises. Recently, a panel of psychiatrists debated whether or not there is a relationship between a woman's beauty and her sexual expressiveness. They agreed the link is a tenuous one. Psychiatrist John L. Schimel (1970) described one way appearances can be deceiving. When he consults with adolescent girls, their "beautiful, sweet, young, vital faces prompt a set of ilusions." These illusions are shattered when he hears of their extensive sexual experiences. Often they are already on their second or third marriage. He has difficulty believing that a sweet, innocent appearance can be linked to hard experience.

Psychiatrist Amnon Issacharaff (1970) observes it is almost impossible to guess much about a woman's sexuality from her appearance. He once had two patients. One was a twenty-two-year-old artist. She possessed the attractiveness of youth and health, but she never made an effort to be attractive in the conventional sense. She never wore makeup, she came to her sessions covered with paint, but she was extremely ardent and proficient sexually. Issachardaff contrasted her with another patient, about the same age and beautiful in the classical sense. She wore makeup, short skirts, and looked just right; however, she had a sexual phobia.

Nathan Stockhamer (1970) echoes this point—that appearances can be deceiving. He described a patient—a twenty-eight-year-old woman who powerfully stimulated men's fantasies. She had no difficulty attracting men, but she ended up having more one night stands than anything else because she was a cold sex partner. She suffered sex. She had little sexual enjoyment herself and deeply resented it if her partner enjoyed himself. Men rarely went near her after the first time.

Other social scientists have also wondered about the link between appearance and sexual behavior. Initially, two quite different theories seemed plausible. The first theory stated that, in general, handsome men and beautiful women probably get more "offers they can't refuse." Thus, we might expect both beautiful women and handsome men to be more sexually experienced than their dowdy counterparts. The second, more complicated, hypothesis seemed equally plausible—that all men are inclined to press their dates for sex, but that only the most appealing men would be successful (Symons 1979). Thus, handsome men were expected to have far more sexual success than homely ones (James Bond versus Woody Allen). Women, however, were traditionally supposed to be coy. For women to engage in sex was seen as evidence, not of desire, but of desperation.

Thus, early researchers were uncertain whether to predict that beautiful women would be unusually sexually experienced (because they had an unusual number of enticing opportunities) or unusually chaste (because they did not have to "put out" to get dates). When push came to shove—when researchers were forced to settle on a hypothesis—they opted for the first theory and predicted beautiful women would be more sexually experienced than their dowdy counterparts. And that is just what they found.

MEASURING SEXUAL INTIMACY

Remember when you were eighteen years of age? Were you dating someone then? Married? How sexually active were you at that time? If someone had asked you to complete Table 6.3, how would you have responded to the items?

Scales like this one have been used since the 1950s to study the sexual attitudes and behaviors of American teenagers. Such studies have looked at how teenagers with different background characteristics vary in their sexual attitudes and behaviors.

Luckily, a few of these studies have investigated whether or not good-looking versus homely men and women differ in sexual experience. In a study at the University of Colorado, Kaats and Davis (1970) assembled four hundred students in an auditorium and asked them a series of questions about their backgrounds, their dating relationships, what they felt about virginity, how sexually active they were (on a scale similar to the preceding one), how sexually active they thought

TABLE 6.3 **How Intimate Is Your Relationship?**

How far have you gone with your partner? (Check all that you have engaged in.)

_____ 1. Necking: kissing and hugging.

_____ 2. French or deep kissing.

_____ 3. Petting: IF A MAN: "I touched her covered breasts."
IF A WOMAN: "He touched my covered breasts."

_____ 4. Petting: IF A MAN: "I touched her naked breasts."
IF A WOMAN: "He touched my naked breasts."

_____ 5. Genital Play: Female
IF A MAN: "I touched her clitoris or vagina."
IF A WOMAN: "He touched my clitoris or vagina."

_____ 6. Genital Play: Male
IF A MAN: "She touched my penis."
IF A WOMAN: "I touched his penis."

_____ 7. Genital Apposition: The man lies prone on female, petting without penetration of her vagina.

_____ 8. Sexual Intercourse.

_____ 9. Cunnilingus: oral contact with woman's clitoris or vagina.

_____10. Fellatio: oral contact with man's penis.

SOURCE: Hatfield, Walster, and Traupmann 1979, 326.

their friends were, and so on (practically everything researchers always wanted to know about sex but were afraid to ask). They assessed women's attractiveness in a simple way. As two investigators collected each woman's questionnaire and answer sheets, they sorted the forms into several piles, depending on whether they considered the woman to be attractive, average, or plain.

What were they women like? Beautiful and homely women were very similar in family background, age, birth order, strength of religion, dating status, and sorority membership. Nor did beautiful versus homely women differ in how often they felt sexual urges, their standards for sexuality, or why they had chosen to indulge in or abstain from premarital intercourse. However, when it came to the bottom line, attractive women turned out to be more sexually experienced. Fifty-six percent of the attractive women were nonvirgins, while only 31 percent of the average-looking and 37 percent of the homely women were sexually experienced.

Attractive women were experienced, but not "promiscuous." Of those who had had sexual intercourse, attractive versus homely women did not differ on the number of times they had tried sex or the number of men with whom they had experimented. Kaats and Davis concluded that attractive women were more likely to have premarital intercourse because they had more opportunities and thus more pressure to experiment. The attractive women had been in love more often, had dated more, and had petted more often. Other studies have also shown that attractive women and men are more popular with the opposite sex and have more dates than their more homely peers (Berscheid and Hatfield [Walster] 1974; Hatfield [Walster] et al. 1966).

Other recent studies indicate that attractive men and women have more permissive sexual attitudes and behaviors. Jonathon Kelley (1978) interviewed a sample of 668 students at the University of California in Berkeley, California. He found attractive men and women to be more permissive than unattractive men and women in their premarital sexual attitudes. For example, attractive men and women did not want to be virgins, nor did they want to marry inexperienced mates. Good-looking men and women were more liberal in their activities as well. For example, attractive men and women were more likely to be having intercourse regularly with a steady date, and occasionally with other persons, than were their less attractive peers.

Finally, Curran (1975) found that attractive men and women had more sexual experience than anyone else *on every item* of the Heterosexual Behavior Scale—a scale similar to the one in Table 6.3. They were more likely to have kissed, frenched kissed, engaged in oral sex, and had intercourse. So, overall, the results are clear. Attractive men and women tend to "do it sooner."

GIVING PLEASURE TO THE PRETTY

Perhaps one reason beautiful people gain more sexual experience is because others are eager to give them pleasure. Imagine you have become privy to the sexual fantasies of an extremely attractive person. You know exactly what would give him/her intense pleasure. All you have to do is play God and push one of eleven buttons, ranging from giving the beautiful/handsome person slight fulfillment of the fantasy and a little pleasure to giving him/her complete fulfillment of the fantasy and ultimate pleasure. Which button would you push? (Remember, you do not get to become part of that fantasy; you may never even meet the gorgeous person to receive his/her thanks.) Now imagine it is not a gorgeous person waiting to have a fantasy fulfilled, but a very homely one. Once again, you have a choice of pressing any button from 0 (giving a little pleasure) to 10 (giving a lot of pleasure). What button would you push?

The above sounds a bit like an adult Disneyland. It is not possible to play God in such a manner (or to be played with in such a manner). However, a few researchers have come close. In research, they use a "Brock Pleasure Machine". The machine gives waves of pleasure to the buttocks and thighs of someone sitting in a specially constructed, attractively upholstered chair. Subjects sit at the control panel, eleven buttons before them. They are told how much pleasure each button, with a touch of the fingers, will give the person sitting in the pleasure chair. Subjects are told they must decide how much reward the learner (who is sitting in the pleasure chair) should receive upon giving either correct or incorrect responses to a forty-five-problem learning task. Sitting in the pleasure chair is an actor/actress who has been told exactly what to say and do. (The machine is not really hooked up.) Sometimes the confederate is dressed attractively, sometimes not.

The researchers (Davis, Rainey, and Brock 1976) found that men and women gave more pleasure to an attractive than to an unattractive confederate of the same sex. There was no difference, however, in the level of pleasure given to an attractive versus unattractive confederate of the *opposite* sex. This result was a surprise. It may suggest that attractive people are more experienced sexually, not because others are unselfishly interested in giving them pleasure, but because these others are interested in *both* the give and take of sex.

WHY ENGAGE IN SEX?

To understand the different sexual lives of attractive versus unattractive people, it is also important to consider why people choose the "sexual scripts" they do. Why do men and women, good-looking or ugly, engage in sexual activities? There are as many reasons as people. Consider, for example, the review by Wallace et al. (1981) of the sex lives of some eminent people:

> Janis Joplin, a blues singer who died of an overdose at age 27, had severe acne, was nicknamed "Pig Face," and was overweight in high school. In college, she was nominated for "Ugliest Man on Campus." This treatment profoundly affected her life.

Wallace then continues Janis' story as a young adult:

> Strung out on Methedrine, broke and alone, she tried to sell her body for five dollars a trick and was devastated when prospective johns either laughed at her or ignored her completely. . . . She said of herself of this period: "I'd have fucked anything, taken anything. . . . I did. I'd take it, suck it, lick it, smoke it, shoot it, drop it, fall in love with it."

Then, Janis as a star:

> She frequently commented that she was too ugly to attract men, and she was heard to lament, "I'm a big star and I can't even get laid." Actually, she got laid quite a bit, but seldom more than a few times by the same person. Once, after a long train trip, she complained that there were over 365 men on board and she'd had sex with only 65 of them. Terrified of rejection, she histrionically faked orgasm at times, feeling that if she didn't have one it was her fault. On other occasions, she wore partners down with demands for nonstop sex. (pp. 277–278)

In contrast, consider Jimi Hendrix, an appealing popular singer and musician with unusual sex appeal, who also died at age twenty-seven:

> The consummate superstud, Hendrix is something of a sexual legend today. His appetite was voracious, and he often indulged it with three or more girls at a sitting (or lying). He was exotically good-looking, very famous, and so sexy. Women flocked to him like bees to honey. And what a honey he was reported to be! One girl said his member was "damn near big as his guitar." He was one of the major black sex symbols for white women of the 1960's. (p. 272)

Finally, consider the beautiful Marilyn Monroe:

> She was the reigning sex symbol of the staid 1950's, the all-American dumb blonde with a campy, exaggerated come-on. Fragile and insecure in her personal life, she sought security in sex, trading up from Hollywood producers to an ill-fated president of the U.S. Marilyn emanated a strong sexual aura, by all counts. She thought about sex all the time, considering it with every man she met, but would describe herself as selectively promiscuous, submitting only to men she liked, the main

requirement being that they be "nice." Her preference was usually for older men, kindly, warm father figures. (pp. 595–596)

In a survey of Wisconsin college students and Madison, Wisconsin, residents, John DeLamater and Patricia MacCorquodale (1979) found that men and women generally cite one of fourteen reasons when explaining why they engaged in a sexual encounter (see Table 6.4).

These fourteen reasons can be broken down into three categories: (1) I wanted to—essentially self-centered reasons for engaging in intercoure (i.e., "I was curious, wanted experience"); (2) my partner wanted to—altruistic reasons for having intercourse (i.e., "Partner wanted/needed it"); and (3) we both wanted it—the desire was mutual (i.e., "Mutual curiosity"; "We are/were in love"; "We like/liked each other"; "Mutual physical desire, enjoyment").

Do good-looking versus ugly people have different reasons for engaging in sexual relations? They might. Possibly, good-looking men and women engage in sexual relations only when *they* want to; homely people may often participate in sex both out of desire and/or out of a desperate need to please their mates. Unfortunately, these researchers

TABLE 6.4   **Reasons for Entering a Sexual Relationship**

People enter sexual relations for different reasons. Following are fourteen possible reasons for becoming sexually involved with someone. Check all of the reasons why you became sexually involved with your partner.

_____   1. I was curious, wanted experience.

_____   2. Partner wanted/needed it.

_____   3. Mutual curiosity.

_____   4. I wanted/needed it.

_____   5. Partner wanted me to prove love.

_____   6. We were/are in love.

_____   7. To provide I am a man/woman.

_____   8. I wanted to prove love.

_____   9. We like/liked each other.

_____10. My friends think it is appropriate.

_____11. Partner convinced me it was appropriate.

_____12. Mutual physical desire, enjoyment.

_____13. I enjoyed it, it felt good.

_____14. Partner enjoyed it.

SOURCE: Hatfield, Walster, and Traupmann 1979, 327.

did not investigate whether attractive versus homely people have different reasons for engaging in sexual activities. It seems likely that they might, however.

So far, we have focused entirely on how people react to the attractive/ugly when the latter are considered as possible sex partners. What happens when the beautiful or ugly are possible rivals or replacements?

SEXUAL JEALOUSY: THE GREEN-EYED MONSTER IS BIASED TOO

Imagine you are at a party. You are sitting on the couch with someone you have been going with for a while. The atmosphere is delightful. You are feeling warm affection for your date, and you offer to get up and refill your wine glasses. Shettel-Neuber, Bryson, and Young (1978) showed men and women just such a scene. The men observers watched the man fetch the wine, while either a devilishly handsome or homely old boyfriend appeared on the scene. Women watched a woman go get the wine, only to be replaced by a strikingly beautiful or plain old girlfriend. Here is an exact description of the film the men and women viewed:

> . . . The scene opened with a scan of the party, stopping at a couple sitting on a couch. After a 45-second segment, during which the couple cuddled, kissed, and toasted each other, one member of the couple got up and left the room to refill their wine glasses. Approximately 15 seconds after this the interloper, introduced as the old boyfriend or girlfriend of the partner remaining on the couch, entered the picture. The partner jumped up, hugged the interloper briefly, and to two of them sat down on the couch. During the next minute they performed progressively more intimate actions, including touching each other and exchanging one brief kiss. Shortly after the kiss the absent partner returned and stopped, standing beside the couch looking down at the two people. At this point, the tape ended. (p. 613)

After the men and women viewed the film, they were given a Jealousy Scale and were asked to "rate the likelihood that each of the listed behaviors would describe what you would do if you were the person who just returned." Some of the items included:

Feel insecure

Feel angry toward the other person

Feel depressed

Feel that my partner had made a mistake

Feel like making my partner jealous

Act as if nothing happened

Become more sexually aggressive with my partner

Hope my partner would end up being hurt

Feel physically ill

When we first heard about this study, we assumed most people would be extremely jealous of stunning rivals (can you really believe someone is "just friends" with Tom Selleck or Brooke Shields?). On the other hand, we thought most individuals could easily believe their dates were just friends with an unappealing old lover. (Of course, they might ask how their dates could *ever* have been attracted to someone like that and may then wonder about their own sex appeal, but make them *jealous*—no.)

We were wrong. Men and women felt most angry and embarrassed when the ex-boyfriend or ex-girlfriend was *homely*. Apparently, it is most upsetting to be jilted for a homely partner. Men and women also differed slightly in their reactions. Men were more likely to report that they would "start going out with the other people" and "become more sexually aggressive with others" if the interloper was attractive. Women, on the other hand, were more likely to report these reactions if the interloper was unattractive. The authors write:

> If we assume that an attractive interloper is seen as more threatening to the relationship, then as the threat increases males become more likely to seek solace or to bolster their ego by pursuing alternative relationships. Females, on the other hand, become less likely to engage in behaviors that might accent the threat to the existing relationship.
> These differences in male and female responses may be attributed to the different roles and differential power traditionally assigned to men and women in heterosexual relationships. It has been more acceptable for males to initiate relationships, verbally threaten the other person, or get drunk or high. Women, whose options for initiating alternative relationships are more restricted, are more likely to use techniques such as making themselves more attractive in order to maintain the existing relationship. (p. 679)

What about when a love affair is over? What happens when you finally break things off and later discover your partner was seeing someone else all the time? What happens when your mate breaks things off, claiming he (or she) can now seek the lover of his dreams and you bump into him/her years later with your replacement? Would it matter what your replacement looked like?

It seems to us it would. In line with our earlier reasoning (which, note, had turned out to be incorrect), we expect that if a partner had been seeing a beauty, the jilted person would be very jealous. If the partner had "cheated" with someone homelier, duller, and less considerate, the rejected individual might be perplexed, but would not be jealous. One member of THE GROUP recounted that, when her husband asked for a divorce, he said, "I've lost all respect for you. I can't love you anymore because you always tried too desperately to give me what I wanted. But I didn't want what I wanted. I love Sylvia because she doesn't give me *anything* I want." Our respondent said, with some glee, "So I gave him just what he wanted again . . . A divorce."

What if an old lover left because he/she had "outgrown you" with an attractive versus a very homely partner? We may well derive some secret satisfaction from knowing that our ex-lovers failed to find anyone as attractive as we are. Said one twenty-seven-year-old, attractive woman from THE GROUP:

> When I ran into *him* (the ex-lover), in a bar, I became very nervous. It brought back a rush of painful feelings because he had been the one to reject me. I politely said hello. He introduced me to the woman on his side, who was obviously his new lover. While it may seem strange, I was smugly pleased that I was more attractive than she was.

As yet, however, there is no evidence that our speculations are correct.

IN BRIEF

Apparently, people do equate good looks with sensual appeal and sexual experience, and they seem to be right. Attractive men and women have more appealing offers, and they end up with more sexual experience than their less appealing counterparts.

Chapter 7

HEIGHT, WEIGHT, AND INCIDENTALS

According to folklore, every aspect of a person—from flame-colored hair to the girth of the big toe—is a clue to their personalities. Not surprisingly, then, most people have definite ideas about who measures up and who doesn't on the traits with which Americans are most concerned—height, weight, and such incidentals as eyes, hair color, and beardedness (in men).

Throughout most of this book, we have been discussing the stereotyping that occurs for physically attractive versus physically unattractive people. Physical attractiveness has been treated as a perceptual gestalt, rather than as linked to any specific physical characteristics. In this chapter, on the other hand, we will consider more specific physical characteristics. We will examine how people with certain physical characteristics are perceived and treated.

What stereotypes do you have about specific physical characteristics? For example, what kind of person do you suspect inhabits a fat body? A thin body? Do you make character judgments based on heigh (someone who towers over you versus someone who barely reaches your navel), hair color (flaming red versus silky blonde), or facial hair (Grizzly Adams versus the Great Gatsby look)? Susan Sprecher once asked some of her students their impressions of people with certain physical characteristics. Here is a sampling of their answers.

Redheads
- mean
- wild
- different and exciting
- fun and spunky, mischievous and not as innocent as they look
- tend to have a hot temper at times

Short People
- just wonderful! Cute and nice, warm people.
- People do not respect them or take them seriously.
- arrogant and defensive

Tall People
- quiet, unassuming
- athletic
- "masculine", quite dominant, take firm control in situations; they get more respect than short people

Fat People
- lazy housewives
- must love to eat
- easygoing
- I feel sorry for

Let's explore just what it means to be tall or short, to be fat or thin, to have a certain hair color, to decide to grow a beard, and so on.

HEIGHT—A GROWING PROBLEM

Short people got no reason to live. . . . They got little hands and little eyes, and they walk around tellin' great big lies. . . . They got grubby little fingers, and dirty little minds. They gonna get you every time. Well, I don't want no short people . . . 'round here.

(Randy Newman 1977)

The song "Short People" was a joke, yet, like all humor, it contains a grain of truth. If you want to be looked up to—grow. Tall men are at a real advantage; short men are discriminated against. Women also seem to benefit from being taller.

Figure 7.1. Robert Wadlow, shown with his brother, was 8 feet 11.1 inches tall, 1936. Photograph courtesy of Robert K. Grant, Alton, Illinois *Telegraph*.

Figure 7.2. The Rose midgets. Courtesy, Circus World Museum, Baraboo, Wisconsin.

Sociologist Feldman (1971) (who stands 5'4" tall) discusses the stigma associated with shortness:

American society is a society with a heightist premise: To be tall is to be good and to be short is to be "stigmatized." When we degrade people, we "put them down" or "belittle" them. Even when we inquire about an individual's stature, we ask, "How tall are you?" The ideal man is viewed as tall, dark, and handsome. In practice, people are "shortsighted," dishonest cashiers "short-change" customers, losers get "the short end of the stick," electrical failures are known as "short circuits," and individuals with little money, no matter their height, will state of their inpecuniousness, "I'm short." A few years ago, a well-known politician spoke at a midwest liberal college and referred to a former head of the Federal Bureau of Investigation as "that short little pervert in Washington." It is rare that one hears of tall perverts, for in many respects, just to be short is to be a "pervert." (p. 1)

In a *Playboy* interview (Playboy: Paul Simon 1984), Paul Simon was asked about himself. How did one of the most successful composers and performers in the history of pop music (Simon and Garfunkel's total album sales exceed 40 million worldwide), describe himself?—As intelligent and *short*. Simon acknowledged a lot of negative feelings about himself.

Playboy: What role has being short played in the negative feelings?

Simon: I think it had the most significant single effect on my existence, aside from my brain. In fact, it's part of an inferior-superior syndrome. I think I have a superior brain and an inferior stature, if you really want to get brutal about it.

(p. 174)

We will examine three areas in which height has been found to make a difference: (1) in career success; (2) in politics and power; and (3) in romance.

Career Success

In Italy, there is a short people law, enacted by dictator Benito Mussolini, that requires government employees to be more than 5'3". Even as recently as December 1983, one young secretary was fired because she was only 5'1" (reported in *Newsweek*, 23 January 1984, 33). Although no such law exists in the United States, short people do seem to be victims of job discrimination.

Evidence indicates that men's height has a critical impact on their career opportunities. In one study, an industrial psychologist (Kurtz 1969) asked 140 corporate recruiters in Michigan to choose between two job applicants. One applicant was 6'1" (and 200 pounds) and the other, 5'5" (and 135 pounds). Otherwise, the men's qualifications were the same. Seventy-two percent of the recruiters said they would rather hire the tall man; 27 percent had no preference. Only one recruiter preferred the short man! Obviously, the recruiters believed "the bigger they are, the better." Indeed, 76 percent of the recruiters believed tall salesmen would impress customers more than short salesmen. Industrial psychologist Kurtz concluded, "What the study showed is that some people think the blond Teutonic giant that comes hulking into your office is more intimidating and therefore a better salesman."

Not only are tall men more likely to be hired, but they are also granted higher salaries and greater prestige. A personnel director at the University of Pittsburgh compared the reported height and starting salary of a sample of Pittsburgh's graduates. He found that the taller students (6'2" and over) received an average starting salary 12 percent higher than those under 6' tall (Deck 1968).

More detailed evidence on the relationship between height and career success was found by survey researcher Robert Quinn (1978).

He examined data from three national surveys conducted at the University of Michigan's Survey Research Center. More than 800 employed men and 470 employed women ranging in age from sixteen up were interviewed about various aspects of their jobs. Interviewers also rated various physical characteristics of the men and women, including their physical attractiveness, height, and weight. As expected, the tallest men made the most money and held jobs with the highest occupational prestige. In general, as men became shorter their income and prestige fell—however, only down to a point. There was an exception: extremely short men were actually a little more successful than one would expect. Wrote Quinn:

> . . . Our day-to-day vocabulary has an apt phrase for describing a very short man who, burdened from often an early age by his little-valued and sometimes deprecated shortness, invests extraordinary energy in demonstrating that he is at least equal to, and possibly better than, any taller man. He is, often disparagingly, said to have a "Napoleonic" orientation. (p. 17)

Incidentally, no relationship between height and occupational success was found for *women* in the above study.

Are not employers, however, just trying to behave rationally? If tall men perform better at their jobs, it only makes dollars and sense to hire them first. However, the tall and short of it is, there is no clear evidence that indicates tall people perform better than short people. Ralph Keyes, who wrote a delightful book about height, reports that, in his search on this matter, he could find no evidence suggesting that tall employees outperform short ones (Keyes 1980). One researcher compared the sales records and height of life insurance salesmen and found that tall salesmen did not sell more insurance than short salesmen (Murrey 1976). Keyes reports that other studies of sales performance have also shown that, although taller men are more likely to be hired, they do not have better performance records than do short men.

Although short men have difficulty finding jobs in certain areas (as basketball players or models), there are always some professions where short men are accepted. For example, it is easier to be a coal miner or an astronaut if one is short. And one could always be a psychologist! It has been said, "Psychologists are just like everybody else, only shorter" (reported in Keyes 1980, 201).

Politics and Power

Michael Korda in a book on power (1975) warned: "Height means something to people, and it's wise not to forget it" (p. 51). Perhaps nowhere has height been more important than in politics. It has been noted that, from 1900 to 1968, the taller of the two major United States presidential candidates has always been elected. Richard Nixon was the first president to be elected who was shorter than his major opponent (George McGovern).

The track record of tall candidates, in fact, has influenced the strategy of more recent campaigns. When Jimmy Carter challenged Gerald Ford for the presidency in 1976, his advisors tried to keep people from realizing that Ford stood "head over shoulders" above Carter. Keyes (1980) observes:

> The climax of Carter's efforts to keep us from realizing his height occurred during his first debate with Gerald Ford. Carter's camp was jittery at the thought of their candidate standing right next to the 6'1" Republican President for all the world to see who was bigger. For this reason they initially demanded that both debaters be seated. Losing on this point, the Democrat's negotiators finally settled for the candidates' lecterns being placed far enough apart that the two men's height difference would not be so apparent. (In return, the Democrats agreed to a background pale enough to camouflage Ford's paucity of hair.)
>
> When the opponents finally faced off on national television, Jimmy Carter made their moment of physical proximity as short-lived as possible—by sticking his arm out stiffly to hold the President at bay as they briefly shook hands, then scurrying back to the safety of his lectern. (pp. 205–206)

Are tall candidates favored—even by their short constituents? Berkowitz and colleagues (1971) examined this issue during the race between tall John Lindsay and short Mario Proccacino for mayor of New York. They asked voters in Manhattan their own height and their mayorial preferences. They found that tall voters clearly favored the tall candidate, Lindsay. Short voters were divided—half were for Lindsay and half were for Proccacino. Apparently, short voters seemed to be in conflict between voting for the taller candidate and voting for someone more similar to themselves (incidentally, Lindsay won).

Not only do taller political candidates receive more votes, but after a decision is made to vote for them, they get even taller. In 1969 Nixon was running against Kennedy for president (This Week, 10 July 1960). Nixon was 5'11"; Kennedy was 6'0". A few weeks before the election, 3,018 registered voters in California were asked, "If the presidential elections were being held today, which one of these men would you vote for—Nixon or Kennedy?" Several questions later in the interview, the voters were asked, "In your opinion, who is taller—Nixon or Kennedy?" Nixon partisans assumed Nixon was taller, while Kennedy partisans assumed Kennedy was taller (Kassarjian 1963).

Other evidence also indicates that, the link between height and power may be so strong in the public's mind that if a short man gains power he somehow comes to seem *taller!* Wilson (1968) demonstrated this link in an ingenious experiment. He introduced a "Mr. England," a visitor, to a series of classes of college students. With each introduction, England's status changed. To one group he was "Mr. England, a student from Cambridge." To a second, he was "Mr. England, a demonstrator in psychology from Cambridge." To a third group, he was "Mr. England, a lecturer in psychology from Cambridge." To yet another group, the visitor was introduced as "Dr. England, senior lecturer from Cambridge." After the visitor left, the students were asked to estimate his height, as well as the height of Wilson, the course instructor.

As Mr. England climbed the academic ladder of success, he gained a full five inches in height in the eyes of the students! He was the shortest when he was a student and the tallest when he was a professor. The height of Mr. Wilson, whose status remained constant, did not change from group to group. (Other studies have secured similar results, see Dannenmaier and Thumain [1964].) It has also been found that the greater a man's aspirations for power, the more likely he is to over-estimate his height (Fisher 1964).

Romance

One final area in which height seems to be critically important is in selecting dates and mates. Apparently, there is an unwritten rule that men must be taller than the women they date. When Elaine Hatfield was conducting a dating study at the University of Minnesota with her colleagues, the research required them to randomly match up freshmen men and women for a dance. They matched partners by simply drawing names out of a fishbowl, but, unthinkingly, they allowed one exception. Whenever they drew a man shorter than his partner, they threw the names back in the fishbowl and drew another, more "appropriate" match. They assumed they simply could not "mismatch" couples in this way.

Luckily, men and women are more relaxed today about men being taller than women. The taboos are breaking down. Few women would refuse to date Woodie Allen (5'6"), Dustin Hoffman (5'6"), or Dudley Moore (5'2") because they are too short. Many men admit to being attracted to taller women. As an example, a 5'10" man interviewed in an early study (Biegel 1954) said he desired a woman of 6'0" weighing 135 pounds, with blonde hair and blue eyes, and

> whom I can walk down the street with and have the entire male popu-
> lace aroused. She would appear as a luscious, scintillating, and yet dig-
> nified individual. To put your arms around her would be like embracing
> a forbidden goddess. My heart would beat like an angry storm, the ex-

ternal world would fade, my every thought and desire would melt as crystals of dew on a spring morn. (p. 267)

Well, perhaps men today are not quite so melodramatic about their desires to date tall women, yet there are men who are willing and who even prefer to date women taller than they are. Following is a list compiled by Keyes (1980) of couples in which the man is shorter than the woman (of course, by the time you read this, some of the pairings may have dissolved):

Paul and Anne Anka
Billy and Sybil Carter
Lynda ("Wonder Woman") Carter and Ron Samuels
Altovise and Sammy Davis, Jr.
Robert De Niro and Diahann Abbott
Dustin and Ann Byrne Hoffman
King Hussein and Lisa Halaby
Mick Jagger and Jerry Hall
Henry and Nancy Kissinger
Sophia Loren and Carlo Ponti
Norman Mailer and Norris Church
Marvin and Jeanne Mandel
Prince Rainier and Grace Kelly
Princess Caroline Rainier and Philippe Junot
Paul Simon and Shelley Duvall
Arthur and Alexandra Schlesinger
Willie and Cynthia Shoemaker
Jerry Stiller and Anne Meara
John and Lilla Tower
Paul and Katie Williams
Robin and Valerie Williams

(pp. 150–151)

Usually, men are taller than their dates (perhaps not surprising since the average American man is 5.4 inches taller than the average woman). Both sexes seem to prefer it that way. Just how tall do women want their dates to be?

If women could have their choice between a man of average height and a man over six feet, would they prefer the tall man? Not necessarily. In one experiment, psychologists (Graziano, Brothen, and Berscheid 1978) found that women preferred men of medium height (5'9" to 5'11") to either short (5'5" to 5'7") or tall men (6'2" to 6'4"). Women were asked to look at photographs of nine men, one at a time, and then give their impressions. Women were asked such questions as: "How attractive do you think the person is?" "How desirable would this person be as a date?" and, "How much do you think you would like this person?" The nine men were all approximately equal in facial attractiveness. Below each photograph was background information about the man, including his height.

Women were found to be most attracted to the medium-tall men. They thought these men were the most desirable dates, liked them most, and rated them more positively on a number of traits. Interestingly, the women's own height had no effect on their valuation. The petites, the average-height women, and the willowy tall all preferred medium-tall men.

The investigators were startled by these results. They had assumed the taller the better. Was it only the scientists who were startled, or do most men make the mistake of assuming that in love, as everywhere else, bigger is better? The researchers speculated that men typically assume women prefer tall men. Tall men overestimate their desirability while medium-sized men underestimate their appeal to women. A second expiriment by the same researchers was then designed to see how men react to other men of various heights.

First, the men "role played" and estimated how attractive and desirable each man would be to a woman. Surprisingly, men did not think height would matter to women. They assumed women would be equally attracted to short, medium, and tall men. Second, the men were asked what they themselves thought of the different men. Here, height did matter, but the tables were turned completely—short men were liked more than tall men. (Perhaps the short men represented less of a threat.)

While the evidence above indicates that women prefer medium-tall men (when reacting to photographs), when forced to specify in inches how tall they want their partners to be, they generally prefer a man about six inches taller than themselves (Gillis and Avis 1980). Men are willing to come closer to eyeball-to-eyeball. They are generally looking for a woman about 4.5 inches shorter than they are. That women prefer a greater height difference is interesting because some observers (Epstein 1974) have argued that the cardinal rule of dating—that men must tower above their wives—is really a reflection of the traditional belief that men must be dominant over their wives. If this notion is true, it is interesting to note that men are willing to have a little more equality here than are women.

Just how closely do people follow the unwritten rule that the man must be taller than the woman? Two investigators (Gillis and Avis 1980) conceived an ingenious way to find out. Some banks require information on the physical features of customers applying for accounts to facilitate identifying the customers. In one such bank, the researchers obtained the heights of husbands and wives from joint checking accounts. They found that almost all couples adhered to the height rule. They calculated that, if men and women are paired up randomly, about one couple in every twenty-nine would have a wife taller than her husband. The bank records, however, revealed only one in 720 couples with the wife towering above her husband.

In sum, although some couples apparently do not mind breaking a traditional taboo for the sake of love, most men and women still prefer the man to be taller than the woman.

Sizing Up Height

The research, then, indicates that, at work, at play, and in the White House, the tall man has the advantages. Of course, the tall are not above having problems and insecurities. One tall man from THE GROUP described his adolescence:

> When I was younger I went through an awkward stage of about 8 years. I'm 6'7" and have always been tall for my age, but around the time I was 7 until the time I turned 15, it seemed that every part of me was growing at different rates. For example, my feet were size 12 by the time I was in 7th grade. I grew 4 inches between the ages of 14 and 15. I feel these changes have marked my self-esteem in such a way that I'm still a bit shy around peers with whom I'm unfamiliar. I've always been sensitive, and I'm pretty sure the fact that many ridiculed my lack of coordination has led me to be somewhat overconcerned about what others think of me.

In general, however, height is an advantage for men. With women the situation is a bit more complicated. Apparently, women should be tall to succeed at work (although there is not much evidence to substantiate this hypothesis) and average height or short to succeed in love. Perhaps because height has traditionally been thought of as a male issue, the effect of height on women's lives has not been thoroughly investigated. No doubt, the latter will be investigated in the future.

WEIGHTY ISSUES

You can never be too rich or too thin.

In chapter 1 we presented the Body Image Questionnaire we published in *Psychology Today*. How satisfied are you with your weight, and with the particular body parts where excess pounds settle—hips (upper thighs), buttocks, and abdomen? Possible answers ranged from "Extremely satisfied" to "Extremely dissatisfied." Many people believe they are too fat and are deeply embarrassed about it. In the study conducted with *Psychology Today* readers, we found that almost 50 percent of women and about 33 percent of men were unhappy about their weight. Because excess weight tends to settle in the midtorso—abdomen, buttocks, hips, and thighs—people were also unhappy about these particular body parts. For example, 50 percent of women were dissatisfied with the size of their hips. Thirty-six percent of men worried about having a "spare tire." A 1980 national poll conducted by the Harris organization found that 36 percent of Americans considered themselves overweight, and 54 percent said they were dieting or had dieted in the past (reported in Hiller 1982).

How much do you actually weigh, and how much would you like to weigh? The Department of Health, Education, and Welfare (see Bray 1979) has provided guidelines for the ideal weight. Compare how much you should weigh with how much you want to weigh, and do weigh (see Table 7.1).

According to the Department of Health, Education, and Welfare, 79 million Americans are significantly overweight—that is, they carry

TABLE 7.1 Acceptable Weights for Men and Women

	MEN		WOMEN	
HEIGHT[a]	AVERAGE WEIGHT[b]	ACCEPTABLE WEIGHT[b]	AVERAGE WEIGHT[b]	ACCEPTABLE WEIGHT[b]
4' 10"	——	———	102	92–119
4' 11"	——	———	104	94–122
5' 0"	——	———	107	96–125
5' 1"	——	———	110	99–128
5' 2"	123	112–141	113	102–131
5' 3"	127	115–144	116	105–134
5' 4"	130	118–148	120	108–138
5' 5"	133	121–152	123	111–142
5' 6"	136	124–156	128	114–146
5' 7"	140	128–161	132	118–150
5' 8"	145	132–166	136	122–154
5' 9"	149	136–170	140	126–158
5' 10"	153	140–174	144	130–163
5' 11"	158	144–179	148	134–168
6' 0"	162	148–184	152	138–173
6' 1"	166	152–189	——	———
6' 2"	171	156–194	——	———
6' 3"	176	160–199	——	———
6' 4"	181	164–208	——	———

[a] without shoes
[b] without clothes
SOURCE: Abraham and John, 1979.

around at least 20 percent extra in body weight (Abraham and John 1979). Americans get off to a slow start in their early twenties—only 7 percent of men and 10 percent of women are overweight in this age group. Soon thereafter, however, the scales begin to climb (see Table 7.2).

Ectomorph, Endomorph, or Mesomorph?

Traditionally, psychologists have identified three body types. For example, long ago, Ernst Kretschmer, in *Physique and Character* (1936), identified three types: the pyknic (or fat) type, the athletic (or muscular) type, and the aesthenic (or skinny) type. He was convinced people with different body types also had different personalities.

In the *Varieties of Human Physique* (1940, 7–8), William Sheldon and his colleagues identified three parallel body types. You may be familiar with Sheldon's labels—the endomorph (fat) type, the mesomorph (muscular) type, and the ectomorph (thin) type (see Illustration 7.3).

The Endomorph (top): The gut dominates; thus, they are inclined to "have comfort, relaxation, sociability, conviviality and sometimes gluttony." If things go awry, they may develop a massive-depressive psychosis.

The Mesomorph (middle): The muscles dominate. Their personalities are "dominated by the will to exertion, exercise, and vigorous self-expression." They tend toward paranoia.

The Ectomorph (bottom): The brain dominates. "The sensory and central nervous systems play dominant roles. He is tense, hyperattentional and under strong inhibitory control. His tendency is toward

TABLE 7.2 **Percent of Men and Women Exceeding Acceptable Weight by 20 Percent or More. A United States Health and Nutrution Examination Survey, 1971–1974**

AGE	MEN 20% OR MORE	WOMEN 20% OR MORE
20–74	14.0%	23.8%
22–24	7.4	9.6
25–34	13.6	17.1
35–44	17.0	24.3
45–54	15.8	27.8
55–64	15.1	34.7
65–74	13.4	31.5

SOURCE: Abraham and John, 1979.

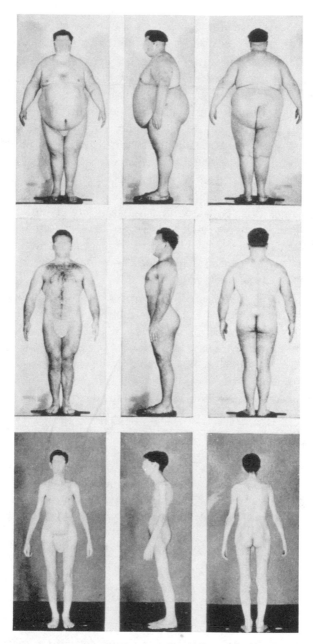

Figure 7.3. Three extreme varieties of human physique (Sheldon et al. 1940).

symbolic expression rather than direct action. They tend toward acute schizophrenic psychosis.

Like Kretschmer, Sheldon was convinced that "anatomy is destiny." He believed that constitution and personality were tightly linked and that most of us are a blending of the different personality/body types.

Although these "constitutional theories" have never become popular in psychology, the work of these psychologists is valuable in one respect. Their work tells us of the stereotypes people in previous generations had about fat, thin, and muscular people. Interestingly, these same stereotypes survive even today. For example, in chapter 1 we discussed what men and women in recent times have considered to be the ideal shape. In general, beauty equals a mesomorphic figure. Nancy Hirschberg and her colleagues (see Wiggins (Hirschberg) et al. 1968) found that men prefer a sort of Golden Mean body. Most men's ideal woman has slightly large breasts, medium to slightly small buttocks, and average-sized legs. Women prefer a tapered "V-look"—men with average shoulders, average waist and hips, and thin legs. Women dislike most the "Alfred Hitchcock, pear-shaped look"—a man with small shoulders and wide hips (Lavrakas 1975).

People not only like the mesomorph's build, they also like their personalities—or what they *assume* are their personalities. In one study, boys were shown full body silhouettes of an endomorph (round, fat body), an ectomorph (thin body), and a mesomorph (muscular, athletic body). It was found that fat boys and girls were likeliest to be seen as cheating, argumentative, being teased a lot, forgetful, unhealthy, lying, sloppy, naughty, ugly, mean, dumb, and dirty. Children with thin bodies were likely to be seen as weak, quiet, lonely, sneaky, afraid, and sad. The child with a muscular body was viewed the most positively (Lerner and Gellert 1969).

In several other studies (Wells and Siegel 1961; and Strongman and Hart 1968) men and women were asked to view silhouettes of people with different body types. Following are some of the traits attributed to each of the different body types.

1. *Round, fat body:* fat, old, short, old-fashioned, physically weak, ugly, talkative, warmhearted, sympathetic, good-natured, agreeable, dependent on others, trusting, greedy for affection, oriented toward people, loves physical comfort, loves eating.

2. *thin body:* thin, young, ambitious, tall, suspicious, tense, nervous, stubborn, difficult, pessimistic, quiet, sensitive to pain, liking privacy, inhibited, secretive.

3. *muscular, athletic body:* strong, masculine, good-looking, adventurous, tall, self-reliant, energetic, youthful, competitive, likes exercise, bold.

A more recent study (Guy et al. 1980) found that in men the mesomorph (muscular) shape is seen as the most "masculine." In women, the ectomorph (thin) type is seen as the most "feminine." For both sexes, the other body types appear to be "androgynous"—associated with personality traits desirable for both men *and* women.

Discrimination Against the Obese

If so many Americans have a weight problem, one would think there would be compassion for people with that same problem. Apparently not. Despite its prevalence, obesity is stigmatized. When THE GROUP was asked what single, physical trait was "disgusting," the trait most often mentioned was "being fat."

Discrimination against the obese begins early. In one study (Richardson et al. 1961), ten- and eleven-year olds were shown drawings of children and asked how much they thought they would like them. Children's preferences, from most likeable to least likeable, were: (1) a normal child, (2) a child with leg braces and crutches, (3) a child in a wheelchair, (4) a child with a hand missing, (5) a child with a facial disfigurement, and, *finally,* (6) a fat child!

This study has been repeated several times with children from different ethnic and social backgrounds and with professional men and women. In every case, the results are the same—the fat child is either ranked last or next to last (Alessi and Anthony 1969; Goodman et al. 1963; Maddox et al. 1968).

Werner Cahnman (1968) discusses the special stigma of obesity:

> . . . contrary to those that are blind, one legged, paraplegic, or dark-pigmented, the obese are presumed to hold their fate in their own hands; if they were only a little less greedy or lazy or yielding to impulse or oblivious of advice, they would restrict excessive food intake, resort to strenuous exercise, and as a consequence of such deliberate action, they would reduce. Actually, the moral factor which is thus introduced aggravates the case. While blindness is considered a misfortune, obesity is branded as a defect. This can be read from familiar patterns of behavior. A blind girl will be helped by her age mates, but a heavy girl will be derided. A paraplegic boy will be supported by other boys, but a fat boy will be pushed around. The embarassing and not infrequently harassing treatment which is meted out to obese teenagers by those around them will not elicit sympathy from onlookers, but a sense of gratification; the idea is that they have got what was coming to them. (p. 294)

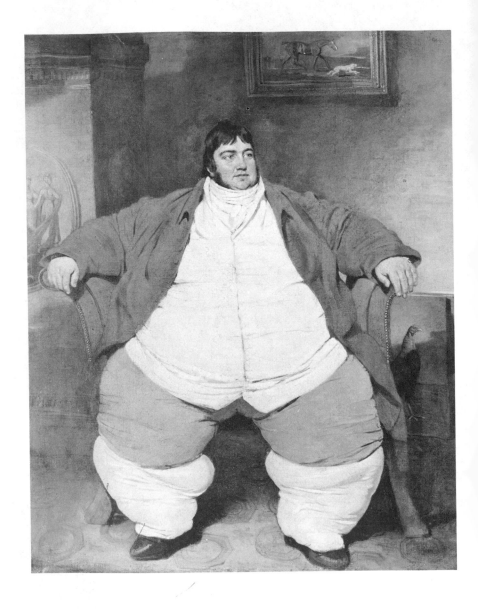

Figure 7.4. Daniel Lambert, 1770–1908. He weighed 52 stone 11 pounds. This painting is by Benjamin Marshall, Leicestershire Museum and Art Gallery, Leicester.

The overweight are not only discriminated against in childhood but also face degradation in adulthood. Fat adults probably face more discrimination—in education, employment, and love—than any other group.

Size: A Weighty Problem

Several years ago, the *New York Times* (24 November 1966, 45) declared: "College Admission Hint: Lose Weight". The startling headline was followed by a startling article reporting on a study conducted in New England by Helen Channing and Jean Mayer on the effect of obesity on college acceptance. They had found that although fat girls and boys were not any less likely than thin boys and girls to apply to college, they were much less likely to be accepted. This finding was particularly true for girls. It was concluded that a fat high school girl has one-third less chance of getting into college than a thin girl, even though of the same intelligence. The researchers thought this inequity occurred because high school teachers and college admission officers were less likely to favorably recommend the fat student.

Other evidence also documents that size can weigh you down. In one study (see Benson, Severs, Tatgenhorst, and Loddengaard 1980), an experimenter, posing as an undergraduate, sent a letter, a resume, and a short questionnaire to seventy male public health administrators, randomly selected from a registry of county public health department officials in a midwestern state. The "undergraduate" wanted to receive career guidance. She stated she was interested in graduate training in public health administration, but needed more information. She asked the administrator three questions: "What graduate schools in Public Health Administration would you suggest I apply to?" "Given my background, do you think I have a good chance of getting into a Public Health graduate program?" and "If I get a degree in Public Health Administration, what kind of chance do you think I'll have of getting a good job in the area of public health?" The enclosed resumé included either a photograph of an obese woman (the resume indicated she was 5'6" and 185 pounds), a photograph of a woman of normal body build (5'6" and 125 pounds), or no photograph (she was 5'6", but no weight was given). The photographs were obtained by photographing two women in their natural states (normal body build) and after placing padding under their shirts.

The discrimination was clearcut. Women of average weight or who did not include a picture got a reply from the public health administrators 57–65 percent of the time. If the bogus applicant was fat, however, the public health administrators generally did not even bother to reply! Such women received an answer less than 25 percent of the time. If they did reply, how did health administrators respond? Even the most friendly administrators warned fat women that their chances of getting into a public health graduate program and of getting a good job later on were poor. Women who did not send a picture and women of normal body build were sent much more positive forecasts.

Discrimination does not end after men and women are admitted to graduate school. Recently, columnist Ellen Goodman (1977) wrote:

> BOSTON—She was brilliant. Everyone involved in the case agreed about that. . . . She was unattractive. Everyone agrees about that, too. . . . She was overweight, whiny, argumentative, unkempt—the list goes on—sloppy, hypercritical, unpopular.
>
> The life of Charlotte Horowitz—whose dismissal from a Missouri medical school became a Supreme Court case this week—has become painfully public. A description of rejection. From all reports, she interacted with the world like a fingernail on a blackboard. She was punished for the crime of being socially unacceptable. Charlotte Horowitz was older than most of the other students when she was admitted to the University of Missouri-Kansas City Medical School in 1972. She was also brighter, a misfit from New York who won her place despite the admissions officer's report that read, "The candidate's personal appearance is against her. . . ." By the school's "merit system," she was tops in her medical school class. Yet, she was dismissed by the Dean on the verge of graduation. The grounds were tardiness, bad grooming and an abrasive personal style. . . . The theme of this difficult, emotional story is prejudice. The most deep-rooted way in which we prejudge each other. The sort of discrimination which is universal, almost unrootable. Prejudice toward appearance. Discrimination against what we "see."
>
> The most unattractive children in the classrooms of our youth had their lives and personalities warped by the fact. Their painful experiences of rejection nurtured in them an expectation of rejection. That expectation, like some paranoia, was almost always fulfilled.
>
> It is a mystery why some "unattractive people" wear it in their souls and others don't. Why one becomes Barbra Streisand and another a reject.
>
> But often, along the way, some people give up trying to be accepted and become defensively non-conforming. They stop letting themselves care. They become "unkempt, argumentative, abrasive." And the list goes on.
>
> Everyone's self-image is formed in some measure by the way they are seen, the way they see themselves being seen. As their image deteriorates, their personality often shatters along with it. At that point, the rest of us smugly avoid them, stamping them "unacceptable," not because of their "looks" but because of their behavior.
>
> It happens all the time.
>
> This case isn't a question of the . . . "life isn't fair" sort of discrimination. It's a story of a university so "blinded" that its officials felt they

had the right to throw away a life and a mind because it was housed in a body that was "overweight, sloppy, hypercritical." "What's been lost in all this," says Dr. Ramey, "is the contribution a brilliant human being might have made in a field which needs all the fine minds we have." You see, Charlotte Horowitz was brilliant. Everyone involved in the case could, at least, see that.

If the overweight survive their education, they then must deal with the work place. Here, discrimination is fierce.

Size Can Weigh You Down

In the business world, it pays to keep trim and in shape. Robert Half, who runs an executive placement organization, surveyed one thousand firms that had used his services to recruit financial and computer executives (Half, *New York Times*, 2 January 1974, 12). From the firms, Half acquired the height, weight, and salaries of the executives hired. In the 1,500 top executive spots (those paying $25,000 to $45,000), only 9 percent of the executives were overweight. On the other hand, nearly 40 percent of the 13,500 executives making between $10,000 to $20,000 were overweight. Half reported that he received thousands of requests for thin men and women, but only once in twenty-five years had anyone asked for a plump executive (and that request came from a company making clothing for overweight men). Half commented, "By exploiting the overweight, too many American companies are literally living off the fat of the land. . . . Some fat people pay a penalty of $1,000 a pound. . . . The overweight have become America's largest, least protected minority group."

Another researcher examined the job success of people in a variety of occupations and found a less gloomy picture for overweight men and women. In chapter 2 and earlier in this chapter, we referred to research conducted by Robert Quinn at the University of Michigan's Survey Research Center (Quinn 1978). He interviewed several hundred employed men and women about various aspects of their jobs. In addition to rating the respondents' physical attractiveness, the interviewers judged the weight of the respondents on a five-point scale: "obese," "overweight," "average for height," "underweight," and "skinny." The results shows a slight tendency for average-weight men and women to have higher paying and more prestigious jobs than either overweight or underweight men and women, but the differences were not significant. A more subtle type of discrimination was detected, but only against women. Overweight and underweight women were unlikely to be hired for jobs requiring interaction with other people. Furthermore, overweight and underweight women reported interpersonal relations with coworkers that were not as good as those reported by women average in weight.

In sum, the portly face discrimination, sometimes very direct and at other times very subtle, throughout their lives.

Why Is There Discrimination Against the Full Bodied?

Probably the main reason people judged the overweight so harshly is because they believe fat people are responsible for their condition—it is assumed the overweight overindulge, are lazy, and lack self-control. It is believed that, if only they had a little more self-discipline, the stout would soon be in perfect shape.

That the obese are seen as personally responsible for their condition was demonstrated in an experiment conducted by Maddox et al. (1968). Men and women were asked to what degree an individual is responsible for several different characteristics. Only 2 percent of them responded a "blind person" was responsible for his/her lack of sight. On the

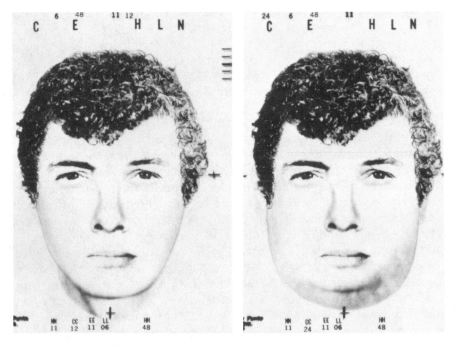

Figure 7.5. Police artists' construction of a suspect at normal weight and overweight.

other hand, 76 percent agreed that a "man with a flabby body" was personally responsible for his poor shape, and 84 percent said a "women needing a girdle" was accountable for her condition.

Most people believe the overweight could easily change and thus evaluate them harshly. Even physicians share this belief. For example, a majority of physicians and student clerks at a public outpatient medical clinic described their obese patients as "ugly" and "weak-willed" (Maddox and Liederman 1969). The following statement from one of THE GROUP members seems typical of the attitudes many hold about the obese:

> I have a very strong stereotype only regarding fat people. I definitely have a "fat prejudice." I feel that fat people are often lazy and lack self-control or the motivation to take responsibility for their cause of obesity. This is probably a very unfair assumption to make, but it is a definite image I have of fat people. I feel people certainly can't change their height or the color of their eyes, but one can do something about a weight problem if they really want to.

Whether or not the overweight are "responsible" for their condition is still being debated (Rodin 1983). Some scientists are convinced there are underlying physical reasons for obesity. They point out that fat cells are laid down in the first few months of life; thus, the potential to gain weight is always greater for the formerly fat than for anyone else (Rodin 1979). Other scientists speculate that metabolic disorders (thyroid problems, glandular problems, or hypoglycemia) are the real causes of obesity. Still others hypotehsize a causal link between diabetes and obesity (Rodin 1979, 1983).

On the other hand, most physicians are skeptical of such claims. In his review of existing evidence, Bayrd (1978) observes:

> Many theories have been proposed over the years to explain obesity, and in general those that have seemed the simplest and gone the farthest to exculpate the individual have held the most appeal. That they have also ranged from the highly implausible to the grossly inaccurate has done little to dim their appeal, and overweight Americans still regularly excuse their overindulgence by insisting that they have a thyroid condition, or a glandular problem, or hypoglycemia. The truth is that only one seriously obese person in a thousand has any kind of glandular problem, and more often than not these metabolic irregularities are a consequence of, rather than a cause of, obesity. (pp. 37–38)

Whether people view obesity as a medical or a moral problem seems to impact profoundly on how sympathetically they respond to the obese. In a series of experiments, DeJong (1980) demonstrated that a heavy woman is viewed very differently, depending on how responsible she is thought to be for her condition. In the first experiment, adolescent girls were asked to look at a folder containing a photograph and a personal statement from another girl and to give their first impressions of her. In half the cases, the photograph was an overweight girl; in the other cases, she was normal in weight. Some of the adolescents were told the girl had a thyroid problem that was causing her weight problem (in the fat girl) or a slight "paleness" (in the normal weight girl). For other respondents, no thryoid problem was mentioned.

When the adolescents described their first impressions of the girl, they rated her on several dimensions—warmth, friendliness, happiness, self-confidence, self-indulgence, self-discipline, and laziness. They also indicated how much they thought they would like her, want to become close friends with her, and introduce her to their friends. The obese girl without a thyroid problem was evaluated more negatively (as having less self-discipline and being lazier) than the normal weight girl. If the obese girl had a thyroid problem, however, she was not derogated. The obese girl was liked much less than the normal weight girl, especially when she did not have a thyroid problem to "excuse" her. In general, the results indicated that an obese person with an "excuse" is tolerated much more than an obese person without an "excuse."

An excuse is not the only thing that can lessen the otherwise harsh evaluations an obese person receives. It may also help if the obese person is able to report recent weight loss (and perhaps suggest that such success will continue). In a second experiment conducted by DeJong (1980), the overweight girl either reported she had already successfully lost twenty-five pounds in the last four months or did not mention anything about weight loss. The obese girl gained a little by losing weight. She was not evaluated as negatively as an obese woman who had not lost weight or who did not have the excuse of a thyroid condition.

There is, then, massive prejudice against the overweight. Although there has been less research examining how the obese fare in the arena of personal relations, we would speculate that here is where the biases against the obese are most often manifested. How do overweight people respond to this prejudice? For most people, the response is mixed. Here is a poignant account by one sensitive woman:

> I firmly believe that the way I look has an impact on how other people relate to me. First of all, in my relationships with females, I'm usually considered to be a great listener. I barely get to talk. One woman, in particular, has treated me just as a sounding board in our relationship. She tells me what a great weekend she had, or about who she's seeing without ever thinking that I might have had fun or something else to tell her. I think her assumptions that I couldn't have had something to tell boils down to the fact that I am fat—and whoever heard of a fat person having a terrific weekend? And who would take a

fat person out? When reading a book about fat women, I have found that many other fat women have said they, too, were considered great listeners, while their friends couldn't believe they may have something fun to talk about. It was comforting to find that I'm not alone in that respect.

My relationships with males are even more bizarre. Lots of men won't give me the time of day because I'm not terribly attractive. Other males treat me like one of the guys. I go out drinking with them and can joke around about sexual things—do really manly stuff. Most men don't deal with me in sexual terms at all, unless we're joking about who is sleeping with whom. So it's a real bind to be fat and female and looking for a guy to be in a boyfriend/girlfriend relationship. In fact, it's practically impossible. So I do have male friends, but that's all they are. We're affectionate, but there is no hugging and kissing allowed, except on very special occasions.

My grandmother and mother are convinced that if I lost weight, I'd get a boyfriend and live happily ever after. The problem is, if I lost weight, I'll still be the same person in a different shell, and who is to say that I'd want a serious relationship, just because I got pretty?

Although the above woman was quite overweight, she seems to have accepted her situation and is almost philosophical about it. Those only slightly overweight, on the other hand, can sometimes be the most miserable and paralyzed by the situation, perhaps they know what it *was* like to be pretty and thin and hate themselves for losing it. Take, as an example, the feelings of the following woman from THE GROUP:

Right now, I feel about the most unattractive I've ever felt in my entire life. The main reason being that I've gained about 30 pounds. It's quite depressing and has affected my relationships with others greatly. I'm not obese. It's just that after being thin and now looking out of shape, wearing two sizes bigger, etc., I hate it and hate myself for getting so out of shape. I've always been obsessed with my weight and dieting ever since I can remember.

I just don't feel self-confident anymore. Everytime I meet someone, I just know they're noticing my weight. Especially guys—I feel like they're thinking, "Hey, she wouldn't be too bad if she were just a little thinner." I'm terribly jealous of any girl who is thin and the first thing I notice when I meet someone is how fat or thin they are.

Some people fight back against the stigma placed on fat people. Magazines such as BBW (*Big Beautiful Woman*) attempt to convince their readers that big is beautiful. They run articles from anthropologists reminding women that in some societies big is beautiful. If only the heavy readers were in that society, they would be stuffing themselves like Strasbourg geese rather than dieting. They run articles from physicians assuring women that weight does not cause high blood pressure, the two factors may just coexist or the stress society puts on overweight may cause physical ills. They run fashion pictures of heavy women. Finally, there is a friendship page where BA (Big Admirers) and BBW and BHM (Big Handsom Men) can find mates.

The ads read like this:

Texas, 32, attractive, green-eyed brunette. Enjoys all life's pleasures. Seeking correspondence with mature male 30–45, 5'10" or over, who considers himself successful personally and professionally, values honesty, warmth, openness. Letters answered. Photo please.   MJ114

Are you a BBW who's getting bigger and more beautiful? Want a BHM who'd love each new pound? MENSAN, 40, likes sharing intelligent conversation, music, travel, theater, gourmet feasts, whatever seems right. Descriptive letters with photos from biggest, tallest, most buxom answered first; all answered. Middle Atlantic preferred; not essential.
                                                        MJ343

Latin male, 36, very handsome. Trim 6' romantic, adventurous, multilingual BBW lover, wishes to meet very buxom, extra large BBW. ND109

Nonsmoking, large BBW, in L.A., seeks newfriends, male/female. Enjoys Scrabble, mysteries, Miss Piggy, drive-in movies, music, laughing. Share love of animals, sense of humor, good times, chocolate chip cookies.
                                                        ND127

"Squeezably soft" BBW, 31, 5'6" enjoys corny jokes, Irish music, Steeler football, slow dancing, Sunday brunch, children, genuine friendships, raquetball ,and "Golden Oldies." Would like to meet tall caucasian BBM who wouldn't mind if I sniffled while watching poignant movies. ND129

Ms: white, 38, 250, 5'6½", far Northern California, poor, nonsmoker, rural extended family lifestyle, trying to farm. Educated, romantic, hardworking, multi-interests, independent, lonely BUT choosey. You should be white 21–50, handyman, jack-of-all-trades type, or willing to learn, hardworking, honest, sincere, relocatable, one woman man, children okay!   ND171

Organizations have also been created to bring fat people together to celebrate how they look (rather than to pressure each other to diet). The National Association to Aid Fat Americans (NAAFA) is a social and political organization with chapters in major cities throughout the United States. The major purposes of the organization are to emphasize that fat is all right and to fight for better treatment of the obese.

One doesn't have to be fat to help fight discrimination against the fat. Researcher Robert Quinn (who investigated how physical attractiveness, height, and weight are related to job success) was thanked by a mother who read a newspaper account of his work on physical deviance:

Dear Mr. Quinn:

Just wish to thank you for the study on job discrimination against the fat people in this world.

The United States government and that State of _____are also guilty as much as private business.

My daughter cannot get a well paying job because of her weight.

1. She passed the written requirements for an Employment Service laboratory technician test, but they said she was too heavy.
2. She passed the requirements for a practical nurse program but was not accepted because of her weight.
3. The United States Army would not accept her because of her weight.

Teachers in school discriminate against fat, pimply-faced kids. They like slim, blonde, clean-cut, clear-complectioned, Anglo-Saxon girls. The only clique left to fat girls is the lowest strata—school skippers, trouble makers, smokers, dropouts, etc. Do you wonder why we have so much delinquency? Because then this pattern and feeling of unworth is ingrained and carried over into adult life: "I am just so fat and ugly. Nobody like me. Why try? I must really be repulsive."

A study like yours is long overdue. This also is a minority group that needs help.

> Sincerely yours,
>
> A mother who has fought the
> world for 25 years to erase
> the scars on an ugly, fat
> daughter.

(from Quinn 1978, 27–28)

The Other Side: Too *Little* of a Good Thing

Recent cultural pressure on Americans (especially on young women) to be thin has sometimes led to the opposite problem—risking one's life to get thin. Men and women who go to extremes to get and stay thin may suffer from one or two types of eating disorders: anorexia nervosa or bulimia.

Those with *anorexia nervosa* are systematically starving themselves. Following is a description of a young woman suffering from the starvation disease:

> At the age of fourteen, Deborah Kaplan developed the syndrome known as anorexia nervosa, or self-starvation. Typically, the illness seems to have begun when she decided to go on a diet in order to pursue a career as a model. At first she followed a normal reducing diet. But over a period of eighteen months she cut out more and more

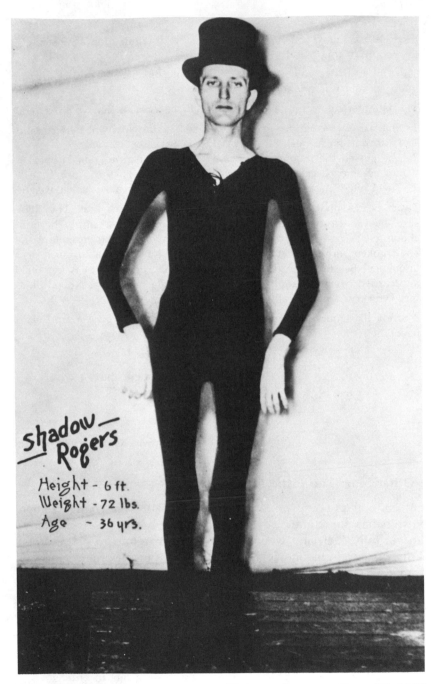

Figure 7.6. Shadow Rogers, Human Skeleton. Courtesy, Circus World Museum, Baraboo, Wisconsin.

foods, until she was eating only apples, cottage cheese, and water. Her weight dropped from 110 pounds to 78 pounds, and amenorrhea [failure to menstruate] developed. At the same time, Deborah's activity increased. Sometimes she would wake up at four or five in the morning and go out to walk for miles until it was time to leave for school. If confined to the house, she ran endlessly up and down the stairs. (Minuchin et al. 1978, 1)

Anorexia is usually found in adolescent girls and young women (Crisp et a. 1976; Diagnostic and Statistical Manual of Mental Disorders 1980). The disease usually begins in the teen years and may continue for months or even years. Some anorexics end up seeking treatment and returning to normal weight. Others eat enough to survive but remain very underweight. As many as 23 percent of the victims of anorexia nervosa actually starve to death or die from complications caused by malnutrition (see Bruch 1978; Maloney and Farrell 1980). (Singer Karen Carpenter, who suffered from anorexia nervosa for several years, died in 1983 from a weakened heart condition.)

Most anorexics suffer from the curse of perfectionism. They are typically intelligent, ambitious, and from cultured, highly educated, middle or upper class families. They are eager to please others. In adolescence, they become obsessed with perfection and with control (Bruch 1980). Some therapists believe young women become anorexic because they fear sexuality and becoming adult women. They lose weight to keep their body at childlike proportions. They engage in physical exercise, often to the point of exhaustion, in order to burn up calories.

Anorexics suffer from a disturbance in their body image. They may weigh less than seventy-five pounds, a "skeleton clad only in skin" (Morton, 1964), but they think they are fat. When they complete the Body Image Questionnaire (that was presented earlier), they express dissatisfaction with their bodies, not because they think they are too thin, but because they think they are too fat.

The incidence of anorexia nervosa appears to be increasing. Recently, such organizations as the National Anorexic Aid Society (NAAS) and Anorexia Nervosa and Associated Disorders have been founded to deal with anorexics.

People with *bulimia* get trapped in a binge-purge syndrome. They regularly engage in uncontrollable eating and then, to avoid gaining weight, force themselves to throw up or to purge themselves with heavy doses of laxatives. Following is a description of the secret life of a woman suffering from bulimia:

Gayle Cappelluti, 29, of Brooklyn, N.Y., knew that something was terribly wrong with her each time she shut herself away in her room to eat.

"I'd have a whole pizza—one of the big ones. And a couple of pounds of candy and more cookies," recalls Gayle, an elementary schoolteacher. "Then I'd telephone a Chinese take-out restaurant and order $30 worth of food."

"It was like being in a dream. I didn't think of anything. I'd just eat all night long."

Yet Gayle never gained much weight. at 5 feet 4½ inches, she weighed 109 pounds. And that was the second part of her guilty secret: Gayle vomited all of the food she ate. (Ubell 1983, 18)

Bulimia is also more common among women than men. It is estimated that as many as 7 million women are trapped at some point in their lives in the binge-purge syndrome (Casper et al. 1980; Garfinkel 1980). Jane Fonda admits she was bulimic as a teenager. Although bulimics may look healthy, they are prone to ailments such as swollen salivary glands, an inflamed pancreas, gallbladder and stomach problems, and eroded tooth enamal. At its worst, bulimia can kill. Purging empties the body of potassium, which weakens the heart. The background of bulimics is much like that of anorexics. They are perfectionists from middle to upper class homes.

Anorexia nervosa and bulimia are increasing in frequency in part because the current idealized image for women in modern Western society is thinness. Recent research has documented the change in the culture's standards for beauty over recent years from a more voluptuous look to a thin shape (Garner, Garfinkel, Schwartz, and Thompson 1980). First, researchers obtained the height, weight, and measurements of 240 monthly playmates from twenty years of *Playboy Magazine*. It was found that the weight of the centerfolds (for age and height) has declined over the twenty years. They also found a shift toward a more androgynous body form (smaller breasts and hips, but larger waist). Second, the researchers collected the same vital statistics from contestants and winners of the Miss America Pageant from 1959 to 1978. An average yearly decline of .28 pounds for contestants and .37 pounds for pageant winners was found. Since 1970, the winners have weighed significantly less than the other contestants! Finally, the researchers examined five popular women's magazines from 1959 through 1978 and found that the number of diet articles has increased significantly over the years. The societal pressure for a thinner ideal shape for women has led some women to go too far to become perfect.

INCIDENTALS

There is much more to the body than overall height and weight. In the rest of this chapter, we will consider some particular parts of the body, as well as a couple nonphysical characteristics of the self (name and smell).

Hair

Surrounding the face is a border—the hair. If carefully styled, hair can bring out the beauty in one's face. However, if hair is left ungroomed or is inappropriately styled, even a person with a very pretty face would not be considered very attractive overall. You may recall several experimental studies in which attractiveness is manipulated by changing the looks of one individual. To make the same individual both particularly appealing and particularly unappealing, one major physical characteristics that is changed is hair. For example, in the "ugly" condition, a woman may have on a stringy, dirty-haired wig, while in the "attractive" condition, her hair is neatly styled. These experiments demonstrated that the "attractive" woman is generally perceived and treated much more favorably than the "ugly" woman.

Even less dramatic changes in hair care can have an effect on the impressions formed of an individual. Men and women were shown photographs of women who had either received hair care or had not received hair care. The men and women rated the hair-treated women more favorably in appearance than the women who had not received hair care. More specifically, they rated the hair-treated women as more tidy, clean, pleasant, and mature looking. The hair-treated women also received more favorable ratings in such aspects of personality as sensitivity, caring, and sincerity (Graham and Jouhar 1980).

Hair comes in different colors. The color of a person's hair may also effect how others view him/her. Everyone has heard the phrases: "Blondes have more fun"; "dumb blonde"; "a fiery redhead." Most of us have definite impressions about what blondes, brunettes, and redheads are like. In fact, research indicates that blondes are expected to have more fun and redheads are expected to be "clowns" (Clayson and Maugham 1976).

What about people's romantic choices? What color of hair would you prefer to stroke? Folk wisdom states that men prefer blondes, while women prefer dark men. In one study (Feinman and Gill 1978), men and women were asked what characteristics they would like in an "ideal" mate. Gentlemen did prefer blondes. Women preferred brown-haired men (the tall, *dark,* and handsome image). Both men and women seemed to have an aversion to redheads.

Blondes, subject to the most stereotyping, have a mixed blessing. Man may prefer blonde-haired women, but they may also be afraid to approach them. Blondes also have to live with the dumb blonde stereo-type. Brian Shapiro, who teaches at the UCLA graduate business school, discusses one of his students.

> One of my students at UCLA was a stunning blonde. She would come up to my office every week and ask questions about the material. They were actually questions that I thought were rather stupid. And so all along I was thinking that it was too bad that she would have to drop the course after she took the midterm.
>
> Well, the midterm exam came. And who do you think got the highest grade? This blonde turned out to be one of the most prolific students I had. But the reason she kept coming off as a dumb blonde—and asking dumb questions—is because she had a dumb blonde syndrome. She had no confidence in herself. She would wake up in the morning, look in the mirror, and say, "I'm a dumb blonde." And I think she really believed it.
>
> One night I had her out for a cocktail, and the subject of dating came up. I asked her who she was dating. She replied that she hadn't had a date in seven months. I was shocked. I asked her why. She said, "No one asks me out." I'm convinced that it was a classic case of a girl being so nice looking that the average insecure guy in this world looks at her and-goes, "Oh shit. I can't ask her out because she's going to turn me down. I'll be rejected."
>
> So this dumb blonde spent a year and a half at UCLA without dates because her only fault was that she was too good-looking. I think being good-looking—and being blonde—are not all that they are cracked up to be.

The Eyes Have It

Try an intriguing experiment: Ask your friends to point to the spot where they are located. At first, they will look at you with puzzlement: "What do you mean, where? I'm everywhere." But if you persist, you will get a reply that is startlingly consistent. Everyone will point to the same spot. We are located right between our eyes. Eyes are indeed the "mirrors of our souls."

Tragically, the importance of eyes is reflected in the behavior of those most off-balance. Dr. Richard Baske, a Wisconsin ophthalmologist, provides emergency treatment to Madison's street people. He reports that during psychotic episodes, many people are overcome by self-loathing. When they set out to destroy themselves, inevitably their eyes are their target. On occasion, Dr. Baske's clients have tried to glue their lids together with rubber cement (so no one can see into their souls), have tried to cleanse their eyes of impurities with industrial solvent

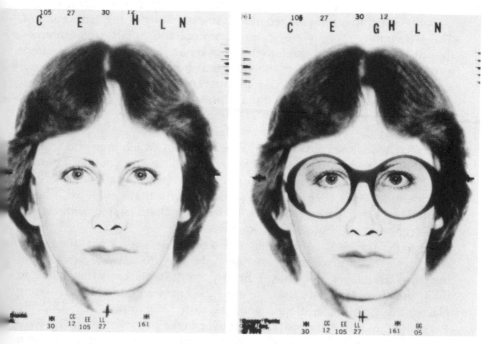

Figure 7.7. Police artists' construction of a suspect, with and without glasses.

(and succeeded only in blinding themselves), and, like King Lear, have tried to gouge their eyes out as an expression of their suffering.

Even children sense that their eyes are important to them. In one study (Vaughan, Stabler, and Clance 1981), 320 gradeschool children were given pictures of seven different body parts and were asked to put a dollar value on each part. The seven body parts were: eyes, leg, foot, hand, finger, arm, and ear. On a range from $0 to $550, the eyes were worth $327 on the average to the children—worth more than any other body part.

People also notice the eyes of others. In a recent survey taken by the Roper Organization, men and women were asked, "When you first meet someone, which one or two things about physical appearance do you tend to notice first?" Especially when meeting a person of the opposite sex, eyes were mentioned as one of the first characteristics to be noticed (reported in *Psychology Today* January 1984, 17). Given the importance of eyes, then, it is surprising that only a smattering of research has examined what makes attractive eyes. The little research that has been done has focused on pupil size, eye color, and the effect of wearing glasses.

The size of the pupils in the eyes can affect how attractive we look. In one study, men looked at two photographs of the same woman. The two photographs were identical, except the pupils were enlarged in one of them. Men preferred the woman and thought her more attractive when her pupils were enlarged; however, the men could not explain why they preferred one photograph over the other—they just knew they did (reported in Graham and Jouhar 1980). Sexual arousal is one way of enlarging pupils, so, understandably, we look more attractive to the one who has captured our heart.

What about the color of eyes? One study, in which men and women described the characteristics of their "ideal" mate, found that men preferred light-colored eyes while women preferred dark-colored eyes (Feinman and Gill 1978). It has also been found that people with light-colored eyes are perceived as more friendly than people with darker eyes (reported in Graham and Jouhar 1980).

Should the near- and farsighted among us ever wear glasses, or should we assume contacts are the only way to salvage any appeal our eyes and faces may have? Beauty consultants are often quick to point out that glasses do damage appeal—Lines all added in the wrong places, the nose looks bigger, and the chin is deemphasized. Dorothy Parker (1936) once quipped: "Guys never make passes at girls who wear glasses." Research has shown that a woman wearing glasses *is* seen as less attractive than a woman who is not wearing glasses. However, if one has to wear glasses, it helps to also have on makeup (reported in Graham and Jouhar 1980).

Glasses may, however, make us appear more intelligent. There is a popularly held belief that men and women wearing glasses are unusually intellectual. Examine the two faces in illustration 7 and choose the one that looks more intelligent to you. A number of studies have demonstrated differences in evaluators' judgments of a person with versus without glasses. One psychologist (Thornton 1944) asked men and women their impressions of others with and without their glasses. People appeared more intelligent and industrious when they had on their glasses. In a more recent study (Elman 1977), people with their glasses on were seen as gentler, more sensitive, and more of a follower.

What about self-perceptions? Are you more likely to feel you could uncover a law of physics or write a symphony when you have glasses on? Students wearing glasses were brought into a laboratory in one study (Kellerman and Laird 1982). One-half the men and women were asked to take their glasses off, while the others were allowed to keep them on. They were then all given a vocabulary test. Although wearing glasses did not affect actual performance on the test, the men and women allowed to keep on their glasses believed they had performed better than those who had taken them off. Those keeping their glasses on also viewed themselves as more stable, scholarly, and competent than those who took them off.

Beards: Some Hair-Raising Facts

A staggering array of women's magazines—*Glamour, Bazaar, Redbook, Madamoiselle*—guide women on how to make over their eyebrows, eyes, eyelashes, cheeks, and lips. Men have fewer options for improving their facial looks. One thing they *can* do, however, is to grow a moustache or beard. The existing research suggests that, to improve their images, men might do well to do just that.

Do women *prefer* facial hair on their mates? In a study we mentioned earlier, men and women were asked what physical characteristics they preferred in a mate (Feinman and Gill 1977). Only 18 percent of the women preferred men with beards, 42 percent liked men with moustaches, and 40 percent preferred clean-shaven men. These results would suggest it does not pay for men to grow beards.

Yet, when psychologists examine how people *react* to clean-shaven versus moustached versus bearded men, they come to quite different conclusions. For example, Pellegrini (1973) persuaded several men to have their beards shaved off. Photographs of the men were taken at each of the following stages: full beard, goatee, moustache, and clean-shaven. Then, individuals were asked to examine one of the photographs and to give their first impressions of the man. The men were perceived to have the most socially desirable characteristics when they had full beards. They were seen as more masculine, mature, good-looking, dominant, self-confident, courageous, likeable, nonconforming, industrious, and older than clean-shaven men. (Now we tell them!) Judgments about men with moustaches and men with goatees fell in between (similar results were found by Kenny and Fletcher 1973).

One ingenious method to study people's perceptions of bearded versus clean-shaven men is the Identi-kit Face Construction technique. Police artists use these kits to help witnesses construct likeliness of suspects. The Identi-kit consists of a set of transparent, celluloid sheets. The artist has several graduated sheets for each possible facial feature—e.g., eyes, nose, lips. The witness keeps making corrections—"The nose is a little wider than that." "The eyes are closer together." "He had a bigger nose." The police artists keeps flipping sheets until the witness says, "Perfect, that's the culprit who snatched my purse."

With her colleagues, Susan Sprecher used Identi-kit faces to examine how people react to a man with varying amounts of facial hair. (Sprecher et al., 1984) (We have used Identi-Kit faces throughout this chapter—for example, in Illustration 7.8. In this trio of sketches, the same man appears clean-shaven, with a moustache, with a beard. In the experiment Smith and Sprecher conducted, faces of several men were constructed, and each face appeared in several forms. The pictures were then shown to young men and women. It was found that both young and middle-aged men did better behind a beard. Regardless of age, bearded men were perceived as unusually intelligent, good-looking, likeable, healthy, physically attractive, popular, sensitive to others, and sexually appealing. (In general, men with moustaches fell between bearded and clean-shaven men in how they were evaluated.)

Although Pellegrini (1973) found that a beard made the young men in his study look older, the young (Identi-kit) men in this study did not look older when they donned a beard. Furthermore, the middle-aged men actually looked younger with a beard, perhaps because it covers up signs of aging.

Otto Friedrick (1982), a writer for *Time* magazine, told how his moustache changed his age appearance and related the trauma of eventually shaving it off. In 1970, Friedrick grew a mustache because he wanted to look older. He was working on a book about Berlin in the 1920s, and he had to interview a number of aged survivors. He hoped they would think of him as a sympathetic listener, a partner of the older generation—thus the moustache.

As he worked on his book, however, mustaches began appearing on all kinds of young men—on probaseball players, policemen, and movie stars. Now, his mustache made him look younger. He observes, "How a mustache dominates a face! If Adolf Hitler had shaved his upper lip and then gone out for a walk, would anyone have recognized him? Or a freshly shaved Erroll Flynn? Or Groucho Marx?" Then, inevitably, a day came when he grew tired of a mustache. He thought of shaving it off, but the idea made him uneasy. Would there be a lot of inane remarks at the office? He delayed. He continues:

> One Saturday in October, just before lunch, I shaved my upper lip bare. To my dismay, I saw in the mirror a face that I had not seen for more than a decade, and I hardly recognized it. The mustache had always provided a certain look of paternal respectability, but now I was only the blankness of middle age.
>
> And how had I acquired those deep vertical lines of discontent across both ends of my mouth, along the outer edges of where the mustache had been? Had they been there before? Or had the mustache somehow caused them to grow there along the edges? Or were they a confession of discontent itself, as though I were a Dorian Gray without a portrait to be hidden in the attic? Who was it who said that every man of 50 has the face he deserves?
>
> . . . If a man's moustache is what dominates his face, and then the moustache is removed, what is left? (p. 19)

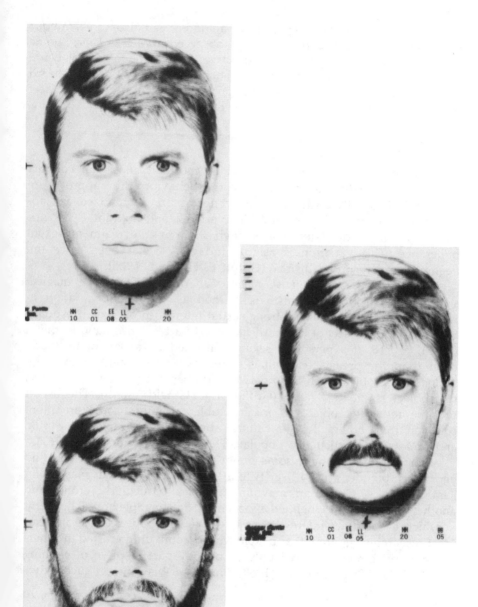

Figure 7.8. Identi-kit illustration of a clean-shaven man, the same man with a mustache, and with a beard.

Facial hair not only covers signs of aging but can also, in a symbolic way, covers the personality. As "Troy" observed in *Men in Love*, "Some women have said that I'm very attractive, even handsome, yet being so damned introspective, it's honestly hard to believe. I wear a beard only to hide as much of my face as possible, which is only one facet of my hiding my true self" (Friday 1980, 316).

The Fetish

All societies have standards for what is "normal" in sexual conduct (H. F. Taylor 1970). Societies assume the behaviors they approve are "natural." Those that vary from their norms are stigmatized as "abnormal," "unnatural," "deviant," "perverted," or "aberrant." Yet, nowhere is human diversity more evident than in the realm of sexual preference. This variation is as true today as it has been since the beginnings of recorded history (Griffitt & Hatfield, 1985b).

Originally, the word *fetish* meant "an object with some magical significance." Today, Fetishism is defined as "A sexual variation in which there is an unusually strong sexual interest in or sexual response to an inanimate object or to a particular body part." (Griffitt and Hatfield, (1985), p. 518. If a person is sexually aroused by a part of the body other than the breasts or genitals—such as hair or feet—or even by an inanimate object such as underwear, rubber boots, gloves, or shoes, that object is called a *fetish* (Griffitt and Hatfield 1985b). The list of possible fetishistic objects is inexhaustible, although some are more common than others. In our culture, shoes, gloves, rubber, fur, silk, and breasts are particularly popular (Thorpe, Katz, and Lewis 1961).

Most individuals have some minor fetishes. One woman may find enormous, blonde, grizzly bear type men arousing. Another may prefer slim brunettes. One man may find freckles particularly erotic, and another may be overwhelmed by a china doll complexion. The point at which a "normal" interest turns into a fetishist obsession is unclear. Most researchers assume that people who become uninterested in others entirely and become focused only on a body part or piece of clothing have a fetish. Paul Gebhard (1969) expresses this opinion succinctly:

> I envision the whole matter of fetishism as a graduated phenomenon. At one end of the range is a slight preference; next is a strong preference; next is the point where the fetish item is a necessity to sexual activity; and at the terminal end of the range the fetish item substitutes for a living sexual partner. . . . This is nicely exemplified by one man who had his first recognition of his own fetishism when he realized he had ignored a beautiful girl to court a plain girl with a particular hair style. The next stage . . . would be the case of a man who is impotent unless his partner wears a certain type of shoe. The ultimate state is the man

who habitually dispenses with the female and achieves orgasm only with the shoe. (pp. 72–73)

As suggested by Gebhard's analysis, female fetishists are extremely rare; almost all fetishists are men (Griffitt and Hatfield 1985b; Stoller 1975, 1979).

BASIC SEXUAL CHARACTERISTICS

In our time, as in all others, the primary and secondary sexual characteristics are powerfully linked to eroticism. People possessing the ideal breasts, penises, and vaginas are naturally "sexy." Since these characteristics are so critically important, throughout the ages people in diverse cultures have tried to adorn the basic body parts. Men and women have padded their bosoms or bound them tight, girdled their waists or exaggerated them, worn girdles or bustles. Since we discussed this issue in chapter 1, we need not consider the research here. Let us just review some of the shapes associated with "sensuality."

AN HOURGLASS FIGURE

During the Victorian era, the "hourglass" figure was the ideal. Beautiful women were expected to wear heavy corseting. Extremely fashionable women had their lower five ribs removed to insure they had a properly tiny, wasp waist. The whalebone corset compressed the waist into a circumference of a few inches. Breasts and buttocks gained in prominence. A bustle completed the illusion.

Such corseting was so common that in the early 1900s physicians began to believe women came that way. Since many women began wearing corsets at six or seven years of age, physicians continually compared men's unfettered bodies with women's deformed figures. As a consequence, Victorian physicians thought men and women's breathing apparatuses functioned differently. Havelock Ellis observed in 1910, "it was commonly supposed that there is a real and fundamental difference in breathing between men and women, that women's breathing is thoraeic and men's abdominal. It is now known that under natural and healthy conditions, there is no difference" (reported in Ellis 1942, 172). Physicians' lack of information had serious consequences. Corsets were seen as necessary to prop up frail women's health when, in fact, they were the cause of women's frailty. They caused permanent liver damage, still birth, and other such problems.

Why would Victorian women work so hard—and suffer so painfully—to get an hourglass figure? Because Victorian men associated the hourglass figure with two desirable (and opposite) traits—purity and sensuality! Thornstein Veblen (1911) observed:

> The corset is an economic theory substantially [an instrument of] mutilation for the purpose of lowering the subjects' vitality and rendering her personally unfit for work. It is true, the corset impairs the personal attractiveness of the wearer [Veblen is referring to the *naked* woman's attractiveness], but the loss suffered on that score is offset by the gain in reputability which comes of her visibly increased expensiveness and infirmity. (p. 172)

Rudofsky in *The Unfashionable Human Body* (1972) added: "Uncorseted women reeked of license; an unlaced waist was regarded as a vessel of sin. A heretic like Isadora Duncan . . . helped only to strengthen further the popular belief that the lack of a corset (and shoes) was the sign of depravity" (p. 111).

THE CINDERELLA COMPLEX—IF THE SHOE FITS

Foot binding is usually dated back to the court of Emperor Li Yu of the late T'ang dynasty, 900 A.D. He insisted his court dancers bind their feet into an arch so they would walk on tiptoes with a seductive sway. The fetish was continued through the Sung and Ming dynasties for the daughters of the aristocracy. The art of foot binding was practiced in China for nearly one thousand years. Lily feet were the ideal.

The pain of binding the foot was excruciating. Girls of six or seven years of age had their toes folded under toward the soles of their feet and bound until the flesh petrified, the toenails fell out, and the bone and muscle structure was completely deformed.

A girl could scarcely move about on the tiny feet produced by this painful procedure. The lines of a girls' body became distorted by her efforts to walk. Women usually had to be carried on a sedan chair or crawled on her hands and knees to move.

Chinese men thought it looked wonderful. Bound feet were considered the sine qua non of beauty and sexuality. According to Lieu Heung Shing (Taylor 1983), "Among the wealthy, unbinding the foot and fondling it was an integral part of lovemaking" (p. C1). Men believed the tilt of the pelvis that binding encouraged created folds in the vagina that intensified a woman's sexual urge and the pleasure of her partner.

The foot-bound wife was satisfying to her husband, psychologically as well as sensually. Dworkin (1974) quotes a Chinese man who admits to being a very ordinary person, "But to my footbound wife, confined for life to her house except when I bear her in my arms to her palanquin, my stride is heroic, my voice is of the sages. To her I am the world;

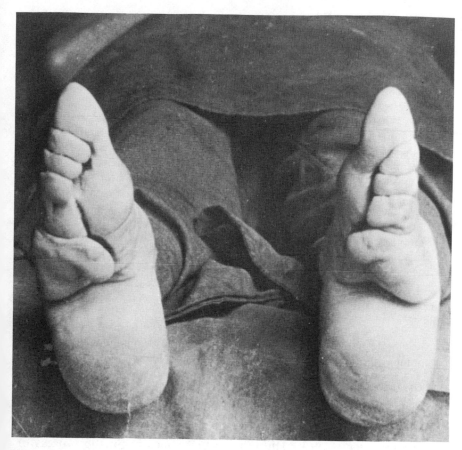

Figure 7.9. Bound feet (Rudofsky 1972, 118).

I am life itself!" (p. 108). As Dworkin remarks, "Chinese men, it is clear, stood tall and strong on women's tiny feet." No man of high rank would consider marrying a woman whose feet had not been bound. Their desirability was in direct proportion to their inability to walk. A woman whose feet had not been bound was doomed to spinsterhood. Andrea Dworkin in her book *Woman Hating* (1974) reported that, in 1931, foot-bound women were captured in war because of their inability to flee. Their foreign captors despised them for their disfigurement and tortured them.

At first glance, the Chinese practice seems bizarre to us. "We would never damage our feet for the sake of fashion," we sniff. But, of course, we do every day. In America, shoes are designed for attractiveness rather than for comfort. (The term "sensible shoes" is, in fact, a condemnation.) A recent article in the *Honolulu Star Bulletin* (Associated Press, 1982, Section C.1) makes this point:

WASHINGTON (AP)—An editor of the Journal of the American Podiatry Association says high heels "May well be the most potent aphrodisiac ever concocted" and advises fellow foot doctors to quit trying to coax women back to earth.

It is "naive and futile" to give women a pitch for nice, sensible, flat footwear, podiatrist William A. Rossi wrote in the journal under the title, "High Heel—The Agony and the Ecstacy."

"When worn by women, the high heel sensuously alters the whole anatomy—foot, leg, thigh, hips, pelvis, buttocks, breasts, etc.

"Further, it alters a woman's self-image in a social, emotional, and psychosensuous sense. She is actually a different person in mood and self-projection in high heels than she is in low or flat heels.

"And for the male, a natural voyeur, the sight of a trim woman in high heels is an intravenous shot in his libido."

Rossi said he agrees with the arguments against high heels. "They throw the body out of kilter," he said. "In order to keep straight, the body bends and the knees and hips and the spine make a curvature, the whole body column has to go through a series of unnatural curves.

"If you do this day after day and year after year, there's got to be a variety of effects—pains in the knees and hip joints, fatigue, backaches, shoulder aches, that sort of thing.

"Women know this," he said. "When they get home they can't get their high heel shoes off fast enough. But that doesn't stop them for a minute from wearing them, and I don't blame them.

"Every doctor in the world could yell from now until Doomsday, and women would still wear them."

Every infant is born with perfect feet. According to a study by the Podiatry Society on the State of New York, 99 percent of all infants have perfect feet at birth. The infant's first shoes begin the process of molding foot to fashion, and permanently dislocating the infant's bones. Eight percent of children develop foot troubles by one year, 41 percent by age five, and 80 percent by age 20. "We limp into adulthood" the report concludes. (reported in Rudofsky 1972, 115)

Like the Victorians, most of us by adulthood are so used to feet that have been molded into "attractive" contours that we have lost all sense of what a normal foot would look like. Take a look at one of your bare feet. It is *not* symmetrical; it is lopsided. The big toe extends one to two inches beyond the little toe. The five toes spread out like a fan. They do *not* converge into a point at the middle toe, as your shoes do. No wonder your feet hurt. Rudofsky (1972) proposes a simple test for finding out how much your toes have been deformed. Place your feet close together. The big toes of undeformed feet are parallel.

There is a folk saying that goes, "Lucky you live Hawaii." If you do your feet may be fairly formed. Otherwise, probably your toes have been twisted, tortured, and mauled into shape, all in the name of

Figure 7.10. The unbound foot (Rudofsky 1972, 114).

beauty. In any case, in modern American society fashionable feet are considered sexy.

We see, then, that almost any aspect of the body can gain erotic significance, and men and women will suffer almost any hardship in order to be appealing.

What's in a Name?

Marilyn Monroe was really Norma Jean Mortenson. Judy Garland was Frances Gumm. Would they have been as successful with their original names? Could you imagine having a sexy pinup of someone called Norma Jean Mortenson? Could you imagine going to a movie that starred Frances Gumm? Although a name is not a physical characteristic, it is something we carry with us for life (our first name, anyway), and it affects the impressions others have of us and the impressions we form of ourselves.

One experiment examined whether beauty was only "name" deep. The researchers placed a large sign at a booth at the student center at Tulane University in New Orleans. "ST JOSEPH'S MARCHING SOCIETY BEAUTY QUEEN. THEY ARE ALL SO PRETTY WE CAN'T DECIDE. PLEASE HELP US BY VOTING FOR YOUR CHOICE AS ST. JOSEPH'S QUEEN."

Students examined photographs of the women supposedly running for St. Joseph's queen. Below each photograph was the woman's first name. All photographs were of attractive women, and the names were actually randomly assigned. Three had female names that had previously been judged desirable. Kathy, Jennifer, and Christine. Three had undesirable female names: Ethel, Harriet, and Gertrude.

Can you guess the voting outcome? Kathy, Jennifer, and Christine received 47, 52, and 59 votes. Ethel, Harriet, and Gertrude received 11, 14, and 14 votes (Garwood et al. 1980).

Scent

Finally, for our last "incidental" we will consider odor. Advertisers spend huge sums to convince us we need perfume or cologne. Apparently we are convinced, because millions of dollars are spent each year to achieve a "pleasant scent." But does smelling good really add to our appeal?

In an experiment at Purdue University (Baron 1981), men were brought into the laboratory to participate in a study about first impressions of others. It was explained that to investigate the process of first impressions they and their partner (actually a woman accomplice of the experimenter) would respond verbally to questions posed by the experimenter. They would then use the information they learned about their partner to form a first impression of her.

For half the men, the woman had placed two drops of perfume behind her ear prior to the session. For the other half, she did not wear any perfume. How the woman looked was also varied. Sometimes she wore a blouse and skirt and sometimes a sweatshirt and jeans.

Surprisingly, the perfume helped most when the woman had on blue jeans and a sweatshirt. Perfume led to more positive perceptions of the woman when she was dressed informally and led to more negative perceptions when she was dressed formally. Possibly, as the authors discussed, the woman was viewed as too formal—as too aloof and unattainable—when she was dressed up *and* wore perfume (remember, the men were in their everyday clothes). In most cases, probably a little dab will do you.

What about natural human body odor? In one very unconventional experiment, male graduate students were given the following: a bar of Ivory soap, a new cotton T-shirt, and a large Ziploc pastic bag. They were told to shower on Friday evening using the Ivory soap and then to wear the T-shirt for forty-eight hours. They were not to use deodorant or to bathe during this period. (Do you wonder how many friends they had left by Sunday night?) On Monday morning they were to remove the shirt (if they could get it off!), seal it in the plastic bag, and return it to the laboratory where it would be kept in a freezer.

Can you guess what happened next? Yes, some lucky set of men and women were asked to come in and smell each shirt and to rate how "bad" the shirt smelled. They also had to rate the person who might have worn the shirt. What was he like? Friendly? Athletic? Fat? Intelligent? Those persons producing unpleasant odors tended to be perceived as unsociable, dirty, unfriendly, unintelligent, nervous, unsophisticated, unpopular, bad-looking, unhealthy, fat, poor, and unattractive to the opposite sex. But a bad odor was not all bad. Persons with unpleasant odors were also rated as active, strong, industrious, and athletic.

There was one final twist to this study. The donors of the T-shirts were brought back into the lab to see if they could identify their own shirt (smell). Only three of the the eleven donors could do so (McBurney, Levine, and Cavanaugh 1977).

On this smelly note, let's end this chapter and go on to more pleasant things.

Chapter 8

PHYSICAL ATTRACTIVE-NESS: THE REALITY

One of Elaine Hatfield's first cases at the Wisconsin Family Studies Institute was the Watson family. The family was bright, imaginative—and impossible. The two daughters, identical twins, had a single problem—their weight. Lee was anorexic, Amanda was enormously overweight. From the time they were infants, the Watsons had referred to Amanda as "the pretty one" and to Lee as "the ugly one." This designation was particularly odd. Both twins had been exceptionally appealing children; now, by their 50's, they had both been equally successful in disguising any remnants of their appeal. Lee, "the ugly one," had managed to starve off her appealing curves; Amanda, "the pretty one," had buried them under layers of fat.

Initially, Elaine Hatfield resisted the family designations, but eventually she began using the terms—first ironically, and then matter-of-factly (as a sort of shorthand) with my colleagues. (When a therapist would ask "Which one did that?" she would gesture, "the pretty one.") Soon the whole clinic identified Lee and Amanda this way. In less

Figure 8.1. Courtesy, Charles Hatfield and Alma Hatfield Francis, 1929.

than a year, we realized we had slowly come to *think* of the identical twins in this way—one was the pretty one the other was ugly.

What do *you* see when you look in a mirror? How do others see you? To what extent has your self-esteem been determined, not by what you *are*, but by what your family, friends, or even strangers *think* you are? To what extent has the shell you happen to inhabit shaped the person you are inside? Too many questions. We will now try to provide some answers.

Psychologists are convinced that people do come to see themselves as others see them . . . to act as others expect them to act. Charles Horton Cooley (1902), a sociologist, suggested that we possess a "looking glass self." Basically, Cooley argued that we become what we see. Our self-esteem is shaped by the esteem others direct toward us. If people generally react positively toward us, we develop a positive self-image. If they generally ignore or shun us, we develop a negative one.

But it does not end there. The kind of person we *think* we are affects the type of person we become. The way we feel about ourselves affects our personality and social interaction style. A self-fulfilling prophecy occurs.

Let's diagram the process we have been discussing:

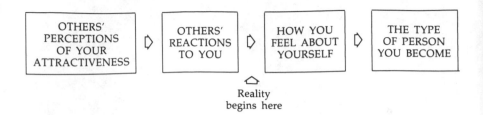

The first part of the book has been devoted to the first two boxes of the diagram—how others perceive you and how they react toward you. As the pointer indicates, we are now ready to understand the reality of physical attractiveness. Let us now consider the first aspect of that reality—how you feel about yourself (your self-esteem/self-concept/self-image).

SELF-ESTEEM

Psychologists have used several terms to refer to how people see themselves—self-esteem, self-concept, self-image, self-confidence, self-perception. (Researchers examining the *reality* of physical attractiveness have focused on either self-concept or self-esteem.) The distinction between these several terms is not always clear.

Self-esteem refers to how positively (or negatively) people evaluate themselves overall. Someone with high self-esteem would agree with statements such as, "On the whole, I am satisfied with myself" and "I take a positive attitude toward myself," but would disagree with "I certainly feel useless at times" and "All in all, I am inclined to feel that I am a failure" (These statements from the Rosenberg [1965] Self-Esteme Scale).

Self-concept refers to how people view themselves on several different dimensions of the self. Someone with a negative self-concept would describe himself/herself as having several negative characteristics—for example, being immature, immoral, unintelligent, bad, weak, and/or dishonest. On the other hand, those viewing themselves as being mature, moral, intelligent, good, strong, and honest would have positive self-concepts. (A few researchers have used self-concept to indicate a person's more or less "objective" evaluation of his/her various characteristics—"I have a large nose.")

Theoretically, people *ought* to develop higher self-esteem and better self-concepts if they come in a beautiful "package." Attractive men and women, who have been evaluated and treated more positively than their peers, ought to end up feeling better about themselves. But does it really happen this way? Maybe not. The evidence suggests that self-esteem and self-concept may not be related to what we are, but rather to what we *think* we are.

We Are Not What We Are—The Relationship Between Appearance and Self-Esteem

Researchers have attempted to determine whether or not our overall self-esteem is affected by what we *actually* look like, as determined by "objective" judges. One scale often used to determine how positively people view themselves is the Rosenberg (1965) Self-Esteem Scale. To review the scale, see chapter 11). Rosenberg defines self-esteem in this way: "By self-esteem we refer to the evaluation which the individual makes and customarily maintains with regard to himself: It expresses an attitude of approval or disapproval" (p. 5).

Is overall self-esteem determined by what people *actually* look like? Surprisingly, the answer is apparently "hardly at all." At most, there may be a tendency for good-looking people to have slightly higher self-esteem than homely individuals, but the tendency is ever so slight (Adams 1975; Berscheid et al. 1971; Coopersmith 1967; Kaats and Davis 1970; and Kasky 1979; Hatfield [Walster] et al. 1966). In general, when attractive and homely people sit down to complete a self-esteem scale, they secure surprisingly similar scores.

Lasky (1979) interviewed forty-six professional men and women ranging in age from sixteen to sixty-one who were strikingly good-looking to unusually homely and assessed their self-esteem via the Jourard-Secord Self and Body Concept Scale. Her conclusion? There is no significant relationship between attractiveness and self-esteem. Lasky sites some typical examples of men and women she interviewed:

THOSE HIGHEST IN SELF-ESTEEM

Alice is 28 years old. She is one of the high self-esteem cases. I rated her physically unattractive. She has a successful career and is living with her boyfriend of 4 years. As a child she had excellent grades in school, was active in student council, went to the Friday night basketball games with a group of kids, was talented in several aristic and creative ways and took several different types of lessons after school hours. In high school and college Alice felt like "an outcast" and assumed she was physically unattractive because she had no dates. She still hates to be photographed and when she looks at a picture of herself she says, "Well, I've seen uglier, but it's not pretty." Nonetheless, Alice has high-self-esteem; it is based on her competencies and her feeling of being loved and accepted. She feels her attractiveness is based on her ability to do and say things. "No one assesses me in terms of my looks; I'm sufficiently attractive to attract anyone I want from sheer force of personality and not from facial features." And indeed she is, for by the time I concluded our interview 1½ hours later, I thought she was a very attractive person. (p. 38)

Betty's story is quite different, although she too has high self-esteem. I rated her as beautiful. . . . Betty, 43, reports that she was a "gorgeous child, a blond angel." Like Alice, Betty was very bright and did well in school. Unlike Alice, Betty was a popular child and teenager who was always included in her group's activities, dated widely and married at 17. She started dating as a teenager. At some point in her modeling career she decided that it was offensive to her to be "a pincushion" . . . as she put it, and therefore she moved on to some other aspect of the fashion world where she had continued to work. (pp. 38–39)

THOSE LOWEST IN SELF-ESTEEM

Esther, 69, is a "fading beauty." I rated her unattractive. She says she was very popular and "never knew what it was like not to be invited to parties." She had always been interested in boys and feels more vital and attractive around men. She has a profession, but it becomes clear from talking to her that men and romance have been the center of life and her work has not been very important to her. She has had two, short-lived, unsuccessful marriages. She wishes she were 35 years old and says that she has hated every year since then. (p. 39)

Fay is 23 and started modeling in college. I rated her as beautiful. She says, "I feel ugly and don't like myself in general." She claims to have been an ugly child, extremely skinny, always sick, and that she was kidded a lot for being skinny. She was popular as a child and did not date in high school at all. "I never had to decide whose house to go over to after school—I had no offers!" She married two years ago and says she was lucky to meet someone who could get along with her! (p. 39)

Lasky concludes that two things are critically important in shaping self-esteem: (1) having a meaningful relationship, and (2) having work you care about. (Freud came to the same conclusion. What was important in life, he argued, was "leiben and arbeiten"—the ability to love and to work.)

Of course, physical attractiveness may help us acquire love and work we care about, but it is *not* a necessity.

But We May Be What We *Think* We Are: Relationship Between What We Think We Look Like and Self-Esteem

We have seen that people's self-esteem has little connection with what they actually look like. What about the relationship between people's self-esteem (self-concept) and what they *think* they look like? Several social psychologists have examined how closely self-concept and body image are intertwined. (In chapter 1, you completed a Body Image Scale. You indicated how satisfied you were with several parts of your body—your face, waist, stomach, hips, and genitals. You may want to check on how high you scored.) Generally, psychologists have found that men and women who are satisfied with their bodies also have a positive self-concept—that is, they consider themselves moral, insightful, honest, fair, likeable, and so on. Those dissatisfied with their body image are likely to have a poor self-concept (see Jourard and Ramy 1955; Secord and Jourard 1954; Sprecher et al. 1981; or Weinberg 1960). Other research has also found that body image is related to self-esteem (Berscheid, Hatfield [Walster] and Bohrnstedt 1973).

Self-concept may depend more on how satisfied we are with certain parts of the body than with other parts. We may not care much what our toes look like, but our whole self-concept may be precariously balanced on our face, our body build, and even on our nose. Research does indicate that certain body parts are more important for self-concept than others. For example, one investigation (Lerner, Karabenick, and Stuart 1973), found that, for both men and women, satisfaction with the following body characteristics was most often related to self-concept: facial complexion, distribution of weight, waist, nose, body build, and face. What body characteristics were not important? For men, characteristics unrelated to self-concept included ears, height, ankles, and chin; for women, unimportant characteristics included hair texture, teeth, arms, and mouth.

Which comes first? Does being satisfied with one's body lead to a higher self-concept, or does having a high self-concept lead one to be satisfied with one's body? Theoretically, we have been arguing that appearances come first and then effects how we evaluate other aspects of ourselves. The opposite is also possible: If we feel good about ourselves, we may end up feeling good about everything—including our looks.

One young women from THE GROUP describes her feelings, "I think the way I feel about myself inside as a person has a lot to do with the way I rate my appearance. If I feel happy with the way life is going and the way I'm treating other people, then I feel good about my looks as well. If I feel ugly inside, I'll feel ugly outside as well."

In sum, the evidence indicates that our body image is related to our overall self-concept (and self-esteem) but that there is only a slight (if any) relationship between actual physical attractiveness and self-esteem. Why? How can beautiful people end up with such low self-esteem? How can physically unappealing men and women manage to maintain their self-regard? Our interviews suggest at least two reasons for this surprising result.

THE COMPANY WE KEEP

A few of the extraordinarily handsome men and beautiful women we interviewed felt badly about themselves because they insisted on comparing themselves with "the best." One striking woman frequented Waikiki beach. She was only interested in comparing herself to the one or two women prettier than she—who had firmer breasts, had flatter stomachs, and were younger. It never occurred to her to compare herself to all the perfectly ordinary tourists on the beach. The "plain" people we met who had a great deal of self-confidence chose their "comparison others" more carefully. They realized many people looked a lot like them—no better and no worse—and went on to other things.

That our evaluations of our own physical attractiveness are influenced by our comparisons was substantialed in a recent investigation (Cash, Cash, and Butters 1983). Women flipped through photographs of either attractice or plain-looking women and then evaluated their own attractiveness. The women exposed to photographs of plain-looking women rated themselves as more attractive than the women who studied photographs of attractive women.

In sum, those banking their self-esteem somewhat on their looks probaby can not help but feel a little less sure of themselves when surrounded by "9's" and "10's". On the other hand, those surrounding themselves with others of the same (or lower) denomination probably manage to maintain a higher self-esteem.

The company we keep can affect our self-esteem in another way. Not only are we making judgments of our own attractiveness, but, of course, others are also judging our attractiveness. It is very harmful to our self-esteem if we keep company with people communicating to us that we are ugly. It is important to seek out those who give us positive feedback. No matter what we look like, someone will like our looks if we look hard and long enough.

A recent Ann Landers column (Ann Landers, *The Salt Lake Tribune*, 22 July 1971, C-1) illustrates this point. An "ugly duckling" reader said she had grown up believing she was the ugliest child in the world. She tried to hide her ugly face behind hunched shoulders. She assumed no one would be interested in being friends with her. Eventually, her teacher asked her to stay after school. She assumed her teacher was going to tell her she was being transferred; she was too ugly to stay in a regular class. Instead, the teacher reassured her—she told her her nose and chin would develop in time. She showed her pictures of models who had weak chins and big noses and explained that irregular features could be interesting. She pointed out she already had nice eyes and pretty hair. Someday she might be considered a beauty. That session changed her life. She began to relax and make friends. Now she is married with two "beautiful children."

Psychologists advise that one way to maintain a healthy self-esteem is to carefully choose the company you keep. People should not surround themselves with others much more attractive than they are (because, in comparison, they can not help but end up feeling unattractive). They should stick with people who like their looks and who love and accept them; they should forget about those who do not (Firebaugh 1980).

THE VALUES WE CHERISH

A second way unattractive people maintain their self-esteem at a healthy level is by accentuating the positive in their personalities or abilities. One of the difficulties of childhood is having to be good at everything— to be cute, smart, obedient, feisty, etc. By the time you reach adulthood you are allowed to specialize. You can pick and choose what you want to be. If you are good-looking, you can focus on that. If you are a scholar with a good sense of humor, you can haughtily disdain "superficial appearances" and focus on your good qualities. By valuing positive traits and ignoring negative ones, it is possible to end up with high self-esteem.

There is evidence that this technique for maintaining self-esteem is common. For example, research indicates that beautiful men and women are far more interested in looks than homely individuals are. One cleverly conducted study found that, the more attractive men and women were, the longer they stared at their own reflections (McDonald and Eilenfield 1980). At North Georgia College there are large reflective windows parallel to a walkway. If passersby want to gaze at their reflections admiringly, they must crane their heads around approximately 90°. One researcher hid behind the windows and recorded, with a stopwatch, how long passersby spent gazing at their reflections. Two other members of the research team were stationed at the end of the walkway and rated the passerbys' attractiveness. The more attractive the passersby, the longer they spent gazing at themselves in the reflective windows.

Charles Cooley was probably right when he suggested we possess "a looking glass self"—that our self-esteem is shaped by the esteem others direct toward us. But, as we have just discussed, it is possible for anyone, regardless of how unattractive they might be, to find people who will give them esteem. Furthermore, it is healthy to value the positive traits we possess and not to worry about what we are not.

Now, let us turn to the next aspect of reality—*do* the physically attractive versus the physically unattractice become different types of people? We will first consider personality.

PERSONALITY

Psychologist David Campbell has spent a lifetime charting the vocational interests, via the Strong Vocational Interest Inventory, of men and women from a variety of occupations—including such diverse occupations as Pulitzer Prize winners, male hair dressers, football coaches, army generals, and navy admirals. One elusive group that intrigued Campbell for some time was top fashion models. He was interested in comparing their vocational interests with those of average-looking women.

He contacted modeling agencies in Minneapolis, New York, and Paris. In all, over one hundred fashion models completed the Strong Vocational Interest Inventory. Campbell (1967) compared their answers with the answers of five hundred women drawn from a variety of occupations. What were some of the unique interests of the beautiful women?

Many of the beautiful women liked activities and occupations in which they could be seen by others. For example, the highest score received by this group of women was on the musician performer scale. Campbell concluded the women might be called "exhibitionistic":

> The girls are pretty, they know it, and they prefer activities that allow them to take advantage of their beauty.
> Perhaps a better summary word to describe their interests would be the term "flourishing," which has various dictionary meanings: to blossom, to thrive luxuriantly, to adorn in a dashing manner. (p. 969)

Beautiful women also showed a preference for exciting, adventuresome careers, for example, as a criminal lawyer or a secrect service woman. Campbell called it the "James Bond syndrome."

What did the beautiful fashion models *dislike?* Said Campbell:

> The major theme that stands out among the *dislikes* is the strong aversion to routine, especially clerical and scientific settings. The models do not like math or science, nor anything of a clerical-bookkeeping nature. The pattern of items suggests that it is the methodical aspect of these areas that repels them, and implies that needs for system, for reg-

ular hours, for accuracy and precision are *not* among the needs of most fashion models. (p. 969)

The Campbell research gives a few clues about the personality traits of the beautiful. However, personality includes far more than vocational interests—it includes a huge array of traits. We will look at many of these traits and see if research has demonstrated any differences between the physically attractice and the physically unattractive. We will also present many of the scales for meaning traits that have been used in the research to measure the traits, so that you can learn about your own personality.

Assertiveness

Here is a chance to discover how assertive you are. This Dating and Assertion Questionnaire was developed by Levenson and Gottman (1978) to measure social competence in dating and assertion situations. Here are some sample questions:

DATING AND ASSERTION QUESTIONNAIRE

We are interested in finding out something about the likelihood of your acting in certain ways. Below you will find a list of specific behaviors you may or may not exhibit. Use the following rating scale:

> 1 = I never do this
> 2 = I sometimes do this
> 3 = I often do this
> 4 = I do this almost always

Now after each of the items on the following list, place the number which best indicates the likelihood of your behaving in that way. Be as objective as possible.

1. Stand up for your rights. _____

2. Maintain a long conversation with a member of the opposite sex. ___

3. Say "no" when you feel like it. _____

4. Assume a role of leadership. _____

5. Be able to accurately sense how a member of the opposite sex feels about you. _____

6. Have an intimate emotional relationship with a member of the opposite sex. _____

7. Have an intimate physical relationship with a member of the opposite sex. _____

The following questions describe a variety of social situations that you might encounter. In each situation you may feel "put on the spot". Some situations may be familiar to you, and others may not. We'd like you to read each situation and try to imagine yourself actually in the situation. The more vividly you get a mental picture and place yourself into the situation, the better.

After each situation circle one of the numbers from 1 to 5 which best describes you using the following scale:

1 = I would be so uncomfortable and so unable to handle this situation that I would avoid it if possible.

2 = I would feel very uncomfortable and would have a lot of difficulty handling this situation.

3 = I would feel somewhat uncomfortable and would have some difficulty in handling this situation.

4 = I would feel quite comfortable and would be able to handle this situation fairly well.

5 = I would feel very comfortable and be able to handle this situation very well.

1. You're waiting patiently in line at a checkout when a couple of people cut right in front of you. You feel really annoyed and want to tell them to wait their turn at the back of the line. One of them, says, "Look, you don't mind do you? But we're in a terrible hurry."

   1   2   3   4   5

2. You are talking to a professor about dropping a class. You explain your situation, which you fabricate slightly for effect. Looking at his grade book the professor comments that you are pretty far behind. You go into greater detail about why you are behind and why you'd like to be allowed to withdraw from his class. He then says, "I'm sorry, but it's against university policy to let you withdraw this late in the semester."

   1   2   3   4   5

3. You meet someone you don't know very well but are attracted to. You want to ask them out for a date.

   1   2   3   4   5

4. You meet someone of the opposite sex at lunch and have a very enjoyable conversation. You'd like to get together again and decide to say something.

   1   2   3   4   5

5. Your roommate has several obnoxious traits that upset you very much. So far, you have mentioned them once or twice, but no no-

ticeable changes have occurred. You still have 3 months left to live together. You decide to say something.

1   2   3   4   5

6. You go to a party where you don't know many people. Someone of the opposite sex approaches you and introduces themself. You want to start a conversation and get to know him/her.

1   2   3   4   5

(pp. 461–462)

As part of a larger study, researcher Harry Reis and his colleagues (Reis, Wheeler, Spiegel, Kernis, Nezlek, and Perri 1982) asked senior men and women at a private northeastern university to complete the Dating and Assertion Questionnaire. They found that handsome men were unusually assertive. Beautiful women were not. In fact, they were *less* assertive than most women. The researchers were not surprised to find beautiful women unassertive in dating and in other situations. Very attractice women are typically in high demand, so they do not have to be assertive to develop an active social life. Less attractive women have to be bold to get what they want.

Although attractive women may not *view* themselves as having an assertive personality, other evidence indicates that, if they are pushed far enough and someone is impolite enough, these women can become very assertive. In one study (Jackson and Huston 1975), psychologists invited a few beautiful and homely women from the campus of the State University of New York at Albany to a faculty lounge to complete separately a questionnaire. Just as the experimenter finished reading the instructions and was about to hand the questionnaire to the woman, he was "interrupted" by someone at the other end of the lounge. Rather than giving the questionnaire to the woman, he mumbled he would be back in a second and set the questionnaire on a table six feet away. The "second" turned into a minute. A minute turned into two minutes, and two minutes into five. The conversation, if uninterrupted by the woman, lasted ten minutes. How did women react to the experimenter who rudely neglected them? Beautiful women were particularly quick to interrupt the experimenter. They interrupted him on the average, about three minutes and twenty-one seconds after he began. Homely women were more likely to suffer in silence; they generally waited over nine minutes before daring to interrupt. These differences were found despite the fact that the attractive women were no more assertive than the unattractive on an assertiveness questionnaire.

In a second study with a female experimenter, the researchers examined the assertiveness of beautiful *versus* homely women in the students' living quarters. Once again, attractive women were much quicker to interrupt the experimenter than were unattractive women.

In sum, attractive men are seemingly more assertive than unattractive men. For women, the relationship between attractiveness and assertiveness seems more complex. Attractive women are less likely than unattractive women to describe themselves as assertive. However, at least in certain situations, attractive women *behave* more assertively than do unattractive women.

Locus of Control: Who Controls Your Fate?

Another aspect of one's inner personality possibly affected by the attractiveness of one's outer appearance is what psychologists term the "locus of control." Some people assume their own actions determine their fate. It is their own intelligence and efforts (or lack thereof) that determine their successes (or failures). These people are called "internals." "Externals," on the other hand, assume that what happens to them is determined by external factors such as luck or fate. Following is a description of a man possessing an external locus of control (as presented by Phares 1976):

> On one occasion, after much therapeutic discussion and coaching, Karl applied for a job and got it. It became obvious following the incident, however, that his expectations for being similarly successful in the future had not changed one bit. Although pleased that he got the job, he regarded it as merely good fortune. He offered a variety of explanations: the employer was partial to veterans, he just happened to feel good that day, or he had not seen any other applicants. Karl was adamant in his unwillingness to accept the responsibility for his success. There were comparable episodes involving asking women for dates. (p. 3)

Are you an "internal" or more of an "external"? When you meet with success (passing an exam, winning a Gold Medal at the Olympics, acquiring the love and adoration of others), do you assume your accomplishment resulted from your talents and efforts, or do you assume your fate was written in the stars? When you get caught for illicit behavior, do you take responsibility for what you did, or do you cry "the devil made me do it"? Various scales have been developed to measure how internal or external people are. Following are a few items taken from the Internal/External Locus of Control Scale developed by Julian Rotter (1966). For each of the following pairs of items, choose the statement that best applies to you:

1. a) In the long run people get the respect they deserve in this world.
   b) Unfortunately, an individual's worth often passes unrecognized no matter how hard he tries.

2. a) Becoming a success is a matter of hard work, luck has little or nothing to do with it.
   b) Getting a good job depends mainly on being in the right place at the right time.

3. a) The average citizen can have an influence in government decisions.
   b) This world is run by the few people in power, and there is not much the little guy can do about it.

4. a) People are lonely because they don't try to be friendly.
   b) There's not much use in trying too hard to please people, if they like you, they like you.

5. a) What happens to me is my own doing.
   b) Sometimes I feel that I don't have enough control over the direction my life is taking.

(pp. 11–12)

A person with an internal locus of control would have chosen the first response (a) to all the items. A person with an external locus of control would have chosen response (b). Of course, most people probably respond with a few a's and a few b's, thus simply seeing the world in all its shades of grey.

One perception study (Miller 1970b) discovered that men and women perceive attractive people as more internal than unattractive people. But are attractive people *really* more internal than unattractive people? In a study conducted with our colleagues Kathleen McKinney and John DeLamater (Sprecher et al. 1982), we examined whether attractive men and women are especially likely to believe they are masters of their fates, controllers of their destinies. A random sample of almost one thousand young adults (both students and nonstudents) from Madison, Wisconsin, part of a larger interview study, rated their own physical attractiveness, completed the Body Image Questionnaire, and completed a locus of control scale similar to the one above. There was a slight tendency for men and women rating themselves as attractive and/or who were satisfied with their body image to have an internal locus of control. Other researchers have also found a tendency for attractive people to be more internal than unattractive people (Adams, 1977 a and b; Cash and Begley 1976).

Why would good-looking people be more likely to feel they have control over what happens to them? Probably because attractive *versus* unattractive people are treated very differently: attractive people are given more opportunities to impose their will in social and achievement activities. (For example, we have already reported that the physically attractive are more likely to be hired for jobs, to be promoted, etc.)

With so many opportunities available to perform effectively, probably the attractive do begin to see associations between their actions and their successes (or failures).

The Personality Potpourri

Personality is made up of several other traits in addition to assertiveness and locus of control, and scales have been developed to measure many of these traits. We will now take you on a whirlwind tour—giving you a slight taste of several personality scales (so you can learn more about your own personality) and then presenting evidence to indicate whether or not the physically attractive and physically unattractive score differently on these scales.

What are Your Expectations For Success and Failure? (see McReynolds and Guevara 1967)

Indicate "true" if the statement is mostly "true" as applied to you.

Indicate "false" if the statement is mostly "false" as applied to you.

1. I have a tendency to give up easily when I meet difficult problems.
   _____

2. I like to fool around with new ideas even if they turn out later to have been a total waste of time. _____

3. I am ambitious. _____

4. It's better to be an observer than a participant because one learns more and gets into less trouble. _____

5. I would rather remain free from commitments to others than risk serious disappointment or failure later. _____

6. When I am in a group or organization, I like to be appointed or elected for office. _____

(If you said true for items, 2, 3, and 6, you have motivation to attain success. If you said true for items 1, 4, and 5, you have motivation to avoid failure.)   (p. 305)

Cash and Smith (1982) found there was a slight tendency for attractive men to be more concerned with success and less afraid of failure than were unattractive men. Beautiful and homely women did not seem to differ in their expectations of success/failure.

Do You Fear Negative Evaluations? (Watson and Friend 1969)

Indicate "true" if the statement is mostly "true" as applied to you.

Indicate "false" if the statement is mostly "false" as applied to you.

1. I rarely worry about seeming foolish to others. _____

2. I worry about what people will think of me even when I know it doesn't make any difference. _____

3. The opinions that important people have often cause me little concern. _____

4. I am frequently afraid of other people noticing my shortcomings. _____

5. I feel that you can't help making social errors sometimes, so why worry about it. _____

6. I worry that others will think I am not worthwhile. _____

(If you answered true for items, 2, 4, and 6, and false for items 1, 3, and 5, you could consider yourself a "social worry wart."   (p. 450)

Adams and Wareham (n.d.) found that those men and women considering themselves attractive were least afraid of negative evaluations.

Do You Experience Social Avoidance and Distress? (Watson and Friend 1969)

Indicate "true" if the statement is mostly "true" as applied to you.

Indicate "false" if the statement is mostly "false" as applied to you.

1. I feel relaxed even in unfamiliar social situations. _____

2. I try to avoid situations which force me to be very sociable. _____

3. It is easy for me to relax when I am with strangers. _____

4. I often want to get away from people. _____

5. I would avoid walking up and joining a large group of people. _____

6. I usually go to whatever social engagements I have. _____

(If you answered true to items 2, 4, and 5, and false for items 1, 3, and 6, you have a tendency to avoid social affairs; they make you distressed.)   (p. 450)

Adams and Wareham (n.d.) found that men and women considering themselves attractive experienced less stress in social settings than did those considering themselves unattractive.

Are You Masculine or Feminine? (Bem 1974)

Indicate on the following 7-point scale how well each of the following personality characteristics describe you.

Never or almost   Always or almost
  never true   1   2   3   4   5   6   7   always true

_____ 1. Acts as a leader

_____ 2. Assertive

_____ 3. Loyal

_____ 4. Self-reliant

_____ 5. Gentle

_____ 6. Compassionate

_____ 7. Independent

_____ 8. Affectionate

_____ 9. Competitive

_____10. Eager to soothe hurt feelings

_____11. Loves children

_____12. Strong personality

(If you score high on items 1, 2, 4, 7, 9, and 12, you tend to have a masculine personality. If you score high on items 3, 5, 6, 8, 10, and 11, you have a feminine personality. If you scored high on both, you have what psychologists call an "androgynous" personality, possessing both feminine and masculine virtues.)   (p. 156)

Cash and Smith (1982) found there was a slight tendency for attractive men and women to have more masculine characteristics than unattractive men and women. No relationship was found between physical attractiveness and feminity.

How Sensation-Seeking Are You? (Zuckerman, Kōlin, Price, and Zoob 1964)

For each of the following pairs of items, choose the statement that best applies to you.

1. a) I would prefer living in an ideal society where everyone is safe, secure, and happy.
   b) I would have preferred living in the unsettled days of our history.

2. a) I can't stand riding with a person who likes to speed.
   b) I sometimes like to drive very fast because I find it exciting.

3. a) If I were a salesman, I would prefer a straight salary, rather than the risk of making little or nothing on a commission basis.

   b) If I were a salesman, I would prefer working on a commission if I had a chance to make more money than I could on salary.

4. a) The most important goal of life is to live it to the fullest and experience as much of it as you can.

   b) The most important goal of life is to find peace and happiness.

5. a) I prefer people who are emotionally expressive even if they are a bit unstable.

   b) I prefer people who are calm and even tempered.

If you responded with an (a) to items 4, 5, and (b) to items 1, 2, 3 consider yourself a "sensation-seeker."   (p. 478–479)

Adams and Wareham (n.d.) found that men and women perceiving themselves as attractive had a greater sensation-seeking tendency.

End of Whirlwind Tour

Now that we have reviewed all the evidence, we can return to the question with which we began: Do attractive people really have especially desirable personalities?

Obviously, this question is difficult to answer. To begin with, it is unclear just what constitutes a "desirable" personality. For example, although many scholars have assumed it is more desirable to have an internal than an external locus of control, such an assumption is questionable. The same questions would apply to other personality traits: Is it really desirable to be a very assertive person? Certainly we can all think of overly assertive people—people who bump our place in line, "assume" we will do them favors, or can not take no for an answer—and such people can infuriate us. Is it more desirable to be masculine or feminine, or to be fearless or prudent in social situations? Our answer is probably, "It depends."

Although we can not make unequivocal judgments about what constitutes a desirable personality (and who has one), we can decide whether The Myth of physical attractiveness is correct (we reviewed The Myth in chapters 2 and 3). Are the good-looking and homely as different as people perceived them to be? The answer appears to be "no." Apparently, The Myth is far greater than reality when it comes to personality. According to The Myth, the beautiful/handsome have far better (or at least different) personalities than do mere mortals; the attractive and unattractive occupy markedly different spheres. According to the evidence we have just reviewed on the reality of physical attractiveness, though, the differences between the personalities of attractive *versus* unattractive people were slight or nonexistent.

We need to consider, however, one more dimension of what people become after experiencing a lifetime of being seen and treated in certain ways. Do attractive and unattractive people end up developing different social interactional styles? Do they have different social lives? Unattractive people may be able to cultivate their own personalities, but they can not manipulate others. They can not force others to invite them to life's cocktail parties.

SOCIAL BEHAVIOR: WHO IS THE LIFE OF THE COCKTAIL PARTY?

We asked men and women from THE GROUP:

> Do you notice any difference in your social relations on the days when you look great *versus* the days when you look just so-so, or even worse?

In general, THE GROUP agreed that when they felt especially good-looking—when they had a new haircut, a new suit, or a new vacation suntan—they were more outgoing than usual, and their gregariousness led others to be more responsive to them than usual. When they felt ugly—when their hair was stringy or they had on smelly jeans—they sort of slunk around. They were not really aware how people responded to them because, as one person put it, "I was too embarrassed to wait around to find out." They suspected that had they waited around, others would have been just as embarrassed and would have moved along too.

Three members of THE GROUP described how their social behavior is affected by their attractiveness:

> It seems to work in a cycle. If I feel good about myself and I look nice, I relate better with others; when I relate better with others they want to get to know me. When I feel unattractive, I feel like no one would want to get to know me, and they don't.

> If I am feeling pretty one day, I generally am more confident, walk with my head up a little higher, and am apt to smile at others more than usual. On the other hand, if I am feeling rather unattractive, I don't care for people to notice me, so I tend to act more reserved around others.

> My appearance definitely affects my relationships with others. For example, a couple weeks ago I had a huge cold sore right in the center

of my bottom lip and my entire daily routine was affected by it. In the library I wouldn't even sit at a table with men at it because I was so embarrassed! Now that's stupid—and I admit it—but I couldn't help it.

We all experience variation in how attractive we feel—on some days we feel unusually attractive, while on other days we feel terribly unappealing. THE GROUP's accounts demonstrate how even slight changes in our appearance can convert us from social butterflies into shy wallflowers. The momentary lows, such as the annoying cold sore, are probably most disruptive to our social confidence.

But many people suffer more than an annoying cold sore. Some people are homely, by most standards, every day of their lives. Not only are such people ill-at-ease about approaching others, but others are equally uneasy about interacting with them. The cumulative effect of such a restricted social life may well be devastating.

The best anecdotal accounts of the effects of an unappealing appearance on social interaction come from case histories of persons with facial deformities. Frances Macgregor (1951), for example, discusses the psychosocial problems associated with facial deformities. Following are excerpts from the case of Tom M.:

> Tom M., 31, had incurred a birth injury which resulted in a complete paralysis of the right side of his face. When in respose, his defect, though noticeable, was not dramatically disfiguring. The lid of his left eye drooped slightly and did not open or close completely when he blinked. When Tom spoke, however, his handicap became most conspicuous. He literally talked "out of the side of his mouth."
>
> If he had not had a facial paralysis, he would have been a rather good-looking man, for his features were most acceptable. He was slim and well built, had nice eyes, good skin and hair. He was neatly dressed, soft spoken, well-mannered, sensitive, and intelligent.
>
> . . . Upon entering school he soon learned that something was "wrong" with his face. "It was my teachers who first made me self-conscious," Tom said. "They would stop me in the middle of a recitation and ask me what was the matter with my face. They would say, 'try and control it and don't talk on one side of your mouth like that'. This embarrassed me because I couldn't help talking the way I did. In trying to help me they crossed me up by mentioning it in front of the other children. If they had only waited until after the class was over."
>
> Tom came home from school every day and did not linger on the streets with other children who had begun to taunt him. "I became self-conscious and shied away from everything and everybody. I hung around my mother in the kitchen. She taught me to cook and did everything she could think of to keep my mind off myself."
>
> In high school, his life was similar to days in grammar school. He preferred poor grades to the ridicule and staring of other students. He

did not try to make friends nor did he participate in school dances or other social activities.

Out of school Tom said he was "driven" into sports in order to prove that he was a good ball player, "so the fellows in that neighborhood would overlook my face." However, when they played with other teams, their opponents would try to upset Tom by calling him "crooked mouth" or admonishing the batter to "hit it (the ball) back to him and straighten out his crooked face." This upset him so much that he would leave the game.

When he was in high school his mother died, and Tom decided to leave home and school to go to work. "But I was always given jobs where I wouldn't meet people . . . so it didn't help much." His ambition was to be a policeman like his father and grandfather. But when he applied to the department, he was turned down. "They gave no reason, just said I failed the physical." Later, a friend told him the physician refused to pass him because of his facial deformity. (pp. 633–634)

Later, Tom gets married and does manage to get odd jobs to support his wife and family. However, he can never forget his face—because other people will not let him.

. . . When Tom is not working, he spends his time at home with his children. He avoids all outside contacts because he can't endure the staring of others or the quick furtive glances toward and away from his face. This self-imposed isolation has resulted in some "serious arguments" with his wife who is very sociable. Tom said, "I just can't enjoy myself when I go anywhere, even with my wife's relatives. If I laugh my mouth goes sideways. It dampens everything for me. I get embarrassed when I talk and so I don't say anything. Other people seem repulsed by my appearance or embarrassed when they talk to me. It seems likely they want to get away. If I do go anywhere I always hear people off in a corner saying, 'What's the matter with him?' If they asked me outright it wouldn't hurt so much." In addition he notices the way they unconsciously draw up their mouths and mimic him while watching him talk. "They don't seem to realize that it's not my fault that I look this way, and one crack about my face stops me cold. I will go home and brood for two months and draw into a shell. I get cross and snap at the kids and my wife and won't talk to any of them." (p. 635)

Frances Macgregor concludes:

While this young man has made a fair adjustment to his life situation, has been able to marry and support a family, he has been crippled psychologically. His feelings of inadequacy and hostility, his periods of depression, are due less to his deformity than to his reactions to the actual and anticipated reactions of others toward his appearance. We see here the influential role the group may play in determining the kind of interpretation an individual makes toward his own deformity.

Given derogatory nicknames by his contemporaries, offered jobs where he would have a minimum of social contact, and characterized as being "tough," seemed to accentuate behavior patterns of a negative nature. No only have his own feelings of frustration, anxiety, and deep hostility prevented him from developing more positive aspects of emotional living, but his personality distortions have in turn been inflicted on his environment. By his periods of depression and short temper, his refusal to enter into social activities, both his wife and children are affected and the family harmony considerably damaged. (p. 636)

The above case of Tom M. illustrates vividly how severe loneliness can have long-term, devastating effects on social opportunities.

The first seven chapters of *Mirror, Mirror* were devoted to reviewing evidence that a physical attractiveness stereotype exists—that people assume "what is beautiful is good and what is ugly is bad." The beautiful/handsome fare better in the dating, mating, and sexual marketplace. To what extent does this occur in the social sphere? Do unattractive people have restricted social lives? Do they become less socially skilled as a consequence? Expectations have a way of being fulfilled. If you expect someone to be a sourpuss, you tend to act in ways that bring out the sourpuss in them. If you expect someone to be a star, you will behave in ways that make the person shine.

The self-fulfilling nature of the physical attractiveness stereotype was demonstrated in an intriguing study by Snyder, Tanke, and Berscheid (1977). Men and women at the University of Minnesota, unacquainted with each other, were scheduled for a study on "the processes by which people become acquainted with each other." The man and woman always arrived from separate corridors and were directed to different rooms (so they would not see each other). There, they were informed that they would be getting acquainted with another student over the phone.

Before the telephone conversation began, the man was given a Polaroid snapshot of his partner along with some biographical information. In truth, the snapshot was not of the partner but of either a good-looking or a homely woman. The man was asked his first impression of his partner from this photo and information. Men who thought they would be talking to an attractive woman expected her to be sociable, poised, humorous, and socially adept. Men who had been led to believe they would be talking to a homely woman expected her to be unsociable, awkward, serious, and socially inept. The formation of these expectations is not surprising. We already know good-looking people make more positive first impressions than homely people.

What is startling is that the men's expectations had a dramatic impact on the *women's* behavior—in the short space of a telephone call. Men thought their partners were unusually good-looking or unattractive. In fact, of course, the women on the other end of the line varied greatly in appearance. Nonetheless, within the space of a telephone conversation, women became what men expected them to be. After the telephone conversation, judges were asked to listen to tapes of the women's portion of the conversation and to guess what the women were like. Women who had been talked to as if they were a beauty, soon began to sound like one. They *became* unusually "animated," "confident," and "adept." Those talked to as if they were homely, soon began acting that way. (They became withdrawn, lacking on confidence, awkward.) Men's expectations were now reflected in women's behavior.

How did this happen? What transpired? When the men's portion of the conversation was analyzed, it was found the men who thought they were talking to a beautiful women, were more sociable, sexually warm, interesting, independent, sexually permissive, bold, outgoing, humorous, obvious, and socially adept than the men who thought they were talking to a homely woman. The men assigned to an "attractive woman" were also more comfortable, enjoyed themselves more, liked their partners more, took the initiative more often, and used their voices more effectively. In a nutshell, the men who thought they had an attractive partner tried harder. Undoubtedly, this behavior caused the women to try harder in return.

If the stereotypes held by the men became reality within only ten minutes of a telephone conversation, one can imagine what happens over several years. If year after year attractive people are given more opportunities and encouragement in social interaction than unattractive people, it is not surprising that attractive and unattractive people become different social beings.

Other evidence indicates that attractive and unattractive people do become different social beings. A study very similar to the one above was conducted (Goldman and Lewis 1977). Pairs of men and women were asked to get acquainted over the phone. This time, however, the telephone partners did not know what each other looked like. Would their real appearance still shine through? In reality, do attractive men and women display more social skills over the phone than unattractive men and women? It was found in this study that attractive men and women were judged by their telephone partners to be more socially skilled than unattractive men and women. Apparently, the physical attractiveness stereotypes does contain a kernal of truth.

Both the above studies were conducted in the laboratory and among strangers. It would also be interesting to find out whether attractive and unattractive people have different everyday social experiences. Before we do that, however, let us find out what *your* social life is like. Imagine you were asked to keep a diary describing your social encounters lasting longer than ten minutes. On the average:

How many different people do you interact with in a day? _____

What percent of your interactions are with the same sex? _____

What percent of your interactions are with the opposite sex? ____

How many hours and minutes a day do you think you spend in social interactions? _____hours _____minutes

Overall, how intimate are your interactions?
Superficial   1 2 3 4 5 6 7   meaningful

Overall, how much do you disclose in your interactions?
very little   1 2 3 4 5 6 7   a great deal

Overall, how satisfying are your interactions.
not at all   1 2 3 4 5 6 7   a great deal

This exercise was actually carried out by freshman men and women at the University of Rochester in New York (Reis, Nezlek, and Wheeler 1980). For forty days (and forty nights) they kept records of their social experiences. At the end of the study, photographs were taken of the men and women who had so carefully kept the diaries. (Later, students at another university judged their attractiveness.) The questions of concern to the investigators were:

1. Does attractiveness affect the *quantity* and *quality* of social participation?

2. Does attractiveness have a greater effect on women's social participation than on men's?

3. Does attractiveness continue to remain important over time?

Based on analysis of the diary entries made by the students, the researchers concluded:

1. Attractiveness affects the *quantity* of social participation, but only for men. It affects the quality of social participation for both men and women.

2. Surprisingly, physical attractiveness seems to be even more important for men than for women.

3. Physical attractiveness remains important over time.

Specifically, handsome men had more interactions and with a *greater number* of women than did homely men. On the other hand, handsome men had fewer social interactions and relations with other men. Attractive men and women were more satisfied with their encounters with the opposite sex than were less appealing people, and this satisfaction increased over time. Attractive people tended to spend more of their interaction time conversing or partying, while less attractive people spent more time in task activities.

A second study was conducted with senior college students (Reis et al. 1982), and somewhat similar results were found. Once again, handsome men got around. They had more encounters with the opposite sex than did homely men. Beautiful *versus* ugly women, on the other hand, did not differ in their number of social encounters. Attractive men and women of both sexes had better quality social encounters. For example, attractive men and women reported that their relationships were more intimate and disclosing than did ugly men and women.

We conclude this section with a long statement made by one, very beautiful young woman from THE GROUP. The young woman is trying to sort out how her good looks have affected her life.

> I know that my looks have affected my relationships with others in many ways. Not only has it affected others' willingness to meet me, give me a chance to prove myself, and be satisfied with my accomplishments, but it also greatly affects my part of the relationship. I have a confidence in myself stemming solely from my looks. I have experienced the reactions of people in regard to my looks, and therefore know just what type of "headstart" I can almost always rely on.
>
> I have learned that people are readily willing to accept assertive and self-confident behavior from one who has an attractive face. Perhaps one of the reasons is that every person likes to have a lot of positive acquaintances and does not like to be rejected by another who appears to be popular and admired. When they initially meet a person of good looks, they subconsciously consider the fact that this good looker probably has many positive acquaintances. They are inclined to see the worthy characteristics of this person because many others probably have. Assertiveness is identified as a definite quality.
>
> However, when meeting a homely person—perhaps our subconscious does not organize these self-protecting attitudes. We almost tend to feel that in order for this person to be effective she/he must have a particularly excellent skill in assertive behavior. The asset of good looks is recovered through extra talent.
>
> I realize that I have been offered jobs, have been introduced to certain people, and have been granted extra conveniences solely on account of my looks. The confidence resulting from these icidents allows me to gain valuable experience and opportunities that others, equally qualified, may not have had.
>
> Also, I realize that, because of this experience concerning my looks, I am not at all overly concerned about looking my best at all times. I feel fine when I let my hair be mattted to my head as I walk to class

in my oldest, most unattractive jeans today because I know that if I *want* to impress tomorrow, I can. I don't always have to be working at it.

Another way that looks affect my behavior is that I know that I already have my foot in the door to relationships. It must be admitted that people are not as willing to become too closely associated romantically with one they find unattractive. Well, I think that most people regard me as attractive and so I usually concentrate on my personality instead of my looks when meeting someone. I have the confidence that at least I do not offend with my looks.

WHEN THINGS GO FROM BAD TO WORSE: MENTAL ILLNESS

Throughout this book, we have emphasized the fact that homely people have to learn to cope with an unusually hostile social environment. They are denied a fair chance for love and work; they are perceived to be dull, incompetent, guilty of crime, cold, and a little bit crazy. You might expect a lifetime of ill treatment to take its toll. Homely people might come to see themselves in a distorted mirror. Do they? Are homely people under more stress? Are they especially likely to develop emotional problems? The answer appears to be yes.

Stress

Evidence indicates that, by adolescense, the homely are under more stress. Blood pressures taken of high school and college students in Ohio (Hanseli, Sparacino, and Ronchi 1982) discovered that homely young women have higher blood pressures than their more attractive peers. To the extent that psychological stress is reflected in blood pressure (and most argue it is), this finding provides compelling evidence for the argument that homely women are experiencing unusual stress. Such differences were not found for high school and college men. Perhaps homely young women feel particularly high levels of emotional stress because, as indicated by other research, a woman's self-concept is more strongly dependent on her appearance than is a male adolescent's (Simmons and Rosenberg 1975).

Mental Illness

In any one year, about 6.3 million Americans are in psychiatric units or are receiving outpatient treatment (Kiesler 1982). Amerigo Farina and his colleagues (1977) wondered if those people hospitalized are less attractive than the rest of us? They took photographs of twenty-three women who had been in the hospital an average of about six years. The researchers then found a comparable group of women in a university setting who were about the same age and took their photographs. The photographs from both samples were then shuffled and shown to a group of judges, asked to rate the beauty of each woman. The patients were rated as being much less attractive than the control women.

Although the above study demonstrates that mental illnesses and unattractiveness are linked, we can not be sure which came first. Do unattractive people become mentally ill and hospitalized (as we have suggested)? Or does mental illness and hospitalization cause people to ignore their appearance? In hospitals, beauty aids are less available, and there is less incentive to look one's best.

A second study by the same researchers examined the consequences of appearance *within* a psychiatric hospital. Are the most unattractive patients the most maladjusted? Indeed, it was found that the least attractive female patients had more severe problems (such as schizophrenia), had more inadequate interpersonal behavior, and received fewer visits from friends and family from the outside than did the better-looking patients.

Other researchers have found even more evidence that a poor appearance can lead to mental illness (Napoleon, Chassin, and Young 1980). The investigators secured high school yearbook pictures for men and women patients at a state mental hospital. Of course, the yearbook pictures were taken long before the hospitalization. The researchers compared the patients' physical attractiveness with those of adjacent photographs of same-sex peers in the yearbook. Those young men and women who eventually became mental patients were the lest attractive in high school.

Not everyone with an emotional problem is hospitalized. Actually, there are 2½ times as many people receiving outpatient care than inpatient care. Furthermore, there are many adults who feel depressed, have ulcers, drink too much, or suffer from migraines yet lead relatively normal lives.

Psychologist Kevin O'Grady (1982) wondered if homely young adults are more likely to see themselves *at risk* for mental disorders. Imagine, for a moment, you were one of the participants in such a study. How much at risk do you perceive yourself to be? You are given the following instructions:

> This survey is concerned with how people feel they might behave in the future. On the following page are descriptions of various individuals. Using a 21-point scale, please indicate in the space to the left of

each description how similar you feel you might be to each person—*at some point in your future*. Use any number between 0 (not at all likely to be similar to this person at any point in your future) to 20 (very likely to be similar to this person at any point in your future). Remember, this questionnaire is concerned with how you might behave later in your life, not what you feel you are like now.

1._____ This person lives in a relatively constant state of tension, worry, and uneasiness. He/she is oversensitive in interpersonal relationships.

2._____ This person has a persistent fear of some object or situation that presents little, if any actual danger. Furthermore, this exaggerated fear becomes the central feature of the person's lifestyle, which is typified by avoidance and apprehension.

3._____ This person is overly concerned with his or her health and with the fear of disease. This person often complains about various ailments, and is sure that he/she is seriously ill, although no physical illness can be found.

4._____ This person has difficulty dealing effectively with his or her frustrations, and the general stress of living. He/she responds to this emotional upset with frequent migraine and tension headaches.

5._____ This person tends to worry too much, and does not deal effectively with his/her anger, resentment, anxiety, and other negative feelings. As a result, he/she develops stomach ulcers.

6._____ This person is often troubled by the intrusion of unwanted thoughts, urges, or actions that he/she seems unable to stop. As a result, this person feels compelled to think continually about something that he/she does not want to think about, or to carry out some action against his or her will.

7._____ This person tends to be selfish, irresponsible, and manipulative. He/she does not seem to experience guilt, is unable to show loyalty to others, and often comes into conflict with society.

8._____ This person is caught up by feelings of unreality and separation from body, self, or environment. This person seems to lose his/her identity, and feels as if he/she is somebody or something else.

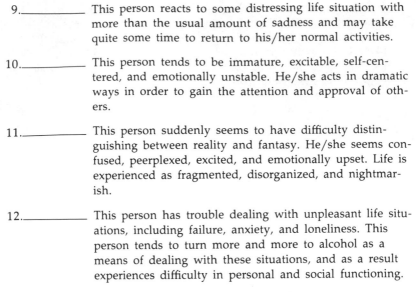

9._____ This person reacts to some distressing life situation with more than the usual amount of sadness and may take quite some time to return to his/her normal activities.

10._____ This person tends to be immature, excitable, self-centered, and emotionally unstable. He/she acts in dramatic ways in order to gain the attention and approval of others.

11._____ This person suddenly seems to have difficulty distinguishing between reality and fantasy. He/she seems confused, peerplexed, excited, and emotionally upset. Life is experienced as fragmented, disorganized, and nightmarish.

12._____ This person has trouble dealing with unpleasant life situations, including failure, anxiety, and loneliness. This person tends to turn more and more to alcohol as a means of dealing with these situations, and as a result experiences difficulty in personal and social functioning.

Following are labels applying to the descriptions above:

1. Generalized anxiety disorder

2. Simple phobia

3. Hypochondriasis

4. Migraine

5. Ulcers

6. Obsessive-compulsive disorder

7. Antisocial personality

8. Depersonalization disorder

9. Episodic unipolar depressive disorder

10. Histrionic personality disorder

11. Schizophrenic disorder

12. Alcohol abuse

(pp. 1066–1067)

A questionnaire similar to the above was distributed to 120 men and 120 women at a large northwestern university (see O'Grady 1982). What sorts of problems did the college students anticipate they might have to face? They ranked their perceived risk in the following way:

1. Generalized anxiety disorder

2. Episodic unipolar depressive disorder

3. Ulcers

4. Obsessive-compulsive disorder

5. Migraine

6. Alcohol abuse

7. Histrionic personality disorder

8. Simple phobia

9. Hypochondriasis

10. Antisocial personality

11. Schizophrenic disorder

12. Depersonalization disorder

Most students were extremely confident about the future of their own mental health, however. On the average, students gave the probability of developing a "generalized anxiety disorder" (their most serious worry) only a 7 on a scale from 0–20. Unattractive men and women were more likely to believe they would suffer a mental disorder in the future. (Although it was expected that homely *women* would feel more at risk for mental disorders than homely men, no sex differences were found.)

IN SUM

In this chapter, we examined the *realities* of beauty. How different are beautiful women and handsome men from the rest of us? We found that the good-looking and homely differ only slightly in self-esteem/self-concept. Self-perceived attractiveness and body satisfaction are more closely linked to self-esteem/self-concept than the way others perceive one's attractiveness.

Next, we consider personality and social behavior. Most therapists consider two areas of life critically important: love and work. In love, beautiful people do seem to have some clear-cut advantages: for example, they have personalities that allow them to relax socially. In work and in the rest of life, however, there is no evidence the good-looking are very different from the rest of us. (For example, they show only a slight tendency toward being more inner directed, being more assertive, seeking success, fearing failure).

Finally, we examined the dark side of life and found that attractive people do seem to experience less stress and mental illness. To be homely seemingly puts one "at risk" as far as adjustment to society is concerned.

In general, however, The Myth of physical attractiveness (which suggests that "what is beautiful is good and what is ugly is bad") is more exaggerated than The Reality. The evidence reviewed here suggests there are no dramatic differences between the attractive and the unattractive in the type of people they become.

Chapter 9

BEAUTY THROUGH THE LIFE SPAN

When Susan Sprecher attended her tenth high school reunion in the summer of 1983, she had a chance to observe the beginnings of the aging process. Conversations often turned to how much they had all changed: "Bill seems to be taller somehow; he was such a shrimp in high school. John certainly has aged; living with Karen would turn anyone's hair grey. Mary Peterson looks a lot prettier now—I wonder why?"

Even the after dinner award ceremonies reflected her classmates' awareness of physical changes. One award was given to the man who lost the most hair since high school. Another to the person who had changed the most. A third to the one who had changed the least. (Many were secretly hoping to win that award.)

Before long, they all realized the class of 1973 differed in one major way from the same class in 1983—the class in 1983 was far better-looking. Almost everyone was at their best. They looked tan and healthy. No one was grossly overweight. Blemishes had vanished and com-

Figure 9.1.   Courtesy, the Thomas and Mary Kalahar family, 1924.

plexions glowed. At first this difference baffled them. They had been led to believe that nature was cruel as soon as one left the teenage years. Then (after about three cocktails), something dawned on them: Not everyone attends class reunions. Those who are pleased with the way they look and the way their lives are going are more likely to show up. Those who have things to be embarrassed about probably stay away. When the group began to run through the list of people who had not attended and to inquire about them, they got a different picture of what had happened to the class of 1973. ''Martha is getting a divorce; she probably didn't want to come because of that. Emily gained almost 100 pounds. Mark has a bad drinking problem—he looks almost twice his age.''

There was a second reason why the class of 1983 looked so good. All of them had made serious efforts to look their best. People did their hair, bought new clothes, and, in some cases, dieted for months. One classmate had been a cheerleader with a good figure in high school. She had never had problems getting dates. The others had always been slightly envious of her. The few times she had been seen since high school revealed that she had gained a great deal of weight. But at the reunion she was as trim and athletic as she had ever been. She confessed she had been on a diet and jogging regime during the months prior to the reunion. She admitted she would not have shown up if she had not been able to get back in shape. But as good as the friends looked at the tenth-year class reunion, there was no denying they were slowly approaching middle age. Hairlines were receding; wrinkles were appearing.

Facing friends one has not seen for a long time is like looking in a special looking glass. You know you have changed, but it happens so gradually you really do not think the changes have been very significant. Then you see old friends, and they all look older. You realize they see you in the same manner. You are getting older, and there is nothing you can do to stop the hands of time.

Changes—that is what this chapter is about. We are interested in the changes in appearances that unfold over the lifespan and their impact on our lives. In this chapter, we explore three questions: What happens to our bodies as we age? How does our self-image change over time? As we age, how do other people's reactions to us change?

WHAT HAPPENS TO OUR BODIES AS WE AGE?

As we age, what changes occur in our faces and bodies? Dig out an old photograph album and retrieve photographs of yourself as a child, a teenager, and on up until now. Look carefully at your face. How did it change over time? Try to be specific (is your nose longer, has your face gotten thinner, have blemishes disappeared only to be replaced by crows'-feet and smile lines?). What changes have occurred in your body?

Changes in your face:

_____

_____

_____

Changes in your body:

_____

_____

_____

What do you think you will look like when you are your parents' age? Can you even begin to imagine what you will look like at ninty years of age? There are ways to find out. First, an obvious way to get ideas on how you will physically change over time is to take a careful look at your parents. Did they get fat? Did their hair grey or go bald? Or, do they look so youthful that people mistake you for siblings? No guarantees, but some of the same changes may be in store for you. To scrutinize pictures from Elaine Hatfield's family album, find the pictures of her mother, Eileen Hatifeld, at eleven years of age sitting on a swing

Figure 9.2. Courtesy, Charles and Eileen Hatfield, 1970.

(see page 96), as a bridesmaid at twenty-two (on page 138), and at 52 and 65 years of age (pages 273–274). You can see how her father, Charles Hatfield's looks have changed with the years by comparing his appearance at seven years of age on Boulevard Dock in Detroit (on page 322), as a policeman at twenty-six, (on page 83), and his appearance at 53 and 66 (pages 273–274).

There is a second, more expensive way to discover how you will look in the future. Journalists are fond of selecting todays' glowing young stars and depicting what the chill of time will do to their appearances. Artist Nancy Burson is a conceptual artist who ages faces via a computer process. (She can also reverse the process, in case you

Figure 9.3.   Courtesy, Charles and Eileen Hatfield, 1981.

want to see your face at a younger age once again.) Her work is reproduced in Illustration 9.4. How does the process work?

> The process is complicated: After freezing an image on a TV screen, Burson matches it with a facial type already in the computer bank. Then she adds characteristics from another bank of aged faces.

> "It's like taking a wrinkle mask off one face and putting in one another," she explains. (Calio 1982, 94).

Finally, a third way to find out how you will age is to review the changes that occur to *most* people. John Tierney of *Esquire* magazine

(May 1928) documented the changes that occur in a man's body as he ages. Many of these changes also apply to women. (For a comprehensive review of the changes that occur in aging, see McGaugh and Kiesler 1981).

30: In most ways, he is at his peak—the tallest, strongest, maybe the smartest he's ever been. And yet he can see the first lines on his forehead, he can't hear quite as well as he could, his skull's circumference has even started swelling. And his degeneration has just begun.

40: He's an eighth of an inch shorter than he was ten years ago, and each hair follicle has thinned two microns, but not everything's shrinking; his waist and chest are ballooning. All over, he's begun to feel the weight of time's passage; his stamina is greatly diminished.

50: His eyes have begun to fail him, particularly at close range. He notices quirky changes; his speaking voice has risen from a C to an E-flat, his thumbnails are growing more slowly, and his erections have dipped below the horizontal mark. His waist is as big as it will get.

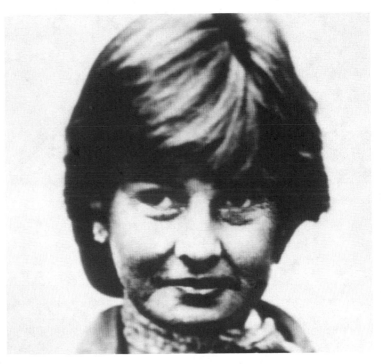

Figure 9.4. Artist Nancy Burson ages Princess Di and Prince Charles via a computer program.

60: By now he has shrunk a full three quarters of an inch, he has trouble telling certain colors, trouble distinguishing between tones, trouble making distinctions among the different foods he tastes. His lungs take in just about half what they could thirty years ago.

70: His heart is pumping less blood, his hearing is worse, vision weakening still; yet if he's made it this far, say the statistics, he'll live another eleven years. And if he has the right attitude, he will look back with awe at the wonders that have made him what he has become.

How Do Our Body Images Change Over Time?

We have seen how men and women's bodies alter as they move from childhood, through adolescence, to old age. What impact do such changes have on the way we think about ourselves? Are we most critical of ourselves when we are young, middle-aged, or old? People of all ages care deeply about appearances. Elaine, with cotherapist Richard Rapson, treated two clients at King Kalakaua Clinic who were

almost fifty years apart in age but identical in their sensitivity about their looks.

Anne was fifteen. When we first encountered her family in the waiting room, we had to smile—its composition was so typical of Hawaii's unique racial mix. Val, the mother, is a forty-five-year-old Russian emigrant. She dresses in vests and colorful peasant dresses. Anne's step-father is a tousel-haired, Japanese man-boy (he is twenty-three). Anne herself is a fifteen-year-old punk-rocker. The family makes a wildly incongruous bunch. (We tried to imagine what Anne's real father must be like. We decided the only person implausible enough to fit into this jumbled family was a dapper Maurice Chevalier type, with patent leather hair and a little moustache.)

One day, when Anne was bemoaning her appearance, we asked her to itemize what she especially liked about herself, and what she disliked. She began a dismal recital—her hair was dull, frizzy, and unmanageable; her eyes were too small (she described them as being like a little pig's eyes); her nose was squat and squashed down. As she talked, before our eyes she changed from a fresh-faced beauty into a drab, squashed-nosed girl. She did not possess one feature with which she was satisfied.

Another one of our clients, a sixty-five-year-old retired tennis pro, systematically reeled off a litany of equally dismal complaints. As he discussed the horrors of old age—failing eyesight, sagging chest muscles, arthritic knees, baldness—we got the same impression. He was a living portrait of Dorian Gray—a man without a single redeeming feature.

Everyone cares about their looks and worries *sometimes* (especially in times of stress) that there is something wrong with his or her looks. Appearance is a concern to everyone. But at what age is the body image lowest? When are men and women most concerned with appearances? If we had to bet, we would say people are cruelest in their self-evaluations in their teens. This notion is especially ironic, since that is precisely the age at which people are at the peak of their health and youthful beauty.

The *evidence* actually indicates that all age groups are equally critical of their body image (see Table 9.1). In the survey of 62,000 Americans we described earlier, Ellen Berscheid, Elaine Hatfield and George Bohrnstedt (1973) examined how men and women of three major age groups— 24 and younger, 24 to 44, and over 45—felt about themselves. They found that young adults (24 and younger) had as many reservations about their bodies as did anyone else. These results are astonishing since these young adults are at age when people are probably most appealing (according to the standards of society). It is poignant to discover that the blooming fourteen-year old feels no better about his or her body than does the faded eighty-seven-year old.

Age, Body Image, and Happiness

What happens to good-looking men and women as they begin to age? There are two popular theories on the matter. The first is the "beauty is a joy forever" argument. This view maintains that men and women who are good-looking in their youth have an advantage throughout their lives. Good-looking men and women have an easier time developing social skills, getting an education, finding just the right mate, and landing the most exciting and prestigious jobs. By the time their attractiveness fades, they can capitalize on *these* advantages. Thus, the theory goes, the good-looking get a head start in youth, which they maintain throughout their lives. The hypothesis that people *believe* beautiful individuals will continue to have fulfilling lives, happier marriages, and more prestigious occupations has been substantiated in first impression studies (Dion et al. 1972).

A second school of thought about the aging beauty proposes a "beauty is short-lived" argument. This view warns that beauty is soon ravaged by time, causing the beautiful to become bitter and miserable. People stunning in youth are tempted to rely on their good looks; when their external attributes fade, they are left with nothing. Opportunities stop knocking, relationships turn sour. Kirkpatrick and Cotton (1951) warned that "husbands (of beautiful but aging women) may feel betrayed and disillusioned, even disgusted with the reliance on charms which have faded with the passing years." (They neglect to mention how wives may feel about their once handsome husbands.)

To complicate things still further, some theorists have taken a third position concerning the link between beauty and happiness. They point out that the bluebird of happiness is an elusive fowl, whose habits have not been fully identified. Often, people's personal feelings of satisfaction with their lot do not show one-to-one correspondence with the "objective" goodness of that lot. Happiness may follow "adaptation" rules. For example, Thibaut and Kelley (1965) pointed out that men and women's happiness in any given relationship depends on what they *expect* to get out of life, as well as what they actually *do* get.

TABLE 9.1 **The Impact of Age Upon Body Image**

	BODY IMAGE		
AGE GROUP	ABOVE AVERAGE	AVERAGE	BELOW AVERAGE
Under 25	26%	51%	24%
25–44	28%	47%	26%
Over 45	30%	45%	25%

SOURCE: Berscheid, Hatfield [Walster], and Bohrnstedt, 1973.

Presumably, then, individuals who have never known anything but exceptionally high rewards in life will come to take such spectacular treatment for granted. Less fortunate people might be bowled over by the things the beautiful take for granted. Thus, Brickman and Campbell (1971) argue, we are all doomed to a kind of hedonic treadmill. We all long for complete happiness, but the more we get, the more we want. Everyone, they assert, ends up being happy about half the time, miserable half the time.

In examining these opposing views Elaine Hatfield and her colleagues (Berscheid, Hatfield [Walster], and Bohrnstedt 1972) asked *Psychology Today* readers a series of questions: How physically attractive did they feel (compared to others of their age) at various ages (in childhood, 13 to 19, 20 to 30, etc.)? The readers were asked how happy they were at this time and how happy they *expected* to be in the future, marking their estimates on a ten-point scale. We have reproduced these questions below. You might indicate how you would answer them.

BODY IMAGE QUESTIONNAIRE

1. Compare your physical attractiveness when you were a child, (one to 12 years), with others of your age. I was:

   ○ A Much more attractive.
   ○ B Considerably more attractive.
   ○ C Slightly more attractive.
   ○ D About the same.
   ○ E Slightly less attractive.
   ○ F Considerably less attractive.
   ○ G Much less attractive.

2. Compare your physical attractiveness when you were an adolescent, (13 to 19 years), with others of your age. I was (am):

   ○ A Much more attractive.
   ○ B Considerably more attractive.
   ○ C Slightly more attractive.
   ○ D About the same.
   ○ E Slightly less attractive.
   ○ F Considerably less attractive.
   ○ G Much less attractive.

3. Compare your physical attractiveness when you were a young adult (20 to 30 years), with others of your age. I was (am):

   ○ A Much more attractive.
   ○ B Considerably more attractive.
   ○ C Slightly more attractive.
   ○ D About the same.
   ○ E Slightly less attractive.
   ○ F Considerably less attractive.
   ○ G Much less attractive.
   ○ H I am not yet 20.

4. Compare your physical attractiveness as a mature adult (31 to 45 years), with others of your age. I was (am):

   ○ A Much more attractive.
   ○ B Considerably more attractive.
   ○ C Slightly more attractive.
   ○ D About the same.
   ○ E Slightly less attractive.
   ○ F Considerably less attractive.
   ○ G Much less attractive.
   ○ H I am not yet 31.

5. Compare your physical attractiveness as a fully mature adult (46 or over) with others of your age. I was (am):

   O A Much more attractive.
   O B Considerably more attractive.
   O C Slightly more attractive.
   O D About the same.
   O E Slightly less attractive.
   O F Considerably less attractive.
   O G Much less attractive.
   O H I am not yet 46.

6. Compare your overall physical attractiveness now with others of your age. I am:

   O A Much more attractive.
   O B Considerably more attractive.
   O C Slightly more attractive.
   O D About the same.
   O E Slightly less attractive.
   O F Considerably less attractive.
   O G Much less attractive.

7. Imagine a ladder with 10 rungs. The top rung (#10) represents the ideal, happy life. The bottom (#1) represents the worst possible life. Put a number by each letter on the answer sheet.

   O A On what rung do you think you are now?_____
   O B On what rung did you think you were as a child (12 or younger)?_____
   O C On what rung were (are) you, as an adolescent (13 to 19 years)?_____
   O D On what rung were you, are your, or do you expect to be as a young adult (20 to 30)?_____
   O E On what rung were you, are you, or do you expect to be as a mature adult (31–45)?_____
   O F On what rung were you, are you, or do you expect to be as a fully mature adult (46 or over)?____

You can compare your feelings to those of people in general by consulting Figure 9.5. You can see whether your good looks (or lack thereof) have brought you the same happiness or misery they have brought others.

Is there a link between beauty and happiness? We found that there is. Childhood and adolescent beauty (see items 1 and 2 of the Body Image Questionnaire) go hand-in-hand with early happiness. The child or teenager who is unattractive is also miserable. "I always thought I was an ugly kid—you know—pimples, crooked teeth, frizzy hair, skinny, glasses, and the worse curse—flat chested," mourned one woman in our study, "and I also remember feeling so depressed."

Childhood beauty (or homeliness), however, has little connection to a person's later happiness. By the time our respondents reached college age, it made little difference whether they were attractive as children or not. "It is only within the last couple of years that I have been able to look in the mirror and say, 'Yes, you are beautiful,'"

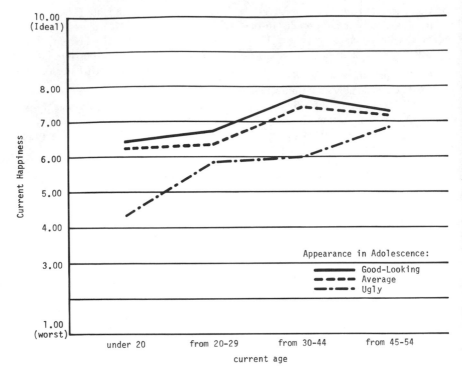

Figure 9.5.   The relationship between looks and happiness.

continued the woman who was an "ugly kid." "And I still have crooked teeth and rotten eye-sight, and I still wear glasses."

Adolescent beauty, on the other hand, leaves its mark for years. People who were unattractive as teenagers are the least happy of all respondents. One is reminded again of Janis Joplin, an early rock star.

Thus far, we have talked about the children and adolescent beauty's happiness *throughout* the lifespan. What about the present? Is *current* appearance (see item 6 of the Body Image Questionnaire) equally important in shaping happiness (or unhappiness) in youth? middle age? old age? The answer that emerges from these data is "yes." Body image and happiness are closely linked at every age.

Moderating Factors: Ugly Swans and Beautiful Ducklings

What about people who change dramatically in their physical appearance? An ugly duckling teenager may turn into a lovely swan in adulthood. The beautiful swan may lose her feathers at puberty. Do people whose appearance undergoes a radical transformation experience a corresponding transformation in self-esteem and happiness?

To find out, Berscheid et al. 1973 looked at how *Psychology Today* readers rated their attractiveness from youth to middle age (see items 1–5 of the Body Image scale). To explore the ugly duckling phenomenon, they contrasted people who felt their attractiveness had changed over the years—for better or worse—with those who had stayed the same. Most respondents believed they had changed. Fewer than half the respondents maintained they were as pretty (or plain) now as they had ever been. For example, some said they were beautiful as children, homely as adolescents, and good-looking again as adults.

To assess the impact of changes in looks, they divided respondents over thirty into five groups: (1) those who felt they had always been beautiful; (2) those who had sometimes been beautiful; sometimes average; (3) those who had always been of average looks; (4) those who vacillated between average and unattractive; and (5) those who had been ugly throughout their lives. They found that the more time one has served in an ugly body, the less self-confident and happy one is (see Table 9.2).

Sometimes it is difficult to forget what we looked like when young. The "ugly duckling" feelings last long after the swan has emerged. "I was praised as an intellectual, quite thoughtful, conscientious, humorous, child of the family—but I desperately wanted to be pretty," wrote one woman. "As a result, I have never believed a single compliment on my looks or appearance, and mistrust people who pay them." For some, remembered comparisons with one's adolescent peers linger. "While I'm above average height," noted one man, "I still think of myself as small, because I was schooled among older boys."

TABLE 9.2 **Consistency of Appearance and Self-Esteem, Body Satisfaction, and Current Happiness**

	NUMBER OF PEOPLE INTERVIEWED	SELF-ESTEEM*	BODY SATISFACTION*	CURRENT HAPPINESS*
Always Beautiful/Handsome	118	38.99	116.94	7.50
Sometimes Beautiful/Handsome Sometimes Average	272	37.59	112.05	7.46
Always Average	315	33.64	105.95	7.10
Sometimes Ugly; Sometimes Average	59	32.28	94.02	6.68
Always Ugly	16	29.00	86.50	6.19

* The higher the number, the more confident, the more satisfied, and the happier men and women are.
SOURCE: Berscheid et al., 1973.

AS WE AGE, HOW DO OTHER PEOPLE'S REACTIONS TO US CHANGE?

Is There a Generation Gap in Perceptions of Beauty?

The next time you are at a family gathering, you might orchestrate a lively discussion among your relatives of different ages. Can your fifteen-year-old cousin agree with your ninety-year-old grandfather on which movie starlet is the best-looking? Can your sister agree with your mother as to which leading man is most attractive?

You might think representatives from different generations would find it hard to agree about *anything*, much less on who is sexy and appealing. But research leads us to a surprising conclusion: There is no generation gap when it comes to judging beauty. You and your siblings are no more likely to agree on what constitutes a perfect "10" than are you and your grandparents.

Fashions in beauty come and go. Clara Bow to Brooke Shields and Rudolf Valentino to Tom Selleck represent quite a change. However, the evidence clearly shows that even those who grew up with Clara Bow and Rudolf Valentino are as likely as the rest of us to skip a heartbeat at the sight of a Brooke Shields or a Tom Selleck. Existing evidence indicates there is substantial agreement between people of different generations as to what is beautiful and what is not.

In one study (Cross and Cross 1971), three hundred men and women ranging in age from seven to fifty were shown photographs of people of three different ages (second graders, high school seniors, and adults) and were asked how pretty or handsome each face was. There was surprising agreement in judges' ratings, regardless of their age or gender. It has also been found that young and old people give similar physical attractiveness ratings to photographs of older people (aged 60–95) (Johnson and Pittenger 1984).

Is There Consistency in Appearance Over the Life Span?

The evidence indicates there is surprisingly little change in who is seen as the least and as the most appealing in a given group of people as they move from childhood to old age. Ugly ducklings generally blossom into ugly ducks. Gerald Adams (1977a) conducted a series of studies to determine how much continuity there is in attractiveness across the life span. In a first study, he secured school pictures of a group of children when they were in kindergarten, first grade, second grade, and so on through the sixth grade. All the children's pictures were rated for attractiveness by a group of college women. He secured strong evidence that *facial* attractiveness is stable throughout grade school. If children were attractive in kindergarten, they were likely to still be attractive in the sixth grade. Children homely in kindergarten were *not* likely to blossom into beautiful roses as they got older.

In the few cases in which dramatic changes in appearance occurred, they were likely to come in the third grade for boys and in the second grade for girls. The reason? Boys and girls got orthodontic corrections (braces, etc.) and lost teeth at that age (other research has found that teeth are important in assessing facial attractiveness [Kleck et al 1974].)

Other researchers (Sussman, Mueser, Grau, and Yarnold 1983) have also found stability in facial attractiveness during childhood. Photographs of thirteen girls, taken during the first, fourth, seventh, and tenth grades, were rated for physical attractiveness by male college students. Some stability of physical attractiveness was found over the large span of childhood and adolescence.

What about even longer time periods—is there also continuity in physical attractiveness throughout adulthood? In a second study, Gerald Adams (1977) studied the stability of men and women's facial and body attractiveness over three stages of adulthood. He had several students dig into old family photo albums and get swimming suit photographs of their parents during adolescence (16–20 years of age), the young married period (30–35), and the middle age years (45–50). Even over these many years, facial attractiveness did not change much. Once a pretty face, always a pretty face. However, there was less stability in bodily attractiveness over the life cycle. A shapely twenty-year-old body sometimes turns into a pudgy forty-five-year-old body.

Overall, there is apparent stability in attractiveness over the life cycle, especially for the face. It is likely, then, that those who are attractive have consistently received positive feedback and will continue to; those who are ugly will probably face a lifetime of negative discrimination.

At What Age Are People Considered to Be Most Appealing?

Do you find a seventeen-year old more attractive than a twenty-seven-year old? a thirty-seven-year old? Does the very youthful, unwrinkled, and innocent face appeal to your sense of aesthetics, or are you more likely to be intrigued by the character in a somewhat older face? Surprisingly, little work has been done to examine if a particular age group has a monopoly on attractiveness. In a study we described earlier, Cross and Cross (1971) asked three hundred men and women of three different age levels—second grade, high school seniors, and adults—how pretty or handsome faces varying in age from 7–37 years of age were. The seventeen-year olds were judged to be the best-looking of

Figure 9.6. Young boy, Takuu Atoll, Papua, New Guinea. Courtesy, Barbara Moir.

the lot. The faces of the seven-year olds and adults were judged as about equal in attractiveness.

Are Good Looks Equally Important Over the Life Span?

One might expect teenagers to be most impressed with appearances, that as people age, they begin to downplay the importance of ap-

Figure 9.7. Grandmother and grandson, Takuu Atoll, Papua, New Guinea, 1983. Courtesy, Barbara Moir.

pearances and begin to realize that other assets are more important to a happy life. The evidence, however, suggests that this assumption is wrong.

People of all ages assume beauty is important. Berscheid et al. (1973) asked a sample of Americans how important they thought looks were in relationships. Twenty-one percent of respondents under twenty-five and 33 percent of respondents over twenty-five responded that physical attractiveness was "very important" for most people. Apparently, they are right.

Earlier in the book we discussed the physical attractiveness stereotype—"What is beautiful is good." We found that most people assume that good looks and appealing personalities are related. The stereotyping process begins early. People are divided on what newborns look like—some insist all babies are cute, others that they are all scrawny and ugly. There is no doubt, however, that prejudice in favor of cute infants begins early. Stephan and Langlois (1984) asked Caucasian, black, and Mexican Americans to rate photographs of infants of various ethnic groups three times—immediately after birth, at three months, and at nine months. They found that the cutest babies were perceived to be the best babies. They were judged to be more likeable and smarter. Homely babies were assumed to cause their parents more problems.

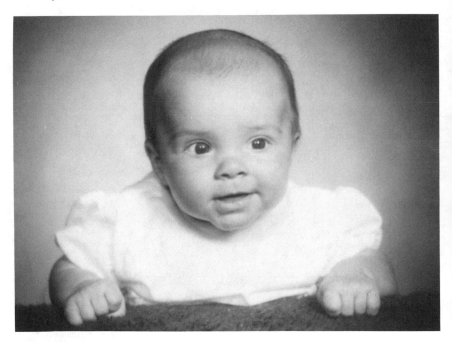

Figure 9.8. Stimulus picture of a three-month-old infant. Courtesy Abagail Fisher, 1984.

In all the research investigations we described in chapters 1–8, young people were rating photographs of other young adults. What happens when elderly people are asked their impressions? Do they also assume "what is beautiful is good?" Furthermore, does age of the target person make a difference? That is, do people (from 5 to 95) attribute positive personality characteristics to others regardless of how young or old the latter are?

In one study (Adams and Huston 1975), both young people (averaging age 25) and elderly people (averaging age 66) gave their first impressions of middle-aged men and women between 48 and 52 years of age. It was found that both the young and the old adhered to the physical attractiveness stereotype for the middle-aged target persons. Physically attractive individuals were judged to have attained higher occupational status, to possess higher self-esteem, to be more socially outgoing, to be more pleasant, and to have several other positive personality characteristics. Actually, the elderly folks held a stronger physical attractiveness stereotype than the younger adults. The elderly were more likely to exaggerate the honesty and vocational status of attractive persons.

In another study, photographs of elderly people (between the ages of sixty and ninety-three) were judged by young and elderly groups of men and women. It was found that attractive old people were perceived by *both* young and old judges as possessing more socially desirable personality characteristics than less attractive old people (Johnson and Pittenger 1984). In conclusion, the physical attractiveness stereotype exists, regardless of the ages of the judges *or* of the targets.

Let us consider the importance of physical appearance in the arena of personal relationships. We know good looks are important in the dating and mating marketplaces for young people, but what about for those no longer experiencing their first love affairs? In a recent study (Jones and Adams 1982), men and women from eighteen to ninety years of age were interviewed about the importance of physical attractiveness. Older people were actually more likely than younger people to believe that physical attractiveness is important for both men and women in marriage selection, friendship formation, marital happiness, and general success. Possibly, as men and women get older they encounter more and more experiences that demonstrate the importance of physical attractiveness.

THE DOUBLE STANDARD OF AGING

Joke
Q: What is this? "10, 9, 8 . . ."
A: Bo Derek growing older.

Since no one can drink from the fountain of youth, neither men nor women are immune from the ravages of aging. One aspect of "masculinity" is power and strength.

As a man ages and loses his physical power, his self-evaluation and prestige may plummett too.

Forty is fun because life has just begun. Age is mind over matter—as long as you don't mind, it don't matter. (Muhammed Ali, before his last fight)

The timing wasn't there and the reflexes weren't there. I could tell I was forty. (Ali, after his last fight)

My batting eye was almost as dependable as ever, but the legs wouldn't carry me around the garden with speed and timing. Old wounds ached constantly. I literally had to grit my teeth and force myself to run. (Ty Cobb at age 42 [quoted in Timm 1982])

Elaine's father is a tall, powerful, rough-hewn man. His style of dealing with the world is with calm authority—a gentle style that works well because it is backed up by his towering size. Once, when some drunken men tried to run his car off the road, he slammed out of his car, threw open the door of their car, and demanded, "What the hell is going on here." They apologized.

Elaine always assumed it was sheer force of character—his bravery—that gave him his authority. In 1981 he developed cancer and had his lung removed. For a few months, his quiet confidence was shaken. He and Elaine's mother live in a rough part of Detroit. During the brief period of his recovery, he was beset with fears that he would no longer be able to protect himself and his wife. During those months, we got a real sense of the effects of aging for a man who has relied on physical size and power for his authority.

If aging is difficult for men, it may be impossible for women. "In Rome we say that it is the duty of every woman to be beautiful. A man is a man—it doesn't matter if he's ugly. But a woman must look as beautiful as she can, because both are happier that way" (Weg 1977). One only has to turn on the television or pick up a magazine to suspect there is a double standard of aging. Women in advertisements, commercials, television shows, and even on the six o'clock news are young and beautiful. Men in the limelight, however, are allowed to get a little old and tarnished.

An example: About the time we were busy writing this book, Christine Craft, a television anchorwoman, was bringing a $1.2 million lawsuit against Metromedia, the former owners of a Kansas City tele-

Figure 9.9.   One aspect of masculinity is power and strength.

vision station (KMBC), for sex discrimination. When Mrs. Craft was thirty-six-years old, she was dropped by KMBC as an anchor because she was "too old, unattractive, and not deferential to men." *Time* magazine (Henry, 22 August 1983, 57) reports:

> During Craft's eight-month tenure, KMBC's news ratings rose from second place to first in the six-station market. . . . Nonetheless, the station hired consultants to test her appeal further. Perhaps the most damaging evidence against Metromedia was an audio tape of a research discussion in which Steve Mechom, A Media Associates employee, said to a group of local viewers, "Let's spend 30 seconds destroying Christine Craft. Is she a mutt?"

The station manager tried to persuade Ms. Craft to change her appearance by wearing heavy makeup and by following a clothing calendar. She reported to the jury, "I found it difficult to be myself with such a radical makeover. . . . I don't think you have to be a beauty queen."

In general, anchor*women* tend to be young (close to twenty) while anchor*men* tend to be older (over forty). Here are some comments on the matter (published in *USA Today*, 27 July 1983, 8A):

> When a man speaks on the television, people listen. But when a woman speaks, people look, and if they like her looks, then they listen. (Pauline Fredrick, first female television correspondent)

> You start a male and a female out in their 20's, and they're both going to get lines, bags, wrinkles covering murder, mayhem, and politics. . . . In a man that's seasoning. In a woman it's disqualification. That's nuts. (Christine Craft, television anchorwoman)

> Television is a youth business, and women feel it more than men. . . . I think women age more gracefully than men. (Dan Rather, CBS Evening News)
>
> Christine Craft won her case. A Kansas City jury awarded Craft $500,000 in damages, but Judge Joseph Stevens threw out the award and ordered a retrial. In that retrial, she was awarded $325,000.
>
> The double standard of aging is also evident in that women are more likely than men to be targets of commercials on how to slow down the aging process by using creams, exercising, and getting the grey out. These commercials suggest that women will be in trouble if they lose the qualities of youthful beauty—smooth skin and slim figures—for which they were most valued. Men, on the other hand, are valued for those things that come with age—money, status, and experience.
>
> Zoe Moss (1970) describes what aging means for women:

It Hurts to Be Alive and Obsolete: The Aging Woman

What, fat, forty-three, and I dare to think I'm still a person? No. I am an invisible lump. I belong in a category labelled *a priori* without interest to anyone. I am not even expected to interest myself. A middle-aged woman is comic by definition.

. . . The mass media tell us all day and all evening long that we are inadequate, mindless, ugly, disgusting in ourselves. We must try to resemble perfect plastic objects, so that no one will notice what we really are. In ourselves we smell bad, shed dandruff, our breath has an odor, our hair stands up or falls out, we sag or stick out where we shouldn't. We can only fool people into liking us by using magic products that make us products, too.

. . . My daughter is a senior in college. She already talks about her "youth" with a sad nostalgia. She is worried because she is not married. That she has not met anyone that she wants to live that close to, does not seem to figure in her anxiety. Everything confirms in her a sense of time passing, that she will be left behind, unsold on the shelf. She already peers in the mirror for wrinkles and buys creams and jellies to rub into her skin. Her fear angers me but leaves me helpless. She is alienated from her body because her breasts are big and do not stand out like the breasts of store mannequins. She looks twenty-one. I look forty-three.

I want to beg her not to begin worrying, not to let in the dreadful daily gnawing already. Everyone born grows up, grows older, and ages every day until he dies. But every day in seventy thousand ways this society tells a woman that it is her sin and her guilt that she has a real living body. How can a woman respect herself when every day she stands before a mirror and accuses her face of betraying her, because every day she is, indeed, a day older.

Everything she reads, every comic strip, every song, every cartoon, every advertisement, every book and movie tells her that a woman over thirty is ugly—and disgusting. She is a bag. She is to be escaped from. She is no longer an object of prestige consumption. For her to have real living sexual desires is obscene. Her touch is thought to contaminate. No man "seduces" women older than him: there is no conquest. It is understood that she would be "glad for a touch of it". Since she would be glad, there can be no pleasure in the act. Either this society is mad or I am mad. It is considered incredible that a woman might have had experiences that are valuable or interesting and that have enriched her as a person. No, men may mature, but women just obsolesce.

(pp. 170–175)

Do people actually judge middle-aged and older women more harshly than men of the same age? In one study (Deutsch, Clark, and Zalenski 1983), elderly men and women provided photographs of themselves at three ages: 19–24 years old; 40–50 years old; and over 60 years olds. Both young men and women and elderly men and women (from a senior citizen housing project) then judged the photographs on various dimensions. The attractiveness of both men and women was perceived to decline as they aged, but the decline was more precipitous for women than for men. Although in youth and middle age men and women were judged to be about equally attractive, in old age (over sixty) the double standard was clearly detected—elderly men were thought to be more attractive than elderly women. This study, then, suggests the double standard begins only in old age.

Another study found that middle-aged women are judged more harshly than middle-aged men in physical attractiveness, but only if judgments are made in public. When physical attractiveness ratings are made privately, the double standard suddenly disappears. In their study, psychologists (Berman, O'Nan, and Floyd 1981) asked college men and women to judge pictures of middle-aged men and women for their "immediate emotional appeal." The men and women judged the pictures either in private or in small groups of all men, all women, or mixed. When men and women formed their judgments privately, they actually judged middle-aged women as more attractive than middle-aged men! However, when judgments were made publically, middle-aged women were thought to be considerably less attractive than middle-aged men. This difference was especially pronounced for men in the all-male groups.

Conceivably, with the new equality and the greying of America, the double standard is beginning to erode. There are some signs of it. In the April 11, 1983 issue of *People* magazine, the lead article was titled "Sexy Forever." It observed that stars such as Jane Fonda, Barbara Streisand, Faye Dunaway, Ann Margaret, Stefanie Powers, Raquel Welch, Julie Christie, Linda Evans, Lee Remick, Rita Moreno, Ursula Andress, Jill St. John, Julie Andrews, Joan Collins, Ali MacGraw are all over forty and are still considered sexy. *People* magazine writes:

> Thirty-five. Not long ago, it was an age that loomed before women, especially in Hollywood, like a fraying rope bridge, with nothing but the pastures of middle age on the far side and a chasm of rejection below. Before she ended her life at 36, Marilyn Monroe had reconciled herself to a future playing "character" roles. Garbo went into permanent seclusion at about the same age. Lana Turner, 63, was dumped at MGM at 36. Ava Gardner, now 60, put it bluntly: "There comes a time when you've simply got to face the fact that you're an old broad."
>
> No longer. These days, age adds depth to glamour. "Broad" is as outmoded as seamed stockings, unless used as an adjective to describe the opportunities that leading ladies in their 30's and 40's now enjoy. (p. 109)

Perhaps, but the 50's, 60's, and 70's still loom ahead. Obviously, it gets a little more difficult to look fantastic, fit, and sexy when we

Figure 9.10. Tish Hooker, a forty-five-year-old decorator from Nashville, Tenn. Ms. Hooker won a recent Germaine Monteil search for an over forty beauty. © Germaine Monteil 1984. Photo: Bert Stern.

nit the last decades of our lives. However, it is possible that people will begin to recognize a new kind of beauty even there. Consider the following news clips.

About Gloria Swanson:

> She looked good. That was what they had come for, really—not to hear about how Cecile B. DeMille had called her "young fellow" or

how Rudolph Valentino got to be her leading man, but to see how time, which had passed over all of them, just as surely, had treated her.

Hundreds of them came, women who had sat in silent-movie theaters as children and had watched her jerk, glamorously, across the screen, women who had seen the costume dramas at a Leow's somewhere in Brooklyn or the Bronx. "We had faces then," Gloria Swanson said in the movie "Sunset Boulevard", and the women who came to the New School to hear Miss Swanson lecture wanted to see her. A number of them were dying to know if it had been lifted.

"I've seen her on Merv and she looks pretty good for a woman of that age who hasn't had a little help," said Myrna Cohen, who, at age 78, is only four years younger than Miss Swanson.

She looked good, and it made them feel wonderful, a constant in a changing world of hemlines and hair styles. She still carries a red carnation. She still wears one glove and carries another. She still dresses like a star. (Quindlen, *New York Times*, 4 November 1981, 15)

On Dolores Del Rio:

"God either gives you a face or doesn't," said Dolores Del Rio. "If he does, then you have a duty to take care of it. But people always make the mistake of worrying about age. Never worry, never be afraid."

When you look like Dolores Del Rio, you can say such things. She is 76 and her beauty can still make people gasp with wonder, as they did when she appeared at the San Francisco International Film Festival following a retrospective of her movies. In a black sequined Oscar de la Renta sheath with white organdy cuffs framing her expressive hands, she appeared as vibrant and as appealing as when she portrayed Madame du Barry in 1934.

The previous evening, in her suite at the Mark Hopkins Hotel, she talked about how to stay beautiful.

"Health is the real secret," she said. "There also has to be a discipline to your life; you cannot be indulgent and expect to look good. But lack of fear is most important. There are lots of advantages to age: You can speak the truth, you have the knowledge and confidence to say what you mean and people listen to you.

"It upsets me to see all these women who worry, who put their faith in the wrong things, believing that some cream or other will help them, or trying to dress too young. Lots of little curls do not make you look younger, nor do frilly clothes." (Byrne, *New York Times*, 20–27 November 1981, 12)

CONCLUSION

In this chapter, we reviewed the changes in physical attractiveness that occur over the lifespan, and their impact on our lives. We first itemized some of the ways our faces and bodies change as we age. We found that adolescent good looks are particularly important for our later vision of ourselves and our happiness, but that good looks remain important throughout the lifespan in shaping self-esteem, in preserving happiness, and in determining the way we will be treated by others.

Chapter 10

THE UGLY TRUTH ABOUT BEAUTY

Throughout most of this book, we have focused on the tremendous benefits of being good-looking. Most people expect the best from good-looking men and women and treat them accordingly. Consequently the strikingly good-looking have a chance to develop the best of everything; yet, every silver lining has its cloud. Note that there are several different ways of viewing the same traits:

I am	You are	He is
firm	obstinate	pigheaded
spontaneous	uncontrolled	a psychopath
careful	compulsive	rigid
interested in people	nosey	a gossip

The preceding commentary reflects an essential truth—any asset is its own liability. In most settings, strong ethical convictions are an asset; yet, carried just a bit too far, "conviction" shades over into fanaticism. Flexibility is fine, except when it becomes indecision and unreliability. Therefore, although the good-looking obviously have some real advantages, like all advantages these must have a dark side too.

Not too surprisingly, handsome men and beautiful women have been most sensitive to the dangers of being too good-looking. A few years ago, *Esquire* magazine (O'Brien 1979) interviewed several handsome men and catalogued the problems they encounter. Others are self-conscious in their presence, other men feel jealous and threatened, women assume the attractive men must be narcissistic and superficial ("They are," sniped some of the women who reviewed this chapter).

Some extremely attractive men and women have even decided to form groups to discuss the problems they face. For example, in California Jerry "I'm a good-looking guy" Lipkin recently formed a Good-Looking People Network. The problems they discuss include finding dates, being perceived as dumb, and being considered sex objects (Jones 1984). Alix Kates Shulman (1972) in *Memoirs of an Ex-prom Queen* points out some of the problems of being too beautiful:

> They say it's worse to be ugly. I think it must only be different. If you're pretty, you are subject to one set of assaults; if you're plain you are subject to another. Pretty, you may have more men to choose from but you have more anxiety too, knowing your looks, which really have nothing to do with you, will disappear. Pretty girls have few friends. Kicked out of mankind in elementary school, and then kicked out of womankind in junior high, pretty girls have a lower birth rate and a higher mortality. It is the beauties like Marilyn Monroe who swallow twenty-five Nembutals on a Saturday night and kill themselves in their thirties. (p. 41)

Rarely, however, do the good-looking get much sympathy for their plight. The average-looking and unattractive among us are tempted to be sarcastic: "Why don't they just quit their limelight jobs if they have it so rough?" "Why don't they stop dating if they can't take the pressure" or "gain a little weight if they don't like being so gorgeous." Nora Ephron (1980) in a chapter titled "On Never Having Been a Prom Queen" agrees:

> . . . It won't wash. There isn't any ugly girl in America who wouldn't exchange her problems for the problems of being beautiful. I don't believe there's a beautiful girl anywhere who would honestly prefer not to be. "They say it's worse to be ugly," Alix Shulman writes. Yes, they do say that. And they're right. It is also worse to be poor, worse to be

orphaned, worse to be fat. Not just *different* from rich, familied, and thin—actually worse. (p. 18)

Without arguing which side of the fence is greener, we recognize beautiful people do face certain problems. In this chapter, we will discuss some of these ugly truths about being beautiful. We will go back and consider the questions we raised before: Do people have different stereotypes about the good-looking versus the ugly? Do they treat them differently? Do attractive versus unattractive men and women have different experiences in their intimate relations? Finally, do the good-looking versus the ugly become different people as a consequence of their different experiences? This time, however, we will focus on the darker side of being attractive.

THE MYTH OF BEAUTY: RECONSIDERED

When we asked THE GROUP what stereotypes they held about *very* attractive people, they countered with a few that were distinctively negative:

Extremely attractive people tend to be arrogant, aloof, and self-indulgent.

Beautiful men and women know it! They are conceited. They aren't interested in associating with average-looking people.

Handsome men are rotten lovers. They demand instant sex. If they don't get everything they want, they just move on. They have no idea of the patience it takes to cement an intimate relationship.

Such critics are not alone. Several recent studies indicate that, although people generally do equate looks with goodness, there are a few exceptions.

WHAT IS BEAUTIFUL IS NOT *ALL* GOOD: A CLASSIC STUDY REVISITED

Remember the classic study we described in chapter 2 (Dion et al. 1972)? This study was the first providing evidence that people generally assume "What is Beautiful is Good." That study found that attractive men and women were perceived to have more desirable personality traits and were expected to have happier lives than the unattractive.

In a variation of that classic study, Marshall Dermer and Darrel Thiel (1975) set out to demonstrate that there are some limits to the fanfare given the physically attractive. Although in the earlier study of men and women rated photographs of both men and women, the replication study included only women—as judges and targets (the authors assumed physical attractiveness is exceedingly important for women). Otherwise, the Dermer and Thiel study was conducted in much the same way as the classic study. In the earlier study, the researchers claimed they were interested in the accuracy of first impressions. The scientists asked the women to look at a variety of photographs of other women (who varied in attractiveness) and to guess what they were probably like. What types of personalities did they probably have? For example, how poised/awkward, warm/cold, sensitive/insensitive, strong/weak were they? What did the future have in store for them— in marriage, children, careers, and life in general?

As was found in the early study, people assumed beautiful and average-looking women possessed more desirable personalities than their homely counterparts. It was also assumed that attractive women would have more social and professional happiness, achieve a higher occupational status, and, in general, have a more pleasant future.

In the Dermer and Thiel study, however, a few additional questions designed to provide possible evidence of the limits to the physical attractiveness stereotype were asked. The researchers asked the women about their stereotyping of beautiful versus ugly women for two traits the classic study had not included: (1) How committed were beautiful versus ugly women to their marriages? Would they have extramarital affairs? Ask for a divorce? (2) How bourgeois was their orientation? To what extent did beautiful versus ugly women sympathize with oppressed peoples (the poor, the disadvantaged, etc.)? How materialistic were they? (For example, did beautiful women believe money and wealth are primary ingredients for a happy life?) Were the attractive social status-seeking snobs?

The researchers found that women were prejudiced against beautiful women. First, they had serious reservations about the faithfulness of beautiful women. They suspected these women would be most tempted to engage in extramarital affairs and would end up divorced. (Perhaps it was assumed stunning women would receive so many offers that sooner or later they would be tempted to say yes. Once they had said yes to an affair, a divorce would be just around the corner.) Beautiful women were also assumed to be more bourgeois—to be unsympathetic with oppressed peoples, to be materialistic and snobbish, and to be more vain and egotistical than other women.

This research tempered the notion that beauty is *always* good. Though beautiful people were seen as having more socially desirable traits and were expected to be happier in life, they were also seen as adulterous, vain, egotistical, greedy, status-seeking, and as unlikely to sympathize with oppressed people. In short, the orientation of the attractive person was seen to be one of selfishness: grab everything for yourself and never mind anyone else.

Since the pioneering research of Dermer and Thiel, other researchers have also found that all that glitters is not good. In one set of studies, for example (Kleinke and Staneski 1980), a woman was described as having either small, medium, or large breasts (one aspect of attractiveness). Attractive, large breasted, women were assumed to be more immoral, selfish, and rude than were women average or below average in breast size. In addition, women with large breasts were assumed to be less intelligent, competent, moral, and modest than women with smaller breasts (clearly one can have too much of a good thing!).

Other evidence documents that handsomeness may fail for men, too. In a study Susan Sprecher conducted with her colleagues, Robert Smith and John DeLamater, men and women were asked to look at a photograph of either a man or a woman and were asked several questions about him/her, including the likelihood that he/she would have an extramarital affair and get a divorce. Handsome men were considered more likely to have an extramarital affair and to get a divorce than less attractive men. The differences were less pronounced for women (Smith, Sprecher, and DeLamater, 1983a).

SOME PEOPLE MAY BE ESPECIALLY BIASED (AND JEALOUS) OF THE GOOD-LOOKING

Anyone Who is Popular is Bound to be Disliked.
(Murphy's Law [Bloch 1982])

In the last section, we found that although most people, most of the time, assume "What is beautiful is good", there may be limits. Although the physically attractive *are* perceived to have several virtues, they are not seen as infallible. In this section, we examine just who is more likely to have reservations about beautiful people—the physically attractive themselves or those less fortunate in looks. Let us evaluate both possibilities:

Perhaps the Good-looking Have More Reasons to Be Jealous of the Beautiful/Handsome.

Obviously, those banking everything on their *own* good looks have reason to resent their closest rivals. Richard Gere may shun Sylvester Stallone. Sophia Loren may not be a fan of Racquel Welch. One of the men in THE GROUP, a model at a large Honolulu agency, observed, "It's extraordinarily hard for me to be civil to Tom Selleck (who is also a Honolulu resident). Every time I look at him, I think there go all the good things that should be coming to me."

One popular television star from THE GROUP described her relations with other soap opera stars.

> Yes, I know that how I look affects my relationships with others. Men want to get to know me because of the way I look . . . and women avoid me for the same reason. At first, women—and even attractive women—feel threatened by me; they assume I'm out to steal the men. Once they get to know me, however, they relax because they can see I'm not trying to steal men.
>
> When I first came to N.B.C., I met a cute girl and we became good friends. However, when we went out together, she would get mad at me because she suddenly wasn't the only center of attention. Previously, she had ugly friends and wasn't used to sharing the spotlight at parties. Now we hardly talk to each other.

There is some anecdotal evidence for the contention that the good-looking are the most critical of their rivals. Several years ago, H. H. Jennings (1943) studied the social choices of adolescents living in the New York Training School for Girls. She found that beautiful girls were the most ambivalent about their feelings for their beautiful rivals. Although the beautiful and popular girls generally chose other beautiful girls as their best friends, the beauties concurrently named other beauties

Figure 10.1. Charles Dana Gibson, *Rival Beauties.* Courtesy Diablo Press.

as the girls they most hated. Jennings noted, "A girl that is another's rival for popularity, prominence, and power, is apt not to like her very much." A love-hate relationship seemingly exists between beautiful rivals.

Not only may the attractive be especially critical of the attractive, but the ugly may be most in awe of the beautiful and most prejudiced against those homely like themselves. As one member of THE GROUP observed:

> I think the ugly are the cruelest critics of other plain people. When you're ugly, your self-esteem is very fragile. You're trying so desperately to be accepted and to just survive, that you have to be totally selfish. If you have terrible acne, a limp, or a grotesque stutter, and if you allowed yourself to be seen with someone like yourself, you would be a joke. So you try to be seen with someone more attractive.

As yet, however, no research evidence exists to support the contention that the ugly are often the most prejudiced against the ugly.

Now let us consider the other possibility.

The Homely Have Even More Reasons to Be Resentful of the Beautiful/Handsome.

Although appealing men and women have *some* reason to resent their closest rivals, ugly men and women should have even *more* reason to be furious at them. For example, Elaine Hatfield once had a friend who was bright and kind but rather on the homely side, so it was difficult for her to attract men. She observed:

> How can I not be jealous of Miriam [a local beauty]? She has no trouble getting a date . . . in fact she's always complaining that men make pests of themselves! Once at work, I spotted this man . . . a salesman for the siding company next door. No one else was interested in him. I made it a point to drop by each day to talk to him. We became friends and started to meet for coffee. I invested 5 months in trying to get him interested. Finally, I thought I had succeeded. Then Miriam walks by, he looks up, and asks her out. He's known her for 15 seconds. I could have cried. How can I not hate her?

Ugly men have equal reason to resent handsome men who seem to easily sweep women off their feet.

Recent research supports the notion that, although everyone has some reason to resent the too good-looking, the ugly actually have the most negative opinions of the beautiful/handsome. In the study we described earlier, Dermer and Thiel (1975) found that the attractive women were the most convinced that "what is beautiful is good"; homely women were more critical. Everyone judged beautiful women as having more desirable personalities and as likely to have more future success than homely women. However, homely women were least likely to put beautiful women on a pedestal. On a few dimensions, the homely women actually assumed that what is beautiful might even be bad. For example, homely women were more likely to assume that beautiful women would make poor parents. (Perhaps they felt that beautiful women—whom they assumed were vain, egotistical, and unconcerned with fidelity—could not be kind, generous, and self-sacrificing mothers.)

In sum, there are limitations to the "what is beautiful is good" stereotype. Not everyone is convinced that the extraordinarily good-looking are wonderful. In fact, most of us assume they have a few character flaws—namely, selfishness and snobbishness. People whose own looks are problematic are the most sensitive to the limitations of the good-looking.

Of course, in some sense whether people are prejudiced in favor of the good-looking or prejudiced against them matter little. Regardless of its shape and direction, prejudice is unfair. One wise young woman from THE GROUP had this to say:

> I think there are some negative stereotypes associated with really good-looking men and women . . . that they are stuck up, conceited, etc. I have to admit that this isn't at all fair. When I think these things toward someone else, it is usually because I am comparing myself to her, and the comparison makes me feel inferior. So I rationalize by saying, "She may be beautiful but she probably isn't very nice." This is supposed to make me feel better, but I have to admit that it usually doesn't work.

Prejudices are unfair, but they do exist and they enormously impact the way people treat beautiful women and handsome men.

PROBLEMS THE PHYSICALLY ATTRACTIVE HAVE IN PERSONAL RELATIONSHIPS

Undoubtedly, it is good to be good-looking when it comes to developing and maintaining personal relationships. Those possessed with good looks seem to have many advantages in their social lives. In earlier chapters, we discussed the evidence indicating that people do desire the company of attractive men and women. In most people's fantasies, the "romantic other" is someone who looks like he/she just stepped out of the pages of *Glamour* magazine. When men and women do not have to worry about the possibility of being rejected, they tend to prefer the most attractive partner possible. Even long after two people meet and decide they belong together as a couple attractiveness remains important. For example, attractiveness can stimulate passion—the best aphrodisiac seems to be an attractive partner. Physical attractiveness can also be used as bargaining power in the intimate relationship; therefore, it is important not to be (or become) much less attractive than one's partner.

But personal relationships are very complex. Although attractive people *do* have some advantages in relationships, they also have to deal with certain problems. In discussing the problems the physically attractive face in their personal relationships, we will be considering not only romantic relationships but also platonic relationships with both the same sex and the opposite sex. We will walk through the friendship/dating/mating process, a step at a time, and review the problems the physically attractive may have. Most of these problems are amplified when the physically attractive relate with people somewhat less attractive than they.

"WHY CAN'T WE JUST BE FRIENDS?"

Problems Being Chums with the Same Sex

Gorgeous people sometimes have problems finding friends of the same sex. People are jealous of them, feel ugly and awkward in their company, and worry they will steal their dates. One of Elaine Hatfield's clients is Vicky Ferenzi. She described how it feels to be intimidated by a friend much more attractive than oneself. She recalled when, as a young girl in Yugoslavia, she agreed to go to a movie with a beautiful village girl. From the start Vicky was nervous because her friend was so striking—she had lovely dark hair and eyes and creamy skin. And she was a nice girl. Vicky spent a long time getting ready for the movie. When she was finally ready and dressed in a new, yellow, polka-dotted dress, she felt lovely. Then her friend arrived. Vicky looked at her glowingly beautiful friend and then at herself—a dowdy village girl in a rumpled, cheap-looking, yellow dress. She could not move—she felt ugly and clumsy. She mumbled she was sick and could not go to the movie. Thirty years later, this episode remained one of her most painful experiences. "I could never stand to see that girl. She reminded me of how ugly I was," she said.

Many women in THE GROUP talked about other problems with becoming friends with extremely attractive women. For example, many admitted that, although they knew their beautiful women friends were probably loyal, they just could not feel comfortable introducing the

beauties to their boyfriends. There was just too much to risk. What if
. . .? And then . . .?

Pat Jordon (1982), a handsome journalist, speaks of parallel problems
handsome men face in their relationships with other men:

> . . . I have been able to develop wonderful friendships with women.
> What I have not been able to do is develop friendships with men. I
> think I threaten men partly because of the ease with which I deal with
> women, an ease acquired to a certain extent, because of my looks. I like
> women, and often they like me. Men who don't like women, or who
> would like to but don't get the chances I do, resent me. Furthermore,
> they feel betrayed by me because I would rather sit in a bar and talk to
> a woman rather than sit with the men and root for a football team on
> the television set over the bar. Men feel I have gone over to the enemy,
> which says volumes about how men view relationships with women. (p.
> 96)

The above personal accounts are substantiated by some research
evidence. The evidence indicates that beautiful women and handsome
men find it especially hard to make friends with the same sex. In one
study (Krebs and Adinolfi 1975), the relationship between physical
attractiveness and social contact with members of the same sex was
examined. Four groups of men and women were selected from a group
of six hundred university freshmen, based on the sociometric ratings
they had received from their same-sex dorm mates. Fifteen men and
fifteen women who had been most frequently mentioned in response
to the sociometric probe, "Would want as a roommate," were placed
in the Accepted Group. Thirty men and women nominated to be
roommates an average number of times were placed in the Control
Group. The Rejected Group was comprised of thirty men and women
most frequently mentioned in response to the sociometric probe, "A
person you try to avoid." Finally, the fourth group was a group of
Isolates—thirty men and women mentioned least overall. Individuals
did not want them as roommates, but neither did they try to avoid
them. These men and women were simply neglected.

The men and women in these four groups were then rated for
physical attractiveness. Four men and four women (unfamiliar with the
groupings) judged the high school graduation photographs of these
individuals for physical attractiveness.

What was the relationship between physical attractiveness and social
popularity with the same sex? As might be expected, the men and
women in the Accepted Group were rated as quite good-looking, better-
looking than those in the Control Group. Those in the Control Group
were judged to be average in attractiveness and better-looking than
those in the Isolated Group, rated as least attractive of all. Surprisingly,

however, *the men and women in the Rejected Group were judged to be the most attractive of all.* These individuals were those peers said they "try to avoid."

Why were the very physically attractive most rejected by their same-sex peers? The researchers came up with several plausible reasons: Perhaps we expect so much from attractive people that when they fail us and we discover they are pretty much like ourselves, we become disillusioned and reject them. Or, possibly, the physically attractive avoid *us*—they may realize their appearances are deceiving and have learned not to allow anyone too close to avoid rejection. Another possible reason we avoid attractive people of the same sex is because we are jealous of them; we are in competition with them for dates and mates and do not want to get close enough to suffer by comparison. Finally, the physically attractive may be rejected because they have an unappealing personality. There was evidence from this study to support this last contention. All the men and women completed several personality questionnaires. The physically attractive were found to have an individualistic, ambitious, and unaffiliative personality style. The less attractive men and women, on the other hand, were more affectionate and sociable.

Mark Salmon (1983) interviewed several models from top modeling agencies in New York City. He concluded that one of the main problems beautiful women face is developing friendships with other women. Many models reported they felt estranged from other women. The beautiful women were always winning men's approval, taking it away from other women. The "rivalry" was unintentional and unwanted, but it alienated other women nonetheless.

Problems Being Chums with the Opposite Sex

Homely men and women often complain that members of the opposite sex offer them friendship instead of romance and passion. They tire of being only a "buddy" when they really want more. Stunningly good-looking men and women have just the opposite problem. They often have a difficult time forming platonic relationships with the opposite sex because potential friends keep trying to become lovers.

As one beautiful woman from THE GROUP observed:

> I am small and blonde. Many men assume, even before they've met me, that I am interested in romance. When men I don't even know start up with me, I get nonresponsive and irritable. I know what it will lead to. It's embarrassing. It's exhausting. No one will take no for an answer. I get tired of saying no, again, and again, even so politely.

Salmon (1983) found that the same problem was experienced by the beautiful models he interviewed from New York City. These women reported that they often felt like "public property" because men approached them without an invitation.

Another member of THE GROUP reported yet another problem—when men finally do realize she really means no, they get angry. They attack her as a snob and tell her she is cold and frigid. Every encounter is therefore made unpleasant. Pat Jordan (1982), the journalist we cited earlier, describes the same problem. Jordan portrays himself as a big man with a full, black beard. He wears sunglasses, jeans, and cowboy boots. He smokes cigars. Women notice him. They react strongly to what they see—although the way they react varies. Once, at a cocktail party, a woman jabbed her finger in his chest and said, "Who are you? Or rather, who do you think you are?" Jordan assumed his good looks threatened her. Another woman, the wife of a man he barely knew, tried to humiliate him in public, because, Jordan assumed, he was good-looking while her husband was bald and fat.

Jordan points out yet another problem with being good-looking. There is always a certain sexual flirtation between men and women. Everyone has fleeting sexual fantasies about one another. For some, however, those fantasies are not enough. When Jordan is not interested, some women feel betrayed and strike out. Friendship is not enough for them. Many beautiful women, attracted to him because of his looks, turned on him when he failed to respond. A teenaged girl with huge breasts, a friend of his daughter, used to flirt with him in front of his wife. Later, when her friendship with his daughter cooled, she accused him of harrassing her. A woman magazine editor in her forties confided to him one day over a business lunch that he had hurt her feelings. After all these years, he had never made a sexual pass at her. A television actress told him he was sexual in a way her husband was not. When he did not pursue her advances, she telephoned his wife at midnight and told her she would destroy him.

To survive the opposite sex, beautiful women and handsome men must develop an array of ingenious techniques for keeping relationships light. For example, when a stunning woman says "no," most men keep right on trying. Yet, if she were to respond to every man expressing an interest in her, she would be labeled a "slut." She's damned if she does, damned if she doesn't. In self-protection, most beautiful women have developed an array of automatic techniques for fending men off, for pushing them away.

This aloof, reluctant style has certain costs. Beautiful women may attract men who have trouble getting close, and find it hard to make *friends* with men. Men may encounter similar problems forming intimate friendships with women.

The attractive may also encounter problems in romantic relation-ships. We will now discuss *these* problems.

Problems Getting Romantic Relationships Started

Earlier, we found that the good-looking have an overwhelming advan-tage in finding romantic partners. Almost everyone, good-looking or not, *prefers* an aesthetically appealing date or mate and will usually risk a great deal to ask them out.

Researchers have found only two instances in which men and women hesitate to approach the good-looking—when it is hard to disguise their intentions and when they fear rejection.

FEAR OF REJECTION

In chapter 4, we reviewed evidence showing that if men and women were assured of any date of their choice, they would choose to date the best—the most stunning, most personable, date possible. When rejection is a very real possibility, however, men and women moderate their dating aspirations and express interest in someone closer to their own level of attractiveness (Berscheid et al. 1971; Huston 1973; Shanteau and Nagy 1979). In life, however, "the best" is rarely available on demand. In 1983, Tom Selleck complained in an article in the *Honolulu Advertiser* that he actually had trouble meeting women because his fame scared women away. He lived to rue that statement. Almost the entire student body at the University of Hawaii decided *they* were not too shy to approach him. Conceivably, a beautiful woman or a handsome man could stay home month after month, year after year, because no one guessed they were lonely, but we doubt it. They could drop a hint to one of their friends.

BYZANTINE APPROACHES

Possibly, the good-looking do not get approached less often, but the problem is they receive "muddy" messages. If we want to date a homely to average looking person we can afford to be reasonably direct in our approach. We may boldly say, "I'm attracted to you and want to date you." "I think you and I could have fun together. Let's go out on Saturday night and see." We can expect to receive direct feedback. The person is either interested or not.

Our approach to a very attractive person may be quite different. We may stutter and stammer and, finally, shyly mention that, since both of us have to study for the trig exam over the weekend, we could study together on Saturday night over a bowl of popcorn. Such an indirect approach reduces the chances of rejection. The other person can decline the offer, and we can assume he/she does not care about getting a good grade or he/she has already studied enough. We do not have to conclude the attractive person is rejecting *us*. We can leave the interaction with our egos intact.

Researchers conducted an experiment to test whether men are more likely to approach an attractive woman if they have a plausible excuse for doing so and if the desire to do so can be kept covert (Bernstein, Stephenson, Snyder, and Wicklund 1983). The experimenter claimed to be examining people's reactions to silent comedy movies. When the man arrived, an attractive woman dressed in a halter top was already seated in front of one of the two television monitors in the room. Although the men undoubtedly assumed the woman was a college student also participating as a subject, she was actually an assistant to the experimenter. Some of the men were randomly assigned to a "low ambiguity" (or no excuse) condition—they were told that, although usually a choice was offered between two films, one of the two videotape machines was broken and, therefore, both television monitors would show the same film. The other men were randomly assigned to a "high ambiguity" (or excuse) condition. These men were told they could choose between two movies, "Slapstick" or "Sad Clowns" (both films were described). The men in both conditions were then told to take a seat in front of whichever monitor they wished. One chair was three inches from the attractive woman, and two free chairs were in front of the other monitor.

In the low ambiguity (or no excuse) condition, 75 percent of the men chose to sit alone. Although they may have wanted to sit next to the attractive woman in the halter top, they really had no excuse to do so since both television monitors were running the same film. However, in the high ambiguity (or excuse) condition, 75 percent of the men chose to sit next to her. They had an excuse to do so—they could pretend they preferred the firm being shown on that television monitor. The results of this study demonstrate that men may only pursue their interest in attractive women if they have a plausible excuse for doing so.

A second experiment was conducted by the same researchers, this time without the attractive woman in the halter top. Instead, male and female subjects were randomly paired to run through a procedure similar to that used in the first study. Thus, the woman in each dyad could range from being quite homely to being very attractive (the attractiveness of both the man and the woman in each dyad was judged by two experimenters). Once again, it was found that men were more likely to sit next to an attractive woman if they had an excuse to do so. If the woman was unattractive, on the other hand, whether or not the men had an excuse did not seem to matter. In general, they avoided her. As might be expected, the men's own physical attractiveness affected their approach tendencies. Extremely attractive men were more likely to approach attractive women than were less attractive men (presumably, they would be less fearful of rejection).

There is no question that others desire to affiliate with attractive women and men. However, good-looking people have to deal with the fact that the desire to affiliate may not always be obvious.

Problems Maintaining Romantic Relationships

When they do find the right mate, beautiful women and handsome men well encounter problems in maintaining their relationships. There are two sides to every relationship. Love can turn sour for either or both partners. Let us first consider very briefly the love felt *by* the attractive partner for his/her mate. Earlier in this chapter, we observed that people *believe* beautiful men and women are more likely to engage in extramarital affairs and to end up divorced (Dermer and Thiel 1975; Smith, Sprecher & DeLamater, 1983b). There is also evidence indicating that attractive people actually do have more extramarital alternatives than do their homely counterparts (White 1980a). If one partner is much more desirable than the other, the more desirable partner is more likely to have extramarital affairs after a few years of marriage than the less desirable partner (Hatfield, Walster, and Traupmann 1979). So, one problem for attractive people in keeping their own love alive is in avoiding temptation. When things get rough in the relationship, it is dangerously easy for them to find "something better." Many therapists agree that beautiful people do not always have the talents and patience required to keep working at intimate relationships. The odds are against their ever learning these skills. It is simply too easy to give up and move along to the next affair; too hard to painfully acquire the complex skills needed to make an intimate relationship work.

Now let us consider what may happen to the love felt *for* the attractive person. Attractive people may have problems *believing* their partner is still in love with them, and they may have difficulties keeping their partner in love with them. Later in this chapter we will discuss how attractive men and women sometimes discount the positive information they receive if they believe the flatterers might have ulterior motives. In the same way, beautiful men and women may discount expressions of love if they believe the other loves only what he/she sees on the outside and not their "real selves." This mistrust can make for a shaky relationship.

The same doubts may actually be going through the mind of the one who loves an attractive person. He may ask, "Do I really love her, or am I just attracted to her physical looks?" Psychologists have suggested that when there is a great deal of extrinsic justification for engaging in an attractive activity, interest in that activity is decreased. This premise has been called the "overjustification effect" (Lepper and Greene 1976; Lepper, Greene, and Nisbett 1973). When applied to romantic relationships, this principle suggests that *if* we think we are attracted to someone in order to obtain extrinsic rewards (such as his/her beauty rubbing off on us), our affection for the person will be less than if the extrinsic rewards were not so obvious.

Two studies were conducted to discover if this premise may actually operate in intimate relationships. In the first study (Seligman, Fazio, and Zanna 1976), men and women heard a tape recording of a man responding to twenty-one questions about his relationship with his girlfriend. Three of the questions dealt with the extrinsic rewards the woman might have to offer. The man either described the girlfriend as wealthy, as physically attractive, and as having an influential father, *or* he described her as not being wealthy or good-looking and as not having an influential father. After listening to the tape recording, the men and women were asked how much they *thought* the man loved his girlfriend. The men and women thought the man loved his girlfriend *less* when she had the extrinsic rewards to offer.

In the second study by these researchers (Seligman, Fazio, and Zanna 1980), men and women were asked to think of their own relationship with a romantic partner. Some of the men and women were made to think of the extrinsic reasons for being involved in the relationship (for example, "I go out with _____because my friends thing more highly of me since I began seeing him/her"). Others were made to think of the intrinsic reasons for being involved in the relationship (for example, "I go out with _____because we share the same interests and concerns"). The men and women then indicated how much they loved their partner, as measured by Rubin's (1970) Loving Scale. It was found that the men and women who focused on the extrinsic rewards of the relationship felt less love for their partner than did the men and women who focused on the intrinsic rewards.

The love for an attractive person can also diminish over time because good looks may lose their appeal. At the start of an affair, good looks may be enough. Eventually, however, lovers begin to take the good looks for granted and begin to demand more. Playwright George Bernard Shaw (1905) observed, "Beauty is all very well at first sight; but who ever looks at it when it has been in the house three days?" (p. 169).

The problem arises, of course, if the beautiful have trouble providing more. It is sometimes easy for the good-looking to get spoiled. Since things are so easy early on, the attractive may come to expect too much and to give too little. By the time stunning men and women realize that more (far more) will be required in an intimate relationship, it may be too late.

As we were writing this book, Elaine Hatfield discussed with her colleagues at King Kalakaua Center in Honolulu the possible disadvantages of being attractive. Most of them, based upon their extensive clinical experiences, argued that the good-looking really do have problems. Our therapist discussed the differences between her two daughters. Her oldest daughter is beautiful and very smart. She became a class leader by just smiling. She is calm, aloof, and pursued by men. She assumes she will marry someone who is good-looking and rich and will spend her days swimming at the country club. Her grades are poor; but she can not see any reason to work and does not. The therapist said her heart just breaks for her daughter—she believes a desperate life is in store for her. Her second daughter is not nearly so good-looking, not nearly so smart; yet, she has already become a good "psychologist." She knows how her friends think and feel. She is attuned to be subtleties of life. She knows how to tiptoe around painful topics, how to encourage her friends to talk about the problems that concern them, how to dodge and dart to make relationships go smoothly. She has the emotional control and the patience to maintain a good relationship. In this example, then, beauty is definitely not for the best.

Eventually, beautiful women and handsome men face a final problem. Extraordinarily good-looking people are likely to attract lovers very concerned about looks. That is fine as long as a person is young and beautiful, but all of us inevitably have off days. Worse yet, we grow older. Many beautiful people, then, face a crisis in their fiftys and sixtys. We discussed this problem in chapter 9, "Beauty Through the Life Span."

In Sum

We can enumerate a number of problems the beautiful *might* face in their intimate relationships. As yet, however, there is surprisingly little research on how widespread such problems are. Surely some beautiful women and handsome men face obstacles, but subsequent research will have to establish whether the ugly truths about beauty are quite so ugly as some people think.

THE REALITY: THE DARKER SIDE

In the first part of this chapter, we considered people's prejudices against good-looking men and women, and the way this stereotyping affects the treatment the attractive receive. Do the good-looking really benefit from the attention they get, or is attractiveness sometimes a handicap?

In chapter 8, we considered some of the strengths good-looking men and women acquire as a consequence of preferential treatment. For example, we found that attractive people end up with a little more confidence, with more control over their own fates, at ease in social situations, and with sounder physical and mental health than do homely people. Are the attractive prone to any weakness of personality or character? Yes. In this section, we will consider the problems the physically attractive may have in developing positive self-esteem and sound mental health. We will end this chapter by presenting an example of how beauty can bring tragedy to a family.

Self-esteem

As we pointed out earlier, the most gorgeous men and women possess only a little more self-esteem than the homely. How can that be? Shouldn't they have *far more* self-esteem? Certainly good-looking people seem to have all the advantages. They start off possessing everything society values. They seemingly receive preferential treatment everywhere, from the classroom to the courtroom. How could they end up with not much more confidence than the rest of us? There are probably several reasons (we already discussed in chapter 8 a few such reasons).

First, in American society, to depend on our looks for all our self-regard probably means trouble. Appearance is not a very stable or permanent basis for self-esteem. Not everyone agrees about who is attractive, so even the best-looking are bound to receive mixed reviews. Furthermore, no matter how attractive people are, there will always be times when they do not feel attractive—when suffering from a cold or when they get old. We can always find the flaws in ourselves. Objective observers may tell us we are cute and adorable, but we are likely to mutter, "Sure, except for my nose." Finally, no matter how good-looking a person is, there will always be others who seem better-looking. Many of the best looking people compare themselves with someone better-looking, someone younger, and conclude they are not good enough.

Yesterday, when my colleague, Dr. Richard Rapson, and I (Elaine Hatfield) were driving to breakfast, we watched the joggers running along Kahala Avenue and delighted in the variation of their bodies. We spotted two women who were particularly appealing, sexy and healthy. We saw a middle-aged woman with a craggy, American Indian face, dark and weather-beaten, with a lithe runner's body, then a blonde girl, with a cute little squat fireplug of a body. Yet, if we had told them honestly how delightful their bodies were, each would have been hurt. In America, advertisers have a vested interest in convincing us there is only *one way* to be good-looking. We have to look the right way and dress the right way. The bland, standard body is the ideal. To have a "weather beaten face," to have a "squat little fireplug of a body" is to be a failure.

What happens if the good-looking recognize it is foolish to base their self-regard on looks? What happens if they choose to rely their self-regard on how personable, bright, and kind they are? Seemingly, the latter would be the better strategy, but it has problems too.

Harold Sigall and John Michela (1976), in an article aptly titled, "I'll Bet You Say That to All the Girls," point out that it is harder for good-looking people (especialy beautiful women) to accept praise at face value. If you are homely and people assure you you are intelligent, witty, and charming, you have every reason to believe them. If you are a gorgeous blonde, however, and a man tells you you have a great personality (and he has one eye on the buttons of your blouse), you may doubt his sincerity. Sigal and Michela discuss this phenomenon in greater detail:

> She [a beautiful woman] may discount the favorable information, think-ing that perhaps it is motivated by the flatterer's attempt to win her over—an attempt which is undertaken primarily on account of her phys-ical attributes. Of course, this would lead the woman to have difficulty in evaluating herself in a general way. On the one hand, she is told that she is intelligent, resourceful, generous, etc. On the other hand, she is not sure whether her exalters are earnest in their praise. . . . While they may get more positive feedback by virtue of their good looks, they often may interpret the feedback as insincere and end up uncertain of their general worth. (pp. 612–613)

The above scientists designed an experiment to test the theory that good-looking women are likely to question any praise for their non-physical characteristics. In their experiment, they ingeniously manipu-lated women's feelings about their own physical attractiveness—leading some to feel particularly appealing and others to feel particularly dowdy. They asked the women to rate for physical and sexual attractiveness several yearbook pictures of women and then to indicate how they felt about their own attractiveness "compared with the average attractiveness of those people pictured." The photographs were rigged. Sometimes all the photographs were of very homely women—by comparison, the women could not help but feel good. At other times, the comparison was depressing—all the photos were of great beauties.

The women were then asked to write "an innovative essay" to be evaluated by a man in an adjacent room. Some women thought they could be seen by this other man through a one-way mirror, while other women believed they could not be seen. In every case, the man evaluated the essay in glowing terms.

It was found that "attractive" women found the man who praised them more credible when they believed he had *not* seen them. For example, the "attractive" women who believed they had not been seen by the evaluator rated him more frank, geunine, and trustworthy, and less deceitful and manipulative than did "attractive" women who believed they had been seen. "Homely" women, on the other hand, were more impressed with the man's credibility when they thought he had seen them than when they thought he had not.

In sum, the physically attractive have their own set of problems in developing a positive self-esteem.

Mental Health

The physically attractive are also not immune to mental health problems. In the book, *Helplessness*, Martin E. Seligman (1975) describes the case of a Golden Girl:

GOLDEN GIRL

Nancy entered the university with a superb high-school record. She had been president and salutatorian of her class, and a popular and pretty cheerleader. Everything she wanted had always fallen into her lap; good grades came easily and boys fell over themselves competing for her attention. She was an only child, and her parents doted on her, rushing to fulfill her every whim; her successes were their triumphs, her failures their agony. Her friends nicknamed her Golden Girl.

When I met her in her sophomore year, she was no longer a Golden Girl. She said that she felt empty, that nothing touched her any more; her classes were boring and the whole academic system seemed an oppressive conspiracy to stifle her creativity. The previous semester she had received two F's. She had "made it" with a succession of young men, and was currently living with a dropout. She felt exploited and worthless after each sexual adventure; her current relationship was on the rocks, and she felt little but contempt for him and for herself. She had used soft drugs extensively and had once enjoyed being carried away on them. But now even drugs had little appeal.

She was majoring in philosophy, and had a marked emotional attraction to Existentialism: like the existentialists, she believed that life is absurd and that people must create their own meaning. This belief filled her with despair. Her despair increased when she perceived her own attempts to create meaning—participation in the movements for women's liberation and against the war in Vietnam—as fruitless. When I reminded her that she had been a talented student and was still an attractive and valuable human being, she burst into tears: "I fooled you, too." (pp. 2–3)

Seligman argues that golden men and women are "at risk" for mental health problems i.e., they are prone to depression. People get depressed, he argues, when they believe nothing they do will have any impact on their lives—i.e., they suffer from "learned helplessness." Golden men and women are loved for what they are (their good looks), not for what they do. They can be charming and work hard or be disagreeable and loaf—no matter, they are loved, treated with respect, given everything. As a consequence, they build up no "immunity" against disaster. They do not think of themselves as competent, energetic people who can actively shape their fates. They have no practice in trying and failing, then trying again until they finally succeed. Thus, when disaster strikes (and eventually it does)—when someone rejects them, when a lover or parent dies, when they fail at school or work, when they merely break a dish—they despair. They feel helpless. Thus, Seilgman believes, to be a golden man or woman is to be mentally at risk.

As yet, there is little evidence in support of Seligman's argument. In fact, the evidence we reviewed in chapter 3 suggests that attractive men and women are *less* likely than others to develop psychological problems. Of course, future research may provide a more balanced assessment.

Next, we will consider a family that was at risk and *did* suffer.

The Sedgwick Family: The Beautiful People

One of the advantages of a pluralistic society is that everyone can emphasize the importance of the traits they possess and end up feeling good about themselves. If you are beautiful, you can convince yourself aesthetics is important. If you are brilliant, you can convince yourself a life dedicated to science is ultimately fulfilling. If you have a sensitivity in dealing with people, you can argue that this asset is what counts. For the beautiful, however, such logic possesses a dark side. If you decide appearances are what matter, you are in trouble when you encounter the harsh realities.

Some beauties do succumb to the temptation to accept such a superficial value system. They accept only a narrow band of "beautiful people" and end up losing all other meaning in life. An example: The Sedgwicks were one of the oldest American families (see Stein and Plimpton 1982). Judge Theodore Sedgwick was a political ally of George Washington and Alexander Hamilton at the time of the American Revolution and became Speaker of the House of Representatives. The descendants continued the tradition: They became the "beautiful people" of the 1960s.

At first glance, this extraordinary family *seemed* eminently successful. Edie (the daughter) became a companion of artist Andy Warhol and of New York cult figures. The boys went to Harvard. Gloria Schiff (director of a New York modeling agency) describes Edie (in Stein and Plimpton 1982):

> Sombody told me that Edie was adorable and available to be photographed for *Vogue*. I remembered from either a previous photograph or a previous description that she was an enchanting, beguiling little girl. We did the session out in Brooklyn Heights, where Gianni Penati photographed her.
>
> On the way out to Penati's studio I remember sitting in the car thinking: "My God, we've got a child! I mean, she's completely child-like."
>
> Penati creates a very nice atmosphere. He flirts, he's mad, he's fun. He says, "Ahhh, you're so beautiful! They never told me you were so beautiful!" That kind of thing. He's a mad Italian. "Ahhh, there is the sex image of all time." He's adorable, and he has tremendous sex appeal. Totally charming and very childlike. He would be totally keen about a girl like Edie because she had a nymphet quality which he always adored.
>
> She loosened up and became very with it . . . giggling and laughing, kind of oblivious to the camera, and you realized what wonderful things could happen to her as a model or a star . . . visualizing her dressed in different outfits or in other locations. I thought, "Oh, God, she'd be so much more beautiful in evening clothes." There was a tremendous range in how she looked and the way she projected.
>
> There was also a paradoxical side to her. She contradicted herself all day long. She'd be flirtatious with Gianni, then she'd be a child, clinging to me: she'd be cocky, then shy, then competent. She'd go through a whole range of emotional behavior, which is typical, isn't it, of a lot of stars. I adored her smile and the fawnlike quality she had. What is amazing is that her face and her looks in these pictures are totally contemporary. They could appear in any fashion magazine tomorrow. They have no date to them. Don't you agree? She was wise with her energy. Surprisingly wise.
>
> I remember going with the pictures to Diana Vreeland, who was the editor-in-chief, saying, "We've got a star! There's no doubt about it, she is terrific! A great model! We should do a whole issue on her." (pp. 296–299)

The Sedgwicks were fine, so long as you were young and beautiful, they could be devastating if you were not. Susan Wilkins, a house guest, described the family attitude toward people who did not measure up—people with odd corners to their minds, those with their own individual looks and feelings, and people who did not match the Sedgwicks' tryannical standards of beauty.

> We arrived and were immediately ushered into the presence of this "man," this father with his exaggerated views about human beauty. Nobody who wasn't beautiful was allowed around. He began by making comments about each of the bridesmaids, the length of our legs, the size of our bosoms. There were two of us he took a particular liking to—Ginny Backus, who was a knockout, and Shelley Dweight, who was Jerry's sister and had that Irish red hair that caught the sun. So while much of that week was spent in tennis and swimming, which should have been fun, all the time you were being made to wonder whether you measured up or not—whether you cut the mustard. It certainly helped if you were beautiful and rich.
>
> There were a lot of tears that week, a lot of us in our rooms crying—bridesmaids, the bride. *Lots* of tension. I remember it as being physically exhausting. We went from dawn to dusk. The tension was phenomenal. *Phenomenal!* There was something almost mythological about what was happening. Duke Sedgwick reminded me of somebody from Mount Olympus. I'm thinking of Titian's *Rape of Europa* in the Isabella Steward Gardner Museum. *That* was the feeling. It was a stud farm, that house, with this great stallion parading around in as little as he could. We were the mares. But it wasn't sex. It was breeding . . . and there's a difference, of course. The air was filled with an aura of procreation. Not carnal lust, but just breeding in the sense of not only re-creating life but a certain kind of life, a certain elite, a superior race. There was no romance. It was stultifying. (p. 88)

Then things fell apart, as they always do. The Sedgwick family had blossomed in the world of dreams, and they lacked the inner resources to deal with the imperfections of reality. When faced with the difficulties of real life, Edie despaired—she plunged heavily into drugs and was in and out of mental hospitals. Henry Gledzahler, a counselor of Edie's, describes what happened:

> I suppose Edie thought of herself as a caterpillar that had turned into a butterfly. She had thought of herself as just another kid in a big, rather unhappy family, and all of a sudden the spotlights were on her and she was being treated as something very, very special, but inside she felt like a lump of dirt. Then when she was being paid less attention to, she didn't know who she was. That possibility of destruction was built into the weakness of her personality. We have to get used to the reality that we're alone. If you can't get used to it, then you go mad. And she went kind of mad.
>
> I came to her apartment a couple of times, which I thought very grim. It was very dark, and the talk was always about how hungover she was, or how high she was yesterday, or how high she would be tomorrow. She was very nervous, very fragile, very thin, very hysterical.

You could hear her screaming even when she wasn't screaming—this sort of supersonic whistling. (p. 279)

Jonathan Sedgwick, Edie's brother, gives his account:

My mother finally took Edie out of Manhattan State Hospital and brought her back to the ranch in the late fall of 1968. She couldn't walk. She'd just fall over . . . like she had no motor control left at all. The doctor did a dye test of some sort and it showed the blood wasn't reaching certain parts of the brain; they said that in the X-ray pictures it looked like a Swiss cheese. She couldn't talk! "kk . . . kk . . . ggg . . . ddd . . . wowo . . . well, uh, well, no, well . . . sa-ay." It was really strange, man, awful. Once in a while three or four words would come out in a rush. Slowly she began to come back. She knew she could do it, but she needed people to have faith in her. I always believed she would make it. I'd say, "Edie, goddam it, get your head together. Man, you have the head to do it. Let it come out." She'd say, "I . . . I . . . I . . . know . . know . . . know . . . I . . . I . . . can . . . but it's ha . . . ha . . . hard." (p. 370)

Edie finally died of a barbiturate overdose in 1971 at the age of twenty-eight. Her brother Minty hung himself; her brother Bobby destroyed himself in a motorcycle accident.

Obviously, good-looking people *can* possess profound values. There are many appealing people who have used their appeal to get in a position to make critical scientific discoveries, to compose masterpieces, or to become humanitarians. Beautiful people do not inevitably develop superficial values; they just have a greater temptation to do so.

Perhaps it was ever this:

Rabbi Joshua, the son of a Hananiah, is described in the Talmud as one of those men whose minds are far more beautiful than their bodies. His great learning, wit, and wisdom had earned for him not only the love and respect of the populace but even the favor of the Emperor Trajan.

Being often in court, one of the princesses remarked on his ugliness.

"How is it," she said, "that such glorious wisdom is enclosed in so ugly a vessel?"

The rabbi, not in the least offended, asked the princess in what sort of vessels her father kept his wines . . .

"Why, in earthen vessels," replied the princess . . .

"Now you should be convinced," said the rabbi, "that wine keeps best in plain vessels. And the same is true of wisdom."

"But," continued the princess, "I know many persons who are both wise and handsome."

"True," replied the sage, "but they would most probably be still wiser were they less handsome." (Mandel 1974, 36)

IN SUMMARY

In this chapter, we have reviewed some of the ugly truths about beauty. Good looks are *generally* an advantage. They can also, however, expose one to some peculiar problems and temptations.

We first demonstrated that the belief "what is beautiful is good" is not universal. Certain character flaws are attributed to the beautiful. People assume the beautiful are self-centered, selfish, unresponsive to others' needs, and adulterous. Understandably, the unattractive are especially likely to point to this darker side in the attractive.

We also enumerated several problems the physically attractive can face in their personal relationships—both in friendship and romance. Finally, we discovered that the physically attractive can experience certain obstacles in developing favorable self-images and sound mental health.

Chapter 11

SUSAN LEE: A CASE HISTORY

Question: "Would you like to be better-looking?"
Answer: (Incredulous) "Of course."

Of course? Maybe you should think a moment before answering. In chapters 1–10, we reviewed the evidence indicating the good-looking men and women have an enormous advantage in life. From this evidence alone, a person might be tempted to conclude that everyone must be profoundly concerned about appearances, that wise individuals should do all they can to make themselves as appealing as possible, and that any other course is foolhardy.

We do not believe that statement. Life is far more complicated than that. A variety of considerations shape men and women's choices about how to look. All of us want to look good, sometimes; but we all have many reasons to look just like ourselves, or sometimes even ugly. In fact, there are a variety of costs and benefits to consider when deciding if you really want to invest a great deal in appearances, thereby sacrificing other things.

In this chapter, we will review the case of Susan Lee and the issues *she* was forced to confront when deciding how much effort she wished

Figure 11.1. Courtesy, George, Alma, and Charles Hatfield, Boulevard Dock, Detroit, 1924.

to expend on appearances. This case history is designed to remind us of the complicated role beauty/ugliness plays in real people's lives.

Chapter 11 is in quite a different form than chapters 1–10. In the preceding chapters, we presented a single theme (i.e., beauty is important) and documented that point by citing a series of studies. Thread by thread we constructed a simple fabric. Chapter 11 will be a richer tapestry. Here, threads will appear, disappear, and reappear. Sometimes ideas will be knotted together, only to be teased apart with patient prodding. Slowly, however, the pattern of our argument will emerge.

By the end of chapter 11, we hope our readers will have an understanding and feeling for our simple thesis: The research literature suggests "beauty is all," but, in real life, things are far more complicated than that—there are many paths to a fulfilling life. In chapter 12 (our concluding chapter) we will return to our usual format. We will discuss the research psychologists have done to answer the question "Self-Improvement—Is It Worth It?"

THE CASE OF SUSAN LEE

For several years, I (Elaine Hatfield) and Richard Rapson have done marital and family therapy at King Kalakaua Center for Psychotherapy in Honolulu, Hawaii.) Our usual procedure in family therapy is to focus on the client (or couple) most interested in change. During the course of therapy, we get acquainted with the grandparents, parents, friends, and acquaintances who populate the clients' lives. This knowledge helps us understand why clients act as they do and gives us some ideas as to which alternative solutions to their problems are possible, given the world in which they find themselves.

One spring day, Susan Lee dropped by to see us at the King Kalakaua Center. (Ms. Lee is actually an amalgam of *many* cases we have seen.) Susan was an exotic woman. Her mother was from New York and was Jewish. Her father was part Chinese, part Hawaiian. She had dark sweeping eyelashes, expressive black eyes, an elfin face, and black hair that fell to her waist. She was fifty pounds overweight. She was hoping we could help her lose weight via hypnosis—or something. The issues Susan confronted when deciding how much she wanted to sacrifice to be better-looking are typical of those most people face when contemplating such changes.

A FAMILY HISTORY

Susan's parents had always had a tumultuous marriage. They claimed to have fallen out of love on their honeymoon. Since then, they had been in bitter conflict. They screamed, shouted, insulted, and threatened to kill one another. Once her mother had thrown a meat cleaver at her father. He shrugged it off. Her mother had had a series of affairs with very young men. Her father "couldn't care less."

Her mother was determined that Susan's future would be right. Susan's mother was pressuring her to get married. She was sure Susan could find someone "just right," if only she could lose weight. But she couldn't, and now, she was desperate. She had seen and rejected five therapists before coming to King Kalakaua. She hoped Dr. Rapson and I could help her attract the lover that was just out of reach.

Our first step was to find out what Susan stood to gain by continuing to be overweight. Most dieters have trouble losing weight because they are fighting a guerilla action with themselves—partly they want to be thin, but partly they do not. And it was that "partly they do not" that we wanted to find out about. We decided to begin long-term therapy to deal with her problems in forming intimate relationships. We would use hypnotherapy to help her lose weight.

In session 1, I began the hypnotic induction:

> Imaging you are in an elevator. The lights on the panel over the elevator door are glaring at you. They're bright green. They mark the

50th floor, the 49th, 48th. Soon the elevator will begin to sink down
. . . down. . . . As it moves, downward . . . downward . . . you can
choose how deep a hypnotic trance *you* wish to sink into.

When Susan reached the "first floor" and was in a deep hypnotic
trance, I asked her to talk, in turn, to two advocates—the Susan who
desperately wanted to be thin and the Susan equally insistent on staying
fat:

> Let them each speak in turn. Let them argue as forcefully as they
> can for each of their positions. *You* can listen to all they have to say
> and make the decision about how much you are going to listen to
> them—how much *you* want to weigh.

The issues Susan raised, in this and subsequent sessions, illuminate
the concerns shaping anyone's rational/emotional decision on what
they want to look like.

Susan #1 Speaks: The Pros of Beauty

Susan #1 was clear. She insisted on becoming beautiful. She said,
"Everyone wants to be good-looking. Why wouldn't I?" She would
certainly get support for this contention. George Masters (1977), a beauty
counselor, in explaining why he wrote his book on beauty, said, "It
was inspired by the memory of Marilyn Monroe's face gazing earnestly
into her mirror and saying wistfully, 'Please, George, make me look
beautiful,' echoing the plaintive secret wish of all women" (p. xiii).

No women is ever rich enough, famous enough, not to care about
beauty. You might think Lillian Hellman (playwright, member of the
National Institute of Arts and Letters, and author of *The Children's
Hour*) or Eleanor Roosevelt (First Lady, United States representative to
the United Nations' General Assembly, and winner of hundreds of
humanitarian awards) would be beyond such concerns, but when asked
if they had any regrets in life, *both* answered, "Just one. I wish I had
been pretty."

Susan had heard horror stories about what happened to women
who did not "measure up." For example, one of her boyfriends told
her that when he was thirteen years old and just beginning to become
interested in girls, he began tentatively exploring his first intimate
relationship. He was painfully shy. His "date" was too. "What do you
really think of me?" she asked. To his horror, he found himself replying,
"You have a nose like Joe Garagiola." She did not ask again.

"Everyone wants to be beautiful," Susan repeated. "Why couldn't
I?" The research we reviewed in chapters 1–10 documents the tremendous importance beauty has for most people. So Susan was not
the only one. Everyone she knew thought beauty matters. If she could

lose fifty pounds, she could be proud of herself, her parents would be relieved, and she could get started on her life. Right now she was disgusted with herself and her body. She felt like a pig, sickenly stuffing herself with food. Susan's reasons for wanting to be beautiful—for wanting to weigh 110 instead of 160—were clear enough.

More interesting were Susan's reasons for wanting to stay just the way she was.

Susan #2 Speaks: It Is Not Worth It

Some of the disadvantages of dieting are obvious, and Susan ticked these off. When you like food, you get a great deal of pleasure out of pouring over cookbooks, planning special dinners, methodically peeling and chopping food with friends, and sitting around eating. Food adds sparkle to a busy life. It is hard to find a substitute.

Susan hated to exercise. The idea of even strolling around the block was unappealing.

> "I joined an exercise class once," she recalled. "The first few days were kind of fun. I was sore. It was fascinating to discover where my muscles were. It was fun to find yourself walking like a duck. (I strained my muscles doing squats.) But the fun soon wore off. Soon, I was dreading the exercise classes. The sweat pouring off my body. My muscles quivering. It was excruciatingly boring. I'd count the seconds, hoping the time was up, and find that just ten minutes had gone by. I never got the pleasure some people do from a vigorous workout. I hated every minute of it and found good excuses not to go."

Part of the reason, then, that Susan did not lose weight was that she was not willing to make any sacrifices. Dorothy Parker, she said, (1944) best described her feelings:

Observation

If I don't drive around the park,
I'm pretty sure to make my mark.
If I'm in bed each night by ten,
I may get back my looks again.
If I abstain from fun and such,
I'll probably amount to much;
But I shall stay the way I am,
Because I do not give a damn.

Under hypnosis, Susan offered other, murkier reasons for being fat, but unless you listened carefully, you would be confused about what she was saying. Her words came out in a troubled jumble:

"My family was always in turmoil.

"My mother is charming. She and I are alot alike—we think alike, dress alike, even look alike—except that she's thin and I'm fat. Everyone thinks my mother and I are the same age. In fact, the man she's having an affair with right now is just a little older than I am.

"I don't know what my dad thinks about that. He always says he doesn't care.

". . . When I was a little girl, I was always confused as to what I was really like. In part, I was a princess. When our family lived in Hong Kong (in my youth) we always had servants. I was always dressed just so. Never a hair was out of place, I knew I was prettier, better, than everyone else. On the other hand, secretly I often felt ugly. When I look at old pictures of myself, I see what other people must have seen. A plain, dowdy, chubby little girl.

"If I were thin, I'd be irresistable. If only I were thin. If I were thin, I could have anyone I wanted.

". . . I had a dream last night. It was horrible. I was on a small raft, trying to negotiate a river. I fell into the water. It was filled with snakes. Thousands of black, frightening snakes, thrashing around. It was disgusting."

Confusing messages—but the better we got to know Susan, the clearer her concerns became. Then, we thought a second reason Susan did not lose weight was that she was desperately afraid to get intimate with anyone—a layer of fat protected her from getting close.

THE THERAPISTS GO OUT FOR COFFEE

Each week after Susan Lee's session, Dick Rapson and I would drop in at Little Jodie's Bakery for coffee and pastry to discuss her case. (There is a certain irony in going to a pastry shop to discuss the problem of obesity.) Our conversations about Susan's case, helps to remind us of the variety of factors, besides looks, that shape the quality of men and women's lives.

Conversation #1: What Is Not the Problem
Susan Lee assumed that her sole problem was her appearance. We disagreed. Twenty years ago, when we began our research on beauty (Berscheid and Hatfield, [Walster] 1974), we seemed to be fighting an uphill battle. In our earlier article, we spent a good deal of time pointing out that good looks are terribly important—that social scientists could not continue to treat the topic as taboo. Its importance, we stated, must be acknowledged.

Somehow, by the 1980s, things changed. In fact, they may have gone too far in the opposite direction. In our 1974 review of the existing attractiveness research, Ellen Berscheid and I could find only a few dozen studies on the topic. In the decade since our review article, *Psychological Abstracts* has reviewed more than a thousand articles on attractiveness. Clearly, scientists can no longer be accused of neglecting the topic. The media, too, openly promote the idea that "looks count." (If one were to believe *Playboy* or *Playgirl*, one would think looks are *all* that matter.)

Paradoxically, now that everyone is convinced good looks are enormously important, we are the ones voicing some reservations. Good looks are important—but they are not everything. We get a flood of letters from distraught men and women who have read newspaper accounts of my research:

> Thank God someone has finally come out and admitted how all important looks are. I have suffered enormously because of my looks— I've never had a proper beard. It is humiliating to walk down the street and have people stare at you. To know that passersby are torn between their desire to be polite—to pretend there is nothing peculiar about me—and their burning desire to sneak a fleeting glance at a freak.
>
> I am desperate. I have considered suicide . . . but I always had some small bit of hope. Now, my hope is you. Please tell me how I can become better looking. (Man in Vancouver, B. C.)

We have also received a few letters from men and women plagued with the problem of being too-good-looking:

> You never mentioned the problems of being too beautiful. I am a tall, blond, willowy, high school girl. I plan to be a model. People often stop to look at me in the street. Maybe in Wisconsin beautiful girls get it all . . . are popular . . . but not here. Not one of the boys at Redford High School has asked me out. Everyone assumes that I am too good-looking for *them*—too aloof . . . too perfect. I'd give anything to be a plain Jane. I am so lonely, I cry myself to sleep almost every night (high school girl from Detroit, Michigan).

We have received dozens of letters from men and women complaining that their looks are the source of all their problems. They usually enclose a photograph to document their claims. They complain about psychiatrists, social workers, and teachers who are skeptical that their sole problem is their looks. Thank God, they say, they have finally found someone who will understand, someone who recognizes the overwhelming importance of looks. The only problem is, we do not understand. Almost always the pictures they enclose are of very ordinary people.

What *is* their problem? Dr. Rapson and I have some ideas. A consideration of Susan Lee's case will suggest some alternative answers as to why her (and their) lives may be so unhappy.

"Life *is* trouble. Death, no" (Nikos Kazantzakis 1952, *Zorba the Greek*, 101)

Conversation #2: "All I Want is Everything".

Susan's first problem was that she had unreasonable expectations. America is a nation of immigrants. Our grandparents probably had a realistic idea of what life has to offer—some joyous times sprinkled with painful experiences.

Part of life's adventure was learning to handle difficult circumstances in a graceful way—to deal with family disagreements, injustice, personal loss, war, the inevitability of old age and death. Most parents, however, dream that life might be better for their children—in fact, not just "better" but "perfect." (See Figure 11.2).

During the course of Susan's therapy, her mother and father continually pointed out how special Susan was—"All I want is for her to be happy." Like tigers they attacked anyone or anything that threatened to cause her pain; however, at times, they attacked her themselves (for not being all they knew she could be).

Paradoxically, the parents' illusion—that Susan was special and deserved the best—was part of her problem. Susan ended up not just having to deal with the same difficulties, disappointments, and irritations her parents had been forced to confront, but she also had to deal with the guilt she felt for not "having it all." Susan assumed that, if she were only better-looking, her problems would disappear. In fact, of course, problems are an inevitable part of life.

Susan recounted a series of disastrous love affairs she had had with local toughs. They were insensitive to her feelings, ordered her around, and stayed out all night with friends riding their motorcycles and drinking. She thought she had to put up with abuse because she was fat, that she simply could not attract the type of man she longed for. In fact, she was capable of attracting sweet, considerate men. Almost in passing she often mentioned men who had been interested in her;

CATHY   by Cathy Guisewite

Figure 11.2. Developing realistic aspirations.

men who seemed to be just what she wanted. She summarily dismissed them however—they were weaklings who "fawned on her." She dismissed (in racist terms) as "your typical Japanese house boy" a gentle man who volunteered to help her around the house.

Susan insisted on believing that if only she were better-looking she could have what she most wanted. She could not give up the dream of the perfect man, a man who was tough *and* gentle, who told her what to do *and* let her do just what she wanted, who was exciting and unpredictable *and* gave her the security she desired. In the course of therapy, we would sometimes observe that no matter how special Susan became, how magical, there was no chance she could fine the flawless man of her dreams. Such discussions were extremely painful for her.

Eventually, Susan became aware that there was a certain comfort in believing all her problems were due to her homeliness. This conviction meant that all she had to do was sit, sadly, wishing things could have been otherwise. When she envisioned giving up this dream, sitting down and deciding what she really wanted, doing a little detective work to figure out how she made her intimate relationships falter, and systematically setting about to change herself, she was overwhelmed.

Conversation #3: Learning to be Intimate

Consciously, Susan *thought* she wanted to be caught up in a passionate, deeply intimate relationship. When men rejected her, she believed there was only one explanation—was ugly, fat, repulsive, and therefore without value. If she could make herself a more valuable commodity, she would be loved.

As family therapists, Dr. Rapson and I were skeptical of her analysis. We were convinced she was far more frightened about getting caught

Figure 11.3. The man/woman of our dreams.
From *Feiffer: Jules Feiffer's America from Eisenhower to Reagan*
© 1982 by Jules Feiffer. Reprinted by permission of Alfred A. Knopf, Inc.

up in an intimate relationship than she thought. (In fact, some men did like her. "Oh them!" They were not her type. Her type of man was a man who did not like her!)

Susan also lacked certain skills—being comfortable with herself and recognizing that men had to be themselves, being comfortable with emotions, being able to push ahead when she and her partners were tempted to withdraw—that made it possible to have an intimate relationship.

Susan's case is typical. Almost every one of our clients who has been convinced their problems were due to the fact they were ugly has turned out to have problems, not in looks, but in relating intimately to mates, friends, and coworkers. Thus, in our coffee break conversations, Dr. Rapson and I spent some time reviewing what psychologists know about intimacy:

What Is Intimacy?

The word "intimacy" is derived from the Latin *intimus*, meaning inner or inmost. To be intimate is to know others and to be known by them.

Hartfield (1984) defines intimacy as, "A *process* in which we attempt to get close to another; to explore similarities (and differences) in the

Figure 11.4.   Mother and son, Takuu Atoll, Papua, New Guinea, 1983. Courtesy, Barbara Moir.

ways we both think, feel, and behave." (Chelune, Robinson, and Kommor [1984] review other possible conceptions of intimacy.)

Intimate relationships have a number of characteristics:

Cognitive Aspect. Intimates are willing to reveal themselves to one another. They disclose information about themselves and listen to their partners' confidences. Research supports the contention that people are willing to reveal far more about themselves in intimate relationships than in casual ones. In casual encounters, most people reveal only the sketchiest, most stereotyped information about themselves. Yet, as the French essayist Montaigne (1948) observed, everyone is complex, multifaced:

> All contradictions may be found in me . . . bashful, insolent; chaste, lascivious; talkative, taciturn; tough, delicate; clever, stupid; surly, affable; lying, truthful; learned, ignorant; liberal, miserly and prodigal: all this I see in myself to some extent according to how I turn. . . . I have nothing to say about myself absolutely, simply and solidly, without confusion and without mixture, or in one word. (p. 242)

In deeply intimate relationships, friends and lovers feel free to reveal far more facets of themselves. They reveal more of their complexities and contradictions. As a result, intimates share profound information about one another's histories, values, strengths and weaknesses, idiosyncracies, hopes, and fears (Altman and Taylor 1973; Huesmann and Levinger 1976; Jourard 1964; Perlmutter and Hatfield 1980; Worthy, Gary, and Kahn 1969).

Emotional Aspect. Intimates care deeply about one another. When discussing intimate encounters, most theorists seem to assume the more intimate a relationship, the more friends and lovers like and love one another. In fact, most scales of liking and loving assume love and intimacy are unidimensional concepts, that human feelings are expressed as either love (the high point), liking, neutrality, dislike, or hatred (the low point) (Berscheid and Hatfield [Walster] 1968). Yet folk wisdom and our own experiences tell us there is something wrong with such a unidimensional view of love—often love and hate go hand in hand. "The opposite of love is not hate, but indifference." It is in intimate relationships that we feel most *intensely*. True, we generally feel more intense love for intimates than for anyone else; yet, because intimates care so much about one another, they have the power to elicit intense pain as well. The dark side of love is jealously, loneliness, depression, and anger. This powerful interplay of conflicting emotions gives vibrancy to the most intimate of relationships (see Berscheid 1979, 1983; and

Hatfield and Walster 1978). Basic to all intimate relationships, however, is trust.

Behavioral Aspect. Intimates are comfortable in close physical proximity. They gaze at one another (Argyle 1967; Exline 1972; Rubin 1970), lean on one another (Galton 1984; Hatfield et al. 1980; Mehrabian 1968), stand close to one another (Allgeier and Byrne 1973; Byrne et al. 1970; Goldberg et al. 1969; Sheflen 1965), and perhaps touch.

For most people, their intimate relationships are the most important thing in their lives (see Berscheid and Peplau 1983; Cook and Wilson 1979; Duck and Gilmour 1981a, 1981b, 1981c, 1982; Fisher and Stricker 1982; Pope and Associates, 1980). Most people are acutely aware that their love relationships are crucially important in shaping the character of their lives. Klinger (1977) found that in response to the question, "What is it that makes your life meaningful?" almost everyone mentioned romantic relationships. Most mentioned the importance of "feeling loved and wanted." In contrast, less than half said that occupational success or religious faith was an important source of meaning for them.

It is not surprising, then, that people also believe their personal happiness is integrally bound to the state of their intimate relationships. In a national survey, psychologists (Campbell, Converse, and Rodgers 1976) found that most people consider it very important to have "a happy marriage," "a good family life," and "good friends." Less importance was given to work, housing, religious faith, and financial security.

Indeed, that close relationships are vital to well-being has been corroborated in research on factors associated with mental and physical health and longevity (see Traupmann and Hatfield 1981 for a review of this research). For example, in their review of available data, Bloom, Asher, and White (1978) concluded there is "an unequivocal association between marital disruption and physical and emotional disorder" (p. 886). Divorced adults are at severely greater risk for mental and physical illness, automobile accidents, alcoholism, and suicide. To take just one example, the mortality rates of divorced, white, American men under sixty-five, as opposed to their married counterparts, are doubled for strokes and lung cancer, ten times higher for tuberculosis, seven times higher for cirrhosis of the liver, and doubled for stomach cancer, according to the American Council of Life Insurance (1978). Premature death from heart disease, too, is significantly more frequent among the "loneliness-prone"—the divorced, widowed, and single, both old and young (Lynch 1977). In fact, people who lack social and community ties were found to be twice as likely to die from any cause during a nine-year period as were people maintaining such relationships (Berkman and Syme 1979). Studies directly assessing feelings of loneliness and social isolation further document the harmful consequences of deficient social relationships.

At King Kalakaua clinic, clients like Susan are usually seeking intimacy, they are eager to find someone to love, want to maintain a faltering love affair, or are adjusting to separation or divorce. Everyone needs intimacy. Why, then, is it so hard to find? Why was Susan reluctant to risk it? To understand Susan's problems, we must focus not just on the advantages of intimacy, but on its *risks*.

The Dangers of Intimacy

Why are people reluctant to become intimate with others? There are many reasons:

a. The Fear of Exposure. In deeply intimate relationships, people disclose far more about themselves than in casual encounters. One reason, then, all of us are afraid of intimacy is that those we care most about are bound to discover all that is wrong with us—that we possess taboo feelings and have done things of which we are deeply ashamed. Such fears are not neurotic. The data clearly show that people who reveal too much to others too soon *are* judged to be a little peculiar (see Derlega and Chaikin 1975 for a review of this literature).

Susan sometimes spoke with arrogance, but deep down she was unsure of herself. She was afraid that, if she allowed others to know her, they would discover her most shameful secrets.

b. The Fear of Abandonment. A second reason people fear exposure is because they think if others get to know them too well, the others will abandon them. Such concerns, too, are sometimes realistic.

We can think of examples: One of my favorite graduate students was a beautiful Swedish woman. At one time, three sociologists at the University of Wisconsin were in love with her. Her problem? She was afraid to let men know who she was. In intimate affairs, each time she tried to admit how uncertain she was, the men lost interest. They wanted to be in love with a *star*, not a mere mortal like themselves. She pretended to be totally self-confident, bright, charming. She knew if she did otherwise she would be "dumped."

A second reason Susan was reluctant to risk intimacy, to admit how needy she was, was that she was terrified that first her parents and then her lovers would abandon her.

c. The Fear of Angry Attacks. Another reason people are reluctant to reveal themselves is the fear that "anything they say will be used against them." Most of us worry that if we reveal confidences to our friends, they will reveal the confidences to their friends, who will reveal them to their friends, etc.

One client, Sara, was a Mexican-American army wife. Her parents had divorced when she was three. Her father was granted custody, and thereafter she was abused both sexually and physically. Sara was justifiably proud of the fact that she learned to be "a perfect lady" in even the most impossible of circumstances. Her voice was always calm, her emotions in control. She took pride in never needing anyone for anything. Her only problem was that she did not have a single friend in which to confide. At long last, she decided to trust one of her sisters. She painfully revealed that her marriage was falling apart and that she was thinking of leaving. Her sister became enraged and denounced her. "What kind of a Catholic are you?"

Similarly, a powerful businessman observed that were he to reveal he was worried about getting old, worried he was not as smart as his computer-aged competition, his competitors would seize his revelations with glee. Sometimes it *is* dangerous to trust.

d. The Fear of Loss of Control.   Men and women are sometimes afraid to risk becoming intimate for yet another reason—they fear losing control. Some theorists have speculated that *men* may be particularly afraid of intimacy and the loss of control it brings (see Hatfield 1982). Traditionally, men are supposed to be in control—of themselves, of other people, and of the situation. The ideal man carefully controls his thoughts, is logical, objective, and unemotional. He hides his feelings, or if he does express any feelings, he carefully telescopes the complex array of human emotions into a single powerful emotion: anger. A "real man" is even supposed to dominate nature.

In contrast, the ideal woman is expressive and warm. She is comfortable expressing a rainbow of feminine feelings—love, anxiety, joy, and depression. (She may be less in touch with anger.) She is responsive to other people and the environment.

Broverman and her colleagues (1972) asked people what men and women *should* be like and what they really *are* like. The answers were clear: Men should be/are in control and instrumental, women should be/are expressive and nurturant. According to theorists there are marked gender differences in three areas: (1) men have a greater desire than women to be "in control"; (2) men have a greater desire to dominate their partners versus submit to them; and (3) men have a greater desire to "achieve" in their love and sexual relations. If such gender differences exist, it is not surprising women feel more comfortable with intimacy than do men. Unfortunately, although a great deal has been written about these topics, there is almost no research documenting that such gender differences exist (see Hatfield 1982; Peplau 1983).

e. The Fear of One's Own Destructive Impulses. Many clients keep a tight lid on their emotions. They fear that if they ever got in touch with what they are feeling, they would begin to cry—or kill.

One Korean client seen at the King Kalakaua clinic was a traditional, macho man. He often explained that men *had* to be cool. He refused to even allude to anything bothering him. To a therapist, it was obvious he was anything but cool. He looked like a seething volcano. He was an enormous, powerful man—a Tai Chi expert. As he explained "analytically' how he felt about things, his eyes blazed, his jaw clenched, he smashed his fist into the palm of his other hand. People were terrified of him. He had to stay cool at all times, he insisted, otherwise he would kill.

He was undoubtedly wrong. Experiences in therapy have shown that as people learn to be more aware of what they are feeling, they find their emotions are not as powerful, not nearly so overwhelming, as they had assumed. They find that somehow they can learn to express their feelings in a controlled way. Yet the fear is real.

f. The Fear of Losing One's Individuality or of Being Engulfed. Theorists believe one of the most primitive fears of intimacy is the feeling that one will be engulfed by another (see Diamond and Shapiro 1981 for a discussion of this point). The Watsons, seen at the King Kalakaua clinic in therapy, demonstrate what it means to fear "engulfment."

The Watsons were a bright, delightful, and thoroughly crazy family. The father and mother insisted they wanted their girls to become independent, to leave home and to build families of their own. However, every time the "girls" (who were in their fifties) showed the least independence, their parents got angry. They complained the girls were not doing "it" right. The girls should be more relaxed about their endeavors. They should be breezy, while succeeding spectacularly. The daughters were the first people I ever heard say they were afraid to get close to anyone for fear that they would be "swallowed up."

Basically, Patti and Ann were confused about what they wanted *versus* what everyone else in the family wanted. Each time they were tempted to express themselves, they would be overtaken by guilt. (They would begin a tortured, internal dialogue. Why were they so ungrateful? Demanding? Their parents would be hurt terribly. Was it fair to do that to them? "No." They inevitably decided to remain mute.)

Nor were Patti and Ann capable of really listening. If they listened, if they permitted themselves to keenly feel their parents need, they would feel responsible for completely sacrificing themselves to provide it. They would lose their freedom. Even then what could they do? They were too weak. So everyone stayed in their own shells. No one could ever be really independent: no one could ever be really intimate with others for fear they would be engulfed.

Susan, too, had such a problem. She assumed that if she ever let people know how desperately she needed to be loved and taken care of, she would be hooked. Her mother was smothering, totally controlling. She assumed love meant you had to think alike, dress alike, do everything together. Susan was afraid if she let anyone get close, she would be trapped. They would make impossible, overwhelming demands. When she thought of saying no to such demands, she felt extremely guilty. She could not even take care of herself, she thought, much less someone else. So she built a barrier between herself and others.

There are a variety of reasons, then, why people are afraid of intimacy. Susan Lee was convinced her problem was her looks; if she were more appealing, she could be intimate with others. In fact, Dr. Rapson and I thought her problem was just the reverse. Susan needed to be fat, in part, because she was terrified of what she said she wanted most—an intimate relationship. Being fat allowed her to hide by keeping others at a distance.

g. How Intimate Are You with Others?   Researchers have developed a variety of scales to assess how intimate people are with those they care about. One team of psychologists (Miller and Lefcourt 1982) has measured intimacy via the Miller Social Intimacy Scale (MSIS). How close do you allow yourself to get to those you care about? The researchers interviewed 216 unmarried men and women and 17 married couples at the University of Waterloo, Ontario, Canada. Their average scores are shown in Table 11.1.

As you might expect, Susan was very timid about getting close to others. She received an unusually low score on the MSIS.

Conversation #5: The Solution
Susan's case highlights many of the issues people face when deciding how much effort they want to spend working on their looks. How did we decide to treat Susan? We decided that, in her case, appearance was not even a small part of her problem in finding a mate. Her problem was that she had a peculiar idea about what intimate relationships are supposed to be like, and she had inadequate skills for getting what life had to offer. In the end, we focused our attention on helping her develop intimacy skills. *NOTE:* We have presented the case of Susan Lee in such detail for a reason—since we have been at King Kalakaua, we have discovered that virtually everyone entering therapy convinced their real problem in finding a date or a mate is their appearance in fact has a more serious problem—they are timid about

Miller Social Intimacy Scale

	VERY RARELY	SOME OF THE TIME	ALMOST ALWAYS
1. When you have leisure time, how often do you choose to spend it with him/her alone?	1 2 3 4 5 6 7 8 9 10		
*2. How often do you keep very personal information to yourself and do not share it with him/her?	10 9 8 7 6 5 4 3 2 1		
3. How often do you show him/her affection?	1 2 3 4 5 6 7 8 9 10		
4. How often do you confide very personal information to him/her?	1 2 3 4 5 6 7 8 9 10		
5. How often are you able to understand his/her feelings?	1 2 3 4 5 6 7 8 9 10		
6. How often do you feel close to him/her?	1 2 3 4 5 6 7 8 9 10		

	NOT MUCH	A LITTLE	A GREAT DEAL
7. How much do you like to spend time alone with him/her?	1 2 3 4 5 6 7 8 9 10		
8. How much do you feel like being encouraging and supporting to him/her when he/she is unhappy?	1 2 3 4 5 6 7 8 9 10		
9. How close do you feel to him/her most of the time?	1 2 3 4 5 6 7 8 9 10		
10. How much is it to you to listen to his/her very personal disclosures?	1 2 3 4 5 6 7 8 9 10		
11. How satisfying is your relationship with him/her?	1 2 3 4 5 6 7 8 9 10		
12. How affectionate do you feel towards him/her?	1 2 3 4 5 6 7 8 9 10		
13. How important is it to you that he/she understand your feelings?	1 2 3 4 5 6 7 8 9 10		
*14. How much damage is caused by a typical disagreement in your relationship with him/her?	10 9 8 7 6 5 4 3 2 1		
15. How important is it to you that he/she be encouraging and supportive to you when you are unhappy?	1 2 3 4 5 6 7 8 9 10		
16. How important is it to you that he/she show you affection?	1 2 3 4 5 6 7 8 9 10		
17. How important is your relationship with him/her in your life?	1 2 3 4 5 6 7 8 9 10		

* Scored in the reverse direction
SOURCE: Miller and Lefcourt (1982).

TABLE 11.1   **Scores on the MSIS**

UNMARRIED		MARRIED	
MEN	WOMEN	MEN	WOMEN
134.9	139.3	152.5	156.2

intimate encounters. Thus, we talk with clients not just about how to improve their appearance, but also about building intimacy.

A PRESCRIPTION FOR INTIMACY

Everyone needs a warm, intimate relationship. At the same time, one must recognize that in every social encounter there are some risks. How, then, can an intimate relationship be established with minimum risk?

Social psychological research and clinical experience gives some hints. We use a basic, theoretical assumption to provide the framework for teaching people how to be intimate with others: People must be capable of independence to be intimate with others, capable of intimacy if they are to be independent. Independence and intimacy are not opposite personality traits, but interlocking skills. People who lack the ability to be independent *and* intimate can never really be either. They are "never really with one another, never really without them." According to theorists, one of the most primitive tasks people face is learning how to maintain their own identity and integrity while engaging in deeply intimate relationships with others (Erikson 1968; Fisher and Stricker 1982; Freud 1922; Hatfield and Walster 1978; Kantor and Lehr 1975; Kaplan 1978; Maslow 1954; Pope and associates 1980). What Dr. Rapson and I set out to do with Susan, then, was to make her comfortable with the notion that she and her intimates are separate people, with separate ideas and feelings, who can sometimes come profoundly close to one another.

Once a person has the skills to be independent/intimate, they must find an appropriate lover or chum on which to practice their art. In a few situations, the only possible way to act is to play out a stereotyped role. In most situations, one has to be at least tactful, in a few, downright manipulative, in order to survive. But on those occasions when real intimacy is possible, men and women can recognize its promise, seize their opportunities, and take a chance.

ARE THERE GENDER DIFFERENCES IN INTIMACY?

It may be that men have the easiest time achieving an independent identity; women have the easiest time achieving closeness with others. Napier (1977) describes two types of people who seem, with uncanny accuracy, to attract one another. Type I (usually a woman) is only minimally concerned with maintaining her independence. What she cares about is achieving emotional closeness. (She seeks "fusion with the partner," "oneness," or "we-ness" in the marriage. She puts much energy into planning "togetherness" activities.) Type I fears rejection and abandonment.

Type I's partner, Type II (usually a man), is most concerned with maintaining his sense of self and personal freedom and autonomy. He feels a strong need to establish his territory within the common household: to have "my study," "my workshop," "my car." Similarly, he fears being "suffocated," "stifled," or "engulfed," or in some manner intruded on by his wife.

Napier observes that men and women's efforts to get close, but not "too close" for each of them, makes matters worse. Women (seeking more closeness) clasp their mates tightly, thereby contributing to the men's anxiety. The men (seeking more distance) retreat further, which increases their wives' panic and induces further "clasping."

There is other evidence that men are less comfortable with intimacy than are women. Researchers find:

(1) *In casual encounters*, women disclose far more to others than do men (Cozby 1973; Jourard 1971). Rubin and his colleagues (1980, 306) point out that the basis for such differences appears to be in socialization practices. In our culture, women have traditionally been encouraged to show feelings; men have been taught to hide their feelings and to avoid displays of weakness (see also Pleck and Sawyer 1974). Kate Millett (1970) observes, "Women express, men repress."

(2) *In their deeply intimate relationships*, however, men and women differ little, if at all, in how much they are willing to reveal to one another. For example, Rubin and his colleagues (1980) asked dating couples how much they had revealed to their partners. Did they talk about their current relationships? Previous opposite-sex affairs? Their feelings about their parents and friends? Their self-concepts and life views? Their attitudes and interests? Their day-to-day activities? The authors found that, overall, men and women did *not* differ in how much they confided in their partners.

There was a difference, however, in the *kind* of confidences men and women were willing to share with those they love. Men were more willing to share their views on politics and their pride in their strengths. Women were more likely to disclose their feelings about other people and their fears. Interestingly enough, Rubin and his colleagues found that such unbalanced forms of communication are most common in traditional men and women.

Some authors have observed that *neither* men nor women may be getting exactly the amount of intimacy they would like. Women may want more intimacy than they are getting; men may want far less. There is evidence that couples negotiate a level of self-disclosure bearable for both. In the words of the movie *My Fair Lady*, this compromise ensures that *"neither* really gets what either really wants at all" (Derlega and Chaikin 1975).

(3) *Women receive more disclosures than do men.* This finding is not surprising in view of the fact that the amount of information people reveal to others has an enormous impact on the amount of information they receive in return (see Altman 1973; Davis and Skinner 1974; Jourard 1964; Jourard and Friedman 1970; Marlatt 1971; Worthy, Gary, and Kahn 1969).

There is some evidence, then, that women feel slightly more comfortable with intense intimacy in their love relationships than do men and are far more comfortable revealing themselves in more casual relationships than do men. Tradition dictates women should be the "intimacy experts." And today, women *are* more comfortable sharing their ideas, feelings, and behavior than are men. What happens if this situation changes? Rubin and his colleagues (1980) suggest such changes have already begun. The prognosis is mixed. Young women usually say they would be delighted if the men they love could be intimate. Change is always difficult however. More than one man has complained that when he finally dared to reveal his weaker aspects to a woman, he soon discovered she was shocked by his lack of "manliness." Family therapists such as Napier (1977) have warned us that the struggle to find individuality *and* closeness is a problem for everyone. As long as men flee from intimacy, women can safely pursue them. Now that men are turning around to face them, women may well find themselves taking flight. In any case, the confrontation is likely to be exciting.

People need intimacy, yet they have every reason to fear it. What advice can social psychologists give men and women on how to secure the benefits of deep encounters while not being engulfed by its dangers? The advice we give follows directly from the theoretical paradigm we offered earlier—one must be independent before one can be intimate, intimate before one can be independent.

Conversation #6: Developing Susan's Independence/Intimacy Skills

a. Encouraging Susan to Accept Herself As She Is

> Good, better, best. Never let it rest, 'till the good is better, and the better is the best.
>
> (Anonymous folk saying)

Susan Lee entered therapy desperately trying to convince herself she was perfect and deeply ashamed that she was not. It is a great temptation to dwell in the realm of absolutes—one is either a saint or a sinner. Many people are determined to be perfect (at least), and they can not settle for less. Yet saintliness/evilness are the least interesting of human conditions. Real life is lived in the middle zone. Real people inevitably have some real strengths and some endearing small quirks, that make them what they are. The real trick to enjoying life is not just accepting diversity, but learning to take pleasure in it.

The first step in learning to be independent/intimate, then, is to accept that you are entitled to be what you are—to have the ideas you have and the feelings you feel, to do the best you can do. What you are is good enough.

In therapy, we tried to shake Susan from the notion that one should come into the world perfect and continue to be that way, to a realization that one can only gain wisdom in small steps. She was told to pick one small goal and work to achieve it. When that goal was accomplished, she could then move on to another. Change is then manageable and possible (Watson and Tharp 1981). We tried to convince Susan that she could never attain perfection, only work toward it.

Psychologist Morris Rosenberg (1965) developed one of the measures most commonly used for discovering how comfortable people feel with themselves. How would you answer these questions? (For a look at some of the literally hundreds of scales that have been developed to measure self-esteem, self-concept, self-acceptance, etc., see Wells and Marwell [1976]; and Wylie [1974 and 1978]).

The Rosenberg Self-Esteem Scale

Please indicate whether you strongly agree, agree, disagree, or strongly disagree with each of the following statements. Please circle the appropriate response.

1. On the whole, I am satisfied with myself.
   a. Strongly agree
   b. Agree
   c. Disagree
   d. Strongly disagree
*2. At times I think I am no good at all.

  a. Strongly agree
  b. Agree
  c. Disagree
  d. Strongly disagree

3. I feel that I have a number of good qualities.
  a. Strongly agree
  b. Agree
  c. Disagree
  d. Strongly disagree

4. I am able to do things as well as most other people.
  a. Strongly agree
  b. Agree
  c. Disagree
  d. Strongly disagree

*5. I feel I do have much to be proud of.
  a. Strongly agree
  b. Agree
  c. Disagree
  d. Strongly disagree

6. I certainly feel useless at times.
  a. Strongly agree
  b. Agree
  c. Disagree
  d. Strongly disagree

7. I feel that I'm a person of worth, at least on an equal plane with others.
  a. Strongly agree
  b. Agree
  c. Disagree
  d. Strongly disagree

*8. I wish I could have more respect for myself.
  a. Strongly agree
  b. Agree
  c. Disagree
  d. Strongly disagree

*9. All in all, I am inclined to feel that I am a failure.
  a. Strongly agree
  b. Agree
  c. Disagree
  d. Strongly disagree

10. I take a positive attitude toward myself.
  a. Strongly agree
  b. Agree
  c. Disagree
  d. Strongly disagree

---

* Items scored in the opposite direction
  Reproduced from Morris Rosenberg, *Society and the Adolescent Self-Image.* (Princeton University Press, 1965, p. 305–307.)

b. Encouraging Susan to Recognize Her Intimates for What They Are.

Individuals may be hard on themselves, but they are generally even harder on their partners. Most people have the idea everyone is entitled to a perfect partner, or at least one slightly better than what is available (see Hatfield et al., 1984). A recent "Cathy" cartoon offered a wry comment on the difficulty of finding the perfect mate. It's Christmas. We see Cathy frantically picking through the merchandise. She observes:

> At first, it all looks so appealing. You want it all.
>
> Then you look a little closer. Eh . . . That's not quite right.
> Nah . . . That won't quite do it.
>
> Pretty soon you realize that of the 42 billion items offered, there's not one thing that's exactly what you want.
>
> Shopping is a lot like dating.
>
> > ("Cathy," *Honolulu Advertiser,* 14 February 1982, C. 3)

To have an intimate relationship, people must learn to enjoy others as they are, without hoping to fix them up. It is extraordinarily difficult, however, to accept that friends are entitled to be the people they are. One of my favorite "Cathy" cartoons [Guisewite (1982)] shows Cathy romantically confiding to her friend Andrea:

> "I know Irving and I are totally different people Andrea . . . but we keep coming back to each other.
>
> "Deep down, I think we both want exactly the same thing!"
>
> Long pause.
>
> "We both want the other person to change."

From our own points of view, clearly life would be far better if our mates were only the people we wanted them to be. It would take so little for them to change their whole character structure. Why are they so stubborn?

When we realize our lover or friend is the person who exists right now—not the person we wish he was, not the person he could be, but what he is—intimacy becomes impossible. Pope (1980) observes, "Romantic love is the recognition and affirmation of both the self and someone else, no matter how flawed both may be."

In James Joyce's *Ulysses,* neither Molly nor Leopold Bloom are idealized. Molly, lying in bed and drifting off to sleep at the end of the book, reflects on herself and her husband (a clumsy, balding, fat, comic man). It would seem that his defects would prevent her from loving and admiring him. And yet:

> The sun shines for you he said the day we were lying among the rhododendrons on Howth head in the grey tweed suit and his straw hat . . . yes first I gave him the bit of seedcake out of my mouth and it was leapyear like now yes 16 years ago my God after that long kiss I near lost my breath yes he said I was a flower of the mountains yes . . . that was one true thing he said in his life and the sun shines for you today yes that was why I liked him because I saw he understood or felt what a woman is . . . and O that awful deepdown torrent O and the sea the sea crimson sometimes like fire and the glorious sunsets . . . and then I asked him with my eyes to ask again yes and then he asked me would I yes to say yes my mountain flower and first I put my arms round him yes and drew him down to me so he could feel my breasts all perfume yes and his heart was going like mad and yes I said yes I will yes.
>
> (Joyce 1914, 782–783)

How accepting of friends and lovers are you? Do you love others as yourself? If not, who are you hardest on—yourself or those you care most about?

c. Encouraging Susan to Express Her Ideas and Feelings. Next, intimates must become more comfortable about expressing their ideas and feelings. This task is harder than one might think. Individuals' intimate relations are usually their most important relationships. When passions are so intense, consequences so momentous, people are often hesitant to speak the truth. From moment to moment, they are tempted to present a consistent picture. If they are in love, they are hesitant to admit their niggling doubts. (What if the person they love is hurt? What if their revelations destroy the relationship?) When they are angry, they are not thinking about their love or their self-doubts, they want to lash out.

Susan's mother, for example, had made Susan feel guilty and frightened about expressing her feelings. By now, Susan had learned to engage in a running commentary each time complicated feelings threatened: (She'd instruct herself: "Don't make a fuss." "You're not perfect either." "Your poor father." "Why do you always make trouble?") In therapy, Susan came to realize that she *should* be more honest than she had been. To be intimate, people have to push toward a more honest, graceful, complete, and patient communication. They must understand that a person's ideas and feelings are necessarily complex, with many nuances, shadings, and inconsistencies. In love, there is time to clear things up.

Interestingly, Susan and other people often discover that their affection increases when they begin to admit their irritations. Sometimes, individuals think they have fallen out of love, that they are "bored" with their marriages but as they begin to express their anger and ambivalence, they feel their love come back in a rush. Therapists Gus Napier and Karl Whitaker (1978) describe such a marital confrontation in *The Family Crucible:*

> When David and Carolyn Brice finally fought it out with each other after the affair was disclosed, the two partners fought and cried, talked and searched for an entire night. The next evening, more exhausting encounters. Feelings that had been hidden for years emerged; doubts and accusations that they had never expected to admit articulated. . . . They felt alive together for the first time in years. Somewhat mysteriously, they found themselves going to bed together in the midst of a great tangle of emotions—continuing anger, and hurt, and guilt, and this new quality: abandon. The lovemaking was, they were to admit to each other, 'the best it had ever been' (p. 153)

Love and hate flow together (Hatfield and Walster 1978; Kaplan 1979).

Psychologist Sidney Jourard (1964) defined intimacy as "a willingness to disclose one's ideas, feelings, and day-to-day activities to lovers, friends, or strangers . . . and to listen to their disclosures in return." He developed one of the most commonly used measures of people's abilities to talk to others about their intimate lives—The Jourard Self-Disclosure Questionnaire (JSDQ). The JSDQ consists of sixty questions in all. It asks people to think about how much they typically disclose to others in six different areas of life. We have reproduced a few of these items below. How much have you disclosed to the person you care most about? How much has he or she disclosed to you?

The Jourard Self-Disclosure Questionnaire

0 Have told my friend nothing about this aspect of me.

1 Have talked in general terms about this item. My friend has only a general idea about this aspect of me.

2. Have talked in full and complete detail about this aspect; my friend could describe me accurately.

Attitudes and Opinions
1. What I think and feel about religion; my personal religious views. _____

2. My views on the present government—the president, government, policies, etc. _____

3. My personal views on sexual morality—how I feel and others ought to behave in sexual matters.   _____

Tastes and Interests
1. My favorite food, the ways I like food prepared, and my food dislikes.   _____
2. The kind of party, or social gathering I like best, and the kind that would bore me, or that I wouldn't enjoy.   _____

Work (or Studies)
1. What I find to be the worst pressures and the strains in my work.   _____
2. What I feel are my special strong points and qualifications for my work.   _____
3. What I feel are my shortcomings and handicaps that prevent me from working as I'd like to, or that prevent me from getting further ahead in my work.   _____

Money
1. How much money I make at my work, or get as an allowance.   _____
2. My most pressing need for money right now, e.g. outstanding bills, some major purchases that is desired or needed.   _____
3. My total financial worth, including property, savings, bonds, insurance, *etc.*   _____

Personality
1. What feelings, if any, that I have trouble expressing or controlling.   _____
2. The aspects of my personality that I dislike, worry about, that I regard as a handicap to me.   _____
3. Things in the past or present that I feel ashamed and guilty about.   _____
4. The kind of things that make me just furious.   _____
5. The kinds of things that make me especially proud of myself, elated, full of self-esteem or self-respect.   _____

Body
1. How I wish I looked, my ideas for overall appearance.   _____
2. Any problems or worries that I had with my appearance in the past.   _____
3. My feelings about different parts of my body—legs, hips, waist, weight, chest or bust, etc.   _____

(From Sidney M. Jourard, *The Transparent Self.* [Princeton, N.J.: D. Von Nostrand, 1964], 161–163.)

d. Teaching People to Listen to Their Intimates. People tend to assume they know just what their dates and mates are thinking. They don't. In therapy, Dr. Rapson and I sometimes try an experiment. We are always startled at the results. We pluck some seemingly trivial sentences out of a conversation such as this from Tom: "Kelley won't make decisions. I tried to get her to stop at C. S. Wo's furniture last Saturday after our session, but she just mumbled something."

We ask couples to slow things down and try to tell us everything they have in mind as this bit of conversation unfolds. Why did Tom want to stop at C. S. Wo's? (There was a sale.) What does he think she was thinking? ("She thinks she deserves to shop at B. J. Furniture: She's pretty and smart and deserves more than bargain basement furniture. If I were a success, we would go there, but I'm not. Why can't she accept that?") Can she recall what she was thinking? (She is amazed. She felt pushed around. "He never warns me what's up. I have no babysitter, the kids are alone, I have dishes to wash, and he wants to shop.") I have never seen such an exercise conducted without couples finding out a great deal about one another. It is hard to listen. (Books such as Gottman et al. [1976] provide suggestions as to how couples can improve their communications.)

e. Teaching Susan to Deal with Her Lover's Reactions. Although you *must* communicate your ideas and feelings to have an intimate affair, your partner is not necessarily going to like it. You can expect that expressing your deepest feelings will hurt. Your lover may well tell you frankly how deeply you have hurt him/her, making you feel guilty, or he/she may react with intense anger.

Susan had to learn to stop responding in automatic fashion to such emotional outbursts—to quit backing up and apologizing for what she had said. She had to learn to stay calm, to remind herself that she was entitled to feel what she felt, to listen to what her partner felt, and to keep on trying. Only then is there a chance of an intimate encounter.

THE OUTCOME

Usually, men and women can learn to be more intimate with their lovers, family, and friends. Susan Lee's case was easy. She was eager for someone to get to know her and equally eager to know someone else intimately. We told her it was too soon to risk intimacy with a potential mate. She should select the three men she liked most and practice being intimate with them. Since she was not serious about any of them, she could afford to make mistakes. As you might guess, in such relaxed circumstances Susan fell in love with one of her trio of friends—John. John was twenty years older than she and had two, college aged children. He was a career diplomat. This Christmas, I got a note from them—they are both in Cairo. With the perseverity of humans, Susan said that now that it didn't matter anymore (since John did not care much about weight one way or the other), she had "somehow" lost forty-five pounds. She didn't know how it happened— maybe because she no longer needed to be protected against intimacy, maybe because she was so busy.

IN SUMMARY

In chapters 1–10, we reviewed evidence that appearances are important. This chapter was designed to reexamine these scientific facts in a real life context. We have seen that real life is somewhat more complicated. Good looks are important, but other factors are even more important. People like Susan Lee make a mistake when they focus overly much on their appearance as the cause of their problems. In searching for a happy life, individuals may do better to focus on developing a talent for love and for exciting, productive work.

Chapter 12

SELF-IMPROVE-MENT—IS IT WORTH IT?

The preceding chapters have documented that people generally perceive the good-looking to be special, that they treat them accordingly, and that, as a consequence, the good-looking become special—different from others in a variety of ways. A superficial reading of chapters 1–10 might lead a reader to conclude one should sacrifice almost everything to improve one's appearance. Yet, there were hints in chapter 10 ("The Ugly Truth About Beauty") and a clear illustration in chapter 11 ("The Case of Susan Lee") that outside the research laboratory, in life, other elements—intelligence, personality, the capacity to be intimate—may vastly overshadow looks in importance.

How does one decide whether to work on one's appearance or to improve one's substance? This chapter is designed to address that question. We will argue that what is needed is balance.

1. It is wise to spend some time improving your appearance. The research in chapters 1–10 makes that clear. In the first section

Figure 12.1.   A Hawaiian woman at the turn of the century.

of this chapter, we will review data that clearly indicates that people can improve their looks, and that such efforts do improve their lives.

2. It is also wise not to spend too much time. In the second section, we will review four reasons that it is a serious mistake to bank too much on good looks. Most people probably should not spend

enormous efforts becoming beautiful women or handsome men. If you invest too much time in achieving and maintaining appeal, your immediate rewards may be great, but you may well end up sacrificing too much in the long run.

3. Finally, in the third part of the chapter we will review a variety of more profitable ways to go about improving your looks and your lives.

Advice to be "moderate" is hard to accept. It is always appealing to see the world more simply. If "what is beautiful is good," it is easy to conclude that "more is better." But things are more complicated than that. Real life is lived in the grey areas—in the realm of complexities, ambiguities, and half truths. In the real world, people are not perfect. (There is a saying: "Wisdom consists in knowing when to avoid perfection.") It is possible, though, to learn to appreciate people for their little corners and quirks. So it is a complex prescription we have to give.

A PRESCRIPTION FOR IMPROVING PHYSICAL APPEARANCE

Chapters 1–10 indicate that it is reasonable to spend *some* time improving your appearance. In adolescence, most of us think of ourselves as "befores," ugly ducklings who could evolve into beautiful swans ("afters") if only we found the right hairstyles, had our teeth straightened, drastically reshaped our noses, etc. We have all tried various techniques to improve our looks. Make a list of the things you have tried.

How did these attempts work out? Did these changes improve your life in any way?

If you were to embark on a self-improvement program today, what aspects of yourself would you try to change? What would it take to improve these defects?

There are no end of magainzes (*Esquire, Glamour, Psychology Today, Self Magazine*), self-help books, Weight Watcher's classes, Jane Fonda exercise records, *Dress for Success* books, teeth-straightening guides, and plastic surgeons that provide detailed guides on how to go about improving yourself. You have probably tried much of this advice already. What teenage boy has not tried a new haircut, a scented after-shave lotion, or body building classes? What teenage girl has not tried eye shadow, padded bras (or no bra at all), horizontal stripes instead of vertical ones, or vice versa?

For some people, beauty is a business. They may embark on more drastic self-improvement programs. For example, both Cher and Loni

Anderson had their breasts reduced; Mariel Hemingway had hers increased. Michael Jackson, Sissey Spacek, Milton Berle, Raquel Welch, and Walter Mondale all had rhinoslasty (a "nose job"). Carol Burnett had jaw reconstruction. Elvis Presley had his eyes and temples lifted. Jackie Onnasis, Jack Lemmon, Betty Ford, Abbie Hoffman, Burt Lancaster, and Queen Elizabeth all had face-lifts (see US Magazine, 16 January 1984, 32–37). All in all, last year 31,000 men and women had eyelid surgery (blepharoplasty), 73,000 had their noses reshaped (rhinoplasty), 42,000 had a face-life (rhytidectomy), 13,000 had dermabrasion/chemical peel, and 15,000 had collegen injections to remove wrinkles and acne scars (Information provided by Mary Mc Grath, Chief of Plastic Surgery, George Washington University Medical Center, Washington, D.C., September, 1984).

How do such attempts work out? Do such efforts change people's lives? How? Let us see:

Do Self-Improvement Programs Really Improve Anything?

FIRST THE GOOD NEWS

Most beauty experts, plastic surgeons, psychologists, and religious leaders insist we can change our appearance/personality/character, and thus our lives, in major ways. For example, Carol Lyn Mithers (1982), a writer for *Mademoiselle* magazine, changed her appearance dramatically in her teens. Did that change affect her life?

> During the summer vacation between my sophomore and junior years in high school, I turned 15 and got a pair of contact lenses.
> When I adjusted to the lenses and could wear them without weeping, I went to a local department store and bought a Dynel "fall" to cover the remaining traces of the last butchery my mother's beautician had committed on my hair. ("I can't cut while your glasses on on," he'd said, which meant I couldn't see what he was doing until it was too late.) And I bought some new clothes.
> My new appearance, I was firmly convinced, would do no less than change my entire life.
> I was right. . . .
> I not only hated the way I looked, I hated the way I was—shy, frightened, self-conscious, socially inept. As someone who had grown up on fairy tales of transformation, I imagined that a change in the way I looked would instantly effect—was the same as—a change in *me*.
> But life is not a fairy tale, and putting on contact lenses . . . is not enough to make an old self melt away. The massive personality changes I had anticipated failed to arrive—I may have looked better than before, but in every other way I was the same person I always had been.

Figure 12.2. Before and after photos, courtesy Frances Loo (stylist). Makeup, Lyle Nelson, photography, Gerald Bishop (Lisa Buhl, model).

That, however, did not seem to be the way others saw it. The football player (who finally stopped staring and made his move) seemed untroubled by my stilted conversation; he was busy brushing the hair back from my cheek and talking about the color of my eyes. After years of unsuccessful drama class auditions (and no appreciable rise in talent), I got a big role in a school play. I was elected to the student council. My quiteness, long mistaken for bookishness or snobbery rather than understood to be acute shyness, began to be seen as evidence of mystery and profundity. And strangers whose eyes once had passed over me with the blank indifference with which they might have observed a billboard, now registered my presence, now wanted to tell me my hair looked nice with the sun on it, that they liked the dress I was wearing, that they wished me a pleasant afternoon, that they wanted to be of service.

When I had imagined a changed life, I had seen the new face leading to a new self which then would change the way others saw and treated me. The face was new, the self was not, yet the change in treatment had come anyway. It seemed some crucial step had been skipped, and in the gap that yawned where that step should have been, I discovered a nasty little secret: All my life I had been told over and over that it was who you were and not what you looked like that mattered. And that had been a lie. (pp. 93–184)

Most beauty counselors agree that great changes *are* possible in our appearances and in our lives. The data suggest that changes may take a little getting used to, but in the end it is worth it. You may recall that in the *Psychology Today* study we referred to in chapter 9 (Bersheid, Hatfield [Walster], and Bohrnstedt 1973) we asked readers to estimate how attractive they were at various ages. We divided readers into five groups: those who had always been beautiful/handsome; those who had vacillated between good-looking and just average; those who always have been just average; those who vacillated between average and homely; and those who felt ugly throughout their lives. The results were clear: The more time men and women had possessed a good-looking body, the more self-confident and happy they were.

Other analyses show there are two determinants for how we feel about ourselves (1) How we looked when we were growing up, and (2) how we look right now. Both are critically important in determining how we feel about ourselves. Homeliness in a child will always have some impact on how that person feels about himself/herself. (One member of THE GROUP said: "I was fat as a child, and even today just when I'm about to walk onstage to M.C. the Emmy awards, beautiful in a $2,500 Halston gown, there's a pudgy little girl inside saying 'What are *you* doing here?' " But change is important too. ("But," the actress added, "I look her in the eye and say smugly 'I'm a Star' and stride on out.")

An aside: It occurred to us that people who have *always* been beautiful, or *always* been homely, might be unaware of the importance of attractiveness. (A beauty might prefer to believe her popularity was due to her sterling personality traits rather than to external attributes. A homely person might rationalize that looks do not count.) But, we reasoned, people who have experienced a major change in their appearance can hardly fail to see how important good looks are. The *Psychology Today* data indicate that this notion is true. People who have experienced a dramatic change in physical appearance at some time in their lives, do rate attractiveness as more important than do those who have never changed at all. Carol Lynn Mithers (1982) described the changes she experienced when she changed from an ugly duckling into a beautiful swan: "When I was plain and unpopular, I wanted desperately to be pretty. I thought being beautiful would change my life. I was right." She, too, argues that, once your looks change, you are forever aware of how much looks matter.

> And during a period not too long ago when I gained a lot of weight, had a disastrous permanent, looked pretty bad and stopped getting preferential treatment from the outside world, I was not at all surprised. It was as I'd always known it would be—"I" wasn't pretty; prettiness was something I'd been given for a while, and now the gift was being reclaimed. My time was up.
>
> As it turned out, it wasn't. But my forebodings made it clear to me that even then, years after I'd wished the "old girl" goodbye, she was still there inside me, alive and well. And it occurred to me that having looks was not dissimilar to having wealth: Only those born rich take what they have for granted. Those to whom it comes later never forget that what has been gained can be lost. No matter how much is in the bank, they never stop counting pennies, checking price tags, anticipating the day when, once again, all the cupboards will be bare. (pp. 93–94)

Minor cosmetic changes, then, can have a positive impact on people's lives. Research by orthodontists, plastic surgeons, etc. confirm that major changes can have an even greater impact on people's lives.

It Is More Important to Become Average Than to Become Beautiful/Handsome

When we are feeling discouraged, many of us pin the problem on our looks. "If only I had a perfect face, a perfect body, *then* I'd be happy." At first glance, the data we presented in chapters 1–10 support that view. In fact, scientists generally summarize the complex research results we reviewed in these chapters with a simple slogan—"What is beautiful is good." This simple summary is fascinating because it is incorrect!

These studies actually demonstrated that "what is beautiful is good; *what is ugly is bad.*"

Americans are so obsessed with beauty that we forget that the spectrum of appearances includes beautiful people, average-looking individuals, ugly folk, and people with disfiguring handicaps. (Illustration 12.3–12.8 may be unsettling . . . but they will enable you in a glance to realize how much humans can vary in appearance. For biographical information of some of these *Very Special People*, see Drimmer [1973].)

Early research on physical attractiveness (Berscheid and Hatfield [Walster] 1974) revealed that good-looking people have an advantage over average individuals who, in turn, have an advantage over homely and disfigured people. *But* subsequent research (for example, see Dermer and Thiel 1975) clearly shows that the emphasis should be on the last half of the sentence. Illustration 12.14 shows the relationship between

Figure 12.3. James Morris, the "elastic skin man." He could pull his cheek skin out eight or more inches, he was able to pull the skin of his chest up to the top of his head, and pull out the skin of one leg and cover the other with it.

Figure 12.4. Charles B. Tripp ("The Armless Wonder"), born 1855, and Eli Bowen ("The Legless Wonder"), born 1844, were a team who appeared in circuses and carnivals. Here they ride a bicycle built for two.

appearance and a host of other variables—self-esteem, job opportunities, dating popularity, happiness.

It is some advantage to be beautiful or handsome rather than average. You would gain something if, through great creativity and sacrifice, you became a stunning person, instead of an extraordinarily ordinary one. You would gain something but not much. Stunning people have only a slight advantage over their more ordinary peers. What is really important is to become at least *average*. The average-looking have a real advantage over the homely or the disfigured.

Plastic surgeons have collected considerable evidence in support of this contention (see Graham and Klingman, in press). One classic experiment was performed by Jurtzberg, Safar, and Cavior (1968). The scientists were eager to find out if plastic surgery might improve prison inmates' psychological adjustment, increase their job success, and reduce prison recidivism. They selected inmates of the New York City jail who seemed (psychologically and surgically) to be good candidates for plastic surgery. These prisoners' disfigurements included knife and burn scars, lop-ears, tatoos, and needle tracks from drug usage. The researcers randomly selected men to receive one of four experimental "treatments":

Figure 12.5.   Myrtle Corbin, "the Four-Legged Girl from Texas."

Figure 12.6. Unzie was born in 1869. He was an Australian aborigine. One in 3,000–9,000 people is born an albino—a birth defect caused by a lack of pigment in the skin. Albinos' skin is white. Their eyes have a pink or blue iris and a dark red pupil. Their hair is white. Sunlight is painful to their eyes. Courtesy, Circus World Museum, Baraboo, Wisconsin.

Figure 12.7. Head, neck, and upper torso of John Merrick, from photos made of him in 1886. Originally printed in *The British Medical Journal*, 11 December 1886, vol. 2, p. 1189. Photograph supplied by Ashley Montagu.

Figure 12.8. Betty Broadbent, Tatoo'd lady. Courtesy, Circus World Museum, Baraboo, Wisconsin.

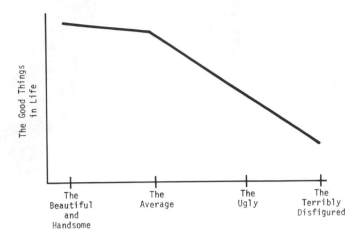

Figure 12.9. The relationship between appearance and the good things in life.

(1) surgery alone (the men received plastic surgery immediately upon release from prison), (2) surgery plus social and vocational services, (3) social and vocational services without surgery or (4) no treatment at all.

The experimenters contacted all inmates one year after their paroles. Cosmetic surgery did give prisoners a head start. As long as prisoners were not drug addicts, plastic surgery dramatically decreased men's recidivism rate. (Surgery produced a 36 percent drop in prison return—an impressive difference.) For some reason, the results for the heroin addicts were not so encouraging. Plastic surgery did not seem to benefit them at all.

The researchers also report that "plastic surgery appeared to help facial disfigurements to a greater extent than those with disfigurements of their bodies" (p. 650). Kurtzberg and his colleagues concluded that, although the cost of plastic surgery in the rehabilitation of adult offenders is relatively high, it "can be considered negligible if the offender is helped to remain out of prison for even one year" (p. 649).

There is also some evidence that as people's looks improve there are corresponding changes in how others treat them. Researchers have asked: If an ugly duckling turns into a beautiful swan, do people continue to treat him/her as they did before (when he/she was unattractive), or do they begin to think of him/her in a new way—corresponding to how she/he now looks? One recent study (Korabik 1981) investigates whether or not changes in adolescent girls' dental attractiveness affects how others react to them. Photographs were taken of adolescent girls, both before and after two years of dental treatment at the St. Louis University Orthodentic Clinic. During the same period of time, photographs were also taken of girls who had not yet been treated.

The girl's photographs were shuffled and shown in random order to men and women who were asked to judge the pictures on four dimensions: intelligence, morality, adjustment, and personal feeling. The men and women were asked to judge the picture twice. Some of the judges saw the pretreatment photos first and the post-treatment photos three weeks later. For the other judges, the order was reversed. It was found that the girls who had received orthodontic treatment were evaluated more positively after treatment than before. Evaluations of the girl's who did not undergo treatment remained uniformly low. This study, like others, demonstrates that improvements in physical attractiveness do change evaluations.

The secret wish of us all is to *become* extraordinarily good-looking; but, the data suggest that if we did we would find, to our disappointment, that our lives had not changed much. What about those who, in spite of their best efforts, can never succeed in becoming other than they are—people with serious physical handicaps. They do face special challenges and difficulties in life; but the data show that even the most disfigured and handicapped individuals have a good chance at happiness if they develop some of the other correlates of inner beauty—compassion, excitement with life, etc. (see Wright 1960).

AND NOW FOR THE BAD NEWS

A few experts insist that even heroic efforts to change people's looks will have very little impact on their lives—"the more things change, the more they remain the same."

At a conference entitled, intimidatingly enough, "The Impact of Craniofacial Changes on Self-Esteem," Dr. Morris Rosenberg reported on a typical case. Jo Ann had been born with a terrible physical defect—her eyes were spaced grotesquely far apart. The spacing was not just the subtle distance that would make a child odd-looking, but a real defect—Jo Ann had the kind of face that makes us gasp in horror. Plastic surgeons did a major reconstruction to recover the distance between her eyes. Dr. Rosenberg expected to find an enormous improvement in Jo Ann's self-confidence after the operation. He found almost none. Jo Ann had been reasonably self-confident before the operation; she remained so after her transformation.

Sociologist Charles Cooley believed our self-esteem is merely a reflection of how others see us. We see ourselves through others' eyes (the "looking glass" self). But this little girl, at such a disadvantage as are many children with serious defects, had cleverly stage-managed *her* mirror. Jo Ann had surrounded herself with people who did not much care about looks. The self *she* saw reflected back was one that said, "You're perfectly fine, thank you" all along. So the operation helped, but not much.

Some experts are convinced that even monumental changes in our looks and personalities can go undetected by those around us. They continue to see us as we were, not as we are.

The Costs of Self-Improvement

Change—even change for the good—is always difficult at first. There is abundant anecdotal evidence that when ugly ducklings turn into swans their delight may well be tinged with sheer terror. The other ducklings sometimes protest the improvements too.

There are some survey data supporting the contention that ugly ducklings who evolve can expect to face some difficult times at first. At first, they will feel singularly out of touch with themselves and uncertain about how to act when offered new dating, sexual, and job opportunities. They will find themselves sabotaged by friends and lovers, uncomfortable with the new them.

A study we touched upon earlier is relevant here. In the *Psychology Today* study we described in chapter 9 (Berscheid et al. 1973), we asked men and women if they had ever experienced a sudden dramatic change in their appearance: for example, rapid weight gain or loss, cosmetic surgery, war injuries, accidents, or the like. We also asked when such changes had occurred.

Have you experienced a sudden and permanent *positive* change in physical attractiveness (cosmetic surgery, dental surgery, rapid weight change, etc.)? (Check all the answers that are applicable.)

_____A Never
_____B Early change (12 years or younger).
_____C Adolescent change (13 to 19 years).
_____D Young adult change (20 to 30 years).
_____E Adult change (31 to 45 years).
_____F Later change (46 or later).

Have you experienced a sudden and permanent *negative* change in physical attractiveness (car accident, war injury, rapid weight change, etc.)? (Check all the answers that are applicable).

_____A Never
_____B Early change (12 years or younger).
_____C Adolescent change (13 to 19 years).
_____D Young adult change (20 to 30 years).
_____E Adult change (31 to 45 years).
_____F Later change (46 or later).

To our surprise, 38 percent of our correspondents had experienced just such a change; in fact, an additional 15 percent of them had had more than one dramatic change!

Were such sudden changes in appearance stressful? Yes. We predicted that, at first, readers who had experienced *one* change—whether for the better or for the worse—would be slightly less confident and happy than those who had never changed. We were right (see Table 12.1).

TABLE 12.1 **The Effect of Dramatic Changes in Appearance**

	NUMBER OF RESPONDENTS	CURRENT SELF-ESTEEM[1]	CURRENT BODY SATISFACTION[1]	CURRENT HAPPINESS[1]
Appearance dramatically improved	(536)	34.09	109.73	6.84
Looks never changed	(893)	34.27	109.83	7.01
Appearance dramatically suffered	(207)	33.02	103.13	6.60

[1] The higher the number, the greater the person's current self-esteem, body satisfaction, and happiness.

SOURCE: Berscheid et al., 1973.

What about the readers who had experienced more than one dramatic change—for better or worse—in appearance? If one change is unsettling (and we have seen it is), these multiple changers should feel less self-confident, have worse body images, and be less happy than those who had changed only once. Again, the data supported our hunch.

The data, then, suggest that in the short run any change, even if an improvement, is unsettling (at first, as things get better they get worse). As ugly ducklings get used to their new status as swans, their lives do improve.

In Sum

The preceding data suggest that people can markedly change their physical appearance and that such changes, although unsettling at first, can have an important impact on their lives. It may well be wise, then, to spend some time improving your appearance. Such efforts can improve your life. But only some time. There are several reasons why you don't want to focus too much on maintaining and improving your physical appearance.

THE PROBLEMS OF BEAUTY

Problem #1: You Could Spend All Your Time Improving Yourself

Beauty counselor George Masters (1977) describes the *first step* in producing a beauty:

> Beauty is much more than hair and makeup. It is a total look. . . . Crucial to your total look of beauty is body control. If you don't have it, start working on it instantly. . . . You start by pretending that you're naked with forty imaginary cameras shooting you from every possible angle—up, down, front, back, sideways—on your cheekbones, chinbone, nose, neckline, shoulderline, hipline, bosoms, stomach, thighs, arms and legs, all over, anywhere and everywhere.
>
> The goal is to make you more conscious of yourself, to help you become aware of your body at all times, whether you're sitting, walking, standing, or bending.
>
> What position are the cameras catching you in? Are you slouching in your chair? Straighten up. Pretend one camera is zooming in from the right side, on your face. Is your neck up? Others are focusing on your middle. Is your stomach in? While your neck is up and your stomach pulled in for this shot, what are you doing with your arms and legs?
>
> While you're at it with the cameras, pay special attention to your hand movements, the way you pick up a fork or wrap your fingers around a glass. Your hand movements can add or detract immensely from your look of total beauty. You do not look at all pretty when your hands grab, clutch, slam, shuffle, or reach awkwardly. Furthermore, the way you hold or bend your wrists can cause wrinkles. (pp. 21–23)

The advice proceeds from there! Masters tells us what we are allowed to eat and what we must refrain from eating, how long we must sleep, how to wash our faces, etc., etc.

After a few pages of Masters' book, most readers have a simple reaction—"Forget it. It's not worth it." Masters, himself, acknowledges that it takes a special person to be so concerned:

> This is the crux of the problem. The women who are most in need of a beauty makeover are those who are too content, too secure in what they already have.
>
> Actors and actresses are notorious for their insecurities. They need to have their egos fed constantly. They do this by making themselves physically attractive, glamorous, ravishing, and sexy.

Insecurity is what made Marilyn Monroe. She had more of it than anyone I've ever met which is why her ego worked overtime. I don't think Marilyn Monroe was ever really in love with anyone but Marilyn Monroe. She was the most narcissistic woman I ever met and the most calculating because she wanted so desperately to be Marilyn Monroe to cure her pathetic insecurity.

She would spend hours in front of her mirror having her makeup done and hours getting herself sewed into her glamorous gowns, all the while letting out little wails that betrayed her constant need of an ego-lift, "George, please make me look beautiful . . . George, do I look beautiful? . . . George, don't you think I look beautiful? Tell me . . . ?"

She needed approval, attention, adulation. She was totally dedicated to overcoming her insecurity. (pp. 4–5)

It is relatively easy to be a fairly good-looking, well-groomed person. It is amazingly time consuming to become a "star," obsessed with looks. Few of us can stand to waste the time.

Problem #2: An All-Out Effort Is Probably Counterproductive

In chapter 1, we cited Webster's definition of beauty/handsomeness. We stressed that a *variety* of factors—self-esteem, an exciting personality, compassion, as well as physical characteristics—have an impact on how good-looking we seem to others. Ironically, if we focus too much on how we look, we are likely to neglect other critically important factors and end up impoverished in appearance—as well as depleted spiritually, personally, and socially. It is a fascinating commentary that those with the most power and the most influence—even those whose occupation is to advise others about beauty, such as George Masters—generally care very little about their own appearance. The same George Masters who has built his career making *others* beautiful gives maintaining the illusion short shrift when it comes to his own appearance. Consider the trouble he took when he went for an important job interview at Saks, on Wilshire Boulevard: He had been out riding and had not even bothered to change. He wore Levi's, a torn shirt, and desert boots. He looked and smelled like a stable boy. "But," he observed, "I was only checking in, not reporting for work" (pp. 24–25). He got the job, however. He is a genius with hair—and that's all that mattered.

One day, I (Elaine Hatfield) was at Sinclair Library working on chapter 2. I had just finished reviewing several dozen studies indicating how critical looks are for job success, and I was just about to add a postscript reminding readers how important it is to "dress for success." Suddenly, I was chagrined to become aware of how I looked. I had not had time to put on any makeup. (I was dying to snatch a few moments to work on the chapter.) I had on an old high school blouse and jeans with a belt with some colored beads spelling out Alaska that my sister Mary had given me. I looked terrible, yet, I was having a great time. I was going to be working all day on things I loved. Like all the times when I have been most absorbed in a project, things in my life were going unusually well. Pardoxically, the more excitement I feel about my work and the more energy I invest in it, the more appealing I seem to be to my mate and friends. When I have spent a bit of time trying to be appealing, I am usually less successful. Probably, I am more stilted, awkward, unapproachable then. (A case of "You only succeed once you stop trying.") I quietly changed my conclusion.

Even those whose main appeal is their beauty are sometimes at their best when they are least concerned with looks. Note the following observations on and by Jacquelline Bisset (De Vries and Weber 1979, reprinted by permission of G. P. Putman's Sons):

> She is almost insolent in her casual disregard for her own intensely physical beauty. Her dismissal of her appeal is, in itself, wildly appealing and enormously sensual. . . . Every touch, every trick, every effort, no matter how calculated, takes a back seat to her very centered sense of self and the electric strength of her ego. Something of this management of her own appeal communicates itself on the screen. In person, it is overwhelming.
>
> "I don't believe in all those myths and rules about beauty. That sort of judgment is arbitrary and destructive. All it causes is insecurity. We really have to get past how we look and on to who we are.
>
> "I don't consider myself in the least bit beautiful. I never have. So I'm at a great advantage in both my business and my life. I've never really lived off my looks. I can feel wonderfully attractive when I feel strong and healthy and loving, but even then, the feeling is intensified by involvement with other people. I feel beautiful when I am making my friends and the people I love comfortable and happy—when I am drawing people out of themselves and helping them to relate positively to themselves and their lives. Being attractive can be a complete waste of time if it refers only to physical appeal, or the prettiness of a certain dress. Isn't it better—far better—to be able to relate to the people around you and communicate good feelings about yourself? To me, that's the real fulfillment. That's the truest beauty." (pp. 22–23)

Problem #3: Sometimes Answered Prayers Are Worse

There is a third problem in sacrificing everything in an effort to be beautiful or handsome: Extraordinarily good-looking people are likely to attract lovers very concerned about looks or to land jobs dependent on appearance. Fine, as long as you are young and beautiful. But all of us inevitably have off days. Worse yet, we grow older.

An example: Elaine Hatfield's secretary in New York, Eileen, always attracted a great deal of attention because she was so good-looking. Eileen was beautiful in a Grace Kelly way. She was ladylike and calm. She was a little cool and standoffish, but men kept after her. There was always someone asking for a stamp or students hanging around when she was trying to get a manuscript done or when the grant budget was due. It is irritating to be wanted by so many people you do not want.

To add insult to injury, at the very same time all this fuss was going on, Eileen was having marital troubles. Her husband had fallen in love with her, not because he wanted a beautiful wife, but because he needed a *perfect* one. Now, as she entered her late twenties, he became obsessed with her imperfections. Couldn't she maintain a better tan? Get a face lift? Eventually, she divorced him. She once observed how terrifying it would be to be sixty and married to a man like that, to know the only hold you have on someone is your beauty—and that that is slipping fast.

Problem #4: The Best Is Never Good Enough

There is a final problem with banking everything on beauty—even the best is never good enough. Ravishing women and handsome men may receive adulation, but they are also targets. ("Oh, Victoria Principal—she's fat. Christopher Reeves—he has such a chicken mouth. I never trust a man with no lips.") Even superstars admit such reviews hurt. It hurts to be nominated "Worst dressed of 1982" or "The most overrated actor of 1985." Consider these reviews: (Sally Quinn 1971, 2)

HERS

"I am very honest," explained George Master, Hollywood's most famous make up man.

"There is no such thing as a natural beauty, at least for women. There are naturally beautiful men, though. I transform a pig into a raving beauty everyday."

. . . Jacqueline Kennedy, he says, "Has eyes so far apart that one of them is on the other side of the room."

. . . Marilyn Monroe, he felt, "had mannish tendencies." Mae West, "I swear she is a man."

. . . "Liza Minelli is a disaster. Too bad, because she's nice, but ugly. Joanne Woodward has a flat nose, and Raquel Welch is silicone from the knees up."

HIS

". . . Alex Karras once told me who had the worst breath in the NFL.

"The worst breath. It belonged to an Italian who played in the line for the Los Angeles Rams—Joe Scihilli. Karras said that for the first three years Scihilli relied heavily on his bad breath until, of course, he developed into a great player. Then he didn't have to breathe on people that much."

. . . "Well, I tell you who had the worst feet. Bubba Smith. The worst feet I ever saw in my life belonged to Bubba Smith. They're about 23 inches long and sort of conically shaped. Remember those pointy-toed shoes that people wore years ago? Well, Bubba's feet were made for those . . . . they'd just slide right in there. He has yellow toenails that crumple under, and they're all wrinkled and just horrid looking. Both feet are perfectly flat; he has no arch whatsoever. He just stands flat on the floor."

. . . "Worst hips go to Don Shinnick," Curry says. "Schinnick did not have any hips. He played linebacker for us on the Colts. He's practically a composite bad body himself. Shinnick had the worst body in the history of the world. His lower stomach protruded; his chest had fallen early in life; his shoulders sloped down to these hairy arms that reached below his knees."

(George Plimpton with Billy Curry, Copyright 1977 by George Plimpton. Excerpted from the book *One More July: A Football Dialogue with Bill Curry,* 1st ed. Published by Harper and Row, New York, NY. Distributed by United Features Syndicate. Reprinted in *The Capital Times.* Madison, Wisconsin, September 17, 1977, p. 9.)

Thus far, we have argued that one is wise to spend some time improving one's appearance (especially if one is less good looking than average), but not too much time. We have seen that one may do better, in the long run, if one concentrates primarily on developing personality/ skills/character. In the third part of this chapter, we will briefly review a variety of the more profitable ways to go about improving your appearance and your life.

REAPING THE REWARDS OF THE GOOD-LOOKING

Beauty: The quality or aggregate of qualities in a person or thing that gives pleasure to the senses or pleasurably exalts the mind or spirit. (*Webster's New World Dictionary,* 1969, 76)

Men and women's appearance and the shapes of their lives are influenced by their structural appearance *and* by their intellect, personality, warmth, and behavior. Thus, once you have decided to embark on a "self-improvement" program, you have a wide choice on how to go about it. First, of course, you can try directly to improve your looks. We have discussed both how to do that and the pros and cons of that choice throughout this chapter. There is also, however, a less direct way to improve your looks. In chapters 1–10, we observed that the beautiful are assumed to be good, whether or not they really are. But research reveals an equally interesting finding—the confusion of beauty with goodness goes two ways. If you are "good," people will come to see you as better-looking than you really are, i.e. "what is beautiful may be good, but what is good seems beautiful too" (see Barak, Patkin, and Dell 1982; Felson and Bohrnstedt 1979; Gross and Crofton 1977; Solomon and Saxe 1977; Hatfield [Walster] 1971).

Here is an example of how profoundly personality can affect the perception of beauty. In one study, Elaine Hatfield found that we tend to think people are unusually good-looking if they share our political attitudes! This study was conducted at the University of Wisconsin at the time of the Vietnam War. At that time, University of Wisconsin students were polarized—most were against the war in Vietnam, but there were a few staunch supporters. Most students had struggled through their positions in numberless arguments, classes, and teachings. They felt deeply about the war; there was no changing their minds. (Their struggle has been documented in the film *The War at Home*.) In this hot political climate, students were invited to discuss their opinions about Vietnam.

When everyone was seated, Elaine handed out a two-page questionnaire designed to catch how the students perceived everyone else— looks included. Then the discussion began: Imagine, the students were told, that a company such as Dow Chemical came to town to recruit students for positions in their company. (During the war, Dow Chemical manufactured napalm, an incendiary chemical).

> "One of the jobs that this company has is making war supplies for the government in Vietnam. For this reason, a large group of students decide to picket against the company. The recruiters refuse to talk to the students when they demand to be heard. A mass rally has been called near the building where the recruiters are and several thousand arrive. The group is incited and are stopped by the police before they do any damage to the building. However, a smaller group goes off and vandalizes the windows of local merchants. Seven students are arrested and charged by both the local and the school authorities with disorderly conduct."

Students were asked a few questions designed to determine whether they favored the student demonstrators, the company, or the policy. (These were not difficult questions for students to answer. Just such demonstrations had occurred at Wisconsin in the spring of 1969). They were asked: "Do you feel students were justified in taking action against the company?" "What role would you have played in the disturbance?" (Would you have intervened against pickets? Watched? Picketed? Gone with the group to break windows?) "What action should be taken against the people arrested?" (Should they be brought to trial? Expelled? Suspended? Reprimanded? Released?) From their reactions, the students were classified as radical or conservative.

Then the debate began. Students soon discovered who was with them, who against. How did that knowledge affect their visions of one another? As we expected, when people discovered others shared their political attitudes—be they radical or conservative—they began to see their political allies as "beautiful people." They continued to see those who disagreed with them as so-so.

Evidence suggests that individuals can improve their appearances in either of two ways: (1) by improving their looks, or (2) by developing more appealing personality traits, developing more honorable characters, or securing higher-status, more exciting jobs. (3) Finally, a wise person may choose to become more appealing by improving his or her skills in any number of areas. What are some of the social and work skills people value most?

Recently, Elaine Hatfield and her colleagues, Jane Traupmann, and Mary Utne (Hatfield et al. 1982; Traupmann and Hatfield 1981) interviewed dating couples, newlyweds, and couples married up to seventy years about the traits they considered critically important in shaping their feelings toward lovers, friends, and coworkers. Surprisingly, there *was* consensus. Almost everyone desires the following traits in others:

Personal Concerns

Appearance

1. Is good-looking (Of course!).

2. Takes care of themselves—dresses right, exercises and eats properly.

Social Grace

3. Is sociable, friendly, and relaxed in social settings.

Intellect

4. Is intelligent and informed.

Emotional Concerns

Liking and loving

5. Seems to like you.

6. Is loving.

Understanding and concern

7. Knows your personal concerns and emotional needs and responds to them.

Acceptance

8. Is accepting. Allows you to express different facets of your personality to be "bossy" sometimes, a "baby" other times, aggressive sometimes, passive others, etc.

Appreciation

9. Is appreciative; doesn't take you for granted.

Physical affection

10. Is appropriately affectionate—hugs you, clasps your shoulders, etc. when it "fits."

Sex

11. Fulfilling sexually.

12. Is faithful sexually.

Security

13. Is committed to friends and family.

14. Supports your need to be free and independent—to be alone sometimes, to work at the kind of jobs you like, to pursue outside interests: to do things with your own friends, etc.

Plans and goals for the future

15. Enjoys planning for and dreaming about the future.

Day-to-Day Concerns

Day-to-day operations

16. Contributing their share of time and effort to housework (grocery shopping, yard work or office work, etc.).

Finances

17. Contributing their share of expenses.

Sociability

18. Is easy to get along with.

19. Is a good companion.

20. Is interested in hearing about your life and in sharing their lives with you.

21. Gets along with your friends and relatives.

Decision making

22. Takes a fair share of the responsibility for making decisions.

Remembering special occasions

23. Is thoughtful about sentimental things; remembers birthdays, anniversaries, and other special occasions.

Opportunities Gained and Lost

Opportunities gained

24. Allows you the opportunity to partake of the many life experiences that depend on being married, having friends, or having work associates—for example, the chance to be included in "married couple" social events; having someone to play tennis with, to count on in difficult financial times, having someone to count on in old age. . . .

Opportunities foregone

25. Marriage, friendships, and business associations require people to give up certain opportunities to be in this relationship. The opportunities could have been other mates, other careers, travel, etc.

If you want to become more appealing, then, you have a wide array of options. You can choose to work on improving your appearance, or you can work on any of the twenty-four other traits people see as critically important in personal relations.

*   *   *

IN CONCLUSION

The evidence is clear: America is possessed by a culture of beauty. In school, business, in love and in life, appearance matters. One must spend some time, then, dealing with the realities. One must spend some time worrying over one's appearance; one must spend some time dealing effectively with discrimination.

Yet, all our experience as professors and therapists, whether in dealing with people whose lives seem to be success stories or the reverse, makes us want to warn people not to focus overmuch on the momentary advantages that good looks provides. Those who play up their superficial assets to get what they want end up with friends and associates who care overmuch about the superficial—and these are usually not especially appealing people. Worse yet, your assets can only dwindle with age and time.

What is a better strategy? If you invest your time in cultivating your intimate relationships and friendships, investing your energies in exciting work, contributing to your community, you will be investing in experiences that last.

The future? America may be a culture of beauty these days, but cultural norms keeps changing. Definitions of beauty do not stay fixed. The women's and men's movements increase the possibilities that in time, the value of good looks will be deemphasized and other values will come to the fore. Even in the last few months, designers like Esprit are beginning to use as their models, not traditional models, carefully selected from the ranks of the most beautiful, but their employees; models who are a little crooked of nose, a little pudgy of thigh.

Given all these facts, only a "pretty face" could fail to conclude that, while one must pay *some* attention to the physical, it is more critical to nurture the mind and the spirit.

BIBLIOGRAPHY

Abbott, A. R., and R. J. Sabastian. 1981. Physical attractiveness and expectations of success. *Personality and Social Psychology Bulletin* 7:481–486.

Abraham, S. and John, C. L. (August 30, 1979) Overweight adults in the United States. *Advanced Data from Vital and Health Statistics of the National Center for Health Statistics.* United States Department of Health, Education and Welfare, 51, pp. 1–10.

Abrams, G. 1983. Even the glitterati dim their flash for court. Focus/Law. *The Honolulu Advertiser*, 1 August B-1.

Adams, G. R. 1975. Physical attributes, personality characteristics, and social behavior: An investigation of the effects of the physical attractiveness stereotype. Ph.D. diss., University of Pennsylvania; Philadelphia. Pa.

Adams, G. R. 1977a. Physical attractiveness, personality, and social reactions to peer pressure. *Journal of Psychology* 96:287–296.

Adams, G. R. 1977b. Physical attractiveness research: Toward a developmental social psychology of beauty. *Human Development* 20:217–239.

Adams, G. R. 1978. Racial membership and physical attractiveness effects on preschool teachers' expectations. *Child Study Journal* 8:29–41.

Adams, G. R. 1982. Physical attractiveness. In *In the eye of the beholder: Contemporary issues in stereotyping,* ed. A. G. Miller. New York: Praeger.

Adams, G. R., and A. S. Cohen. 1974. Children's physical and interpersonal characteristics that affect student-teacher interaction. *Journal of Experimental Education* 43:1–5.

Adams, G. R., and A. S. Cohen. 1976a. Characteristics of children and teacher expectancy: An extension to the child's social and family life. *Journal of Educational Research* 70:87–90.

Adams, G. R., and A. S. Cohen. 1976b. An examination of cumulative folder information used by teachers in making differential judgements of children's abilities. *Alberta Journal of Educational Research* 22:216–225.

Adams, G. R., and P. Crane. 1980. An assessment of parents' and teachers' expectations of preschool children's social preference for attractive or unattractive children and adults. *Child Development* 51:224–231.

Adams, G. R., and S. M. Crossman. 1978. *Physical attractiveness: A cultural imperative.* Roslyn Heights, N.Y.: Libra.

Adams, G. R., and T. L. Huston. 1975. Social perception of middle-aged persons varying in physical attractiveness. *Developmental Psychology* 11:657–658.

Adams, G. R., and J. C. LaVoie. 1974. The effect of student's sex, conduct, and facial attractiveness on teacher expectancy. *Education* 95:76–83.

Adams, G. R., and J. C. LaVoie. 1975. Parental expectations of educational and personal-social performance and child-rearing patterns as a function of attractiveness, sex, and conduct of the child. *Child Study Journal* 5:125–142.

Adams, G. R., and J. C. LaVoie. 1977. Teacher expectations: A review of the student characteristics used in expectancy formation. *Journal of Instructional Psychology Monographs* 4:1–28.

Adams, G. R., and J. Wareham. n.d. Beautiful is good: Mechanism of self and others' perceptions. Photocopy. College of Family Life, Utah State University. Logan, Utah.

Agarwal, P., and N. Prakash. 1977. Perceived physical attractiveness as related to attitudes towards women's liberation movement. *Indian Psychological Review* 15:31–34.

Alessi, D. F., and W. A. Anthony. 1969. The uniformity of children's attitudes toward physical disabilities. *Exceptional Children* 35:543–545.

Algozzine, R., and J. Salvia. 1976. Attractiveness and psychological development. *Teacher Education Forum* 4:368–388.

Allen, B. P. 1976. Race and physical attractiveness as criteria for white subjects' dating choices. *Social Behavior and Personality* 4:289–296.

Allgeier, E. R. 1981. The influence of androgynous identification on heterosexual relations. *Sex Roles* 7:321–330.

Allgeier, E. R., and D. Byrne. 1973. Attraction toward the opposite sex as a determinant of physical proximity. *Journal of Social Psychology* 90: 213–219.

Allport, G. W. and H. S. Odbert. 1936. Trait names: A psycho-lexical study. *Psychological Monographs: General and Applied.* 47, (1 whole No. 221) Washington: American Psychological Assoc. pp 1–171.

Aloia, G. F. 1975. Effects of physical stigmata and labels on judgments of subnormality by preservice teachers. *Mental Retardation* 13:17–21.

Altemeyer, R. A., and K. Jones. 1974. Sexual identity, physical attractiveness and seating position as determinants of influence in discussion groups. *Canadian Journal of Behavioural Science* 6:357–375.

Altman, I. 1973. Reciprocity of interpersonal exchange. *Journal for the Theory of Social Behavior* 3:249–261.

Altman, I., and D. A. Taylor. 1973. *Social penetration: The development of interpersonal relationships.* New York: Holt, Rinehart and Winston.

Amir, M. 1971. *Patterns in forcible rape.* Chicago: University of Chicago Press.

Andersen, S. M., and S. L. Bem. 1979. Sex roles in dyadic interaction: Sometimes beauty equals goodness. Paper presented at the Annual Convention of the American Psychological Association, New York City, September. Abstract in *Personality and Social Psychology Bulletin* 5 (1979):256.

Andersen, S. M., and S. L. Bem. 1981. Sex typing and androgyny in dyadic interaction: Individual differences in responsiveness to physical attractiveness. *Journal of Personality and Social Psychology* 41:74–86.

Anderson, R. 1978. Physical attractiveness and locus of control. *Journal of Social Psychology* 105:213–216.

Anderson, R., and S. A. Nida. 1978. Effect of physical attractiveness on opposite- and same-sex evaluations. *Journal of Personality* 46:401–413.

Angell, R. C. 1936. *The family encounters the depression.* New York: Charles Scribner's Sons.

Anton, J. L., and M. L. Russell. 1974. *Employer attitudes and opinions regarding potential college graduate employees.* Hayward, Calif.: Research Committee of the Western College Placement Association.

Appleford, B. et al. 1976. Teacher-child interactions as related to sex, socio-economic status and physical attractiveness. Paper presented at the Annual Meeting of the Canadian Psychological Association, Toronto, Canada, June 9–11.

Archer, D. 1973. The face of power: Physical attractiveness as a nonverbal predictor of small group stratification. *Proceedings of the 81st Annual Convention of the American Psychological Association* (Montreal, Canada) 8:177–178.

Argyle, M. 1967. *The psychology of interpersonal behavior.* Baltimore, Maryland: Penguin Books.

Argyle, M. 1981. *The psychology of social situations.* Oxford, England: Pergamon Press.

Argyle, M., and R. McHenry. 1971. Do spectacles really affect judgements of intelligence? *British Journal of Social and Clinical Psychology* 10:27–29.

Arkowitz, H., R. Hinton, J. Perl, and W. Himadi. 1978. Treatment strategies for dating anxiety in college men based on real-life practice. *Counseling Psychologist* 7:41–46.

Aronson, E. 1969. Some antecedents of interpersonal attraction. In *Nebraska symposium on motivation,* ed. W. Arnold and D. Levine, vol. 17, 143–177. Lincoln: University of Nebraska Press.

Aronson, E., and V. Aronson. Nov. 1971. Does a woman's attractiveness influence men's nonsexual reactions? *Medical Aspects of Human Sexuality* 5:12–27.

Aronson, E., and D. Linder. 1965. Gain and loss of esteem as determinants of interpersonal attractiveness. *Journal of Experimental Social Psychology* 1:156–171.

Aronson, E., B. Willerman, and J. Floyd. 1966. The effect of a pratfall on increasing interpersonal attractiveness. *Psychonomic Science*, 4, 157–158.

Asher, J. J. 1970. How the applicant's appearance affects the reliability and validity of the interview. *Educational and Psychological Measurement* 30:687–695.

Athanasiou, R., and P. Greene. 1973. Physical attractiveness and helping behavior. *Proceedings of the 81st Annual Convention of the American Psychological Association* (Montreal, Canada) 8:289–290.

Atkins, C., C. Morse, and R. Zweigenhaft. 1978. The stereotype and recognition of female athletes. *Journal of Psychology* 100:27–31.

Bailey, R. C., and J. P. Price. 1978. Perceived physical attractiveness in married partners of long and short duration. *Journal of Psychology* 99: 155–161.

Bain, A. 1868. *Mental and moral science.* London: Longmans, Green and Co.

Baker, M. J. 1974. The effects of inequity on heterosexual behavior: A test for compensation in inequitable dating relationships. (Master's thesis) University of Wisconsin, Madison, Wisc.

Baker, M. J., and G. A. Churchill. 1977. The impact of physically attractive models on advertising evaluations. *Journal of Marketing Research* 14:538–555.

Banziger, G., and L. Hooker. 1979. The effects of attitudes toward feminism and perceived feminism on physical attractiveness ratings. *Sex Roles* 5:437–442.

Barak, A., J. Patkin, and D. M. Dell. 1982. Effects of certain counselor behaviors on perceived expertness and attractiveness. *Journal of Counseling Psychology* 29:261–267.

Barbach, L. G. 1975. *For yourself: The fulfillment of female sexuality.* New York: New American Library.

Barclay, A. M. 1969. The effect of hostility on physiological and fantasy responses. *Journal of Personality* 37:651–667.

Barefoot, J. C., and R. B. Straub. 1971. Opportunity for information search and the effect of false heartrate feedback. *Journal of Personality and Social Psychology* 17:154–167.

Barker, R. G. 1942. The social interrelations of strangers and acquaintances. *Sociometry* 7:169–179.

Barocas, R., and H. K. Black. 1974. Referral rate and physical attractiveness in third-grade children. *Perceptual and Motor Skills* 39:731–734.

Barocas, R., and P. Karoly. 1972. Effects of physical appearance on social responsiveness. *Psychological Reports* 31:495–500.

Barocas, R., and F. L. Vance. 1974. Physical appearance and personal adjustment counseling. *Journal of Counseling Psychology* 21:96–100.

Baron, R. A. 1981. Olfaction and human social behavior: Effects of a pleasant scent on attraction and social perception. *Personality and Social Psychology Bulletin* 7:611–616.

Baron, R., and D. Byrne. 1983. *Social psychology.* 4th ed. Newton, Mass.: Allyn and Bacon.

Barrell, J. J. 1974. Sexual arousal in the objectifying attitude. *Review of Existential Psychology and Psychiatry* 13:98–105.

Bar-Tal, D., and L. Saxe, 1974. Effect of physical attractiveness on the perception of couples. *Personality and Social Psychology Bulletin* 1:30–32.

Bar-Tal, D., and L. Saxe. 1976a. Perceptions of similarly and dissimilarly attractive couples and individuals. *Journal of Personality and Social Psychology* 33:772–781.

Bar-Tal, D., and L. Saxe. 1976b. Physical attractiveness and its relationship to sex-role stereotyping. *Sex Roles* 2:123–133.

Baumeister, R. F., and J. M. Darley. 1982. Reducing the biasing effect of perpetrator attractiveness injury simulation. *Personality and Social Psychology Bulletin* 8:286–292.

Bayrd, E. 1978. *The thin game.* (In consultation with Clifford F. Gastineau and Edwin Bayrd). 1st ed. New York: Newsweek Books.

Beck, S. B., C. I. Ward-Hull, and P. M. McLear. 1976. Variables related to women's somatic preferences of the male and female body. *Journal of Personality and Social Psychology* 34:1200–1210.

Beigel, H. G. 1954. Body height in mate selection. *Journal of Social Psychology* 39:257–268.

Bell, I. P. 1979. The double standard: Age. In *Women: A feminist peerspective,* 2d ed., ed. Jo Freeman, 233–244. Palo Alto, Calif.: Mayfield Publishing Co.

Bem, A. P. 1979. *Social behavior: Fact and falsehood.* Chicago: Nelson Hall.

Bem, S. L. 1974. The measurement of psychological androgyny. *Journal of Consulting and Clinical Psychology* 42:155–162.

Benson, P. L., S. A. Karabenick, and R. M. Lerner. 1976. Pretty pleases: The effects of physical attractiveness, race, and sex on receiving help. *Journal of Experimental Social Psychology* 12:409–415.

Benson, P. L., D. Severs, J. Tatgenhorst, and N. Loddengaard. 1980. The social costs of obesity: A non-reactive field study. *Social Behavior and Personality* 8:91–96.

Berg, D. H. 1975. Sexual subcultures and contemporary heterosexual interaction patterns among adolescents. *Adolescence* 10: 543–548.

Berkman, L. F., and S. L. Syme. 1979. Social networks, host resistance, and mortality: A nine-year follow-up study of Alameda County residents. *American Journal of Epidemiology* 109:186–204.

Berkowitz, L., and A. Frodi. 1978. Reactions to a child's mistakes as effected by her/his looks and speech. Photocopy. Department of Psychology. University of Wisconsin. Madison, Wisc.

Berkowitz, L., and A. Frodi. 1979. Reactions to a child's mistakes as affected by his/her looks and speech. *Social Psychology Quarterly* 42:420–425.

Berkowitz, W. R., J. C. Nebel, and J. W. Reitman. 1971. Height and interpersonal attraction: The 1969 mayoral election in New York City. *Proceedings of the 79th Annual Convention of the American Psychological Association* 6:281–282.

Berman, J. J., and P. Brickman. 1971. Standards for attribution of liking: Effects of sex, self-esteem, and other's attractiveness. *Proceedings of the 79th Annual Convention of the American Psychological Association* 6:271–272.

Berman, P. W., B. A. O'Nan, and W. Floyd. 1981. The double standard of aging and the social situations: Judgments of attractiveness of the middle-aged women. *Sex Roles* 7:87–96.

Bernard, J. 1964. The adjustments of married mates. In *Handbook of marriage and the family*, ed. H. T. Christensen, 675–739. Chicago: Rand McNally & Co.

Berne, E. 1964. *Games people play: The psychology of human relationships*. New York: Grove Press.

Bernstein, W. M., B. O. Stephenson, M. L. Snyder, and R. A. Wicklund. 1983. Casual ambiguity and heterosexual affiliation. *Journal of Social Psychology*, 19:78–92.

Berscheid, E. 1979. Affect in close relationships. Photocopy. Department of Psychology, University of Minnesota, Minneapolis, Minn.

Berscheid, E. 1983. Emotion. In *Close relationships*, ed. H. H. Kelley, E. Berscheid, A. Christensen, J. H. Harvey, T. Huston, G. Levinger, E. McClintock, L. A. Peplau, and D. Peterson. 742–775. New York: W. H. Freeman.

Berscheid, E., K. Dion, E. Hatfield (Walster), and G. W. Walster. 1971. Physical attractiveness and dating choice: A test of the matching hypothesis. *Journal of Experimental Social Psychology* 7:173–189.

Berscheid, E. and L. A. Peplau. 1983. The emerging science of relationships. In *Close relationships* ed. Harold H. Kelley et al., E. Berscheid, A. Christensen, J. H. Harvey, T. Huston, G. Levinger, E. McClintock, L. A. Peplau, and D. Peterson, 1–19. New York: W. H. Freeman.

Berscheid, E., and E. Hatfield (Walster). 1968. *Interpersonal attraction*. Reading, Mass.: Addison Wesley.

Berscheid, E., and E. Hatfield (Walster). 1974. Physical attractiveness. In *Advances in experimental social psychology*, ed. L. Berkowitz, vol. 7, 157–215. New York: Academic Press.

Berscheid, E., E. Hatfield (Walster), and G. Bohrnstedt. 1972. A *Psychology Today* questionnaire: Body image. *Psychology Today*, 6 (July):57–66.

Berscheid, E., E. Hatfield (Walster), and G. Bohrnstedt. 1973. The happy American body: A survey report. *Psychology Today* 7:119–131.

Bickman, L. 1974. Social roles and uniforms: Clothes make the person. *Psychology Today*, (April):45–51.

Biegel, H. G. 1954. Body height in mate selection. *The Journal of Social Psychology* 39:257–268.

Black, H. K. 1974. Physical attractiveness and similarity of attitude in interpersonal attraction. *Psychological Reports* 35:403–406.

Blass, T., L. Alperstein, and S. H. Block. 1974. Effects of communicator's race and beauty and of receiver's objectivity-subjectivity on attitude change *Personality and Social Psychology Bulletin* 1:132–134.

Blau, P. M. 1964. *Exchange and power in social life*. New York: Wiley & Sons

Bloc, A. 1982. *Murphy's law*. Los Angeles: Price/Stern/Stone Publishers.

Bloom, B. L., S. J. Asher, and S. W. White. 1978. Marital disruption as a stressor: A review and analysis. *Psychological Bulletin* 85:867–894.

Blumstein, P., and P. Schwartz. 1983. *American couples*. New York: William Morrow.

Bohannan, P., ed. 1971. *Divorce and after*. Garden City, N.Y.: Doubleday Anchor

Bonney, M. W. 1943. Personality traits of socially successful and socially un-successful children. *Journal of Educational Psychology* 34:449–472.

Boor, M. 1976. Beautiful is not dangerous, beauty is not talent: Two failures to replicate physical attractiveness effects. *Catalog of Selected Documents in Psychology* 6:109.

Boor, M., and F. R. Zeis. 1975. Effect of physical attractiveness on IQ estimation: A failure to extend results of prior research. *Catalog of Selected Documents in Psychology*, no. 929:234–235.

Boukydis, C., L. Ford, L. Celhoffer, and K. Minde. 1978. Nurses' judgements of the attractiveness of premature infants. *Infant Behavior and Development* 1:373–380.

Bowman, G. 1962. The image of a promotable person in business. Ph.D. diss., New York University, New York City.

Bowman, G. 1964. What helps or harms promotability? *Harvard Business Review* 42:6–196.

Bramel, D., B. Taub, and B. Blum. 1968. An observer's reaction to the suffering of his enemy. *Journal of Personality and Social Psychology* 8:384–392.

Bray, G. A., ed. 1979. November. *Obesity in America* Department of Health, Education, and Welfare. Public Health Service. National Institutes on Health. NIH Publication no. 79–359.

Brehm, J. W. 1966. *A theory of psychological reactance.* New York: Academic Press.

Brickman, P., and D. T. Campbell. 1971. Hedonic relativism and planning the good society. In *Adaptation-level theory: A symposium,* ed. M. H. Appley, 287–304. New York: Academic Press.

Brislin, R. W., and S. A. Lewis. 1966. Dating and physical attractiveness: A replication. *Psychological Reports* 22:976.

Brock, T. C., S. K. Edelman, D. C. Edwards, and J. R. Schuck. 1965. Seven studies of performance expectancy as a determinant of actual performance. *Journal of Experimental Social Psychology* 1:295–310.

Brody-Johansen, R. 1968. *Body and clothes.* New York: Reinhold.

Broverman, I. K., S. R. Vogel, D. M. Broverman, F. E. Clarkson, and P. W. Rosenkrantz. 1972. Sex role stereotypes: A current appraisal. *Journal of Social Issues* 28:59–78.

Brown, N. W., and P. Renz. 1973. Altering the reality self-concept of seventh grade culturally deprived girls in the inner city. *Adolescence* 8:463:474.

Brown, R. D. 1970. Experienced and inexperienced counselors' first impressions of clients and case outcomes: Are first impressions lasting? *Journal of Counseling Psychology* 17:550–558.

Brownmiller, S. 1975. *Against our will: Men, women, and rape.* New York: Simon and Schuster.

Bruch, H. 1978. *The golden cage: The enigma of anorexia nervosa.* Cambridge, Mass.: Harvard University Press.

Brundage, L. E., V. J. Derlega, and T. F. Cash. 1977. The effects of physical attractiveness and need for approval on self-disclosure. *Personality and Social Psychology Bulletin* 3:63–66.

Brunner, E. 1945. *Justice and the social order.* London: Luderworth Press.

Buckley, H. M., and M. E. Roach. 1974. Clothing as a nonverbal communicator of social and political attitudes. *Home Economics Research Journal* 3:94–102.

Bull, R., and C. Hawks. 1979. Judging politicians by their faces. *Bulletin of the British Psychological Society* 32:188.

Bunting, G. 1981. Is there love after mail-order marriage? *California Today*, 19 April, 9.

Burke, E. 1909. On the sublime and beautiful. In *The Harvard Classics*, ed. Charles W. Eliot, vol. 24, pt. 3, sec. 9, 90. New York: P. H. Collier and Son.

Byrne, B. 1981. Delores Del Rio. *The New York Times*, 20–27 November, 12–21.

Byrne, D. 1971. *The attraction paradigm.* New York: Academic Press.

Byrne, D. C. R. Ervin, and J. Lamberth. 1970. Continuity between the experimental study of attraction and "real life" computer dating. *Journal of Personality and Social Psychology* 16:157–165.

Byrne, D., O. London, K. Reeves. 1968. The effects of physical attractiveness, sex, and attitude similarity on interpersonal attraction. *Journal of Personality* 36:259–271.

Byrne, D., D. P. J. Przybyla, and A. Infantino. 1981. The influence of social threat on subsequent romantic attraction. Paper presented at the meeting of the Eastern Psychological Association, April, New York City.

Cahnman, W. J. 1968. The stigma of obesity. *The Sociological Quarterly* 9:283–299.

Calhoun, L. G., J. W. Selby, A. Cann, and G. T. Keller. 1978. The effects of victim physical attractiveness and sex of respondent on social reactions to victims of rape. *British Journal of Social and Clinical Psychology* 17:191–192.

Calio, J. 1982. Inventors: Artist Nancy Burson and her age machine are making people old before their time. *People*, 93–96.

Campbell, A., P. E. Converse, and W. L. Rodgers. 1976. *The quality of American life.* New York City: Russell Sage Foundation.

Campbell, D. P. 1967. The vocational interests of beautiful women. *Personnel and Guidance Journal* 45:968–972.

Campbell, D. T. 1965. *The results of counseling: Twenty-five years later.* Philadelphia: Saunders.

Campbell, D. T., and J. C. Stanley. 1963. Experimental and quasiexperimental designs for research on teaching. In *Handbook of research on teaching*, ed. N. L. Gage, 171–246. Chicago: Rand McNally.

Campbell, R. T. 1979. The relationship between children's perceptions of ability and perceptions of physical attractiveness: Comment on Felson and Bohrnstedt's "Are the good beautiful or the beautiful good?" *Social Psychology Quarterly* 42:393–398.

Cann, A., W. D. Siegfried, and L. Pearce. 1981. Forced attention to specific applicant qualifications: Impact on physical attractiveness and sex of applicant biases. *Personnel Psychology* 34:65–75.

Caprio, F. S. 1973. Fetishism. In *Encyclopedia of sexual behavior*, ed. A. Ellis and A. Abarbanel, 435–438. New York: Jason Aronson.

Carducci, B. J., P. C. Cozby, and C. D. Ward. 1978. Sexual arousal and interpersonal evaluations. *Journal of Experimental Social Psychology* 14:449–457.

Carnegie, D. 1936. *How to win friends and influence people.* New York: Simon and Schuster.

Carter, J. A. 1978. Impressions of counselors as a function of counselor physical attractiveness. *Journal of Counseling Psychology* 25:28–34.

Cash, T. F. 1978. Self-disclosure in initial acquaintanceship: Effects of sex, approval motivation, and physical attractiveness. *Catalog of Selected Documents in Psychology* 8, no. 1642:11.

Cash, T. F. 1979. Behavioral science and the benefits of beauty. Paper presented to the Symposium on Cosmetic Benefits, sponsored by the Cosmetic, Toiletry, and Fragrance Association, 16 November, New York City. (Available from the author)

Cash, T. F., and P. J. Begley. 1976. Internal-external control, achievement orientation and physical attractiveness of college students. *Psychological Reports* 38:1205–1206.

Cash, T. F., P. J. Begley, D. A. McCown, and B. C. Weise. 1975. When counselors are heard but not seen: Initial impact of physical attractiveness. *Journal of Counseling Psychology* 22:273–279.

Cash, T. F., and D. S. Burns. 1977. The occurrence of reinforcing activities in relation to locus of control, success-failure expectancies, and physical attractiveness. *Journal of Personality Assessment* 41:387–391.

Cash, T. F., D. W. Cash, and J. W. Butters. 1983. Mirror, mirror, on the wall . . . ?: Contrast effects and self-evaluations of physical attractiveness. *Personality and Social Psychology Bulletin* 9:351–358.

Cash, T. F., and V. J. Derlega. 1978. The matching hypothesis: Physical attractiveness among same-sexed friends. *Personality and Social Psychology Bulletin* 4:240–243.

Cash, T. F., B. Gillen, and D. S. Burns. 1977. Sexism and "beautyism" in personal consultant decision-making. *Journal of Applied Psychology* 62:301–310.

Cash, T. F., and J. Kehr. 1977. Influence of nonprofessional counselors' physical attractiveness and sex on perceptions of counselor behavior. *Journal of Counseling Psychology* 25:336–342.

Cash, T. F., J. A. Kehr, J. Polyson, and V. Freeman. 1977. Role of physical attractiveness in peer attribution of psychological disturbance. *Journal of Consulting and Clinical Psychology* 45:987–993.

Cash, T. F., and R. F. Salzbach. 1978. The beauty of counseling: Effects of counselor physical attractiveness and self-disclosures on perceptions of counselor behavior. *Journal of Counseling Psychology* 25:283–291.

Cash, T. F., and E. Smith. 1980. Physical attractiveness and personality: More than skin deep? Old Dominion University, Norfolk, Virginia. (Available from first author upon request)

Cash, T. F., and E. Smith. 1982. Physical attractiveness and personality among American college students. *The Journal of Psychology* 111:183–191.

Cash, T. F., and D. Soloway. 1975. Self-disclosure: Correlates of physical attractiveness: An exploratory study. *Psychological Reports* 36:579–586.

Cash, T. F., and C. A. Trimer. 1980. Sexism and beautyism in women's evaluations of peer performance. Old Dominion University, Norfolk, Virginia. (Available from first author)

Casper, R. C., E. D. Eckert, K. Halmi, S. C. Goldberg, and J. M. Davis. 1980. Bulima: Its incidence and clinical importance in patients with anorexia nervosa. *Archives of General Psychiatry* 37:1030–1035.

Cavan, R. S. 1959. Unemployment: Crisis of the common man. *Marriage and Family Living* 21:139–146.

Cavior, H. W., S. C. Hayes, and N. Cavior. 1974. Physical attractiveness of female offenders: Effects on institutional performance. *Criminal Justice and Behavior* 1:321–331.

Cavior, N. 1970. Physical attractiveness, perceived attitude similarity and interpersonal attraction among fifth and eleventh grade boys and girls. Ph.D. diss., University of Houston, Houston.

Cavior, N., and P. J. Boblett. 1972. Physical attractiveness of dating versus married couples. *Proceedings of the 80th Annual Convention of the American Psychological Association* 7:175–176.

Cavior, N., and P. R. Dokecki. 1971. Physical attractiveness self-concept: A test of Mead's hypothesis. *Proceedings of the 79th Annual Convention of the American Psychological Association* 6:319–320.

Cavior, N., and P. R. Dokecki. 1972. Physical attractiveness, perceived attitude similarity, and academic achievement as contributors to interpersonal attraction (popularity) among fifth and eleventh grade boys and girls. Mimeo. available from the senior author.

Cavior, N., and P. R. Dokecki. 1973. Physical attractiveness, perceived attitude similarity, and academic achievement as contributors to interpersonal attraction among adolescents. *Development Psychology* 9:44–54.

Cavior, N., and I. R. Howard. 1973. Facial attractiveness and juvenile delinquency among black and white offenders. *Journal of Abnormal Child Psychology* 1:202–213.

Cavior, N., R. L. Kurtzberg, H. Safar, and D. S. Lipton. 1967. The community's response to substance misuse. *International Journal of the Addictions* 2:139–142.

Cavior, N., and D. A. Lombardi. 1973. Developmental aspects of judgement of physical attractiveness in children. *Developmental Psychology* 8:67–71.

Cavior, N., K. Miller, and S. H. Cohen. 1975. Physical attractiveness, attitude similarity, and length of acquaintance as contributors to interpersonal attraction among adolescents. *Social Behavior and Personality* 3:133–141.

Centers, R. 1949. *The psychology of social classes: A study of class consciousness.* Princeton, N.J.: Princeton University Press.

Chadwick-Jones, J. K. 1976. *Social exchange theory: Its structure and influence in social psychology.* London: Academic Press.

Chaiken, S. 1979. Communicator physical attractiveness and persuasion. *Journal of Personality and Social Psychology* 37:1387–1397.

Chaiken, S., A. H. Eagly, D. Sejwacz, W. L. Gergory, and D. Christiansen. 1978. Communicator physical attractiveness as a determinant of opinion change. *Catalog of Selected Documents in Psychology* 8, no. 1639 (February) 9–10.

Chaikin, A. L., V. J. Derlega, B. Bayma, and J. Shaw. 1975. Neuroticism and disclosure reciprocity. *Journal of Consulting and Clinical Psychology* 43:13–19

Chaikin, A. L., H. B. Gillen, V. Derlega, J. Heinen, and M. Wilson. 1978. Students' reactions to teachers' physical attractiveness and nonverbal behavior: Two exploratory studies. *Psychology in the Schools* 15:588–595.

Chakrabarti, T. K. 1974. Attitudes reflected in matrimonial advertisements. *Australian and New Zealand Journal of Sociology* 10:142–143.

Chappel, D., and J. James. 1978. Victim selection and apprehension from the rapist perspective: A preliminary investigation. Paper presented at the Second International Symposium on Victimology, September, 1976, Boston. Reported in Schram, D. D. (1978) Rape. In *Victimization of Women*, ed. J. R. Chapman and M. Gates, 53–79. Beverly Hills: Sage.

Chelune, G. J.; J. T. Robison, and M. J. Kommor. 1984. In V. J. Derlega *Communication, intimacy, and close relationships.* New York: Academic Press, 11–40.

Child, I. L. 1968. Esthetics. In *The Handbook of Social Psychology*, ed. G. Lindzey and E. Aronson, vol. 3, 853–915. Reading, Mass.: Addison Wesley.

Christie, R., and F. L. Geis. 1970. *Studies in Machiavellianism.* New York: Academic Press.

Clanton, G., and L. G. Smith. eds. 1977. *Jealousy.* Englewood Cliffs, N.J.: Prentice-Hall.

Clark, R. D., III, and E. Hatfield. 1981. Gender differences in receptivity to sexual offers. Photo copy. Department of Psychology. Florida State University: Tallahassee, Fla.

Clayson, D. W., and M. Maugham. 1976. *Blond is beautiful: Status and preference by hair color.* Paper presented at the Rocky Mountain Psychological Association Convention, Phoenix, Arizona.

Clifford, M. M. 1975. Physical attractiveness and academic performance. *Child Study Journal* 5:201–209.

Clifford, M. M., and E. Hatfield (Walster). 1973. Research note: The effects of physical attractiveness on teacher expectations. *Sociology of Education* 46:248–258.

Clifton, R. A., and I. J. Baksh. 1978. Physical attractiveness, year of university, and the expectations of student-teachers. *Canadian Journal of Education* 3:37–46.

Coleman, J. S. 1974. *Youth: Transition to adulthood.* Report of the Panel on Youth of the President's Science Advisory Committee. Chicago: University of Chicago Press.

Conger, J. J. 1975. Sexual attitudes and behavior of contemporary adolescents. In *Contemporary issues in adolescent development*, ed. John J. Conger. New York: Harper and Row.

Connor, B. H., K. Peters. and R. H. Nagasawa. 1975. Person and costume: Effects on the formation of first impressions. *Home Economics Research Journal* 4:32–41.

Cook, M., and G. Wilson, eds. 1979. *Love and attraction: An international conference.* Oxford: Pergamon Press.

Cooley, C. H. 1902. *Human nature and the social order.* New York: Charles Scribner's Sons.

Coombs, R. H., and W. F. Kenkel. 1966. Sex differences in dating aspirations and satisfaction with computer-selected partners. *Journal of Marriage and the Family* 28:62–66.

Coopersmith, S. 1967. *The antecedents of self-esteem.* San Francisco: W. H. Freeman.

Cordwell, J. M. 1976. Human arts of transformation. *CTFA Cosmetic Journal* 8 (October/December):22–28.

Corliss, R. 1982. Sexes: The new ideal of beauty. *Time,* 30 August, 72–73.

Corrigan, J. D., D. M. Dell, K. N. Lewis, and L. D. Schmidt. 1980. Counseling as a social influence process: A review. *Journal of Counseling Psychology* 27:295–441.

Cortes, J. B., and F. M. Gatti. 1965. Physique and self-description of temperament. *Journal of Consulting Psychology* 29:432–439.

Cozby, P. C. 1973. Self-disclosure: A literature review. *Psychological Bulletin* 79:73–91.

Crespi, L. P. 1942. Quantitative variation in incentive and performance in the white rat. *American Journal of Psychology* 55:467–517.

Crisp, A. H., R. L. Palmer, and R. S. Kalucy. 1976. How common is anorexia nervosa? A prevalance study. *British Journal of Psychiatry* 128:549–554.

Critelli, J. W. 1978. Physical attractiveness in dating couples. Paper presented at the Annual Convention of the American Psychological Association, September, Chicago.

Critelli, J. W., L. R. Waid, and L. J. Schneider. 1979. Inequity in physical attractiveness as a predictor of dominance and romantic love. Paper presented at the Annual Convention of the American Psychological Association, September, New York City. Abstract in *Personality and Social Psychology Bulletin* 5:259.

Cross, J. F., and J. Cross. 1971. Age, sex, race, and the perception of facial beauty. *Developmental Psychology* 5:433–459.

Crouse, B. B., and A. Mehrabian. 1977. Affiliation of opposite-sexed strangers. *Journal of Research in Personality* 11:38–47.

Cunningham, J. D. 1976. Boys meet girls: Patterns of interaction and attribution of heterosexual attraction. *Journal of Personality and Social Psychology* 34:334–343.

Cunningham, M. R. 1981. Sociobiology as a supplementary paradigm for social and psychological research. In *Review of personality and social psychology,* ed. L. Wheeler, vol. 2. Beverly Hills, Calif.: SAGE.

Curran, J. P. 1973. Correlates of physical attractiveness and interpersonal attraction in the dating situation. *Social Behavior and Personality* 1:153–157.

Curran, J. P. 1975. Convergence toward a single sexual standard? *Social Behavior and Personality* 3:189–195.

Curran, J. P., and S. Lippold. 1975. The effects of physical attractiveness and attitude similarity on attraction in dating dyads. *Journal of Personality* 43:528–539.

Curran, J. P., S. Neff, and S. Lippold. Correlates of sexual experience among university students. *The Journal of Sex Research* 9:124–131.

Cutrona, E. E. 1982. Transition to college: Loneliness and the process of social adjustment. In *Loneliness*, ed. L. A. Peplau and D. Perlman, 291–309. New York City: Wiley.

Dabbs, J. M., Jr., and N. A. Stokes, III. 1975. Beauty is power: The use of space on the sidewalk. *Sociometry* 38:551–557.

D'Addario, L. J. 1977. Sexual relation between female clients and male therapists. Ph.D. diss., California School of Professional Psychology, San Francisco, Calif.

Dailey, D. A. 1952. The effects of premature conclusion upon the acquisition of understanding a person. *Journal of Psychology* 33:133–152.

Dailey, W. F., G. J. Allen, J. M. Chinsky, and S. Veit. 1974. Attendant behavior and attitudes toward institutionalized retarded children. *American Journal of Mental Deficiency* 78:586–691.

Dally, P., and W. Sargant. 1966. Treatment and outcome of anorexia nervosa. *British Medical Journal*, October: 793–795.

Dannenmaier, W. D., and F. J. Thumain. 1964. Authority status as a factor in perceptual distortion of size. *Journal of Social Psychology* 63:361–365.

Darley, J. M., and J. Cooper. 1972. The "clean for Gene" phenomenon: The effect of students' appearance on political campaigning. *Journal of Applied Social Psychology* 2:24–33.

Darwin, C. 1952. The origin of species by means of natural selection. The descent of man and selection in relation to sex. *Great books of the western world: 49, Darwin*. Chicago: Encyclopedia Britannica.

Data matter: Tips for landing that job. 1975. *Journal of Systems Management* 5 (October).

Davenport, D. 1982. Dating by want ad. Lifestyles, *Madison*, June, 7.

Davis, D., H. G. Rainey, and T. C. Brock. 1976. Interpersonal physical pleasuring: effects of sex combinations, recipient attributes, and anticipated future interaction. *Journal of Personality and Social Psychology* 33:89–106.

Davis, J. B., and A. E. Skinner. 1974. Reciprocity of self disclosure in interviews: Modeling of social exchange. *Journal of Personality and Social Psychology* 29:779–784.

Deaux, K. 1974. Woman in management: Causal explanations of performance. Paper presented at the 82nd Annual Meetiing of the American Psychological Association, August, New Orleans, Louisiana.

Deaux, K. 1976. *The behavior of men and women*. Belmont, Calif.: Wadsworth Publishing.

Deck, L. 1968. Reported in *Journal of College and University Personnel Association* 19:33–37.

Deck, L. 1971. Short workers of the world unite. *Psychology Today*, August, 102.

Deitz, S. R. and L. E. Byrnes. 1981. Attribution of responsibility for sexual assault: The influence of observer empathy and defendant occupation and attractiveness. *The Journal of Psychology* 108:17–29.

DeJong, W. 1980. The stigma of obesity: The consequences of naive assumptions concerning the causes of physical deviance. *Journal of Health and Social Behavior* 21:75–87.

Delafield, G. 1979. Reactions to priase and specificity in self-esteem. *Bulletin of the British Psychological Society* 32:221.

De Lamater, J. 1982. Gender differences in sexual scripts. *American Sociological Association Meetings.* San Francisco, Calif.

DeLamater, J., and P. MacCorquodale. 1979. *Premarital sexuality: Attitudes, relationships, behavior.* Madison, Wis.: The University of Wisconsin Press.

Dembo, A., and I. Imbeloni. 1938. *Deformaciones intencionales del humano de character etnico.* Buenos Aires: J. Anesi.

DeMeis, D. K., and R. Turner. 1978. Effects of students' race, physical attractiveness, and dialect on teachers' evaluations. *Contemporary Educational Psychology* 3:77–86.

Derlega, V. J., and A. L. Chaikin, 1975. *Sharing intimacy: What we reveal to others and why.* Englewood Cliffs, N.J.: Prentice-Hall.

Dermer, M. 1973. *When beauty fails.* Ph.D. diss., University of Minnesota, Minneapolis.

Dermer, M., and D. L. Thiel, 1975. When beauty may fail. *Journal of Personality and Social Psychology* 31:1168–1176.

Deseran, F. A., and C. S. Chung. 1979. Appearance, role-taking, and reactions to deviance: Some experimental findings. *Social Psychology Quarterly* 42:426–430.

Deutsch, F. M., M. E. Clark, and C. M. Zalenski. 1983. Is there a double standard of aging? Paper presented at Eastern Psychological Association Convention, Philadelphia.

De Vries, M., and E. Weber. 1979. *Body and beauty secrets of the superbeauties.* New York: G. P. Putnam.

Diagnostic and Statistical Manual of Mental Disorders. 1980. 3d ed. (DSM-III). Washington, D.C.: American Psychiatric Association.

Diamond, M. J., and J. L. Shapiro. 1981. *The paradoxes of intimate relating.* Honolulu: King Kalakaua Center for Humanistic Psychology, Ltd. (Available from Dr. J. L. Shapiro, King Kalakaua Center for Humanistic Psychology, Ltd., Suite 121, Aina Haina Professional Building, 850 West Hind Drive, Honolulu, Hawaii, 96821.)

Dibiase, W. J., and L. A. Hjelle. 1968. Body-image stereotypes and body-type preferences among male college students. *Perceptual and Motor Skills* 27:1143–1146.

Dillon, W. S. 1968. *Gifts and nations.* The Hague: Mouton.

Dion, K. K. 1972. Physical attractiveness and evaluation of children's transgressions. *Journal of Personality and Social Psychology* 24:207–213.

Dion, K. K. 1973. Young children's stereotyping of facial attractiveness. *Developmental Psychology* 9:183–188.

Dion, K. K. 1974. Children's physical attractiveness and sex as determinants of adult punitiveness. *Developmental Psychology* 10:772–778.

Dion, K. K. 1977. The incentive value of physical attractiveness for young children. *Personality and Social Psychology Bulletin* 3:67–70.

Dion, K. K., and E. Berscheid. 1972. Physical attractiveness and social perception of peers in preschool children. Mimeo. (Available from the authors)

Dion, K. K., and E. Berscheid. 1974. Physical attractiveness and peer perception among children. *Sociometry* 37:1–12.

Dion, K., E. Berscheid, and E. Hatfield (Walster). 1972. What is beautiful is good. *Journal of Personality and Social Psychology* 24:285–290.

Dion, K. K., and S. Stein. 1978. Physical attractiveness and interpersonal influence. *Journal of Experimental Social Psychology* 14:97–108.

Dipboye, R. L., R. D. Arvey, and D. E. Terpstra. 1977. Sex and physical attractiveness of raters and applicants as determinants of resume evaluations. *Journal of Applied Psychology* 62:288–294.

Dipboye, R. L., H. L. Fromkin, and K. Wiback. 1975. Relative importance of applicant sex, attractiveness, and scholastic standing in evaluation of job applicant resumes. *Journal of Applied Psychology* 60:39–43.

Donley, B., and B. Allen. 1977. Influences of experimenter attractiveness and ego-involvement on paired-associates learning. *Journal of Social Psychology* 101:151–152.

Dorman, M. 1969. *King of the courtroom: Percy Foreman for the defense.* New York: Delacorte Press, 151–211.

Dosey, M. A., and M. Meisels. 1969. Personal space and self-protection. *Journal of Personality and Social Psychology.* 11:93–97.

Dostoyevsky, F. 1958. *The Brothers Karamazov.* Vol. 1. Baltimore, Md.: Penguin Books.

Douvan, E. 1977. Interpersonal relationships—Some questions and observations. In G. Levinger & H. L. Raush. (Eds.) *Close relationships: Perspectives on the meaning of intimacy.* Amherst University of Mass. 1977, 17–32.

Drimmer, F. 1973. *Very special people.* N.Y. City: Amjon Publishers.

Duck, S. and R. Gilmour, eds. 1981a. *Personal relationships.* Vol 1, *Studying personal relationships.* London: Academic Press.

Duck, S., and R. Gilmour, eds. 1981b. *Personal relationships.* Vol. 2, *Personal relationships in disorder.* London: Academic Press.

Duck, S., and R. Gilmour, eds. 1981c. *Personal relationships.* Vol. 3, *Personal relationships in disorder.* London: Academic Press.

Duck, S., and R. Gilmour. 1982. *Personal relationships.* Vol. 4, *Dissolving personal relationships.* London: Academic Press.

Dushenko, T. W., R. P. Perry, J. Schilling, and S. Smolarski. 1978. Generality of the physical attractiveness stereotype for age and sex. *Journal of Social Psychology* 105:303–304.

Dutton, D., and A. Aron. 1974. Some evidence for heightened sexual attraction under conditions of high anxiety. *Journal of Personality and Social Psychology* 30:510–517.

Dworkin, A. 1974. *Women hating.* New York: Dutton.

Edgemon, C. K., and J. R. Clopton. 1978. The relationship between physical attractiveness, physical effectiveness and self-concept. *Psychosocial Rehabilitation Journal* 2:21–25.

Efran, M. G. 1974. The effect of physical appearance on the judgment of guilt, interpersonal attraction, and severity of recommended punishment in a simulated jury task. *Journal of Research in Personality* 8:45–54.

Efran, M. G., and E. W. J. Patterson. 1974. Voters voted beautiful: The effect of physical appearance on a national election. *Canadian Journal of Behavioural Science* 6: 352–356.

Ehrmann, W. (1956) *Premarital dating behavior.* New York: Holt, Rinehart & Winston.

Eiseman, R., and H. Huber. 1970. Creativity, insolence, and attractiveness of female experimenters. *Perceptual and Motor Skills* 30: 515–520.

Ekman, P. 1972. Universals and cultural differences in facial expressions of emotion. In *Nebraska symposium on motivation,* ed. J. K. Cole, vol. 19. Lincoln: University of Nebraska Press.

Ekman, P. 1973. Cross-cultural studies of facial expression. In P. Ekman (ed) *Drawin and facial expression: A century of research in review,* 169–222. New York: Academic Press.

Ekman, P., and W. V. Friesen. 1975. *Unmasking the face.* Englewood Cliff, N.J.: Prentice-Hall.

Ekman, P., W. V. Friesen, and S. S. Tomkins. 1971. Facial affect scoring technique: A first validity study. *Semiotica* 3(1): 37–38.

Elder, G. H., Jr. 1969. Appearance and education in marriage mobility. *American Sociological Review* 34: 519–533.

Ellis, H. 1942. *Studies in the psychology of sex.* Vol. 2, pt. 1. New York: Random House, 172.

Ellis, H. D. 1975. Recognizing faces. *British Journal of Psychology* 66: 409–426.

Elman, D. 1977. Physical characteristics and the perception on masculine traits. *Journal of Social Psychology* 103: 157–158.

Elman, D., T. J. Killebrew, and C. Oros. 1978. How sexual orientation and physical attractiveness affect impressions of males. Paper presented at the Annual Convention of the American Psychological Association, August, Toronto. Abstract in *Personality and Social Psychology Bulletin* 4: 352.

Emerson, R. W. 1971. *The Collected Works of Ralph Waldo Emerson.* Vol. 1, *Nature, Addresses, and Lectures.* Edited by A. R. Ferguson, Cambridge, Mass.: The Belknap Press of Harvard University Press, p. 15.

Ephron, N. 1980. *Crazy salad.* New York: Bantam, pp. 18–19.

Epstein, C. F. 1974. Commentary on a paper by R. Seidenberg. In *Sexual behavior,* ed. L. Gross. Flushing, N.Y.: Spectrum.

Epstein, Y. M., E. Krupat, and C. Obudho. 1976. Clean is beautiful: Identification and preference as a function of race and cleanliness. *Journal of Social Issues* 32: 109–118.

Equality for uglies. 1972. *Time,* 21 February, 8.

Erikson, E. H. 1968. *Childhood and society.* Rev. ed. New York: W. W. Norton.

Exline, R. 1972. Visual interaction: The glances of power and preference. In *Nebraska symposium on motivation 1971,* ed. J. Cole. Lincoln: University of Nebraska Press.

Farina, A., E. Fischer, S. Sherman, W. Smith, T. Groh, and P. Nermin. 1977. Physical attractiveness and mental illness. *Journal of Abnormal Psychology* 86: 510–517.

Feiffer, J. 1982. In *Jules Feiffer's America,* ed. S. Heller. New York: Alfred A. Knopf.

Feinman, S., and G. W. Gill. 1977. Females' response to males' beardedness. *Perceptual and Motor Skills* 44: 533–534.

Feinman, S., and G. W. Gill. (1978) Sex differences in physical attractiveness preferences. *Journal of Social Psychology* 105: 43–52.

Feldman, S. 1971. The presentation of shortness in everyday life—Height and heightism in American society: Toward a sociology of stature. Paper presented at the Annual Convention of the American Sociological Association, Chicago.

Felson, R. B. 1980. Physical attractiveness, grade and teachers' attributions of ability. *Representative Research in Social Psychology* 11: 64–71.

Felson, R. B. 1981. Physical attractiveness and perception of deviance. *The Journal of Social Psychology* 114: 85–89.

Felson, R. B., and G. W. Bohrnstedt. 1979. Are the good beautiful or the beautiful good?: The relationship between children's perceptions of ability and perceptions of physical attractiveness. *Social Psychology Quarterly* 42: 386–392.

Festinger, L. 1957. *A theory of cognitive dissonance.* Evanston, Ill.: Row, Peterson.

Finck, H. T. 1887. *Romantic love and personal beauty.* Vol. 2. London: MacMillan and Company.

Firebaugh, G. 1980. Groups as contexts and frog ponds. *New Directions for Methodology of Social and Behavioral Science* 1: 43–52.

Firestone, S. 1970. *The dialectic of sex.* New York: Morrow Paperbacks.

Fisher, M., and G. Gricker, eds. 1982. *Intimacy.* New York: Plenum.

Fisher, S. 1964. Power orientation and concept of self-height in men: Preliminary note. *Perceptual and Motor Skills* 18: 732.

Fitzgerald, B. J., R. A. Paseward, and S. Fleisher. 1974. Responses of an aged population on the Gerontological and Thematic Apperception tests. *Journal of Personality Assessment* 38: 234–235.

Fleishman, J. J., M. L. Buckley, M. J. Klosinsky, N. Smith, and B. Tuck. 1976. Judged attractiveness in recognition memory of women's faces. *Perceptual and Motor Skills* 43: 709–710.

Ford, C. S., and F. A. Beach. 1951. *Patterns of sexual behavior.* New York: Harper & Row.

Francaeur, R. T. 1982. *Becoming a sexual person.* New York: John Wiley & Sons.

Frazier, A., and L. Sisonbee. 1950. Adolescent concerns with physique. *School Review* 58: 397–405.

Freedman, D. G. 1969. The survival value of the beard. *Psychology Today,* October, 36–39.

Freedman, D. G. 1979. *Human sociobiology: A holistic approach.* New York: Free Press.

Freidman, M. 1974. *Buried alive: The biography of Janis Joplin.* N.Y. City: Morrow.

Freud, S. 1922. *Group psychology and the analysis of the ego.* London: Hogarth.

Friday, N. 1980. *Men in love.* New York: Dell.

Freidrick, O. 1982. When I shaved off my mustache. *New York Times,* 6 November, 19.

Friend, R. M., and M. Vinson. 1974. Leaning over backwards: Jurors' responses to defendants' attractiveness. *Journal of Communication* 24: 124–129.

Fromm, E. 1956. *The art of loving.* New York: Harper & Row.

Fugita, S. S., T. A. Agle, I. Newman, and N. Walfish. 1977. Attractiveness, self-concept, and a methodological note about gaze behavior. *Personality and Social Psychology Bulletin* 3: 240–243.

Fugita, S. S., P. E. Panek, L. L. Balascoe, and I. Newman. 1977. Attractiveness, level of accomplishment, sex of rater, and the evaluation of feminine competence. *Representative Research in Sociol Pyschology* 8: 1–11.

Furlong, A., H. Laforge. 1975. Manifest anxiety and self-concept: Further investigations. *Journal of Genetic Pyschology* 127: 237–247.

Gacsaly, S. A., and C. A. Borges. 1979. The male physique and behavioral expectancies. *The Journal of Psychology* 101: 97–102.

Gage, N. (1976) *Sexual assault: Confronting rape in America.* New York City: Grosset & Dunlap.

Gagnon, J. H., and W. Simon. 1973. *Sexual conduct: The social services of human sexuality.* Chicago: Adline.

Gall, F. J., and J. G. Spurzheim. *Recherches sur le systeme nerveux.* Paris: Schoell.

Galton, F. 1884. Measurement of character. *Fortnightly Review* 36: 179–185.

Garfinkel, P. E., H. Moldofsky, and D. M. Garner. 1980. Behavioral treatment of an anorexic male: Experimental analysis of generalization. *Behavior Analysis and Modification* 4(2): 152–168.

Garham, D., and R. P. Perry. 1976. Limitations in generalizability of the physical attractiveness stereotype: The self-esteem exception. *Canadian Journal of Behavioural Science* 8: 263–274.

Garner, P. M., P. E. Garfinkel, D. Schwartz, and M. Thompson. 1980. Cultural expectations of thinness in women. *Psychological Reports* 47: 483–491.

Garwood, S. G., L. Cox, V. Kaplan, N. Wasserman, and J. L. Sulzer. 1980. Beauty is only "name" deep: The effect of first-name in ratings of physical attraction. *Journal of Applied Social Psychology* 10: 431–435.

Gebhard, P. H. 1969. Fedishism and sadomasochism. *Science and Psychoanalysis* 15: 71–80.

Geller, J. D., and R. A. Haurenstine. 1980. In *On love and loving,* ed. Kenneth S. Pope and Associates. San Francisco: Jossey-Bass.

Geller, M. I., J. A. Kelley, W. T. Traxler, and F. J. Marone. 1978. Behavioral treatment of an adolescent female's bulimic anorexia: Modification of consequences and antecedent conditions. *Journal of Clinical Child Psychology* 7(2): 138–142.

Gellert, E., J. S. Girgus, and J. Cohen. 1971. Children's awareness of their bodily appearance: A developmental study of factors associated with the body percept. *Genetic Psychology Monographs* 84: 109–174.

Gergen, K. J. 1974. The self and interpersonal behavior. In *Social psychology for sociologists,* ed. D. Fields, 83–100. New York: John Wiley & Sons.

Gibbins, K. 1969. Communication aspects of women's clothes and their relation to fashionability. *British Journal of Social and Clinical Psychology* 8: 301–312.

Gibson, C. D. 1968. In *The Gibson girl,* ed. S. Warshaw. Berkeley, Calif.: Diablo Press.

Giddon, D. 1980. Through the looking glass, economically: The socioeconomic implications of esthetically motivated behavior of consumers and producers of health care. Photocopy. *Symposium on Facial Esthetics Behaviors,* 6 June, Osaka, Japan.

Gilbert, K. E., and H. Kuhn. 1939. *A history of esthetics.* New York: Dover.

Giles, H., and W. Chavasse. 1975. Communication length as a function of dress style and social status. *Perceptual and Motor Skills* 40: 961–962.

Gilley, M. 1975. Don't the girls all get prettier at closing time. In *The Best of Mickey Gilley*. Vol. 2. Columbia Recording Co. Written by Baker Knight, Singleton Music Company: BMI. #0871551 CBS. N.Y., N.Y.

Gillis, J. S., and W. E. Avis. 1980. The male-taller norm in mate selection. *Personality and Social Psychology Bulletin* 6: 396–401.

Glasgow, R. E., and H. Arkowtiz. 1975. The behavioral assessment of male and female social competence in dyadic heterosexual interactions. *Behavior Therapy* 6: 488–498.

Glass, G. V., and J. C. Stanley. 1970. *Statistical methods in education and psychology*. Englewood Cliffs, N.J.: Prentice-Hall.

Glenwick, D. S., L. A. Jason, and D. Elman. 1978. Physical attractiveness and social contact in the singles bar. *Journal of Social Psychology* 105: 311–312.

Goebel, B. L., and V. M. Cashen. 1979. Age, sex, and attractiveness as factors in student ratings of teachers: A developmental study. *Journal of Educational Psychology* 71: 646–653.

Goffman, E. 1952. On cooling the mark out: Some aspects of adaptation to failure. *Psychiatry* 15: 451–463.

Going, M., and J. D. Read. 1974. Effects of uniqueness, sex of subject, and sex of photograph on facial recognition. *Perceptual and Motor Skills* 39: 109–110.

Goldberg, G. N., C. A. Kiesler, and B. E. Collins. 1969. Visual behavior and face-to-face distance during interaction. *Sociometry* 32: 43–53.

Goldberg, P. A., M. Gottesdiener, and P. R. Abramson. 1975. Another putdown of women. Perceived attractiveness as a function of support for the feminist movement. *Journal of Personality and Social Psychology* 32: 113–115.

Goldman, W., and P. Lewis. 1977. Beautiful is good: Evidence that the physically attractive are more socially skillful. *Journal of Experimental Social Psychology* 13: 125–130.

Goldstein, R. E. 1979. Clinical considerations in prosthodontics. Paper presented at the American Dental Association's 120th Annual Session, 21–25 October, Dallas, Texas.

Goodman, E. 1980. At large. *Albuquerque Journal*, 4 October, 11.

Goodman, M. J., and L. E. Goodman. 1980. *Sex differences in the human life cycle*. Los Angeles, Calif.: Gee Tee Bee.

Goodman, N., S. A. Richardson, S. I. Dornbusin, and A. H. Hastorsf. 1963. Variant reactions to physical disabilities. *American Sociological Review* 28: 429–435.

Gottman, J. N., C. Notarius, J. Gonso, and H. A. Markman. 1976. *A couples' guide to communication*. Champaign, Ill.: Research Press.

Graham, D., and R. P. Perry. 1976. Limitations in generalizability of the physical attractiveness stereotype: The self-esteem exception. *Canadian Journal of Behavioral Science* 8: 263–274.

Graham, J. A., and A. J. Jouhar. 1980. Cosmetics considered in the context of physical attractiveness: A review. *International Journal of Cosmetic Science* 2: 77–101.

Graham, J. A., and A. M. Klingman (Eds.) (In Press.) *The psychology of cosmetic treatments*. New York City: Praeger.

Gray, D. B., and R. D. Ashmore. 1976. Biasing influence of defendants' characteristics on simulated sentencing. *Psychological Reports* 38: 727–738.

Graziano, W., T. Brothen, and E. Berscheid. 1978. Height and attraction: Do men and women see eye-to-eye? *Journal of Personality* 46: 128–145.

Green, S. K., and P. Sandos. 1980. Perceptions of male and female initiators of relationships. Paper presented at the meeting of the American Psychological Association, Montreal.

Green, W. P. and H. Giles. 1973. Reactions to a stranger as a function of dress style: The tie. *Perceptual and Motor Skills* 37: 676.

Greenwald, D. P. 1977. The behavioral assessment of differences in social skill and social anxiety in female college students. *Behavior Therapy* 8: 925–937.

Greenwell, M. E. 1983. Development of the juvenile love scale. Master's thesis, University of Hawaii, Honolulu, Hawaii.

Griffiths, R. D., and P. Gillingham. 1978. The influence of videotape feedback on the self-assessments of psychiatric patients. *British Journal of Psychiatry* 133: 156–161.

Griffitt, W., and E. Hatfield. 1985a. Gender identities and gender roles: Psychosocial determinants. In *Human sexual behavior*, ed. W. Griffitt and E. Hatfield. Glenview, Ill.: Scott, Foresman.

Griffitt, W., and E. Hatfield. 1985b. *Human Sexual Behavior*. Glenview, Ill.: Scott, Foreman.

Gronlund, N. E., and L. Anderson. 1957. Personality characteristics of socially accepted, socially neglected, and socially rejected junior high school pupils. *Educational Administration and Supervision* 43: 329–339.

Gross, A., E., and C. Grofton. 1977. What is good is beautiful. *Sociometry* 40: 85–90.

Gross, A. E., I. M. Piliavin, B. S., Wallston, and L. Broll. 1972. When humanitarianism is not humane: Helping—the recipients' view. Paper presented to the American Psychological Association Meeting, 7 September, Honolulu. (Revised April 1973)

Guesewite, C. 1981. I think I'm having a relationship with a blueberry pie! *The Cathy Chronicles*. Vol. 2. New York: Bantam, p. 125.

Guesewite, C. 1982. *Another Saturday night of wild and reckless abandon*. New York: Andrews & McMeel, Inc.

Guilford, J. P. 1954. *Psychometric methods*. New York: McGraw-Hill.

Gunderson, E. K. E. 1965. Body size, self-evaluation, and military effectiveness. *Journal of Personality and Social Psychology* 2: 902–906.

Guralnik, D. B. 1982. *Webster's New World Dictionary: Ed. 2*. New York: Simon and Schuster.

Guthrie, R. D. 1976. *Body hotspots*. New York: Van Nostrand Reinhold.

Guy, R. F., B. A. Rankin, and M. J. Norvell. 1980. The relation of sex role stereotyping to body image. *The Journal of Psychology* 105: 167–173.

Hagen, R. 1979. *The bio-sexual factor*. New York: Doubleday.

Hagiwara, S. 1975. Visual versus verbal information in impression formation. *Journal of Personality and Social Psychology* 32: 692–698.

Haley, E. G., and N. J. Hendrickson. 1974. Children's preferences for clothing and hair styles. *Home Economics Research Journal* 2: 176–193.

Half, R. (January 2, 1974) Pay of fat executives is found leaner than checks of others. *New York Times Vol. 73*, (No. 42) p. 12.

Halmi, K. A., P. Powers, and S. Cuningham. 1975. Treatment of anorexia nervosa with behavior modification: Effectiveness of formula feeding and isolation. *Archives of General Psychiatry* 32: 93–96.

Hambidge, J. 1920. *Dynamic symmetry.* New Haven: Yale University Press.

Hamid, P. N. 1968. Style of dress as a perceptual cue in impression formation. *Perceptual and Motor Skills* 26: 904–906.

Hamid, P. N. 1969. Change in person perception as a function of dress. *Perceptual and Motor Skills* 29: 191–194.

Hamid, P. N. 1972. Some effects of dress cues on observational accuracy, a perceptual estimate, and impression formation. *The Journal of Social Psychology* 86: 279–289.

Hanseli, S., J. Sparacino, and D. Ronchi. 1982. Physical attractiveness and blood pressure: Sex and age differences. *Personality and Social Psychology Bulletin* 8: 113–121.

Hansson, R. C., and B. J. Duffield. 1976. Physical attractiveness and the attribution of epilepsy. *Journal of Social Psychology* 99: 233–249.

Harada-Stone, D. 1983. What you wear to address the jury. Focus/law. *The Honolulu Advertiser,* 1 August, B-1.

Harari, H., and J. W. McDavid. 1969. Situational influence on moral justice: A study of "finking." *Journal of Personality and Social Psychology* 11: 240–244.

Harding, J., H. Proshansky, B. Kutner, and I. Chein. 1968. In *The handbook of social psychology,* ed. G. Lindzey and E. Aronson, vol. 5, 1–76. Reading Mass.: Addison-Wesley.

Harrell, W. A. 1978. Physical attractiveness, self-disclosure, and helping behavior. *Journal of Social Psychology* 104: 15–17.

Harrell, W. A. 1979. Physical attractiveness and public intimacy of married couples: An observational study. *Social Behavior and Personality* 7: 65–75.

Harris, M. B., and H. Baudin. 1973. The language of altruism: The effects of language, dress, and ethnic group. *The Journal of Social Psychology* 91: 37–41.

Harris, M. B., and G. Bays. 1973. Altruism and sex roles. *Psychological Reports* 32: 1002.

Harrison, A. A., and L. Saeed. 1977. Let's make a deal: An analysis of revelations and stipulations in lonely hearts advertisements. *Journal of Personality and Social Psychology* 35: 257–264.

Hartnett, J., and D. Edler. 1973. The princess and the nice frog: Study in person perception. *Perceptual and Motor Skills* 37: 863–866.

Hartnett, J. J., J. Gottlieb, and R. L. Hayes. 1976. Social facilitation theory and experimenter attractiveness. *Journal of Social Psychology* 99: 293–294.

Hartup, W. W. 1970. Peer interaction and social organization. In *Carmichael's manual of child psychology,* ed. P. H. Mussen, vol. 2, 361–456. New York: Wiley.

Hatfield (Walster), E. (1974) Did you ever see a beautiful conservative? A note. Reported in E. Berscheid & E. Hatfield (Walster), Physical attractiveness. In L. Berkowitz (Ed.) *Advances in Experimental Social Psychology.* New York: Academic Press, 7, 184.

Hatfield (Walster), E. (1970) The effect of self-esteem on liking for dates of various social desirabilities. *Journal of Experimental Social Psychology*, 6, 248–253.

Hatfield (Walster), E., & Berscheid, E. (1978) *Interpersonal attraction* (ed. 2). Reading Massachusetts: Addison-Wesley.

Hatfield (Walster), E., & Berscheid, E. (1974) A little bit about love: A minor essay on a major topic. In T. Huston (ed.), *Foundations of interpersonal attraction*, 355–381. New York: Academic Press.

Hatfield, E., Traupmann, J., & Walster, G. W. (1979) Equity and extramarital sex. In M. Cook & G. Wilson (Eds.), *Love and attraction: An international conference*. Oxford: Pergamon Press, 309–322.

Hatfield (Walster), E., Walster, G. W., Pilliavin, J., & Schmidt, L. (1973) Playing hard-to-get: Understanding and elusive phenomenon. *Journal of Personality and Social Psychology*, 26, 113–121.

Hatfield, E. 1982. What do women and men want from love and sex? In *Gender roles and sexual behavior: The changing boundaries*, ed. E. R. Allgeier and N. B. McCormick. Palo Alto, Calif.: Mayfield Publishing.

Hatfield, E. 1983. Equity theory and research: An overview. In *Small groups and social interaction*, ed. H. H. Blumberg, A. P. Hare, V. Kent, and M. Davies, vol. 2, 401–411. London: John Wiley & Sons.

Hatfield, E. 1984. Physical attractiveness in social interaction. In *The psychology of cosmetic treatments*, ed. J. Graham, & A. M. Kligman. New York: Praeger.

Hatfield, E. 1984. The dangers of intimacy. In *Communication, intimacy, and close relationships*, ed. V. Derlaga. New York City: Praeger, 207–220.

Hatfield, E., D. Nerenz, D. Greenberger, P. Lambert, and S. Sprecher. 1982. Passionate and companionate love in newlywed couples. Photocopy. Department of Psychology. University of Hawaii at Manoa, Honolulu, HI.

Hatfield, E., and M. S. Perlmutter. 1983. Social psychological issues in bias: Physical attractiveness. In *Handbook of bias in psychotherapy*, ed. J. Murray and P. Abrahamson, 53–83. New York: Praeger.

Hatfield, E., D. Roberts, and L. Schmidt. 1980. The impact of sex and physical attractiveness on an initial social encounter. *Recherches de psychologie sociale* 2: 27–40.

Hatfield, E., and S. Sprecher. 1986. *Mirror, mirror: the importance of looks in everyday life*. Albany: State University of New York Press.

Hatfield, E., J. Traupmann, S. Sprecher, M. Utne, and J. Hay. 1984. Equity and intimate relations: Recent research. In *Compatible and incompatible relationships*, ed. W. Ickes. New York: Springer Verlag. pp. 1–27.

Hatfield, E., and G. W. Walster. 1978. *A new look at love*. Lantham, Mass.: University Press of America.

Hatfield, E., G. W. Walster, and J. Piliavin. 1978. In *Altruism, sympathy, and helping*, ed. L. Wispe, New York: Academic Press.

Hatfield, E., G. W. Walster, and J. Traupmann. 1979. Equity and premarital sex. In *Love and attraction: An international conference*, ed. M. Cook and G. Wilson, 323–336. Oxford: Pergamon Press.

Heilman, M. E., and L. R. Saruwatari. 1979. When beauty is beastly: The effects of appearance and sex on evaluations of job applicants for managerial and nonmanagerial jobs. *Organizational Behavior and Human Performance* 23: 360–372.

Heiman, J., L. LoPiccolo, and J. LoPiccolo. 1976. *Becoming orgasmic: A sexual growth program for women.* Englewood Cliffs, New Jersey: Prentice-Hall.

Hellman, L. 1953. *The children's hour* (Acting ed.). New York: Dramatists Play Service.

Helmreich, R., Aronson, E. M. & Lefan, J. (1970) To err is humanizing—sometimes: Effects of self-esteem competence and pratfall on interpersonal attraction. *Journal of Personality and Social Psychology, 16,* 259–264.

Helson, H. 1964. *Adaptation-level theory: An experimental and systematic approach to behavior.* New York: Harper.

Henry, W. 1983. Requiem for T.V.'s gender gap? *Time,* 22 August, 57.

Henze, L. F., and J. W. Hudson. 1969. Campus values in mate selection: A replication. *Journal of Marriage and the Family* 31: 772–775.

Hershorn, L. 1979. Clinical considerations: Orthodontics. Paper presented at the 120th Annual Session of the American Dental Association, 21–25 October, Dallas.

Herter, G. L. 1974. *How to live with a bitch.* Waseca, Minn.: Herter's.

Hess, E. H. 1965. Attitude and pupil size. *Scientific American* 212: 46–54.

Hewitt, L. E. 1958. Student perceptions of traits desired in themselves as dating and marriage partners. *Marriage and Family Living* 20: 344–349.

Hickling, E. J., R. C. Noel, and F. D. Yutzler. 1979. Attractiveness and occupational status. *Journal of Psychology* 102: 71–76.

Hildebrandt, K. A., and H. E. Fitzgerald. 1977. Facial feature determinants of perceived infant cuteness. Paper presented at the meeting of the Midwestern Psychological Association, May, Chicago.

Hildebrandt, K. A., and H. E. Fitzgerald. 1978. Adults' responses to infants varying in perceived cuteness. *Behavioral Processes* 3: 159–172.

Hilderbrandt, K. A., and H. E. Fitzgerald. 1979. Adult's perceptions of infant sex and cuetness. *Sex Roles* 5: 471–481.

Hill, M. K., and H. A. Lando. 1976. Physical attractiveness and sex-role stereotypes in impression formation. *Perceptual and Motor Skills* 43: 1251–1255.

Hill, R. 1945. Campus values in mate selection. *Journal of Home Economics* 37.

Hiller, D. V. 1982. Overweight as master status: A replication. *The Journal of Psychology* 110: 107–113.

Himmelfrab, S., and M. Fishbein. 1971. Studies in the perception of ethnic group members: II. Attractiveness, response bias, and antisemitism. *The Journal of Social Psychology* 83: 289–298.

Hinckley, E. D., and D. Rethlingshafer. 1951. Value judgements of heights of men by college students. *Journal of Psychology* 31: 257–262.

Hite, S. 1981. *The Hite report on male sexuality.* New York: Alfred A. Knopf.

Hobfall, S. E., and L. A. Penner. 1978. Effect of physical attractiveness on therapists' initial judgements of a person's self-concept. *Journal of Consulting and Clinical Psychology* 46: 200–201.

Hochberg, J., and R. E. Galper. 1974. Attribution of intention as function of physiognomy. *Memory and Cognition* 2(1–A): 39–42.

Hochberg, J. E. 1964. *Perception.* Englewood Cliffs, N.J.: Prentice-Hall.

Hochschild, A. R. 1975. Attending to, codifying, and managing feelings: Sex differences in love. Paper presented at the American Sociological Association meetings, 29 August, San Francisco.

Holahan, C. K., and C. W. Stephan. 1981. When beauty isn't talent: The influence of physical attractiveness, attitudes toward women, and competence on impression formation. *Sex Roles* 7: 867–876.

Hollander, N. 1980. *Ma, can I be a feminist and still like men?: Lyrics from life.* New York: St. Martin's Press.

Holmes, S. J., and C. E. Hatch. 1938. Personal appearance as related to scholastic records and marriage selection in college women. *Human Biology* 10: 65–76.

Homans, G. C. 1974. *Social behavior: Its elementary forms.* Rev. ed. New York: Harcourt, Brace Jovanovich.

Hood, A. B. 1963. A study of the relationship between physique and personality variables measured by the MMPI. *Journal of Personality* 31: 97–107.

Hoon, P. W. Wincze, J. P. and Hoon, E. F. 1977. A test of reciprocal inhibition: Are anxiety and sexual arousal in women mutually inhibitory? *Journal of Abnormal Psychology* 86(1): 65–74.

Horai, J. 1976. The effects of sensation seeking: Physical attractiveness of stimuli, and exposure frequency on liking. *Social Behavior and Personality* 4: 241–246.

Horai, J., N. Naccari, and E. Fatoullah. 1974. The effects of expertise and physical attractiveness upon opinion agreement and liking. *Sociometry* 37: 601–606.

Hore, T. 1971. Assessment of teaching practice: An attractive hypothesis. *British Journal of Educational Psychology* 41: 327–328.

Horvath, T. 1979. Correlates of physical beauty in men and women. *Social Behavior and Personality* 7: 145–151.

Horvath, T. 1981. Physical attractiveness: The influence of selected torso parameters. *Archives of Sexual Behavior* 10: 21–24.

Howard, C. R., S. H. Cohen, and N. Cavior. 1974. More results on increasing the persuasiveness of a low prestige communicator: The effects of the communicator's physical attractiveness and sex of the receiver. *Personality and Social Psychology Bulletin* 1: 393–395.

Hoyt, L. L. and J. W. Hudson. 1981. Personal characteristics important in mate preference among college students. *Social Behavior and Personality* 9: 93–96.

Hsu, L. K. G. 1980. Outcome of anorexia nervosa: A review of the literature (1954–1978). *Archives of General Psychiatry* 37: 1041–1046.

Hudson, J. W., and L. F. Henze. 1969. Campus values in mate selection: A replication. *Journal of Marriage and the Family* 31: 772–775.

Hudson, J. W., and L. L. Hoyt. 1981. Personal characteristics important in mate preference among college students. *Social Behavior and Personality* 9: 93–96.

Huesmann, L. R., and G. Levinger. 1976. Incremental exchange theory: A formal model for progression in dyadic social interaction. In *Equity theory: Toward a general theory of social interaction,* ed. L. Berkowitz and E. Hatfield-Walster, vol. 9, 192–230. New York: Academic Press.

Hunt, M. 1974. *Sexual behavior in the 1970s.* New York: Dell.

Hunt, M., and B. Hunt. 1977. *The divorce experience.* New York: McGraw Hill.

Huntley, C. W. 1940. Judgements of self based upon records of behavior. *Journal of Abnormal and Social Psychology* 35: 398–427.

Huston, T. L. 1972. From liking to affiliation: Empirical tests of a two-factor model of social choice. Ph.D. diss., State University of New York at Albany.

Huston, T. L. 1973. Ambiguity of acceptance, social desirability and dating choice. *Journal of Experimental Social Psychology* 9: 32–42.

Iliffe, A. H. 1960. A study of preferences in feminine beauty. *British Journal of Psychology* 51: 267–273.

Illsley, R. 1955. Social class selection and class differences in relation to stillbirths and infant deaths. *British Medical Journal* (December): 1520–1524.

Illsley, R. 1959. Social class selection and class differences in relation to stillbirths and infant deaths. In S. M. Lipset & R. Bendix (Eds.) *Social Mobility in Industrial Society*. Berkeley: University of California Press.

Insko, C. A., V. D. Thompson, W. Stroebe, K. F. Shaud, B. E. Pinner, and B. D. Lwyton. 1973. Implied evaluation and the similarity-attraction effect. *Journal of Personality and Social Psychology* 25: 297–308.

Issacharaff, A. 1970. Is there a relationship between a woman's physical appearance and her sexual behavior? *Medical Aspects of Human Sexuality* (October): 14.

Istvan, S., W. Griffitt, and G. Weidner. 1983. Sexual arousal and the polarization of perceived sexual attractiveness. *Basic and Applied Social Psychology*, 4, 307–318.

Isvan, J., and W. Griffitt. 1978a. Emotional arousal and sexual attraction. Kansas State University, Manhattan. Photocopy.

Izard, C. E. 1971. *The face of emotion*. New York: Appleton-Century-Cross.

Izett, R., and L. Fishman. 1976. Defendant sentences as a function of attractiveness and justifications for actions. *Journal of Social Psychology* 100: 285–290.

Izzett, R. R., and W. Leginski. 1974. Group discussion and the influence of defendant characteristics in a simulated jury setting. *Journal of Social Psychology* 93: 271–279.

Jackson, D. J., and T. L. Huston. 1975. Physical attractiveness and assertiveness. *Journal of Social Psychology* 96: 79–84.

Jackson, D. N., and H. L. Minton. 1963. A forced-choice adjective preference scale for personality assessment. *Psychological Reports* 12: 515–520.

Jackson, M. (1982) Muscles. Performed by D. Ross. Published by MiJac Music (MIB). c. 1982 RCA Records VIC45 PB–13348.

Jacobson, M. B. 1981. Effects of victim's and defendant's physical attractiveness on subjects' judgements in a rape case. *Sex Roles* 7: 247–255.

Jacobson, M. B., and W. Kock. 1978. Attributed reasons for support of the feminist movement as a function of attractiveness. *Sex Roles* 4: 169–174.

Jacobson, S. K., and C. R. Berger. 1974. Communication and justice: Defendant attributes and their effects on the severity of his sentence. *Speech Monographs* 41: 282–286.

James, C. 1984. Beauty is as beauty does. *Psychology Today*, no. 2, 14.

Janda, L. H., K. E. O'Grady, and S. A. Barnhart. 1981. Effects of sexual attitudes and physical attractiveness on persona perception of men and women. *Sex Roles* 7: 189–199.

Jennings, H. R. 1943. *Leadership and isolation*. New York: Longmans, Green.

Joffe, N. F. 1953. Non-reciprocity among East European Jews. In *The study of culture at a distance,* ed. M. Mead and R. Metraux, 386–387. Chicago: University of Chicago Press.

Johnson, D. F., and J. B. Pittenger. 1984. Attribution, the attractiveness stereotype, and the elderly. Dept. of Psychology University of Arkansas at Little Rock. Photocopy.

Johnson, R. W., D. Doiron, G. P. Brooks, and J. Dickinson. 1978. Perceived attractiveness as a function of support for the feminist movement: Not necessarily a put-down of women. *Canadian Journal of Behavioral Science* 10: 214–221.

Johnson, R. W., S. W. Holborn, and S. Turcotte. 1979. Perceived attractiveness as a function of active versus passive support for the feminist movement. *Personality and Social Psychology Bulletin* 5: 227–230.

Jones, C. and E. Aronson. 1973. Attribution of fault to a rape victim as a function of responsibility of the victim. *Journal of Personality and Social Psychology* 26: 415–419.

Jones, E. E., and K. E. Davis. 1965. From acts to dispositions: The attribution process in person perception. In *Advances in experimental social psychology,* ed. L. Berkowitz, vol. 2, 219–266. New York: Academic Press.

Jones, M. C. 1957. The later careers of boys who were early or late maturing. *Child Development* 28: 113–128.

Jones, M. C., and P. H. Mussen. 1958. Self conceptions, motivations and interpersonal attitudes of early and late maturing girls. *Child Development* 29: 491–501.

Jones, Q. R., and I. S. Moyel. 1971. The influence of iris color and pupil size on expressed affect. *Psychonomic Science* 22: 126–127.

Jones, R. M., and G. R. Adams. 1982. Assessing the importance of physical attractiveness across the life-span. *The Journal of Social Psychology* 118: 131–132.

Jones, W. H., R. O. Hannson, and A. L. Phillips. 1978. Physical attractiveness and judgments of psychopathology *Journal of Social Psychology* 55: 79–84.

Jonson, B. 1975. Love freed from ignorance and folly. In *The works of Ben Jonson,* vol. 3, 195. London: Bickers and Son, Henry Sotheran and Co.

Jordan, P. 1982. Confessions of a handsome devil. *Madamoiselle,* June, 95–186.

Josselin de Jong, J. P. 1952. *Levi-Strauss' theory on kinship and marriage.* Leiden, Holland, Brill.

Jourard, S. M. 1964. *The transparent self.* Princeton, N. J.: D. Van Nostrand Co., Inc.

Jourard, S. 1971. *Self-disclosure: An experimental analysis of the transparent self.* New York: Wiley.

Jourard, S., and R. Friedman. 1970. Experimenter-subject distance in self-disclosure. *Journal of Personality and Social Psychology* 15: 278–282.

Jourard, S., and R. Ramy. 1955. Perceived parental attitudes, the self and security. *Journal of Consulting Psychology* 19: 364–366.

Joyce, J. 1914. *Ulysses.* New York: The Modern Library.

Jue, J. June, 1981. Body image: The value of snails and puppy-dogs' tails: $76. *Psychology Today,* 26.

Kaats, G. R., and K. E. Davis. 1970. The dynamics of sexual behavior of college students. *Journal of Marriage and the Family* 32: 390–399.

Kagan, J. 1964. Acquisition of significance of sex typing and sex role identity. In *Review of Child Development Research*, ed. M. Hoffman and L. Hoffman, vol. 1, 137–167. New York: Russell Sage.

Kagan, J., B. A. Henker, A. Hen-Tou, J. Levine, and M. Lewis. 1966. Infants' differential reactions to familiar and distorted faces. *Child Development* 37: 519–532.

Kahn, A., J. Hottes, and W. I. Davis. 1971. Cooperation and optimal resonding in the prisoner's dilemma game: Effects of sex and physical attractiveness. *Journal of Personality and Social Psychology*, 17, 267–279.

Kalick, S. M. 1978. Toward an interdisciplinary psychology of appearances. *Psychiatry* 41: 243–253.

Kanekar, S., and R. B. Ahluwalia. 1975. Academic aspirations in relation to sex and physical attractiveness. *Psychological Reports*, 36: 834.

Kanfer, F. H., P. Karoly, and A. Newman. 1974. Source of feedback, observational earning, and attitude change. *Journal of Personality and Social Psychology* 29: 30–38.

Kantor, K., and W. Lehr. 1975. *Inside the family*. San Francisco: Jossey-Bass.

Kaplan, H. S. 1974. *The new sex therapy*. New York: Brunner/Mozel.

Kaplan, H. S. 1979. *Disorders of sexual desire*. New York: Simon and Schuster.

Kaplan, J. F., and N. H. Anderson. 1973. Information integration theory and reinforcement theory as approaches to interpersonal attraction. *Journal of Personality and Social Psychology* 28: 301–312.

Kaplan, L. J. 1978. *Oneness and separateness: From infant to individual*. New York: Simon and Shuster.

Kaplan, R. M. 1978. Is beauty talent? Sex interaction in the attractiveness halo effect. *Sex Roles* 4: 195–204.

Kassarjian, H. H. 1963. Voting intentions and political perception. *The Journal of Psychology* 56: 85–88.

Katz, D., and K. W. Braly. 1933. Racial stereotypes of 100 college students. *Journal of Abnormal and Social Psychology* 28: 280–290.

Katz, M., and P. Zimbardo. 1977. Making it as a mental patient. *Psychology Today* 10: 122–126.

Kaye, E. 1979. On starving oneself to death: A well-known writer tells her own story. *Family Health* 11: 38–44.

Kanzantzakis, N. 1952. *Zorba the Greek*. Trans. C. Wildman, New York: Simon and Schuster, p. 101.

Kehle, T. J., W. J. Bramble, and E. J. Mason, 1974. Teachers' expectations: Ratings of student performance as biased by student characteristics. *Journal of Experimental Education* 43: 54–60.

Kellerman, J. M., and J. D. Laird. 1982. The effect of appearance on self-perceptions. *Journal of Personality* 50: 296–315.

Kelley, E., S. Jones, D. A. Hatch, and R. Nelson. 1976. How to help your students be successful at job hunting. *Journal of Home Economics* 68: 32–35.

Kelley, H. H., E. Berscheid, A. Christensen, J. H. Harvey, T. Huston, G. Levinger, E. McClintock, L. A. Peplau, and D. Peterson. 1983. *Close relationships*. New York: Freeman.

Kelley, J. 1978. Sexual permissiveness: Evidence for a theory. *Journal of Marriage and the Family* 40: 455–468.

Kellogg, M. A. 1982. Could it be love at first cassette? *TV Guide,* 26 June, 33–36.

Kendrick, D. T., and R. B. Cialdini. 1977. Romantic attraction: Misattribution vs. reinforcement explanations. *Journal of Personality and Social Psychology* 35: 381–391.

Kennedy, R. D., Jr. 1980. A Marxist perspective: The production of cooperative intimate relations. Photocopy. Dept. of Sociology, Univ. of Wisc., Madison, Wisc.

Kenny, C. T., and D. Flectcher. 1973. Effects of beardedness on person perception. *Perceptual and Motor Skills* 37: 413–414.

Kenrick, D. T., and S. Gutierres. 1978. Influence of mass media on judgments of physical attractiveness: The people's case against Farrah Fawcett. Paper presented at the Annual Convention of the American Psychological Association, Toronto, Canada. Abstract in *Personality and Social Psychology Bulletin* 4: 358.

Kenrick, D. T., and S. E. Gutierres. 1980. Contract effects and judgments of physical attractiveness: When beauty becomes a social problem. *Journal of Personality and Social Psychology* 38: 131–140.

Kerber, K. W., and M. G. Coles. 1978. The role of perceived physiological activity in affected judgments. *Journal of Experimental Social Psychology* 14: 419–433.

Kernis, M. H., and L. Wheeler. 1981. Beautiful friends and ugly strangers: Radiation and contrast effects in perceptions of same-sex pairs. *Personality and Social Psychology* 7: 617–620.

Kerr, B. A., and D. M. Dell. 1976. Perceived interviewer expertness and attractiveness: Effects of interviewer behavior and attire and interview setting. *Journal of Counseling Psychology* 23: 553–556.

Kerr, N. L. 1978. Beautiful and blameless: Effects of victim attractiveness and responsibility on mock jurors' verdicts. *Personality and Social Psychology Bulletin* 4: 479–482.

Kerr, N. L., and S. T. Kurtz. 1978. Reliability of the eye of the beholder: Effects of sex of the beholder and sex of the beheld. *Bulletin of the Psychonomic Society* 12: 179–181.

Keyes, R. 1980. *The height of your life.* New York: Warner Books.

Kiesler, C. A. 1982. Public and professional myths about mental hospitalization. *American Psychologist* 37: 1323–1329.

Kiesler, S. B., and R. L. Baral. 1970. The search for a romantic partner: The effects of self-esteem and physical attractiveness on romantic behavior. In *Personality and Social Behavior,* ed. K. J. Gerger and D. Marlow, 155–165. Reading, Mass.: Addison-Wesley.

Kiker, V. L., and A. R. Miller. 1967. Perceptual judgment of physiques as a factor in social image. *Perceptual and Motor Skills* 24: 1013–1014.

Kinsey, A., W. B. Pomeroy, and C. Martin. 1948. *Sexual behavior in the human male.* Philadelphia: W. B. Saunders.

Kinsey, A., W. Pomeroy, C. Martin, and P. Gebhard. 1953. *Sexual behavior in the human female.* Philadelphia: Saunders.

Kirch, A. M., ed. 1960. *The anatomy of love.* New York: Dell.

Kirkpatrick, C., and J. Cotton. 1951. Physical attractiveness, age, and marital adjustment. *American Sociological Review* 16: 81–86.

Kleck, R. E., S. A. Richardson, and L. Ronald. 1974. Physical appearance cues and interpersonal attraction in children. *Child Development* 45: 305–310.

Kleck, R. E., and C. Rubenstein. 1975. Physical attractiveness, perceived attitude similarity, and interpersonal attraction in an opposite-sex encounter. *Journal of Personality and Social Psychology* 31: 107–114.

Kleinke, C. L. 1975. *First impressions: The psychology of encountering others.* Englewood Cliffs, N.J. Prentice-Hall.

Kleinke, C. L., and R. A. Staneski. 1980. First impressions of female bust size. *Journal of Social Psychology* 110: 123–134.

Kleinke, C. L., R. A. Staneski, and D. E. Berger. 1975. Evaluation of an interviewer as a function of interviewer gaze, reinforcement of subject gaze, and interviewer attractiveness. *Journal of Personality and Social Psychology* 31: 115–122.

Kleinke, C. L., R. A. Staneski, and S. L. Pipp. 1975. Effects of gaze, distance, and attractiveness on male's first impressions of females. *Representative Research in Social Psychology* 6: 7–12.

Klinger, E. 1977. *Meaning and void: Inner experience and the incentives in people's lives.* Minneapolis: University of Minnesota Press.

Komarovsky, M. 1971. *The unemployed man and his family.* New York: Octagon Books.

Kopera, A. A., R. A. Maier, and J. E. Johnson. 1971. Perception of physical attractiveness: The influence of group interaction and group coaction on ratings of the attractiveness of photographs of women. *Proceedings of the 79th Annual Convention of the American Psychological Association* 6: 317–318.

Korabik, K. 1981. Changes in physical attractiveness in interpersonal attraction. *Basic and Applied Social Psychology* 2: 59–65.

Korda, M. 1975. *Power; How to get it, how to fight it!* New York: Random House.

Koulack, D., and J. A. Tuthill. 1972. Height perception: A function of social distance. *Canadian Journal of Behavioral Science* 4: 50–53.

Kramer, C. 1982. How your looks shape your life. *Parade,* 4 July, 11.

Krebs, D., and A. A. Adinolfi. 1975. Physical attractiveness, social relations, and personality style. *Journal of Personality and Social Psychology* 31: 245–253.

Kretschmer, E. 1936. *Physique and character.* London; Kegan, Paul, Trench, Trubner and Co.

Krohn, M., G. P. Waldo, and G. Theodore. 1974. Self-reported delinquency: A comparison of structured interviews and self-administered checklists. *Journal of Criminal Law and Criminology* 65: 545–553.

Kulka, R. A., and J. B. Kessler. 1978. Is justice really blind? The influence of litigant physical attractiveness on judicial judgment. *Journal of applied Social Psychology* 8: 366–381.

Kupke, T. E., S. A. Hobbs, and T. H. Cheney, 1979. Selection of heterosocial skills: I. Criterion-related validity. *Behavior Therapy* 10: 327–335.

Kurtz, D. . 1969. Physical appearance and stature: Important variables in sales recruiting. *Personnel Journal* 48: 981–983.

Kurtzberg, R. L., H. Safar, and N. Cavior. 1968. Surgical and social rehabilitation of adult offenders. *Proceedings of the 76th Annual Convention of the American Psychological Association* 3: 649–650.

Kury, H., and S. Bauerle. 1977. The personality structure of popular and unpopular schoolchildren. *Psychologie in Eriziehung and Unterricht* 24: 244–247.

Lambert, S. 1972. Reactions to a stranger as a function of style of dress. *Perceptual and Motor Skills* 35: 711–712.

Landau, S., and G. S. Leventhal. 1976. A simulation study of administrators' behavior toward employees who receive job offers. *Journal of Applied Social Psychology* 6: 291–306.

Landers, A. 1975. *The Wisconsin State Journal.* Madison, Wisconsin, (November), 4.

Landers, A. 1979. *Ann Landers encyclopedia . . . A to Z.* New York: Ballantine Books.

Landy, D., and E. Aronson. 1969. The influence of the character of the criminal and his victims on the decisions of simulated jurors. *Journal of Experimental Social Psychology* 5: 141–152.

Landy, D., and H. Sigall. 1974. Beauty is talent: Task evaluation as a function of the performer's physical attractiveness. *Journal of Personality and Social Psychology* 29: 299–304.

Langlois, J. H., and A. C. Downs. 1979. Peer relations as a function of physical attractiveness: The eye of the beholder or behavioral reality? *Child Development* 50: 409–418.

Langlois, J. H., and C. Stephan. 1977. The effects of physical attractiveness and ethnicity on children's behavior attributions and peer preferences. *Child Development* 48: 1694–1698.

Langlois, J. H., and L. E. Styczynski. 1979. The effects of physical attractiveness on the behavioral attributions and peer preferences of acquainted children. *International Journal of Behavioral Development* 2: 325–341.

Lanier, H. B., and J. Byrne. 1981. How high school students view women: The relationship between perceived attractiveness, occupation, and education. *Sex Roles* 7: 145–148.

Larkin, J. C., and H. A. Pines. 1979. No fat persons need apply. Experimental studies of the overweight stereotype and hiring preference. *Sociology of Work and Occupations* 6: 312–327.

Lasch, C. 1977. *Haven in a heartless world: The family besieged.* New York: Basic Books.

Lasky, E. 1979. Physical attractiveness and its relationship to self-esteem: Preliminary findings. In *Love and attraction: An international conference,* ed. M. Cook and G. Wilson. Oxford: Pergamon Press.

Lasswell, M., and M. Lobsenz. 1980. *The styles of loving: Why you love the way you do.* New York: Doubleday.

LaVoie, J. C., and G. R. Adams. 1974. Teacher expectancy and its relation to physical and interpersonal characteristics of the child. *Alberta Journal of Educational Research* 20: 122–132.

LaVoie, J. C., and R. Andrews. 1976. Facial attractiveness, physique, and sex role identity in young children. *Development Psychology* 12: 550–551.

LaVoie, J. C., and G. R. Adams. 1978. Physical and interpersonal attractiveness of the model and imitation in adults. *Journal of Social Psychology* 106: 191–202.

Lavrakas, P. 1975. Female preferences for male physiques. *Journal of Research in Personality* 9: 324–334.

Lawson, E. D. 1971. Hair color, personality, and the observer. *Psychological Reports* 28: 311–322.

Layton, B. D., and C. A. Insko. 1974. Anticipated interaction and the similarity-attraction effect. *Sociometry* 37: 149–162.

Lederer, W. J., and D. D. Jackson. 1968. *The mirages of marriage.* New York: W. W. Norton & Co.

Lefebvre, L. M., and S. P. McNeel. 1973. Attractiveness, cost and dependency in the exchange of unlike behaviors. *European Journal of Social Psychology* 3: 9–26.

Leonard, J. 1980. Private lives. *New York Times,* 13 February, C16.

Lepper, M. R., and D. Greene. 1976. On understanding "overjustification": A reply to Reiss and Sushinsky. *Journal of Personality and Social Psychology* 33: 25–35.

Lepper, M. R., Greene, D., & Nisbett, R. E. (1973) Undermining children's intrinsic interest with extrinsic rewards: A test of "overjustification" hypothesis. *Journal of Personality and Social Psychology, 28,* 129–137.

Lerner, M. J. 1965. Evaluation of performance as a function of performer's reward and attractiveness. *Journal of Personality and Social Psychology* 1: 355–360.

Lerner, R. M. 1969. The development of stereotyped expectancies of body build-behavior relations. *Child Development* 40: 137–141.

Lerner, R. M. 1972. Richness analysis of body build stereotype development. *Developmental Psychology* 7: 219.

Lerner, R. M., and B. E. Brackney. 1978. The importance of inner and outer body parts attitudes in the self-concept of late adolescents. *Sex Roles* 4: 225–238.

Lerner, R. M., and E. Gellert. 1969. Body build identification, preference, and aversion in children. *Developmental Psychology* 1: 456–462.

Lerner, R. M., S. Iwawaki, and T. Chihara. 1976. Development of personal space schemata among Japanese children. *Developmental Psychology* 12: 466–467.

Lerner, R. M., and S. A. Karabenick. 1974. Physical attractiveness, body attitudes, and self-concept in late adolescents. *Journal of Youth and Adolescence* 3: 307–316.

Lerner, R. M., S. A. Karabenick, and J. L. Stuart. 1973. Relations among physical attractiveness, body attitudes, and self-concept in male and female college students. *Journal of Psychology* 85: 119–129.

Lerner, R. M., and J. V. Lerner. 1977. Effects of age, sex, and physical attractiveness on child-peer relations, academic performance, and elementary school adjustment. *Development Psychology* 13: 585–590.

Lerner, R. M., and T. Moore. 1974. Sex and status effects on perception of physical attractiveness. *Psychological Reports* 34: 1047–1050.

Lerner, R. M., J. B. Orlos, and J. R. Knapp. 1976. Physical attractiveness, physical effectiveness, and self-concept in late adolescents. *Adolescence* 11: 313–326.

Lerner, R. M., and K. B. Pool. 1972. Body-build stereotypes: A cross cultural comparison. *Psychological Reports* 31: 527–532.

Levenkron, S. 1978. *The best little girl in the world.* Chicago: Contemporary Books.

Levenson, H., and C. N. Harris. 1980. Love and the search for identity. In *On love and loving*, ed. K. S. Pope and Associates. San Francisco: Jossey-Bass.

Levenson, R. W., and J. M. Gottman. 1978. Toward the assessment of social competence. *Journal of Consulting and Clinical Psychology* 46: 453–462.

Leventhal, G., and R. Krate. 1977. Physical attractiveness and severity of sentencing. *Psychological Reports* 40: 315–318.

Levin, E. 1983. [Reported by David Wallace]. Staying fit and fantastic at any age. *People*, 11 April, 108–115.

Levine, N. B. 1976. *Hardcore crafts.* New York: Ballantine Books.

Levinger, G. 1972. Little sandbox and big quarry: Comment on Byrne's paradigmatic spade for research on interpersonal attraction. *Representative Research in Social Psychology* 3: 3–19.

Levinson, D. J., C. N. Darrow, E. B. Klein, M. H. Levinson, and B. McKee. 1978. *The seasons of a man's life.* New York: Knopf.

Lewin, K., T. Dembo., L. Festinger, and P. Sears. 1944. Level of aspiration. In *Personality and the behavior disorders*, ed. J. McV. Hunt, vol. 1, 333–378. New York: Ronald Press.

Lewis, K. N., and W. B. Walsh. 1978. Physical attractiveness: Its impact on the perception of a female counselor. *Journal of Counseling Psychology* 25: 210–216.

Libby, R. 1977. Creative singlehood as a sexual lifestyle: Beyond marriage as a rite of passage. In *Marriage and attractiveness: Exploring intimate relationships*, ed. R. W. Libby and R. Whitehurst. Glenview, Ill.: Scott, Foresman.

Liggett, J. 1974. *The human face.* New York: Stein and Day.

Light, L., S., Hollander, and F. Kayra-Stuart. 1981. Why attractive people are harder to remember. *Personality and Social Psychology Bulletin* 7: 269–276.

Lindzey, G. 1965. Morphology and behavior. In *Theories of personality: Primary source and research*, ed. G. Lindzey and C. S. Hall. New York: Wiley.

Lipton, D. N., and R. O. Nelson. 1980. The contribution of initiation behaviors to dating frequency. *Behavior Therapy* 11: 59–64.

Liu, A. 1979. *Solitaire.* New York: Harper and Row.

Lowenstein, L. F. 1978. The bullied and nonbullied child: A contrast between the popular and unpopular child. *Home and School* 12: 3–4.

Luce, C. B. September 1971. The beautiful girl syndrome. *Cosmopolitan*, New York City: Cosmopoliton Books, 171, 90–192.

Lucker, G. W., W. E. Beane, and K. Guire. 1981. The idiographic approach to physical attractiveness research. *The Journal of Psychology* 107: 57–67.

Lucker, G. W., W. E. Beane, and R. L. Helmreich. 1981. The strength of the halo effect in physical attractiveness research. *The Journal of Psychology* 107: 69–75.

Lucker, G. W., and L. W. Graber. 1980. Physiognomic features and facial appearance judgments in children. *The Journal of Psychology* 104: 261–268.

Lynch, J. J. 1977. *The broken heart: The medical consequences of loneliness.* New York: Basic Books, Inc.

MacCorquodale, P., and J. DeLamater. 1979. Self-image and premarital sexuality. *Journal of Marriage and the Family* 41: 327–339.

Mace, K. C. 1972. The "overt-bluff" shoplifter: Who gets caught? *Journal of Forensic Psychology* 4: 26–30.

Macgregor, F. C. 1951. Some psycho-social problems associated with facial deformities. *American Sociological Review* 16: 629–638.

Macy, D. J. 1973. Effect of verbal praise and reproof on balance board performance of college males and females. *Perceptual and Motor Skills* 37: 488.

Maddox, G. L., K. Back, and V. Liederman. 1968. Overweight as social deviance and disability. *Journal of Health and Social Behavior* 9: 287–298.

Maddox, G. L., and U. Liederman. 1969. Overweight as a social disability with medical implications. *Journal of Medical Education* 44: 210–220.

Mahoney, E. R. 1978. Subjective physical attractiveness and self-other orientations. *Psychological Reports* 43: 277–278.

Major, B. N., and R. C. Sherman. 1975. The competitive woman: Fear of success, attractiveness, and competitor sex. Paper presented at the Annual Convention of the American Psychological Association, 30 August to 2 September, Chicago, Illinois.

Malcolm, H. 1971. *Generation of narcissus.* New York: Little, Brown.

Malinowski, B. 1929. *The sexual life of savages in North-Western Melanesia.* 2 vols. New York: Harcourt, Brace, Jovanovich.

Maloney, J. J., and M. K. Farrell. 1980. Treatment of severe weight loss in anorexia nervosa with hyperalimentation and psychotherapy. *American Journal of Psychiatry* 137(3): 310–313.

Mandel, M. (Ed.) 1974. *A complete treasury of stories for public speakers,* Middle Village, N.Y.: Jonathan David Publishers, p. 36.

Marcus, M. G., and K. I. Hakmiller. 1975. Effects of frequency, duration of study trial, and total duration of exposure on affective judgments. *Psychological Reports* 37: 195–200.

Markmann, J. J., K. J. Jamieson, and F. J. Floyd. 1983. In *Advances in family intervention: Assessment and theory,* ed. J. Vincent, vol. 3. Greenwich, Conn.: JAI Press.

Marks, E. S. 1943. Skin color judgments of Negro college students. *Journal of Abnormal and Social Psychology* 38: 370–376.

Marlatt, G. A. 1971. Exposure to a model and task ambiguity as determinance of verbal behavior in an interview. *Journal of Consulting and Clinical Psychology* 36: 268–276.

Martin, P. J., M. H. Friedmeyer, and J. E. Moore. 1977. Pretty patient-healthy patient? A study of physical attractiveness and psychopathology. *Journal of Clinical Psychology* 33: 990–994.

Martindale, C., M. Ross, D. Hines, and L. Abrams. 1978. Independence of interaction and interpersonal attraction in a psychiatric hospital population. *Journal of Abnormal Psychology* 87: 247–255.

Martinek, T. J. 1981. Physical attractiveness: Effects on teacher expectations and dyadic interactions in elementary age children. *Journal of Sport Psychology* 3: 196–205.

Maruyama, G., and N. Miller. 1980. Physical attractiveness, race, and essay evaluation. *Personality and Social Psychology* 6(3): 384–390.

Marwell, G., S. Sprecher, R. McKinney, J. DeLamater, and S. Smith. 1982. Legitimizing factors in the initiation of heterosexual relationships. Paper presented at the First International Conference on Personal Relationships, July, Madison, Wisconsin.

Marwit, K. L., S. J. Marwit, and E. F. Walker. 1978. Effects of student race and physical attractiveness on teachers' judgments of transgressions. *Journal of Educational Psychology* 70: 911–915.

Mashman, R. C. 1978. The effect of physical attractiveness on the preception of attitude similarity. *Journal of Social Psychology* 106: 103–110.

Maslow, A. H. 1954. *Motivation and personality.* New York: Harper.

Masters, G. 1977. *The Masters way to beauty.* New York: Signet.

Masters, W. H., and V. E. Johnson. 1966. *Human sexual response.* Boston: Little, Brown, & Co.

Masters, W. H., and V. E. Johnson. 1970. *Human sexual inadequacy.* Boston: Little, Brown, & Co.

Masters, W. H., and V. E. Johnson. 1976. *The pleasure bond.* New York: Bantam Books.

Mathes, E. W. 1975. The effects of physical attractiveness and anxiety on heterosexual attraction over a series of five encounters. *Journal of Marriage and the Family* 37: 769–773.

Mathes, E. W., and L. L. Edwards. 1978. Physical attractiveness as an input in social exchanges. *Journal of Psychology* 98: 267–275.

Mathes, E. W., and A. Kahn. 1975. Physical attractiveness, happiness, neuroticism, and self-esteem. *Journal of Psychology* 90: 27–30.

Mathews, A. M., J. H. J. Bancroft, and P. Slater. 1972. The principal components of sexual preference. *British Journal of Social and Clinical Psychology* 11: 35–43.

Matthews, C., and R. C. Clark, III. 1982. Marital satisfaction: A validation approach. *Basic and Applied Social Psychology* 3: 169–186.

Matthews, L. B. 1975. Improving the self-image of the socially disabled. *Journal of Home Economics* 67: 9–12.

May, J. L., and P. A. Hamilton. 1980. Effects of musically evoked affect on women's interpersonal attraction toward and perceptual judgments of physical attractiveness of men. *Motivation and Emotion* 4: 217–228.

McBurney, D. H., J. M. Levine, and P. H. Cavanaugh. 1977. Psychophysical and social ratings of human body odor. *Personality and Social Psychology Bulletin* 3: 135–138.

McCall, M. M. 1966. Courtship as social exchange: Some historical comparisons. In *Kinship and family organization*, ed. B. Farber, 190–200. New York John Wiley & Sons, Inc.

McCandless, B. R., and H. R. Marshall. 1957. A picture-sociometric technique for preschool children and its relation to teacher judgments of friendship. *Child Development* 28: 139–149.

McCandless, B. R., W. S. Persons, III., and A. Roberts. 1972. Perceived opportunity, delinquency, race, and body build among delinquent youths. *Journal of Consulting and Clinical Psychology* 38: 281–287.

McCartney, J. L. 1966. Overt transference. *Journal of Sex Research* 2: 227–237.

McCauley, C., and C. L. Stitt. 1978. An individual and quantitative measure and stereotpyes. *Journal of Personality and Social Psychology* 36: 929–940.

McCormack, E. 1975. Maximum tumescence and repose. *Rolling Stones*, 9 October, 36–71.

McCormick, N. B., and C. J. Jesser. 1982. The courtship game: Power in the sexual encounter. In *Changing Boundaries*, ed. E. R. Allegier, and N. B. McCormick, 64–86. New York: Mayfield.

McCullers, J. C., and J. Staat. 1974. Draw an ugly man: An inquiry into the dimensions of physical attractiveness. *Personality and Social Psychology Bulletin* 1: 33–35.

McDonald, P. J., and V. C. Eilenfield. 1980. Physical attractiveness and the approach/avoidance of self-awareness. *Personality and Social Psychology Bulletin* 6: 391–395.

McFatter, R. M. 1978. Sentencing strategies and justice: Effects of punishment philosophy on sentencing decisions. *Journal of Personality and Social Psychology* 36: 1490–1500.

McGarry, M. S., and S. G. West. 1975. Stigma among the stigmatized: Resident mobility, communication ability, and physical appearance as predictors of staff-resident interaction. *Journal of Abnormal Psychology* 84: 399–405.

McGaugh, J. L., and S. B. Kiesler, eds. 1981. *Aging: Biology and behavior.* New York: Academic Press.

McGinnis, R. 1959. Campus values in mate selection: A repeat study. *Social Forces* 36: 368–373.

McGrath, M. (September 1984) A mini-guide to plastic surgery. *Ladies Home Journal*, New York City. 119.

McKeachie, W. J. 1952. Lipstick as a determiner of first impressions of personality: An experiment for the general psychology course. *Journal of Social Psychology* 36: 241–244.

McKelvie, S. J. 1976. The role of eyes and mouth in the memory of a face. *American Journal of Psychology* 89: 311–323.

McKelvie, S. J., and S. J. Matthews. 1976. Effects of physical attractiveness and favorableness of character on liking. *Psychological Reports* 38: 1223–1230.

McReynolds, P., and C. Guevara. 1967. Attitudes of schizophrenics and normals toward success and failure. *Journal of Abnormal Psychology* 72: 303–310.

Mead, G. H. 1934. *Mind, self and society: From the standpoint of a social behaviorist.* Chicago: University of Chicago Press.

Meehl, P. E. 1970. Nuisance variables and the ex post facto design. In *Minnesota studies in the philosophy of science*, ed. M. Radner, and S. Winokur, vol. 4, 373–402. Minneapolis: University of Minnesota Press.

Mehrabian, A. 1968. Relationship of attitude to seated posture, orientation, and distance. *Journal of Personality and Social Pyschology* 10: 26–30.

Meiners, M. L., and J. P. Sheposh. 1977. Beauty or brains: Which image for your mate? *Personality and Social Psychology Bulletin* 3: 262–265.

Melamed, L., and M. K. Moss. 1975. The effect of context on ratings of attractiveness of photographs. *Journal of Psychology* 90: 129–136.

Mencken, H. L. 1931. *The aesthetic recoil* New York: American Mecury, p. 288.

Merchlenhard, C. L., and R. M. McFall. 1981. Dating initiation from a woman's perspective. *Behavior Therapy* 12: 682–691.

Meredith, M. 1972. The influence of physical attractiveness, independence and honesty on date selection. Dept. of Psychol. Western Illinois University. Photocopy. Macomb, Illinois.

Mettee, D. R., and E. Aronson. 1974. Affective reactions to appraisal from others. In *Foundations of interpersonal attraction*, ed. T. L. Huston, 235–283. New York: Academic Press.

Meyers, R. 1976. Broom-Hilda. *Los Angeles Times*, 16 May.

Miller, A. G. 1970a. Role of physical attractiveness in impression formation. *Psychonomic Science* 19: 241–243.

Miller, A. G. 1970b. Social perception of internal-external control. *Perceptual and Motor Skills* 30: 103–109.

Miller, A. G. 1972. Effects of attitude similarity-dissimilarity on the utilization of additional stimulus inputs in judgments of interpersonal attraction. *Psychonomic Science* 26:199–203.

Miller, A. G., B. Gillen, C. Schenker, and S. Radlove. 1974. The prediction and perception of obedience to authority. *Journal of Personality* 42:23–42.

Miller, H. L., and W. H. Rivenbark, III. 1970. Sexual differences in physical attractiveness as a determinant of heterosexual liking. *Psychological Reports* 27:701–702.

Miller, N., and G. Maruyama. 1977. The effects of physical attractiveness and race on essay evaluations. *Psychonomic Society Bulletin* 10:253.

Miller, R. S., and H. M. Lefcourt. 1982. The assessment of social intimacy. Photocopy. Department of Psychology, University of Waterloo; Waterloo, Ontario, Canada.

Millett, K. 1970. *Sexual politics.* New York: Avon books.

Mills, J. 1958. Changes in moral attitudes following temptation. *Journal of Personality.* 26:517–531.

Mills, J., and E. Aronson. 1965. Opinion change as a function of the communicator's attractiveness and desire to influence. *Journal of Personality and Social Psychology* 1:173–177.

Mills, J., and M. S. Clark. 1980. Communal and exchange relationships. Paper presented at the 1980 meetings of the Society of Experimental Social Psychologists, Palo Alto, California.

Mills, J., and J. Harvey. 1972. Opinion change as a function of when information about the communicator is received and whether he is attractive or expert. *Journal of Personality and Social Psychology* 21:52–55.

Milord, J. T. 1978. Aesthetic aspects of faces: A (somewhat) phenomenological analysis using multidimensional scaling methods. *Journal of Personality and Social Psychology* 36:205–216.

Mims, P. R., J. J. Hartnett, and W. R. Nay. 1975. Interpersonal attraction and help volunteering as a function of physical attractiveness. *Journal of Psychology* 89:125–131.

Minuchin, S., B. L. Roseman, and L. Baker. 1978. *Psychosomatic families: Anorexia nervosa in context.* Cambridge, Mass.: Harvard University Press.

Mitchell, K. R., and F. E. Orr. 1976. Heterosexual social competence, anxiety, avoidance and self-judged physical attractiveness. *Perceptual and Motor Skills* 43:553–554.

Mithers, C. L. 1982. I wasn't always pretty. *Mademoiselle*, June, 93–184.

Molloy, J. T. 1975. *Dress for success*. New York: Warner Books.

Molloy, J. T. 1977. *The woman's dress for success book*. New York: Warner Books.

Montagu, A. 1971. *The elephant man*. New York: Outerbridge and Dienstfrey.

Montaigne, M. de. 1948. Of the inconsistency of our actions. In *Complete essays of Montaigne*, trans. D. M. Frame, 242. Stanford, Calif.: Stanford University Press.

Monthei, P. 1981. Can a "6" woman find happiness with a "10" man? *Big Beautiful Women*, December.

Moore, S. G. 1967. Correlates of peer acceptance in nursery school children. *Young Children* 22:281–297.

Morris, D. 1981. *Manwatching*. New York: Harry Abrams.

Morrison, D. E., and C. P. Holden. 1971. The burning bra: The American breast fetish and women's liberation. In *Deviance and change*, ed. P. K. Manning. Englewood Cliffs, N. J.: Prentice Hall.

Morse, C. 1982. College yearbook pictures: More females smile than males. *The Journal of Psychology* 110:3–6.

Morse, S., and K. J. Gergen. 1970. Social comparison, self-consistency and the concept of self. *Journal of Personality and Social Psychology* 16:148–156.

Morse, S. J., J. Gruzen, and H. Reis. 1976. The eye of the beholder: A neglected variable in the study of physical attractiveness? *Journal of Personality* 44:209–225.

Morse, S. J., H. T. Reis, J. Gruzen, and E. Wolff. 1974. The "eye of the beholder": Determinants of physical attractiveness judgments in the U. S. and South Africa. *Journal of Personality* 42:528–542.

Morton, R. 1964. *Ptthisiologica—Or a treatise of consumption*. London: Smith and Walford.

Moss, M. K., R. Miller, and R. A. Page. 1975. The effects of racial context on the perception of physical attractiveness. *Sociometry* 38:525–535.

Moss, M. K., and R. A. Page. 1972. Reinforcement and helping behavior. *Journal of Applied Social Psychology* 2:360–371.

Moss, Z. 1970. It hurts to be alive and obsolete, or the aging woman. In *Sisterhood is powerful*, ed. R. Morgan. New York: Vintage.

Muehlenhard, C. G., and R. M. McFall. 1982. Assertiveness breeds attempt. *Psychology Today*, 75. December.

Muirhead, S. 1979. Therapists' sex, clients' sex, and client attractiveness in psycho-diagnostic assessments. Paper presented at the meetings of the American Psychological Association, September, New York.

Murphy, M. J., and D. T. Hellkamp. 1976. Attractiveness and personality warmth: Evaluations of paintings rated by college men and woman. *Perceptual and Motor Skills* 43:1163–1166.

Murrey, J. 1976. The role of height and weight in the sales performance of salesmen of ordinary life insurance. Dept. of Psychology Ph. D. diss., North Texas State University, Denton, Texas.

Murstein, B. I. 1970. Stimulus—value—role: A theory of marital choice. *Journal of Marriage and the Family* 32:465–481.

Murstein, B. I. 1971. Critique of models of dyadic attraction. In *Theories of attraction and love*, ed. B. I. Murstein, I–30. New York: Springer.

Murstein, B. I. 1972. Physical attractiveness and marital choice. *Journal of Personality and Social Psychology* 22(1):8–12.

Murstein, B. I. 1977. The stimulus-value-role (SVR) theory of dyadic relationships. In *Theory practice in interpersonal attraction*, ed. S. Duck, 105–127. New York: Academic Press.

Murstein, B. I. 1980. The limit of exchange in equity theories. Psychology dept. Conn. College, New London, CT.

Murstein, B. I., and P. Christy. 1976. Physical attractiveness and marriage adjustment in middle-aged couples. *Journal of Personality and Social Psychology* 34:537–542.

Murstein, B. I., M. Goyette, and M. Cerreto. 1974. A theory of the effect of exchange orientation on marriage and friendship. Photocopy. Department of Psychology, Connecticut College, New London, Conn.

Murstein, B. I., and M. G. MacDonald. 1977. *The relationship of 'exchange orientation' and 'commitment' scales to marriage adjustment.* Dept. of Psychol., Connecticut College. Photocopy. New London, Conn.

Musa, K. E., and M. E. Roach. 1973. Adolescent appearance and self concept. *Adolescence* 8:385–394.

Mussen, P. H., and M. C. Jones. 1957. Self-conceptions, motivations, and interpersonal attitudes of late and early maturing boys. *Child Development* 28:243–256.

Mussen, P. H., and M. C. Jones. 1958. The behavior of inferred motivations of late and early maturing boys. *Child Development* 29:61–67.

Nadler, A. 1980. Good looks do not help. Effects of helper's physical attractiveness and expectation for future interaction on help-seeking behavior. *Personality and Social Psychology Bulletin* 6:378–383.

Nadler, A., R. Shapira, and S. Ben-Itzhak. 1982. Good looks may help: Effects of helper's physical attractiveness and sex of helper on males' and females' help-seeking behavior. *Journal of Personality and Social Psychology* 42:90–99.

Napier, A. Y. 1977. The rejection-intrusion pattern: A central family dynamic. School of Family Resources, University of Wisconsin-Madison. Photocopy.

Napier, A., and C. Whitaker. 1978. *The family crucible.* New York: Harper & Rowe.

Napoleon, T., L. Chassin, and R. D. Young. 1980. A replication and extension of physical attractiveness and mental illness. *Journal of Abnormal Psychology* 89:250–253.

Napolitane, C., and V. Pellegrino. 1977. *Living and loving after divorce.* New York: Rawson Associates.

Nesdale, A. R., B. G. Rule, and M. McAra. 1975. Moral judgments of aggression Personal and situational determinants. *European Journal of Social Psychology* 5:339–349.

Newcomb, T. M. 1947. Autistic hostility and social reality. *Human Relations* 1:69–86.

Newcomb, T. M. 1961. *The acquaintance process.* New York: Holt, Rinehart and Winston.

Newman, R. 1977. Short people. Hightree Music. International copyright secured, PV 119412-5.

New woman. Her looks are often deceptive. 1982. *New Woman,* June, 58–59.

New York Times. 1968. Ten thousand wait in vain for reappearance of Wall Street's sweater girl. 21 September, 14.

Nicoletis, C. 1972–1973. Morphology and psychology. *Psychotherapy and Psychosomatics* 21:101–104.

Nida, S. A. and J. E. Williams. 1977. Sex-stereotyped traits, physical attractiveness and interpersonal attraction. *Psychological Reports* 41:1311–1322.

Nielson, J. P., and A. Kernaleguen. 1976. Influence of clothing and physical attractiveness in person perception. *Perceptual and Motor Skills* 42:775–780.

Nisbett, R. E., and N. Bellows. 1977. Verbal reports about casual influences on social judgments: Private access versus public theories. *Journal of Personality and Social Psychology* 35:613–624.

Nisbett, R. E., and T. D. Wilson. 1977. The halo effect: Evidence for unconscious alteration of judgments. *Journal of Personality and Social Psychology* 35:250–256.

Nordholm, L. A. 1980. Beautiful patients are good patients: Evidence for the physical attractiveness stereotype in first impressions of patients. *Social Science and Medicine* 14A:81–83.

Norman, R. 1976. When what is said is important: A comparison of expert and attractive sources. *Journal of Experimental Social Psychology* 12:294–300.

Novak, W. 1983. *The great American man shortage and other roadblocks to romance.* New York: Rawson Associates.

O'Brien, P. 1979. The dangers of being too good-looking. *Esquire,* September, 19–23.

O'Grady, K. E. 1982. Sex, physical attractiveness, and perceived risk for mental illness. *Journal of Personality and Social Psychology* 43:1064–1071.

Old nursery rhyme. 1964. In *A family book of nursery rhymes,* ed. G. and P. Opie. New York: Oxford University Press, p. 157.

Orgega y Gasset, J. 1957. *On love.* New York: New American Library.

Ovid. 1963. *The art of love.* Trans. R. Humphries. Bloomington: Indiana University Press.

Owens, G., and J. G. Ford. 1978. Further consideration of the "what is beautiful" finding. *Social Psychology* 41:73–75.

Palardy, J. M. 1969. What teachers believe—what children achieve. *Elementary School Journal* 69:370–374.

Palmer, M. 1974. Marriage and the formerly fat: The effect of weight loss has on your life together. *Weight Watchers,* 7(2):23–50.

Pancer, S. M., and J. R. Meindl. 1978. Length of hair and beardedness as determinants of personality impressions. *Perceptual and Motor Skills* 46:1328–1330.

Panferov, V. N. 1974. The perception and interpretation of personal appearance. *Voprosy Psikhologii* 2:59–64.

Parke, R. D., and C. W. Callmer. 1975. Child abuse: An interdisciplinary review. In *Review of child development research*, ed. M. Hetherington, vol. 5, 509–590. Chicago: University of Chicago Press.

Parker, D. 1936. *Collected poetry.* New York: Random House, The Modern Library.

Parker, D. 1944. *The portable Dorothy Parker.* New York: The Viking Press.

Paterson, D. G., and K. E. Ludgate. 1922. Blond and brunette traits: A quantitative study. *Journal of Personnel Research* 1:122–127.

Patterson, G. R. 1971. *Families: Applications of social learning to family life.* Champaign, Ill.: Research Press Co.

Pavlos, A. J., and J. D. Newcomb. 1974. Effects of physical attractiveness and severity of physical illness on justification seen for attempting suicide. *Personality and Social Psychology Bulletin* 1:36–38.

Pellegrini, R. J. 1973. Impressions of the male personality as a function of beardedness. *Psychology* 10:29–33.

Pellegrini, R. J., R. A. Hicks, S. Meyers-Winton, and B. G. Antal. 1978. Physical attractiveness and self-disclosure in mixed-sex dyads. *Psychological Record* 28:509–516.

Pennebaker, J. W., M. A. Dyer, R. S. Caulkins, D. L. Litowitz, P. L. Ackerman, D. B. Anderson, and K. M. McGraw. 1979. Don't the girls get prettier at closing time: A country and western application to psychology. *Personality and Social Psychology Bulletin* 5:122–125.

Peplau, A. 1979. Developing a social-psychological theory of loneliness. Paper presented at the 87th Annual Convention of the American Psychological Association, September, New York.

Peplau, L. A. 1983. Roles and gender. In *Close relationships*, ed. H. H. Kelley, E. Berscheid, A. Christensen, J. H. Harvey, T. L. Huston, G. Levinger, E. McClintoch, L. A. Peplau, and D. Petersen, 220–264. New York: W. H. Freeman.

Peplau, L. A., and D. Perlman. 1982. *Loneliness.* New York: John Wiley and Sons.

Perlman, D., W. Josephson, W. T. Hwang, H. Begum, and T. L. Thomas. 1978. Cross-cultural analysis of students' sexual standards. *Archives of Sexual Behavior* 7:545–558.

Perlmutter, M. 1978. *Therapists' reactions to their clients' appearance.* Photocopy. Dept. of Social Work. University of Wisconsin, Madison, Wisc.

Perlmutter, M., and E. Hatfield. 1980. Intimacy, intentional metacommunication and second-order change. *American Journal of Family Therapy* 8:17–23.

Perper, T. and V. S. Fox. 1980. Special focus: Flirtation behavior in public settings. Paper presented at the meeting of the Eastern Region of the Society for the Scientific Study of Sex, April, Philadelphia.

Perrin, F. A. C. 1921. Physical attractiveness and repulsiveness. *Journal of Experimental Psychology* 4:203–217.

Peters, A. 1971. Gefuhl and wiederhennen. *Fortschr. Psychology* 4:120–133.

Peterson, J. A., and B. Payne. 1975. *Love in later years.* New York: Association Press.

Peterson, J. L., and C. Miller. 1980. Physical attractiveness and marriage adjustment in older American couples. *Journal of Psychology* 105:247–252.

Peterson, K., and J. P. Curran. 1976. Trait attribution as a function of hair length and correlates of subjects' preferences for hair style. *Journal of Psychology* 93:331–339.

Petrarca, F. 1968. De remediis utriusque fortunae. *Francisci Petrachae de Remediie.* Venice: Paganino 1515 Bk ii.

Phares, E. J. 1976. *Locus of control in personality.* Morristown, N. J.: General Learning Press.

Pheterson, M., and J. Horai. 1976. The effects of sensation seeking, physical attractiveness of stimuli, and exposure frequency on liking. *Social Behavior and Personality* 4:241–247.

Piehl, J. 1977. Integration of information in the courts: Influence of physical attractiveness on amount of punishment for a traffic offender. *Psychological Reports* 41:551–556.

Pigache, F. P. May 17, 1978. Are you anti-facial discrimination—or an unrepentant lookist pig? *World Medicine, p.* 13, 79–89.

Pilkonis, P. A. 1977. The behavioral consequences of shyness. *Journal of Personality* 45:596–611.

Piliavin, I. M., J. A. Piliavin, and J. Rodin. 1975. Costs, diffusion, and the stigmatized victim. *Journal of Personality and Social Psychology* 32:429–438.

Place, D. M. 1975. The dating experience for adolescent girls. *Adolescence* 10:157–174.

Plato. 1925. *Plato: Philebus.* Trans. H. N. Fowler. Cambridge: Harvard University Press, p. 389.

Playboy: Paul Simon. 1984. *Playboy,* 174.

Playboy's complete book of party jokes. 1972. New York: Playboy.

Pleck, J. H., and J. Sawyer, eds. 1974. *Men and masculinity.* Englewood Cliffs, N. J.: Prentice-Hall.

Plimpton, G. 1977. *One more July: A football dialog with Bill Curry,* 1st ed. New York: Harper and Row.

Pocs, O., A. Godow, W. L. Tolone, and R. H. Walsh. 1977. Is there sex after 40? *Psychology Today* 11(1):54–56, 87.

Poling, T. H. 1978. Sex differences, dominance, and physical attractiveness in the use of nonverbal emblems. *Psychological Reports* 43:1087–1092.

Polivy, J., R. Hackett, and P. Bycio. 1979. The effect of perceived smoking status on attractiveness. *Personality and Social Psychology Bulletin* 5:401–404.

Pomeroy, K. & J. A. Broussard. 1984. *How to write to Oriental ladies* Honokaa, Hawaii: Rainbow Ridge Publications.

Pomeroy, W. B., and A. C. Kinsey. 1972. Man and method. In *Human sexuality,* ed. O. Pocs, vol. 82/83, 14. Annual Editions. Guilford, Conn.: The Duskkin Publising Group. [From *Psychology Today,* March, 1972. Abridged and adapted from Chapter 7, "Interviewing." In *Dr. Kinsey and the Institute for Sex Research.* The Harold Matson Co.]

Pope, K. 1980. Defining and studying romantic love. In *On love and loving,* ed. K. Pope and Associates. San Francisco: Jossey-Bass.

Pope, K. S., and Associates 1980. *On love and loving.* San Francisco: Jossey-Bass Publishing.

Pope, K. S., H. Levenson, and L. R. Schover. 1979. Sexual intimacy in psychology training: Results and implications of a national survey. *American Psychologist* 34:682–689.

Powell, P. H., and J. M. Dabbs. 1976. Physical attractiveness and personal space. *Journal of Social Psychology* 100:59–64.

Price, R. A. 1978. Family resemblances in physical attractiveness. *Behavior Genetics* 8:562.

Price, R. A., and S. G. Vandenberg. 1977. Assortative mating for physical attractiveness. *Behavior Genetics* 7:84–85.

Price, R. A., and S. G. Vandenberg. 1979. Matching for physical attractiveness in married couples. *Personality and Social Psychology Bulletin* 5:398–400.

Prieto, A. G., and M. C. Robbins. 1975. Perceptions of height and self-esteem. *Perceptual and Motor Skills* 40:395–398.

Purdy, S., C. Gates, and W. Stewart. 1976. A behavioral analysis of fashion. *Perceptual and Motor Skills* 43:239.

Quindlen, A. 1981. About New York: A woman, a carnation, a glove, & memories. *New York Times.* 4 November.

Quinn, R. P. 1978. Physical deviance and occupational mistreatment: The short, the fat, and the ugly. Master's thesis, University of Michigan Survey Research Center, University of Michigan, Ann Arbor.

Quinn, R., J. Tabor, and L. Gordon. 1968. *The decision to discriminate.* Ann Arbor, Mich.: Survey Research Center.

Quinn, S. 1971. *The Capital Times.* Madison, Wisconsin, 24 July 2.

Rapson, R. L. 1980. *Fairly lucky you live Hawaii.* Honolulu: University Press of America, p. 67.

Rasberry, W. (1982, Feb. 21). Equality for uglies. *Time,* New York. p. 8.

Reis, H. T., J. Nezlek, and L. Wheeler. 1980. Physical attractiveness in social interaction. *Journal of Personality and Social Psychology* 38:604–617.

Reis, H. T., L. Wheeler, N. Spiegel, M. H. Kernis, K. J. Nezlek, and M. Perri. 1982. Physical attractiveness in social interaction: I. Why does appearance affect social experience? *Journal of Personality and Social Psychology* 43:979–996.

Reiss, A. J., Jr., O. D. Duncan, P. K. Hatt, and C. C. North. 1961. *Occupations and social status.* New York: Free Press.

Reiss, I. L. 1967. *The social context of premarital sexual permissiveness.* New York City: Holt, Rinehart, Winston.

Reynolds, D. E., and M. S. Sanders. 1975. Effect of defendant attractiveness, age, and injury on severity of sentence given by simulated jurors. *Journal of Social Psychology* 96:149–150.

Rican, P., and A. Richter. 1971. Self-assessment in the reference frame of a concrete social group. *Ceskosvolenska Psychologie* 15:253–256.

Rich, J. 1975. Effects of children's physical attractiveness on teacher's evaluations. *Journal of Educational Psychology* 67: 599–609.

Richardson, S., A. Hastorf, N. Goodman, and S. Dornbusch. 1961. Cultural uniformity in reaction to physical disabilities. *American Sociological Review* 26:241–247.

Riordan, C. A., and J. T. Tedeschi. 1983. Attraction in aversive environments: Some evidence for classical conditioning and negative reinforcement. *Journal of Personality and Social Psychology* 44:683–692.

Rist, R. C. 1970. Student social class and teacher expectations: The self-fulfilling prophecy in ghetto education. *Harvard Educational Review* 40:411–451.

Robertiello, R. C. 1976. The myth of physical attractiveness. *Psychotherapy: Theory, Research and Practice* 13:54–55.

Roberts, A. C. 1971. *Facial prostheses: The restoration of facial defects by prosthetic means.* London: Henry Kimpton.

Rockman, M. 1982. Know how to interview for a job. *Wisconsin State Journal,* 18 July, 22.

Rodin, J. 1979. Pathogenesis of obesity: Energy intake and expenditure. In *Obesity in America,* ed. G. A. Bray. N.I.H. Publication No. 79–359. U.S. Department of Health, Education, and Welfare.

Rodin, J. 1983. *Exploding the weight myths.* London: Century Press.

Roff, M. 1960. Relations between certain preservice factors and psychoneurosis during military duty. *Armed Forces Medical Journal* 11:152–169.

Roff, M. 1961. Childhood social interactions and young adult bad conduct. *Journal of Abnormal and Social Psychology* 63:333–337.

Roff, M., and D. S. Brody. 1953. Appearance and choice status during adolescence. *Journal of Psychology* 36:347–356.

Rogers, C. R. 1951. *Client-centered therapy.* Boston: Houghton Mifflin.

Rogers, E. M., and A. E. Havens. 1960. Prestige rating and mate selection on a college campus. *Journal of Marriage and Family Living* 22:55–59.

Rokeach, M. 1943. Studies in beauty: 1) The relationship in beauty in women, dominance, security. *The Journal of Social Psychology* 17:181–189.

Rokeach, M. 1945. Studies in beauty: 2) Some determinants of the perception of beauty in women. *Journal of Social Psychology* 22:155–169.

Roll, S., and J. S. Verinis. 1971. Stereotypes of scalp and facial hair as measured by the semantic differential. *Psychological Reports* 28:975–980.

Rom, P. 1973. Hair style and life style. *Individual Psychologist* 10:22–25.

Romano, J. M., and A. S. Bellack. 1980. Social validation of a component model of assertive behavior. *Journal of Consulting and Clinical Psychology* 48:478–490.

Rosen, G. M., and A. O. Ross. 1968. Relationship of body image to self-concept. *Journal of Consulting and Clinical Psychology* 32:100.

Rosenberg, M. 1965. *Society and the adolescent self-image.* Princeton, N. J.: Princeton University Press.

Rosenberg, M., and R. G. Simmons. 1971. *Black and white self-esteem: The urban school child.* Washington, D.C.: American Sociological Association.

Rosenkrantz, P., S. Vogel, H. Bee, I. Broverman, and D. M. Broverman. 1968. Sex-role stereotype and self-concept in college students. *Journal of Consulting and Clinical Psychology* 32:287–295.

Rosenthal, R., and L. Jacobson. 1968. *Pygmalion in the classroom.* New York: Holt.

Ross, M. B., and J. Salvia. 1975. Attractiveness as a biasing factor in teaching judgments. *American Journal of Mental Deficiency* 80:96–98.

Rotter, J. B. 1966. Generalized expectancies for internal versus external control of reinforcement. *Psychological Monographs* 80.

Rougement, D. de 1974. *Love in the western world.* Trans. M. Belgion. Rev. and augmented ed. New York: Harper and Row.

Rubenstein, C., and P. Shaver. 1982. *In search of intimacy.* New York: Delacorte Press.

Rubin, Z. 1970. Measurement of romantic love. *Journal of Personality and Social Psychology* 16–265–273.

Rubin, Z. 1973. *Liking and loving: An invitation to social psychology.* New York: Holt, Rinehart and Winston.

Rubin, Z., C. T. Hill, L. A. Peplau, and C. Dunkel-Schetter. 1980. Self-disclosure in dating couples: sex roles and the ethic of openness. *Journal of Marriage and the Family* 42:305–317.

Rucker, M., D. Taber, and A. Harrison. 1981. The effect of clothing variation and first impressions of female job applicants; what to wear when. *Social Behavior and Personality* 9:53–64.

Rudofsky, B. 1972. *The unfashionable human body.* London: Rupert Hart-Davis.

Rule, B. G., R. Dyck, M. McAra, and A. R. Nesdale. 1975. Judgments of aggression serving personal versus prosocial purposes. *Social Behavior and Personality* 3:55–63.

Rumsey, N., R. Bull, and D. Gahagan. 1982. The effect of facial disfigurement on the proxemic behavior of the general public. *Journal of Applied Social Psychology* 12:137–150.

Rusianoff, P., and H. J. Freudenberger. January, 1982. Risking intimacy, *Psychology Today* Cassette #20227. Copyright Ziff-Davis Publishing Company.

Russell, D., L. A. Peplau, and C. E. Cutrona. 1980. The revised UCLA loneliness scale: Concurrent and discriminant validity evidence. *Journal of Personality and Social Psychology* 39:153–166.

Russell, D., L. A. Peplau, and M. L. Ferguson. 1978. Developing a measure of loneliness. *Journal of Personality Assessment* 42:290–294.

Rutzen, S. R. 1973. The social importance or orthodontic rehabilitation: Report of a five year follow-up study. *Journal of Health and Social Behavior* 14:233–240.

Safilios-Rothschild, C. 1977. *Love, sex, and sex roles.* Englewood, Cliffs, N. J. Prentice-Hall, Spectrum Books.

Sager, C. 1976. *Marriage contracts and couple therapy.* New York: Bruner-Mazel

Salmon, M. 1983. *Beauty as elite stigma: Note on an ambivalent indentity.* Paper presented at the 78th meeting of the American Sociological Association Detroit, Michigan.

Salvia, J., R. Algozzine, and J. B. Sheare. 1977. Attractiveness and school achievement. *Journal of School Psychology* 15:60–67.

Salvia, J., J. B. Sheare, and B. Algozzine. 1975. Facial attractiveness and personal social development. *Journal of Abnormal Child Psychology* 3:171–178.

Samuel, W. 1972. Response to bill of rights paraphrases as influenced by the hip or straight attire of the opinion solicitor. *Journal of Applied Psychology* 2:47–62.

Sappenfield, B. R., and B. Balogh. 1970. Perceived attractiveness of social stimuli as related to their perceived similarity to self. *The Journal of Psychology* 74:105–111.

Sappho. 1965. Fragments 101. In *Poems and fragments.* Trans. with an introduction by G. Davenport. Ann Arbor: University of Michigan Press.

Sarason, I. G., J. H. Johnson, and J. M. Siegel. 1978. Assessing the impact of life changes: Development of the Life Experience Survey. *Journal of Consulting and Clinical Psychology* 46:932–946.

Saxe, L. 1978. The ubiquity of physical appearance as a determinant of social relations. In *Love and attraction*, ed. M. Cook and G. Wilson, 9–14. Oxford, U.K.: Pergamon.

Scanzoni, J. 1972. *Sexual bargaining: Power politics in the American marriage.* Englewood Cliffs, N.J.: Prentice-Hall.

Schachter, S. 1964. The interaction of cognitive and physiological determinants of emotional state. In *Advances in experimental social psychology*, ed. L. Berkowitz, vol. 1. New York: Academic Press.

Schachter, S., and J. Singer. 1962. Cognitive, social and physiological determinants of emotional state. *Psychological Review* 69: 379–399.

Shafer, R. B., and P. M. Keith. 1980. Equity and depression among married couples. *Social Psychology Quarterly* 43:430–435.

Scheflen, A. E. 1965. Quasi-courtship behavior in psychotherapy. *Psychiatry* 28:245–257.

Scherwits, L., and R. Helmreich. 1973. Interactive effects of eye contact and verbal content on interpersonal attraction in dyads. *Journal of Personality and Social Psychology* 25:6–14.

Schiavo, R. S., B. Sherlock, and G. Wicklund. 1974. Effect of attire on obtaining directions. *Psychological Reports* 34:245–246.

Schiller, J. C. F. 1982. *Essays, esthetical and philosophical, including the dissertation on the "Connections between the animals and the spiritual in man."* London: G. Bell.

Schimel, J. L. 1970. Is there a relationship between a woman's physical appearance and her sexual behavior. *Medical Aspects of Human Sexuality*, October, 15.

Schoedel, J., W. A. Frederickson, and J. M. Knight. 1975. An entrapolation of the physical attractiveness and sex variables within the Byrne attraction paradigm. *Memory and Cognition* 3:527–530.

Schofield, M. 1965. *The sexual behavior of young people.* Boston: Little, Brown, and Company.

Schofield, W. 1964. *Psychotherapy: The purchase of friendship.* Englewood Cliffs: Prentice-Hall.

Schonfeld, W. A. 1969. The body and the body-image in adolescents. In *Adolescence: Psychosocial perspectives*, ed. G. Caplan and S. Lebovici. New York: Basic Books.

Schuler, H., and W. Berger. 1979. The impact of physical attractiveness and on an employment decision. In *Love and attraction*, ed. M. Cook and G. Wilson, 33–36. New York: Pergamon Press.

Schulz, C. M. 1960. *Go fly a kite Charlie Brown.* New York: Holt, Rinehart, and Winston.

Schumann, R. Cited in Baron, R., and D. Byrne. 1983. *Social psychology.* 4th ed. Newton, Mass.: Allyn and Bacon.

Schwartz, J. M., and S. I. Abramowitz. 1978. Effects of female client physical attractiveness on clinical judgment. *Psychotherapy: Theory, Research and Practice* 15:251–257.

Schwarzbaum, L. and L. Whisnant (eds.) 1982. Can you find true love on campus? *Nutshell*, 41–46. Knoxville, Tenn.: 13–30 Corporation.

Secord, P. F., and C. W. Backman. 1974. *Social psychology*. New York: McGraw Hill.

Secord, P. F., W. F. Dukes, and W. Bevan. 1954. Personalities in faces: I. An experiment in social perceiving. *Genetic Psychology Monographs* 49:231–279.

Secord, P. F., and S. M. Jourard. 1954. The appraisal of body cathexis; body cathexis and the self. *Journal of Consulting Psychology* 17:343–347.

Secord, P. F., and J. E. Muthard. 1955. Personalities in faces: II. Individual differences. *Journal of Abnormal Social Psychology* 50:238–242.

Seidenberg, R. 1973. Psychosexual adjustment of the unattractive woman. *Medical Aspects of Human Sexuality* 7:60–81.

Seligman, C., J. Brickman, and D. Koulack. 1977. Rape and physical attractiveness: Assigning responsibility to victims. *Journal of Personality* 45:554–563.

Seligman, C., R. H. Fazio, and M. P. Zanna. 1980. Effects of salience of extrinsic rewards on liking and loving. *Journal of Personality and Social Psychology*, 38:453–460.

Seligman, C., R. H. Fazio, and M. P. Zanna. 1976. *Consequences of extrinsic rewards for impressions of liking and loving*. Unpublished manuscript, Princeton University.

Seligman, C., N. Paschall, and G. Takata. 1974. Effects of physical attractiveness on attribution responsibility. *Canadian Journal of Behavioral Science* 6:290–296.

Seligman, C., N. Paschall, and G. Takat. In press. Attribution of responsibility for a chance event as a function of physical attractiveness of target person, outcome and likelihood of event.

Seligman, M. E. P. 1975. *Helplessness: On depression, development, and death*. San Francisco: W. H. Freeman.

Sempe, J. J. 1981. *Displays of affection*. Trans. Edward Koren. New York: Workman.

Shantaeu, J., and C. Nagy. 1976. Decisions made about other people: A human judgment analysis of dating choice. In *Cognition and social behavior*, ed. J S. Carroll and J. W. Payne. Hillsdale, N.J.: Lawrence Erlbaum.

Shanteau, J., and G. F. Nagy. 1979. Probability of acceptance in dating choice *Journal of Personality and Social Psychology* 37:522–533.

Shapiro, A. K., E. L. Struening, H. Barten, and E. Shapiro. 1973. Prognostic factors in psychotherapy: A multivariate analysis. *Psychotherapy: Theory Research and Practice* 10:93.

Shapiro, A. K., E. Struening, E. Shapiro, and H. Barten. 1976. Prognostic correlates of psychotherapy in psychiatric outpatients. *American Journal of Psychiatry* 133:802–808.

Sharf, R. S., and J. B. Bishop. 1979. Counselors' feelings toward clients a related to intake judgments and outcome variables. *Journal of Counseling Psychology* 26:267–269.

Shaw, G. B. 1905. *Man and superman*. New York: Brentanos, Act IV, p. 169.

Shaw, M. E., and P. J. Wagner. 1975. Role selection in the service of self presentation. *Memory and Cognition* 3:481–484.

Shea, J., S. M. Crossman, and G. R. Adams. 1978. Physical attractiveness an personality development. *Journal of Psychology* 99:59–62.

Sheldon, W. H., C. W. Dupertuis, and E. McDermott. 1954. *Atlas of men: A guide for somatotyping the adult male of all ages.* New York: Harper & Row.

Sheldon, W.H., and S. S. Stevens. 1942. *The varieties of temperament: A psychology of constitutional differences.* New York: Harper & Row.

Sheldon, W. H., S. S. Stevens, and W. B. Tucker. 1940. *The varieties of human physique: An introduction to constitutional psychology.* New York: Harper & Row.

Shepard, M. 1973. The effects of physical attractivenes and trustworthiness in long- and short-term dating selection. Department of Psychology, Western Illinois University, Macomb, Illinois. Photocopy.

Shepherd, J. W., and H. D. Ellis. 1972. Physical attractiveness and selection of marriage partners. *Psychological Reports* 30:1004.

Shepherd, J. W., and H. D. Ellis. 1973. The effects of attractiveness on recognition memory for faces. *American Journal of Psychology* 86:627–633.

Shettel-Neuber, J., J. B. Bryson, and L. E. Young. 1978. Physical attractiveness of the "other person" and jealousy. *Personality and Social Psychology Bulletin* 4:612–615.

Shinar, E. H. 1978. Person perception as a function of occupational and sex. *Sex Roles* 4:679–693.

Shoemaker, D. J., and D. R. South. 1978. Nonverbal images of criminality and deviance: Existence and consequence. *Criminal Justice Review* 3:65–80.

Shulman, A. K. 1972. *Memoirs of an ex-prom queen.* New York: Knopf.

Sigall, H. L., and E. Aronson. 1969. Liking for an evaluator as a function of her physical attractiveness and nature of the evaluations. *Journal of Experimental Social Psychology* 5:93–100.

Sigall, H., and D. Landy. 1973. Radiating beauty: The effects of having a physically attractive partner on person perception. *Journal of Personality and Social Psychology* 28:218–224.

Sigall, H., and J. Michela. 1976. I'll bet you say that to all the girls: Physical attractiveness and reactions to praise. *Journal of Personality* 44:611–626.

Sigall, H., and N. Ostrove. 1975. Beautiful but dangerous: Effects of offender attractiveness and nature of the crime on juridic judgment. *Journal of Personality and Social Psychology* 31:410–414.

Sigall, H., and R. Page. 1972. Reducing attenuation in the expression of interpersonal affect via the bogus pipeline. *Sociometry* 35:629–642.

Sigall, H., R. Page, and A. C. Brown. 1971. Effort expenditure as a function of evaluation and evaluator attractiveness. *Representative Research in Social Psychology* 2:19–25.

Silverman, I. 1971. Physical attractiveness. *Sexual Behavior,* September, 22–25.

Silvestro, J. R. 1982. Attractiveness and its effect on medical students' rank order for seeing patients. *Psychological Reports* 50:115–118.

Simmons, R. G., L. Brown, D. M. Bush, and D. A. Blyth. 1978. Self-esteem and achievement of black and white adolescents. *Social Problems* 26:86–96.

Simmons, R. G., and F. Rosenberg. 1975. Sex, sex roles, and self-image. *Journal of Youth and Adolescence* 4:229–258.

Simms, T. M. 1967. Pupillary response of male and female subjects to pupillary difference in male and female picture stimuli. *Perception and Psychophysics* 2:553–555.

Singer, J. E. 1964. The use of manipulative strategies: Machiavellianism and attractiveness. *Sociometry* 27:128–150.

Singh, B. N. 1964. A study of certain personal qualities as preferred by college students in their marital partners. *Journal of Psychological research* 8:37.

Singleton, R., and S. Hofacre. 1976. Effects of victim's physical attractiveness on juridic judgments. *Psychological Reports* 39:73–74.

Sinha, P. 1973. Development of feminine role concept inventory. *Indian Psychological Review* 10:18–19.

Siperstein, G. N., and J. Gottlieb. 1977. Physical stigma and academic performance as factors affecting children's first impression of handicapped peers. *American Journal of Mental Deficiency* 81:455–462.

Smedley, J. W., and J. A. Bayton. 1978. Evaluative race-class stereotypes by race and perceived class of subjects. *Journal of Personality and Social Psychology* 36:530–535.

Smith, E. D., and A. Hed. 1979. Effects of offenders' age and attractiveness on sentencing by mock juries. *Psychological Reports* 44:691–694.

Smith, J. W., and S. S. Baker. 1973. *Doctor make me beautiful.* New York: Bantam Books.

Smith, R. J., S. Sprecher, and J. DeLamater. 1983a. The impact of physical attractiveness and gender on perceptions of sexuality. Dept. of Sociology University of Wisconsin-Madison. Photocopy.

Smith, R. J., S. Sprecher, and J. DeLameter. 1983b. Perceptions of the intimacy of matched vs. mismatched couples. Department of Sociology, University of Wisconsin-Madison. Photocopy.

Smits, G. J., and I. M. Cherhoniak. 1976. Physical attractiveness and friendliness in interpersonal attraction. *Psychological Reports* 39:171–174.

Snyder, M., and M. Rothbart. 1971. Communicator attractiveness and opinion change. *Canadian Journal of Behavioural Science* 3:377–387.

Snyder, M., E. D. Tanke, and E. Berscheid. 1977. Social perception and interpersonal behavior: On the self-fulfilling nature of social stereotypes. *Journal of Personality and Social Psychology* 35:656–666.

Soble, S. L., and L. H. Strickland. 1974. Physical stigma, interaction, and compliance. *Bulletin of the Psychonomic Society* 4:130–132.

Solomon, M. R., and J. Schopler. 1978. The relationship of physical attractiveness and punitiveness: Is the linearity assumption out of line? *Personality and Social Psychology Bulletin* 4:483–486.

Solomon, S., and L. Saxe. 1977. What is intelligent, as well as attractive, is good. *Personality and Social Psychology Bulletin* 3:670–673.

Somerville, B. T. 1894. Notes on some islands of the New Hebrides (IV) Clothing, Ornaments, etc. *The Journal of the Anthropological Institute.* London: Kegan, Paul, Trench, Trübner, and Co., p. 368.

Sontag, S. 1972. The Double standard of aging. *Saturday Review* 55:29–38.

Sorenson, R. C. 1973. *Adolescent sexuality in contemporary America.* New York World Publishing.

Sorokin, P. A. 1959. *Social and cultural mobility.* New York: Free Press of Glencoe.

Sparacino, J., and S. Hansell. 1979. Physical attractiveness and academic performance: Beauty is not always talent. *Journal of Personality* 47:449–469.

Spence, J. T., and R. L. Helmreich. 1972. The attitudes toward women scale: An objective instrument to measure attitudes toward the rights and roles of women in contemporary society. *JSAS Catalog of Selected Documents in Psychology* 2:66. (Ms. No. 153)

Spence, J. T., R. Helmreich, and J. Stapp. 1973. A short version of the attitudes toward women scale. *Psychonomic Bulletin* 2:219–220.

Spreadbury, C. L., and J. B. Reeves. 1979. Physical attractiveness, dating behavior, and implications for women. *Personnel and Guidance Journal* 57:338–340.

Sprecher, S. 1980. Men, women, and intimate relationships: A study of dating couples. Master's thesis, University of Wisconsin-Madison.

Sprecher, S., J. DeLamater, N. Neuman, M. Neuman, P. Kahn, and D. Orbuch. In press. The girls (and boys) may not get prettier at closing time—and other interesting results from asking questions in bars. *Personality and Social Psychology Bulletin.*

Sprecher, S., and E. Hatfield. 1985. Interpersonal attraction. In *From research to clinical practice,* ed. G. Stricker and R. H. Keisner. New York: Plenum, 179–217.

Sprecher, S., K. McKinney, and G. DeLamater. 1981. Body satisfaction, physical attractiveness and self-concept. Dept. of Sociology. Photocopy. University of Wisconsin, Madison, Wisc.

Sprecher, S., R. J. Smith, and K. Johnson. 1984. What is bearded is beautiful and good: The effects of age on the beardedness stereotype. Dept. of Sociology. Photocopy. University of Wisconsin, Madison, Wisc.

Springbett, B. M. 1958. Factors affecting the final decision in the employment interview. *Canadian Journal of Psychology* 12:13–22.

Sroufe, R., A. Chaikin, R. Cook, and V. Freeman. 1977. The effects of physical attractiveness on honesty: A socially desirable response. *Personality and Social Psychology Bulletin* 3:59–62.

Staffiere, J. R. 1967. A study of social stereotype of body image in children. *Journal of Personality and Social Psychology* 7:101–104.

Stanford-Binet Intelligence Scale. 1973. 2nd rev. Described and reviewed in *The eight mental measurements yearbook,* ed. O. K. Burus, vol. 1, 227–229. Highland Park, N.J.: The Aryphon Press.

Stannard, U. 1971. The mask of beauty. In *Women in sexist society; Studies in power and powerlessness,* ed. V., Gormick and B. K. Moran, 118–130. New York: Basic Books.

Starfield, B., and I. B. Pless. 1980. Physical Health. In *Constancy and change in human development,* ed. O. G. Brim, Jr. and J. Kagan, 272–324. Cambridge, Mass.: Harvard Univ. Press.

Steffen, J. J., and J. Redden. 1977. Assessment of social competence in an evaluation-interaction analogue. *Human Communication Research* 4:30–37.

Steffensmeier, D. J., and R. H. Steffensmeier. 1976. Advocates of law and order: Villains or guardians of justice. *Criminal Justice and Behavior* 3:273–286.

Steffensmeier, D. J., and R. M. Terry. 1973. Deviance and respectability: An observational study of reactions to shoplifting. *Social Forces* 51:417–426.

Steig, W. 1951. *The rejected lovers.* New York: Knapf.

Stein, J., and G. Plimpton, eds. 1982. *Edie: An American biography*. New York: Alfred A. Knopf.

Stephan, C., and J. C. Tully. 1977. The influence of physical attractiveness of a plaintiff on the decisions of simulated jurors. *Journal of Social Psychology* 101:149–150.

Stephan, C. W. and J. H. Langlois. 1984. Baby beautiful: Adult attributions of infant competence as a function of infant attractiveness. *Child Development* 55:576–585.

Stephan, W., E. Berscheid, and E. Hatfield. [Walster] 1971. Sexual arousal and heterosexual perception. *Journal of Personality and Social Psychology* 20:93–101.

Stephenson, S. D. 1978. The effect of physical attractiveness on the attribution of leadership. Paper presented at the Annual Convention of the American Psychological Association, Toronto. Abstract in *Personality and Social Psychology Bulletin* 4:369.

Sternglanz, S. H., J. L. Granz, and M. Murakami. 1972. Adult preferences for infantile facial features: An ethnological approach. *Animal Behavior* 25:108–115.

Sternlicht, M. 1978. Perceptions of ugliness in the mentally retarded. *Journal of Psychology* 99:139–142.

Stewart, J. E. 1980. Defendant's attractiveness as a factor in the outcome of criminal trials: An observational study. *Journal of Applied Social Psychology* 10:348–361.

Stewart, J. E., and S. Rosen. 1974. Mediating effects of cost to audience and audience attractiveness on response to counterattitudinal role taking. *Journal of Social Psychology* 92:251–257.

Stewart, R. A., S. J. Tutton, and R. E. Steele. 1973. Stereotyping and personality: I. Sex differences in perception of female physiques. *Perceptual and Motor Skills* 36:811–814.

Stockhamer, N. 1970. Is there a relationship between a woman's physical appearance and her sexual behavior. *Medical Aspects of Human Sexuality*, October, 14.

Stogdill, R. M. 1948. Personal factors associated with leadership: A survey of the literature. *Journal of Psychology* 25:35–71.

Stokes, S. J., and L. Bickman. 1974. The effect of the physical attractiveness and role of the helper on help seeking. *Journal of Applied Social Psychology* 4:286–294.

Stoller, R. J. 1975. *Pervasion: The erotic form of hatred*. New York: Pantheon Books.

Stoller, R. J. 1979. *Sexual excitement*. New York: Pantheon Books.

Stolz, H. R., and L. M. Stolz. 1951. *Somatic development of adolescent boys*. New York: Macmillan.

Storck, J. T., and H. Sigall. 1979. Effect of a harm-doer's attractiveness and the victim's history of prior victimization on punishment of the harm-door. *Personality and Social Psychology Bulletin* 4:344–347.

Strane, K., and C. Watts. 1977. Females judged by attractiveness of partner. *Perceptual and Motor Skills* 45:225–226.

Stretch, R. H., and C. R. Figley. 1980. Beauty and the beast: Predictors of interpersonal attraction in a dating experiment. *Psychology, A Quarterly Journal of Human Behavior* 17:35–43.

Strickland, B. R., J. A. Doster, and J. S. Thrope. 1969. Early impressions and later confirmation of interpersonal judgments. *Perceptual and Motor Skills* 28:105–106.

Stroebe, W., C. A. Insko, V. D. Thompson, and B. D. Layton. 1971. Effects of physical attractiveness, attitude similarity, and sex on various aspects of interpersonal attraction. *Journal of Personality and Social Psychology* 18:79–91.

Strongman, K. T., and C. J. Hart 1968. Stereotyped reactions to body build. *Psychological Reports* 23:1175–1178.

Strupp, H. H. 1963. The outcome problem in psychotherapy revisited. *Psychotherapy: Theory, Research and Practice* 1:1–13.

Styczynski, L. E., and J. H. Langlois. 1977. The effects of familiarity on behavioral stereotypes associated with physical attractiveness in young children. *Child Development* 48:1137–1141.

Suedfeld, P., A. Bochner, and C. Matas. 1971. Petitioner's attire and petition signing by peace demonstrators: A field experiment on reference group similarity. *Journal of Applied Social Psychology* 1:278–283.

Suedfeld, P., S. Bochner, and D. Wnek. 1972. Helper-sufferer similarity and a specific request for help: Bystander intervention during a peace demonstration. *Journal of Applied Social Psychology* 2:17–23.

Sussman, S., K. T. Mueser, B. W. Grau, and P. R. Yarnold. 1983. Stability of females facial attractiveness during childhood. *Journal of Personality and Social Psychology.* 44:1231–1233.

Symons, D. 1979. *The evolution of human sexuality.* New York: Oxford Press.

Szondi, L., U. Moser, and M. W. Webb. 1959. *The Szondi test.* Philadelphia: J. B. Lippincott.

Taguiri, R. 1968. Personal perception. In *The handbook of social psychology,* ed. G. Lindsey and E. Aronson, vol. 3. Reading, Mass.: Addison Wesley.

Tanke, E. D. 1982. Dimensions of the physical attractiveness stereotype: A factor/analytic study. *The Journal of Psychology* 110:63–74.

Tavris, C. 1977. Men and women report their views on masculinity. *Psychology Today,* January, 34–82.

Taylor, G. R. 1970. *Doomsday book.* London: Thames and Hudson.

Taylor, H. F. 1070. *Balance in small groups.* New York: Van Vostrand, Teingold Co.

Taylor, L. 1981. Anorexia nervosa. *Honolulu Star Bulletin,* 4 June, D-1.

Taylor, L. 1983. Sunday today: The finest of the east. *The Sunday Star-Bulletin and Advertiser,* 24 July, C1.

Taylor, P. A., N. D. Glenn. 1976. The utility of education and attractiveness for females' status attainment through marriage. *American Sociological Review* 41:484–498.

Taylor, P. A., and D. G. Norvall. 1976. The utility of education and attractiveness for females' status attainment through marriage. *American Sociological Review* 41:484–497.

Tennis, G. H., and J. M. Dabbs. 1975. Judging physical attractiveness: Effects of judges' own attractiveness. *Personality and Social Psychology Bulletin* 1:513–516.

Tennov, D. 1979. *Love and limerence.* New York: Stein and Day.

Terman, L. M., and M. A. Merrill. 1973. *Stanford-Binet Intelligence Scale.* Boston: Houghton Mifflin Co.

Terman, L. M., and M. A. Merrill. 1973. *Measuring intelligence: A guide to the administration of the new revised Stanford-Binet tests of intelligence.* Boston: Houghton Mifflin.

Terry, R. L. 1975. Additional evidence for veridicality of perceptions based on pgysiognomic cues. *Perceptual and Motor Skills* 40:780–782.

Terry, R. L. 1977. Further evidence on components of facial attractiveness. *Perceptual and Motor Skills* 45:130.

Terry, R. L., and C. S. Brady. 1976. Effects of framed spectacles and contact lenses on self-ratings of facial attractiveness. *Perceptual and Motor Skills* 42:789–790.

Terry, R. L., and J. S. Davis. 1976. Components of facial attractiveness. *Perceptual and Motor Skills* 43:918.

Terry, R. L., and D. L. Kroger. 1976. Effects of eye correctives on ratings of attractiveness. *Perceptual and Motor Skills* 42:562.

Terry, R. L., and E. Macklin. 1977. Accuracy of identifying married couples on the basis of similarity of attractiveness. *Journal of Psychology* 97:15–20.

Tesser, A., and M. Brodie. 1971. A note on the evaluation of a computer date. *Psychonomic Science* 23:300.

Thibaut, J. W., and H. H. Kelley. 1965. *The social psychology of groups.* New York: Wiley.

Thomas J. 1982. Disturbing documentary on J. Edgar Hoover. *The Sunday Star-Bulletin and Advertiser, T.V. Week,* 6 June, 6.

Thornton, B. 1977. Effect of rape victim's attractiveness on jury simulation. *Personality and Social Psychology Bulletin* 3:666–669.

Thornton, G. R. 1944. The effect of wearing glasses upon judgments of personality traits of persons seen briefly. *Journal of Applied Psychology* 28:203–207.

Thorpe, L. P., B. Katz, and R. T. Lewis. 1961. *Psychology of abnormal behavior.* New York: Ronald Press.

Tieger, T. 1981. Self-rated likelihood of raping and the social perception of rape. *Journal of Research in Personality* 15:147–158.

Tierney, J. 1982. The aging body. *Esquire,* May, 45–57.

Time. 1971. Heightism. 4 October, 64.

Time. 1981. Caught in the line of fire. 13 April, 48.

Timm, M. 1982. Another look at aging. *The Star Bulletin & Advertiser,* 6 July, H-8.

Tolstoi, L. N. 1967. *The Kreutzer Sonata.* Trans. Ivan Lepinski. Rev. ed. New York: Brentano's, graf, 1823–1910.

Tompkins, R. C., and M. Boor. 1980. Effects of students' physical attractiveness and name popularity on student teachers' perceptions of social and academic attributes. *The Journal of Psychology* 106:37–42.

Touhey, J. C. 1979. Sex-role stereotyping and individual differences in liking for the physically attractive. *Social Psychology Quarterly* 42:285–289.

Traupmann, J., and E. Hatfield. 1981. Love and its effect on mental and physical health. In *Aging: Stability and change in the family,* ed. R. Fogel, E. Hatfield, S. Kiesler, and E. Shanas, 253–274. New York: Academic Press.

Traupmann, J., E. Hatfield, and S. Sprecher. 1981. The importance of "fairness" for the marital satisfaction of older women. Photocopy. Department of Psychology. University of Hawaii at Manoa, Honolulu, HI.

Traupmann, J., E. Hatfield, and P. Wexler. 1983. Equity and sexual satisfaction in dating couples. *British Journal of Social Psychology* 22:33–40.

Traupmann, J., R. Peterson, M. Utne, and E. Hatfield. 1981. Measuring equity in intimate relations. *Applied Psychological Measurement* 5:467–480.

Trudeau, G. B. 1981. Doonesbury. *Honolulu Star Bulletin.*

Turkat, D., and J. Dawson. 1976. Attributions of responsibility for a chance event as a function of sex and physical attractiveness of target individual. *Psychological Reports* 39:275–279.

Tymm, M. 1982. Another look at aging. *The Sunday Star Bulletin and Advertiser,* 6 June, H8.

Ubell, E. (Oct. 23, 1983) When staying thin is a sickness. *Parade,* p. 18.

Udry, J. R. 1971. Commentary. *Sexual Behavior,* September, 23.

Udry, J. R. 1977. The importance of being beautiful: A re-examination and racial comparison. *American Journal of Sociology* 83:154–160.

Udry, J. R., and B. K. Eckland. 1982. The benefits of being attractive: Differential payoffs for men and women. Paper presented at American Sociological Association, September.

Uesato, G. 1968. Esthetic facial balance of American-Japanese. *American Journal of Orthodontics,* 54: 601–611.

Unger, R. K., M. Hilderbrand, and T. Madar. 1982a. Physical attractiveness and assumptions about racial deviance. *Personality and Social Psychology Bulletin* 8:293–301.

Unger, R. K., M. Hilderbrand, and T. Madar. 1982. Physical attractiveness and assumptions about social deviance. Some sex-by-sex comparisons. *Personality and Social Psychology Bulletin* 8(2):293–301.

USA Today. 1983. Anonymous quotelines, 27 July, 8A.

Utne, M. K., E. Hatfield, J. Traupmann, and D. Greenberger. 1984. Equity, marital satisfaction and stability. *Journal of Social and Personal Relationships* 1(3):323–332.

Vagt, G. 1979. The relationship between looks and personality: Consider yourself beautiful, that is what matters. *Zeitschrift fur Experimantalle und Angewandte Psychologie* 26:355–363.

Vail, J. P., V. M. Staudt. 1950. Attitudes of college students toward marriage and related problems: I. Dating and marriage selection. *Journal of Psychology* 30:171–182.

Valins, S. 1966. Cognitive effects of false heart-rate feedback. *Journal of Personality and Social Psychology* 4:400–408.

Valins, S. 1967. Emotionality and information concerning internal reactions. *Journal of Personality and Social Psychology* 6:458–463.

Van Buren, A. 1976. *The Capital Times* 26 November, 11.

Van Buren, A. 1981. *The best of Dear Abby.* Kansas City: Andrews and McMeel, 181.

Van Buskirk, S. S. 1977. A two-phase perspective on the treatment of anorexia nervosa. *Psychological Bulletin* 84(5):529–538.

Vandenberg, S. G. 1972. Assortative mating, or who marries whom? *Behavioral Genetics* 2:127–157.

Vargas, A. M., and J. G. Borkowski. 1982. Physical attractiveness and counseling skills. *Journal of Counseling Psychology* 29:246–255.

Vaughan, S. L., J. R. Stabler, and P. R. Clance. 1981. Children's monetary evaluations of body parts as a function of sex, race, and school grade. *The Journal of Psychology* 107:203–207.

Veblen, T. 1911. *The theory of the leisure class. An economic study of institutions.* New York: MacMillan, p. 172.

Villemez, W. J., and J. C. Touhey. 1977. A measure of individual differences in sex-stereotyping and sex discrimination. *Psychological Reports* 41:411–415.

Vockell, E. ., and J. W. Asher. 1972. Dating frequency among high school seniors. *Psychological Reports* 31:381–382.

Von Hentig, H. 1974. Redhead and outlaw: A study in criminal anthropology. *Journal of Criminal Law and Criminology* 38:1–6.

W.Newspaper (Nov. 20–27, 1981). N.Y. City Fairchild Publications. p. 12.

Wagatsuma, E., and C. L. Kleinke. 1979. Ratings and facial beauty by Asian-American and Caucasian females. *Journal of Social-Psychology* 109:299–300.

Walker, D. N., and D. L. Mosher. 1970. Altruism in college women. *Psychological Reports* 27:887–894.

Walker, R. N. 1962. Body build and behavior in young children: I. Body build and nursery schoolteachers' ratings. *Monographs of the Society for Research in Child Development* 27:2–94.

Walker, R. N. 1963. Body build and behavior in young children: II. Body build and parents' ratings. *Child Development* 34:1–23.

Wallace, I., ed. 1981. *The intimate sex lives of famous people.* New York: Delacorte Press.

Wallace, I., A. Wallace, D. Wallechinsky, and S. Wallace. 1981. *The intimate sex lives of the famous people.* New York: Dell.

Waller, W. 1937. The rating and dating complex. *American Sociological Review* 2:727–734.

Waller, W. 1938. *The family: A dynamic interpretation.* New York: Dryden.

Wall Street Journal. 1969. Tall hiring. 25 November, 1.

Ward, C. D. 1967. Own height, sex, and liking in the judgment of the heights of others. *Journal of Personality* 35:381–401.

Wasserman, J., N. Wiggins, L. Jones, and S. Itkin. 1974. A cross-cultural study of the attribution of personological characteristics as a function of facial perception. *Personality and Social Psychology Bulletin* 1:45–47.

Waters, J. 1980. The Cinderella syndrome. *Farleigh Dickinson University Magazine,* winter.

Watson, D., and R. Friend. 1969. Measurement of social-evaluation anxiety. *Journal of Consulting and Clinical Psychology* 33:448–457.

Watson, D. L., and R. G. Tharp. 1981. *Self-directed behavior: Self-modification for personal adjustment.* 3rd ed. Monterey, Calif.: Brooks/Cole Publishing Co.

Webster's Seventh New Collegiate Dictionary. 1969. Springfield, Mass.: G. & C. Merriam.

Weg, R. 1977. More than wrinkles. In *In looking ahead, a woman's guide to problems and joys of growing older*, ed. E. Troll, J. Israel, and K. Israel. Englewood Cliffs, N. J.: Prentice-Hall, Inc.

Weil, W. B. 1977. Current controversies in childhood obesity. *Journal of Pediatrics* 91:175–187.

Weinberg, J. A. 1960. A further investigation of body catrexis and the self. *Journal of Consulting Psychology* 24:277.

Wells, L. E., and G. Marwell. 1976. *Self-esteem: Its conceptualization and measurement*. Beverly Hills: Sage Publications.

Wells, W., and B. Siegel. 1961. Stereotyped somatypes. *Psychological Reports* 8:77–78.

West, S. G., and T. J. Brown. 1975. Physical attractiveness, the severity of the emergency and helping: A field experiment and interpersonal simulation. *Journal of Experiment Social Psychology* 11:531–538.

Wexler, P. 1980a. A critical social analysis. Photocopy. Department of Sociology, University of Wisconsin, Madison, Wisc.

Wexler, P. 1980b. The social psychology of progressive individualism: A critique of equity theory. Photocopy. Department of Sociology, University of Wisconsin, Madison, Wisconsin.

White, G. L. 1980a. Inducing jealousy: A power perspective. *Personality and Social Psychology Bulletin* 6:222–227.

White, G. L. 1980b. Physical attractiveness and courtship progress. *Journal of Personality and Social Psychology* 39:660–668.

White, G. L., S. Fishbein, and J. Rutstein. 1981. Passionate love and the misattribution of arousal. *Journal of Personality and Social Psychology* 41:56–62.

Widgery, R. N. 1974. Sex of receiver and physical attractiveness of source of determinants of initial credibility perception. *Western Speech* 38:13–17.

Wiggins, J. S. 1971. Men's preferences for different types of female figures. *Medical Aspects of Human Sexuality*, September, 100–116.

Wiggins, J. S., N. Wiggins (Hirshberg), and J. C. Conger. 1968. Correlates of heterosexual somatic preference. *Journal of Personality and Social Psychology* 10:82–90.

Williamson, R. L. 1966. *Marriage and family relations*. New York: Wiley.

Wilson, D. W. 1978. Helping behavior and physical attractiveness. *Journal of Social Psychology* 104:313–314.

Wilson, D. W., and E. Donnerstein. 1977. Guilty or not guilty? A look at the "simulated" jury paradigm. *Journal of Applied Social Psychology* 7:175–190.

Wilson, E. O. 1975. *Sociobiology*. Cambridge, Mass.: The Belknap Press.

Wilson, G. D., and A. H. Brazendale. 1974. Psychological correlates of sexual attractiveness: An empirical demonstration of denial and fantasy gratification phenomena? *Social Behavior and Personality* 2:30–34.

Wilson, G., and D. Nias. 1976. Beauty can't be beat. *Psychology Today*, September, 96–103.

Wilson, G. D., D. K. Nias, and A. H. Brazwndale. 1975. Vital statistics, perceived sexual attractiveness, and response to risque humor. *Journal of Social Psychology* 95:201–205.

Wilson, M., T. F. Cash, and S. G. West. 1978. Divergent effects of physical attractiveness on impression formation as a function of situational context. Paper presented at the Annual Convention of the Eastern Psychological Association, April, Washington, D.C. Available from second author, Old Dominion University, Norfolk, Virginia.

Wison, P. R. 1968. Perceptual distortion of height as a function of ascribed academic status. The Journal of Social Psychology 74:97–102.

Woods, T. L. 1975. Comments on the dynamics and treatment of disfigured children. Clinical Social Work Journal 3:16–23.

Worral, N., V. M. Taylor, J. P. Ricketts, and A. P. Jones. 1974. Personal hygiene cues in impression formation. Perceptual and Motor Skills. 38:1269–1270.

Worthy, M. A., L. Gary, and G. M. Kahn. 1969. Self-disclosure as an exchange process. Journal of Personality and Social Psychology 13:63–69.

Wright, B. A. 1960. Physical disability: A psychological approach. New York: Harper and Row.

Wyer, R. S., Jr., M. Henninger, and M. Wolfson. 1975. Informational determinants of females' self-attributions and observers' judgments. of them in an achievement situation. Journal of Personality and Social Psychology 32:556–570.

Wylie, R. 1974. The Self-concept: Revised edition. Vol. I. A review of methodological considerations and measuring instruments. Lincoln, Neb.: University of Nebraska Press.

Wylie, R. 1978. The self-concept: Revised edition. Vol. 2. Theory and research on selected topics. Lincoln, Neb.: University of Nebraska Press.

Yeats, W. B. 1950. For Anne Gregory, Collected poems. London: MacMillan & Co. Limited, St. Martin's Street, p. 277.

Young, J. W. 1979. Symptom disclosure to male and female physicians: Effects of sex, physical attractiveness, and symptom type. Journal of Behavioral Medicine 2:159–169.

Young, N. 1979. Full stomachs and empty lives. Glamour, September, 204–208.

Zajonc, R. B., and P. Brickman. Expectancy and feedback as independent factors in task performance. Journal of Personality and Social Psychology 11:148–150.

Zelnick, M., and J. E. Kantner. 1977. Sexual and contraceptive experience of young unmarried women in the United States, 1976 and 1971. Family Planning Perspectives 9:55–7.

Zilbergeld, B. 1978. Male sexuality: A guide to sexual fulfillment. Boston: Little, Brown, and Co.

Zirkel, P. A. 1971. Self-concept and the "disadvantage" of ethnic group membership and mixture. Review of Educational Research 41:211–225.

Zirkel, P. A., and E. G. Moses. 1971. Self-concept and ethnic group membership among public schoolchildren. American Educational Research Journal 8:253–265.

Zuckerman, M. 1974. The sensation seeking motive. In Progress in experimental personality research, ed. B. Maher, Vol. 7, 79–148. New York: Academic Press.

Zuckerman, M., E. A. Kolin, L. Price, and I. Zoob. 1964. Development of a sensation seeking scale. Journal of Consulting Psychology 28:477–482.

Index